Praise for *Voices for the Islands*

"In *Voices for the Islands*, Sheila Harrington chronicles the legacy of the many dedicated, local activists who worked for over fifty years to build the land trusts, conservancies, and precious wild sanctuaries that now safeguard the very soul of BC's Gulf Islands. She documents what these nature heroes did against daunting odds, employing land covenants, scientific research, innovative fund-raising, and effective advocacy, to save nature from development. As such, she also provides a how-to guide.

This is an impressive, engaging book. I highly recommend it. If you care about passing nature onward, *Voices for the Islands* is a must-read that I suspect may inspire you too to join the action."

RIC CARELESS OBC, founding member of the Sierra Club of BC and BC Parks Foundation

"As a sailor, I have had the privilege of visiting every one of the islands in this book and hiked many trails in the parks and protected areas. Each Gulf Island holds a distinct beauty where orange Arbutus trees reach for the sun off rocky cliffs while towering Douglas fir support Bald Eagles in their treetop nests. Orca, humpback whales and seals wander the deep waters. It is a delight to follow in the wake of fellow sailor Sheila Harrington as she meets the people and organizations that have fought tirelessly to preserve these unique ecosystems for future generations to enjoy."

BOB MCDONALD OC, author, journalist, and host of CBC's *Quirks & Quarks*

"The interconnected islands of the Salish Sea present wonderful diversity—from arbutus groves to intertidal ecosystems, camas meadows, and vital wetlands. But these delicate zones are threatened by biodiversity loss, land clearing, and climate change. As a fellow island dweller invested in conservation, I appreciated learning more about the differences between reserves, conservancies, covenants, and parks, as well as how the Islands Trust movement began. Sheila Harrington reminds us that islands are a construct and draws our attention to the waterways and desire trails that connect these jewels. Reading about the many individuals and groups working to preserve these lands helps me feel a little less alone, the distances easier to cross."

AMANDA LEWIS, author of *Tracking Giants: Big Trees, Tiny Triumphs, and Misadventures in the Forest*

"At last, a Good New Story. This book details the ongoing successful battles to preserve the natural spaces on the treasured Islands of the Salish Sea. Engagingly written, part chronology, part inspiration and part guide for the future. It details the battles and sacrifices of the many dedicated crusaders for Mother Gaia."

BOBBI HUNTER, Greenpeace co-founder and editor/contributor of *Mr. Mindbomb: A Life in Stories*

"Aboard her small sailboat, Sheila Harrington takes us to the islands in the Salish Sea to tell a remarkable story. As developments began to threaten unique ecosystems, local activists rallied round to preserve them. Determined, creative, and savvy, they often succeeded. Their fights contain lessons for all of us—both timeless and timely!"

CLAUDIA CORNWALL, author of British *Columbia in Flames: Stories from a Blazing Summer*

"A beautifully crafted, comprehensive tour of these iconic, fragile islands, seen through the eyes and hearts of those who tend them. Indigenous and Settler. Through colourful photos, and conversations with colourful locals, Sheila Harrington shows us restoration is possible."

PAULINE LE BEL, author of *Whale in the Door: A Community Unites to Protect BC's Howe Sound*

"Conservation does work. From philanthropy to volunteer hours to policy campaigns, regular people who care about community have shaped and reshaped the Western land and seascape. This book is a beautiful tribute to those people—past and present—who have continuously engaged in the hard work of protecting nature. It is celebration and inspiration."

ANDREA OLIVE, University of Toronto Mississauga professor and author of *Protecting the Prairies: Lorne Scott and the Politics of Conservation*

"In *Voices for the Islands*, Sheila Harrington takes readers on a delightful sailing journey through the Salish Sea. As Harrington visits each jewel on the long necklace of Gulf Islands, detailing their rich conservation history, she shines a light on the passionate residents who have dedicated so much of their lives to protecting nature in doggedly creative ways. Voices for the Islands unflinchingly documents the mounting threats facing the islands in the Salish Sea and describes on-going efforts at reconciliation with First Nations, the original stewards of the waters and land. In these troubling times of climate change and biodiversity loss, Harrington's book is an uplifting testament to how individuals and communities working together to protect what they cherish can make an incalculable difference."

SARAH COX, author of *Signs of Life* and *Breaching the Peace*

"*Voices for the Islands* will be an important contribution to understanding how conservation has and will happen on the Salish Sea Islands."

DUANE WEST, former superintendent of Parks Canada, former director of Gabriola Lands and Trails Trust, and current director of Lasqueti Island Nature Conservancy

"The telling of the history of conservation on Bowen Island, capturing all its details and personalities, is a real gift to our community. We, Bowen Island, need to know our conservation history. Good things don't just happen—people work hard to make them happen, and Sheila Harrington tells that story well. I learned a lot reading it."

BOB TURNER, former mayor of Bowen Island and current director of Bowen Island Conservancy

"An enjoyable trip down memory lane for sure, and inspiration to keep on going!"

DR. KATHY DUNSTER, former director and co-chair of Land Trust Alliance of BC, former board member of the Islands Trust Fund (Conservancy), and lead Urban Ecosystems faculty at Kwantlen Polytechnic University.

Voices for the Islands

Thirty Years of Nature Conservation on the Salish Sea

HERITAGE

Sheila Harrington

*"Island life just has a different pacing
and value system than a lot of what I see on
the mainland, and everywhere. I think there's
a wisdom embedded in island communities
that is valuable to the wider world."*

BOB TURNER
Bowen Island

Copyright © 2024 Sheila Harrington
Foreword copyright © 2024 Briony Penn

All rights reserved. No part of this publication may be reproduced, stored in a retrieval system, or transmitted in any form or by any means—electronic, mechanical, audio recording, or otherwise—without the written permission of the publisher or a licence from Access Copyright, Toronto, Canada.

Heritage House Publishing Company Ltd.
heritagehouse.ca

Cataloguing information available from Library and Archives Canada
978-1-77203-492-9 (paperback)
978-1-77203- 493-6 (e-book)

Edited by Andrea Lister
Proofread by Jess Klaassen-Wright
Cover design by Sara Loos
Cover images: "Faux-Tsuga de Douglas; Pseudotsuga douglasii" (P. Mouillefert, Arbres, p. 80), courtesy of the LuEsther T. Mertz Library, New York Botanical Garden
Interior photographs by Sheila Harrington unless otherwise indicated
Maps by Danielle Morrison courtesy of The Nature Trust of BC

The interior of this book was produced on FSC®-certified, acid-free paper, processed chlorine free, and printed with vegetable-based inks.

Heritage House gratefully acknowledges that the land on which we live and work is within the traditional territories of the Lkwungen (Esquimalt and Songhees), Malahat, Pacheedaht, Scia'new, T'Sou-ke, and W̱SÁNEĆ (Pauquachin, Tsartlip, Tsawout, Tseycum) Peoples.

We acknowledge the financial support of the Government of Canada through the Canada Book Fund (CBF) and the Canada Council for the Arts, and the Province of British Columbia through the British Columbia Arts Council and the Book Publishing Tax Credit.

Canadä   Canada Council   Conseil des arts
          for the Arts   du Canada

BRITISH COLUMBIA   BRITISH COLUMBIA ARTS COUNCIL
                    An agency of the Province of British Columbia

28 27 26 25 24   1 2 3 4 5

Printed in China

CONTENTS

FOREWORD

IF YOU'VE PICKED UP THIS BOOK, chances are that you've fallen in love with the islands in the Salish Sea. You might have wondered how the heck they've retained their natural beauty against the hostile tsunami of contemporary clear-cuts, cookie cutter suburbs, and mindless malls that are encroaching elsewhere. The answer is the collective efforts of thousands of people defending and tending these islands over generations. This book is the most recent chapter of a long history of strong matriarchs, fearless fishermen, hippie accountants, loud librarians, gutsy hairdressers, energetic ecoforesters, senior shit disturbers, activist artists, organized kindergarten teachers, tireless biologists and all the other islanders who roll up their sleeves for beauty, future generations, and the natural world in a culture that doesn't value these things. I love every one of these islanders and only have to look out the window to have deep gratitude for their ongoing efforts to defend this wider community for all of us. I'm also grateful to Sheila for having put all these valiant defenders together into one crew list (with all their duties) to show how we can work together to turn this crazy ship around.

Voices for the land and sea have always been essential but never more than now. Canadian historian Margaret MacMillan argued in her 2015 Massey Lecture series that the histories of environmental struggles are lagging in Canadian historical scholarship. Jack (J. I.) Little suggests that his fellow historians are starting to realize "that a deeper understanding of the growth in popular environmental consciousness requires detailed analysis of locally organized protests against large-scale economic development projects as well as against unsustainable logging and fishing."[1] Sheila Harrington's personal account of the land trust and conservation movement throughout the Gulf Islands is one such addition to Canadian history. It is one great model of protecting the natural world within the juggernaut of urbanization.

One of the reasons these histories are not typically celebrated is that they are local, collaborative, slow, and mostly held together by volunteers in committees of local land trusts. It requires skill sets that are often viewed as globally unmarketable: long-term commitment to a place, understanding the legalese of land laws, and learning ecological principles. Not the stuff of dramatic novels, but a quiet revolution. Occasionally, islanders rise up into the protests that Jack Little refers to in his research, but these are only when the quiet revolution meets a wall. For example, my fifteen minutes on a horse riding naked down Howe Street as Lady Godiva to protest a corporation putting profits ahead of endangered species was only after thousands of people had spent years before that on committees across Canada quietly working to protect those endangered species. Sheila brings the story of both the exhilaration of protests and the quiet revolution alive as she sails through these unique and beloved islands. She is one of those volunteers who will sit through years of meetings until all other options are exhausted. Then watch out.

Sheila's narrative complements the unfolding of the political vision of 1975 that created the Islands Trust, a unique legal framework that aims to preserve and protect the natural world and rural communities on these islands for all British Columbians. For "all people" is an important point; islanders have been welcoming visitors here for millennia to share the beauty, to rest and to heal. The most recent events that Sheila has captured in her account is what SELILIYE Belinda Claxton, a Tsawout First Nation Elder, calls ȻENEṈITEL—working together to heal the land and ourselves. Dana Lepofsky, one of the scholars featured, exemplifies the type of islander who brings her professional lens as an archaeologist to support the work of Knowledge Keepers. Tara Martin is an ecologist who helped arrange one of the first Land Backs through TLC The Land Conservancy of BC for SISȻENEM (Halibut Island). We are at a time in history when it is essential that we work together to respect and heal the land and ourselves. As William Rees, the UBC professor who helped coin the term "ecological footprint," wrote recently, this is not a climate or biodiversity crisis, it is a behavioural crisis and the solution is to heal our connection to the land that supports us.[2] I hope this little sliver of history will help other communities chart a better course upon this gentle earth and seas.

BRIONY PENN

Brooks Point, Pender Island, with Mt. Baker behind. Protected by local islanders as a nature reserve through their dedicated fundraising and partnerships. MYLES CLARKE

INTRODUCTION

*"The Penelakut people told me that they don't see these
as 'islands.' Rather they see them as shorelines,
with the ocean as the highway. I see it all as a Gift."*
LOREN WILKINSON
Galiano Island

I'M AT HOME ON THE ISLANDS IN THE SALISH SEA. I came here as a young teenager, and it took some time to identify the natural wonders that grabbed my heart. As I lived, fished, and sailed around the islands, I marveled at their incredible beauty and learned about the life-giving seeds and berries of the arbutus, fir, hemlock, yew, Garry oak, and cedars. Salal, Oregon grape, and huckleberry soon became part of my diet, along with the cod and salmon, crab, clams, and oysters. I heard the herons, gulls, sea ducks, juncos, and warblers call.

As the years passed, I began to see loss and fragmentation. In the '80s and early '90s, fights were strong over clear-cut logging, slash burning, and development. Mega corporations like MacMillan Bloedel, Weldwood-Westply, and other numbered companies were ravaging forests and trashing streams, once the home of wild creatures living on these precious islands.

People were moving to the islands in droves. The forests, wildlife, and rural refuges were fast disappearing. There were a few provincial parks, at Montague Harbour and Mount Maxwell, but the majority of the land was being sold and developed. Most newcomers did not realize that their land clearing resulted in degradation and loss of sensitive ecosystems found nowhere else in the world. The land and its wildlife had no voice to object. I started to feel "solastalgia"—a form of emotional or existential grief caused by environmental change, linked to mourning what is lost.

While I was living on Salt Spring Island in the '90s, I joined others who were promoting positive alternatives—green building, community recycling, and composting projects. Learning how to change our human practices to integrate with the cycles of life means we have to cross that boundary of separation we erect between ourselves and the natural world. We are more than kin with nature—we are part of her. To feel and experience this kinship with the natural world, we need to open to it, enter into its realm, learn its rhythms of tide, fresh and salt water, the connections between the tree and mycelium and the birds that eat the berries.

One of my many mentors, Michael Dunn from Mayne Island, encouraged me to notice the edges—between ecosystems and different habitats, and all of the living earth around. In the mid '90s, with Michael and Briony Penn, we invited island residents to walk their lands and map the unique natural and cultural features of their own home places. We held showings of the maps on a few islands and published the methods and a sampling of them in a small book, *Giving the Land a Voice: Mapping Our Home Places.*

In response to a new millennium, in 2000, Judi Stevenson, Briony, and I invited people from eighteen of the larger populated islands to create artistic community maps, revealing what islanders knew about their island's ecology. We especially wanted them to record what they cherished at this turning of a new century. We held exhibitions showing these beautiful community maps and published them with their stories in the *Atlas of the Islands in the Salish Sea.* People were truly inspired by the diversity and preciousness displayed in these maps, and the book sold out.

Then like a bad dream, suddenly the changes came barreling down the strait to my home island. The extensive Garry oak woodlands above Burgoyne Bay on Salt Spring were under threat of logging and development.

Like many other people featured in this book, I rose to the call of the land and its creatures—determined that it would be saved. With hundreds of other advocates of nature, we worked with the local land trust, often called conservancies, that enable people to legally protect these unique and threatened places in perpetuity. This book chronicles the story of how we succeeded in protecting most of the threatened areas on Salt Spring island, working with our local land trust, a water preservation society, a larger BC land trust, and with BC Parks. This book captures many other similar stories of locals banding together to protect threatened natural areas in their communities.

Most of the Islands in the Salish Sea are within a very small ecological niche, the critically imperiled Coastal Douglas-fir Biogeoclimatic zone (CDF), the smallest and most at-risk ecological community in Canada.[1] This bioregion is unique within Canada and home to the highest number of ecosystems and species at risk in the province, many of which are ranked as critically imperiled at a national and global scale. Sadly, less than 1 percent of the original forest in the CDF is left, with less than 10 percent of the young forested lands protected. The highest elevations of Salt Spring, the islands in Howe Sound, and the northern-most islands in the Salish Sea are in another biogeoclimatic zone—the Coastal Western Hemlock zone (CWH) a much wetter area, also threatened by logging and development. All of these islands are within the coastal region where logging first took place, one of the earlier areas to be colonized and developed. The wetlands, riparian ecosystems, and estuaries that depend on these forests have been so modified by human activities that they too, are at significant risk. Yet, something changed in the '80s. People started to notice what was going on, and what was being lost—especially as they wanted what was being torn asunder.

The '70s to mid '80s were a time of rampant industrial logging in British Columbia. From Meares Island to the Indigenous-led protests in the Stein Valley and Haida Gwaii, then onto the famous record-breaking number of arrests in Clayoquot Sound, huge public protests were flaring up over industrial logging. The wilderness preservation movement arose in BC between 1975 and 1995 resulting in large parks in the Valhalla Valley, Stein Valley, Clayoquot Sound, Carmanah and Walbran Valleys, and the Tatshenshini River. But at home on the islands, logging and development were picking up the pace. And people on the islands heard that same call to action spawned from other regions of the province. These local land trusts arose out of a very activist time in BC. What could they do at home?

Starting with islands like Galiano, Pender, Denman, and Salt Spring, individuals joined together to form conservation land trusts, which could legally protect the land. They provide the legal means to purchase, covenant, and conserve land for the larger community and to protect the habitats of other species. These island land trusts, started in the '90s, have now been working for twenty-five to thirty years.

This book grew out of the recent passing of some of the pivotal founders of these local land trusts—charitable organizations that are part of the larger conservation movement. The regional focus of this book is on the islands in the Salish Sea within Canada, a coastal area of international ecological significance.[2] Based on my interviews with founders and current staff and directors of the more than fifteen local land trusts that developed from the mid '90s to the present, this book provides an in-depth view of their timely emergence, multiple successes, hard lessons, human interest stories, and case studies.

As conservation on the islands includes both national and provincial parks, as well as regional and local nature reserves, I talked with people directly involved in their creation and continued management to provide some broader perspectives. This historical review describes how these intrepid people came together to conserve land on the islands in the Salish Sea in a myriad of ways. As climate change and development are dramatically altering the landscape and way of life on the coast, particularly on these unique islands, I hope their voices and stories will provide insight and motivation to conserve more of the natural areas that sustain life.

In early 2021, the loss of one of my mentors, John Scull, a founder of the Cowichan Community Land Trust and the Land Trust Alliance of BC, woke me to the reality that these elders' voices would soon be silenced. I decided to visit other founders and capture their stories, their motivations and inspirations that led them to create these land trusts, before they were lost. So began my exploration and sailing journey to the more populated islands in the Salish Sea to meet with the founders, to learn about their successes and challenges. I also talked with many who now carry these island conservation organizations forward. This is a time of the passing of the guard.

After twelve years away from the Southern Gulf Islands, in July 2021, I began a three year sailing voyage to many of the islands in the Salish Sea to interview the unsung heroes behind these conservation land trusts. As I recorded the voices of many of the initiators and people now working with these organizations, I learned about new places that had been conserved, new educational, science, and restoration projects, and new Indigenous partnerships—along with the growing threats to the biodiversity of the islands.

The recent United Nations biodiversity conference held in Montreal set a goal to conserve 30 percent of land and water by 2030. In order to meet this objective, we need to conserve more land, awaken to a larger view, and recognize that it really does matter what we do, especially in our own backyards. All aspects of nature, including ourselves, are interrelated and interdependent. With the climate and biodiversity crisis upon us, human civilization and the natural ecosystems we depend on hang in the balance.

Through this collection of stories about conservation on the islands—the land acquisitions, legal battles, lessons learned, and areas protected through landowner (or landholder) agreements, such as conservation covenants—I hope to inspire readers, turn apathy or cynicism to action, and support conservation in an era of restoration and reconciliation. Thanks to the generosity of landowners and donors, since the early '90s, conservation organizations have protected thousands of hectares on these small islands.[3] They have made formidable partnerships with senior and local governments to create parks and nature reserves. They have undertaken unique restoration and innovative educational and science projects to help bring other islanders and visitors to an appreciation of the intricate biodiversity that needs conserving and protecting.

This book shares these "voices for the islands" from the people who founded the land trusts in the Salish Sea, those working in land and marine conservation today, and those who worked in both federal and provincial agencies who helped create federal and provincial parks on the islands.

Today we understand more about how land was taken from Indigenous people and the dire ramifications. In naming the islands, I've used the colonial names and included the Indigenous place names for the islands and other places in the text where possible. Indigenous place names are still being fully recognized for some islands, and many islands are in the shared traditional territories of more than one First Nation. As well, some First Nations do not separate discrete islands from the waters around them.

With human population and wealth growing exponentially on the West Coast, the impacts and changes in the Salish Sea and the islands are significant—from loss of herring and salmon to homelessness for those people at the bottom end of the capitalistic spectrum. Yet, more and more people and organizations are resisting the singular economic driver that has led us here. Promoting individual stewardship of land and working with conservation land trusts—stepping up to protect nature—is a hopeful way forward for the future.

May fair winds be with us as I take you in my small sailboat across the Salish Sea to the islands to meet their passionate defenders.

Sailing in the Southern Gulf Islands of the Salish Sea.
HEATHER CRAWFORD

Conservation Areas within the Salish Sea - Secured as of 2000

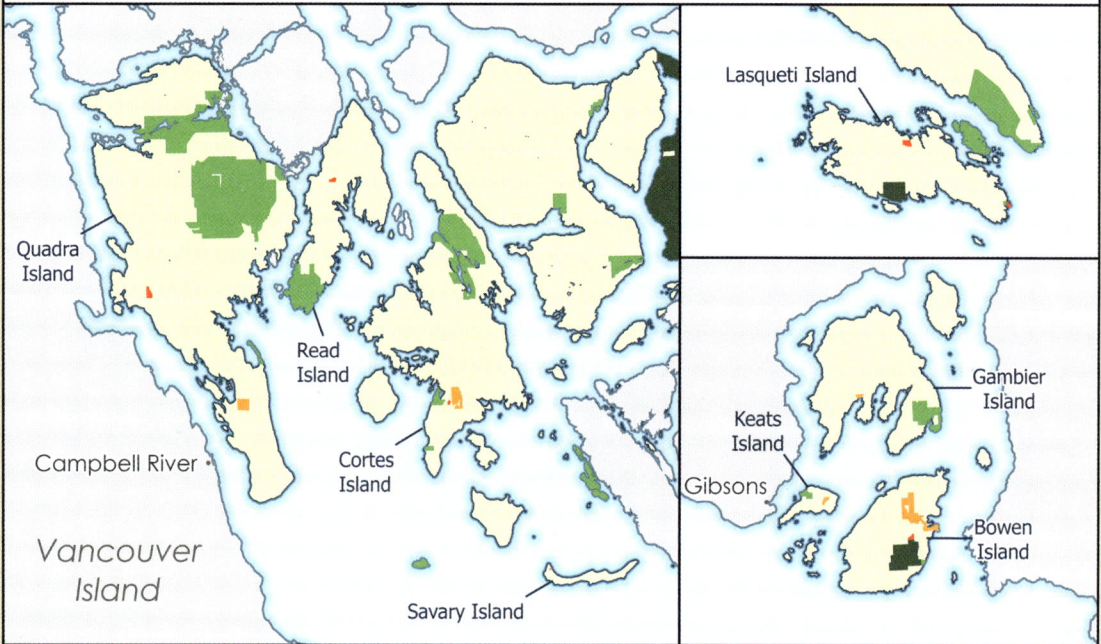

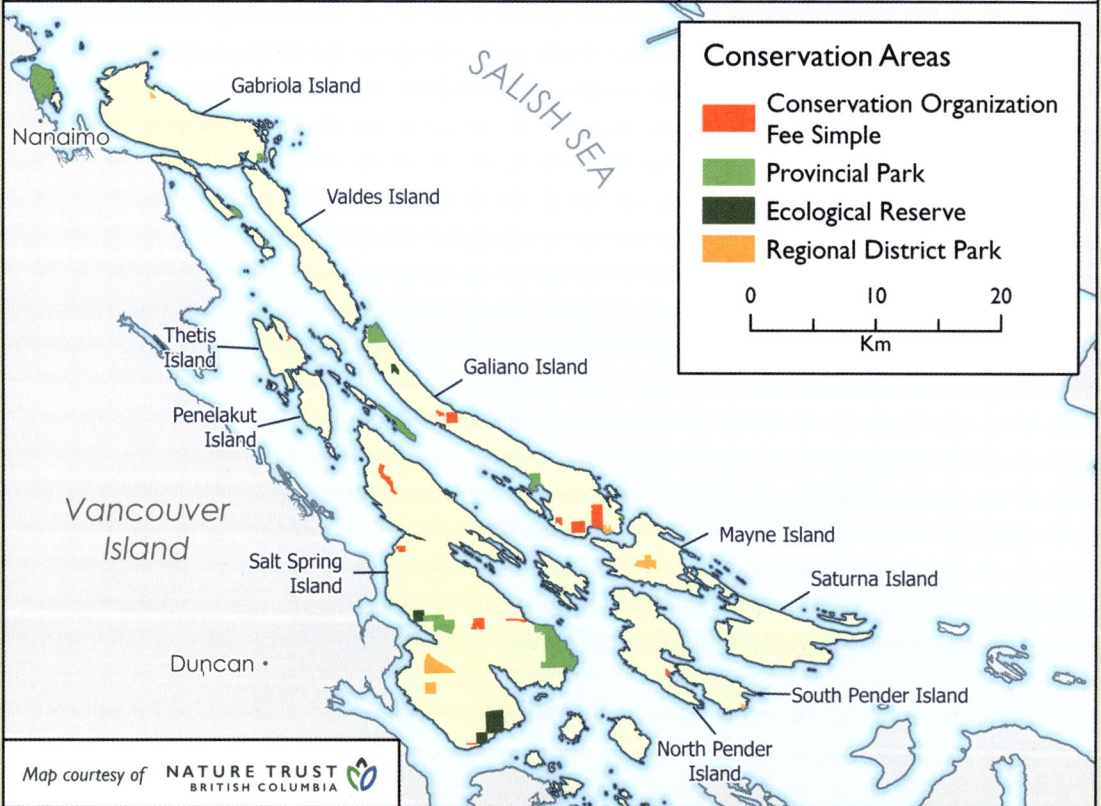

Quadra Island

Read Island

Campbell River

Cortes Island

Vancouver Island

Savary Island

Lasqueti Island

Keats Island

Gibsons

Gambier Island

Bowen Island

Gabriola Island

Nanaimo

SALISH SEA

Valdes Island

Thetis Island

Galiano Island

Penelakut Island

Mayne Island

Saturna Island

Salt Spring Island

Vancouver Island

Duncan

North Pender Island

South Pender Island

Conservation Areas

- Conservation Organization Fee Simple
- Provincial Park
- Ecological Reserve
- Regional District Park

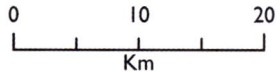

0   10   20
Km

Map courtesy of **NATURE TRUST**
BRITISH COLUMBIA

Conservation Areas within the Salish Sea - Secured as of 2022

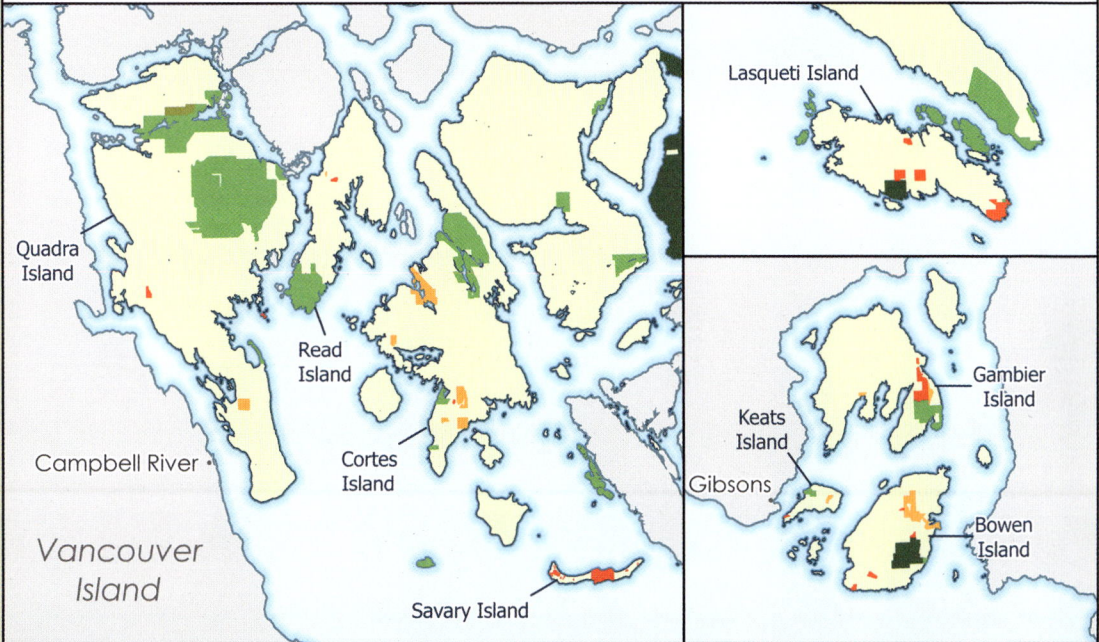

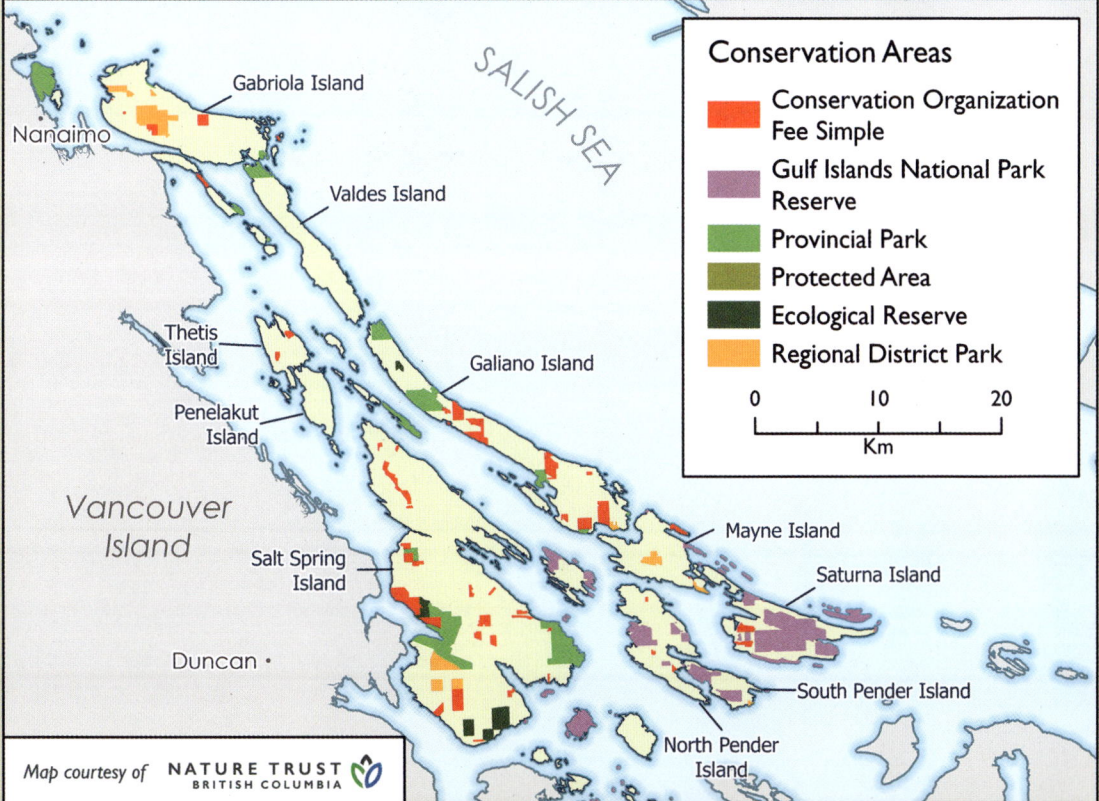

Lasqueti Island

Quadra Island

Read Island

Campbell River

Cortes Island

Vancouver Island

Savary Island

Keats Island

Gibsons

Gambier Island

Bowen Island

Gabriola Island

Nanaimo

SALISH SEA

Valdes Island

Thetis Island

Penelakut Island

Galiano Island

Vancouver Island

Salt Spring Island

Duncan

Mayne Island

Saturna Island

South Pender Island

North Pender Island

Conservation Areas

- Conservation Organization Fee Simple
- Gulf Islands National Park Reserve
- Provincial Park
- Protected Area
- Ecological Reserve
- Regional District Park

0   10   20
Km

Map courtesy of **NATURE TRUST BRITISH COLUMBIA**

Spared from much of the logging that has occurred on Gabriola Island, this large cedar may be one of the guardians looking over this protected forest.

CHAPTER ONE

GABRIOLA ISLAND
In Trails We Trust

"It's not up to governments! Lovely people have
joined in this work, and we've had huge success!"

ROB BROCKLEY
President, Gabriola Land and Trails Trust

WE SLIPPED OUT OF SQUITTY BAY on the south end of Lasqueti Island with a gentle northwest breeze tickling the Salish Sea. The long summer sky was that deep blue that seems to go on forever. As we left our home port, my first mate, friend, and long-time islander, Doane Grinell, wryly commented, "Let's get these sails up, and let the adventure begin."

I turned back to look at Lasqueti—situated right in the centre of Georgia Strait. My friend Dana Lepofsky calls it "the island in the middle of everywhere." Prior to the last century of colonial exploration and industrial resource extraction, people travelled between islands, to the mainland, or to Vancouver Island by canoes or small boats. Dana has learned from archeological evidence that Lasqueti Island, being right in the middle, was a common stopping point in trade and travel. So, it seemed appropriate that I begin my journey here—in the middle of the islands in the Salish Sea.

I was brimming with excitement as I was returning to the Southern Gulf Islands after many years away. I hoped there was still time to locate and interview the founders of the islands' land trusts and nature conservancies. Twenty-five plus years had passed since these pioneering people had established their local conservancies. What motivated these early directors to voluntarily spend hours on the phone, go to meetings, write letters and grant applications, raise money and find help to further land conservation on their islands? What inspired people to donate their land, give their hard-earned money to support purchase of other areas, or give away partial rights to protect their own properties through a conservation covenant? What stories did they have? What worked? What needed changing, and most importantly, what were their messages of hope and hard-won experience for the next generations to follow?

These were some of the questions that rattled around in my brain as Doane and I set our course for the island archipelago known as the Southern Gulf Islands. Gabriola Island was our first stop on the journey. Having lived on Lasqueti Island for the past twelve years, and previously on Salt Spring and Galiano Island, I was excited to revisit the southern islands.

As we headed south, a fifteen- to twenty-knot northwest wind picked up. We seemed to fly down the Strait with the sails set, wing on wing. We rejoiced in this first perfect day on the journey south. Nearing Gabriola, I was reminded of the beauty of these emerald-like southern islands. Captain George Vancouver's master's mate Thomas Manby, aboard the HMS *Discovery*, expressed a feeling I shared:

> Never was contrast greater on this day's sailing than with what we had been long accustomed to. It had more the aspect of enchantment than reality, with silent admiration each discerned the beauties of Nature, and nought was heard on board but expressions of delight murmured from every tongue. Imperceptibly our bark skimmed over the glass surface of the deep, about three miles an hour. The shore on either side glow'd with foliage, pleasingly variegated with every shade a cheerful spring can give the forest.[1]

Sailing past Nanaimo with its belching mills, square networks of urban roads and houses, and anchored freighters, the contrast was not with weather today, but with the modern industrialization that has happened since. Passing Nanaimo and nearby Newcastle (Saysutshun) and Protection Islands, we kept east of Gabriola's forested shores and sailed into Silva Bay, a haven for wooden boat and sailing aficionados.

THE NEXT MORNING, firmly anchored in the bustling Silva Bay, we decided to go ashore to search out a bathroom and ice. We were gone for a long time, past the hungry pangs of lunch, as we walked to Drumbeg Provincial Park on the shores of Gabriola Passage. The park has extensive middens, evidence of past use by the Snuneymuxw and Lyackson people. This beautiful 52 hectare park (21 hectare upland and 35 hectare foreshore) was established in 1971.

The northwest wind scooped up the water and slammed it into the rocks and islets of the pass. We swam in the tepid waters, and walked around the classic weather-etched rocks of the island. The tall sandstone cliffs are divided up like a puzzle, with intense light on the facets of their exposed sides. These erratic islets with Douglas-fir trees leaning over the beach offered shade to intertidal creatures. Only a week ago the shorelines had been exposed to 30- to 40-degree weather, now called a "heat dome," which left a smelly residue of millions of dead mussels and other intertidal creatures all along the Salish Sea. Those that survived were tucked in north-facing rock crevices or under the life-giving shade of the overhanging Douglas-fir and arbutus trees.

We savoured a full day of hiking, swimming, and paddling around the shores and islets surrounding Silva Bay and Gabriola Passage. Like the many tourists and boaters who come here annually, we marveled at the fast currents which create a unique habitat for abundant marine life. The transparent water revealed life at both the high and low intertidal zones—home to limpets, barnacles, rockweed, sea stars, chitons, sculpins, sea cucumbers, and numerous types of crabs. We saw the forage fish that a great blue heron was feeding on.[2] Sailboats slipped by, and we watched several paddlers fight the current in the pass. The sandstone rocks edged the shore with their eroding circular forms, a result of salt and wave action, reminiscent of bones and the dinosaurs from the Late Cretaceous period from which these rocks were formed. Like most of these once jewel-like islands, Gabriola had been logged by industrial and small-scale loggers within the last century. Slash piles of burning logs, clear cuts, and eroded hillsides are not as common today. The story of how locals on Gabriola protected some of their own lands starts with Weldwood-Westply, the forestry company that owned 1,133 hectares (2,800 acres), a quarter of the island.

The first day was glorious as a strong northwest wind blew us toward Gabriola Island—sailing wing on wing.

Long-time nature advocate and Gabriola Island Trustee Susan Yates played a major role in Weldwood's departure. Dyan Dunsmoor-Farley highlighted Susan photographing diesel fuel on the ground and taking this evidence to the larger community.[3] They had to clean up their practices or leave town.

In response, Weldwood approached the regional government, the Islands Trust, with an offer. With the help of a hired contract facilitator, who had experience with MacMillan Bloedel on other islands, their goal was to work with the community to raise $12.5 million—their assessment of the value of the lands they were willing to sell. The rest they wanted zoned for subdivision. Their idea was to create a ~8 hectare (20 acre) lot subdivision on seventy-five lots, leaving the rest for the community, which included protection of the forested watershed areas.

Unfortunately, Dyan explained to me during our phone interview, the island was going through a review of its local official community plan (OCP) at the same time. Things fell apart as divisions in philosophy and methods deepened. Eventually, the company decided to quit negotiations and sell the land to two buyers. The federal government bought ~405 hectares (1,000 acres), which they held for Treaty negotiations with the neighbouring Snuneymuxw First Nation. The second buyer was an American, who in turn sold it to another character famous in many of the islands' logging history books—Mike Jenks.

According to Dyan, Jenks clear-cut literally everything except 30 metres (98 feet) on both sides of North Road, which locals now call Tunnel Hill. "It took a few years for the dust to settle, but acrimony persisted and eventually Jenks started selling to developers, and each time he did this, the owners of the development were required by the Islands Trust to donate land for community purposes, as every time a big development came in a deal was made. Along with confusion over the OCP and differing perspectives over what Weldwood wanted to do, it all resulted eventually in 1,300 acres of conserved land." Dyan noted that "if the original proposal from Weldwood had gone through, the community would have acquired 2,000 acres of land. This was more than we would have gotten but all at one time, instead of almost thirty years of successive developers giving up chunks."[4]

Dyan was disappointed over it all. She felt that they lost an opportunity to have a community resolution in the beginning. "Because with all these large chunks set up for development, we lost—as soon as the land is sold and privatized, that gets extinguished." However, the federal purchase she feels was "very prescient because we are now in Treaty negotiation for that 1,000 acres sold to the Crown.[5] That's there and the remainder of 1,300 acres is now held by the Regional District of Nanaimo."

By the time I made my way to the island in 2021, three provincial parks and several community and regional parks were connected by a trail network. In the eastern end are Drumbeg Provincial Park and Petroglyph Heritage Park, plus a small community park on South Road. Toward the western end of the island lies the 707 Community Park which connects through the village to Cox Community Park and Descanso Bay Regional Park and campground. Several smaller waterfront and community parks dot the northern shoreline of the island, including Sandwell Provincial Park and Gabriola Sands Provincial Park on the northwest end, locally nicknamed "twin beaches" because the isthmus is bordered by two beaches facing east and west.[6]

The regional Islands Trust Conservancy (ITC) owns an additional three nature reserves on the island. These include two small nature reserves: Burren's Acres (not open to the public) and Coats Millstone, and the larger Elder Cedar (S'ul-hween X'pey).

> The Islands Trust Conservancy (ITC) is a regional land trust associated with the Islands Trust. The ITC often partners with local conservancies on land acquisition projects. Having been in operation since 1992, they have now worked with other conservation land trusts to protect over sixty nature reserves on the islands as of 2022.

Gabriola Island Lands and Trails Trust past and current presidents at Silva Bay. From left: Rob Brockley, current president; Norm Harburn, past president; Kerry Marcus, past president; current board member; Tom Cameron, past president; Anne Landry, past president, current board member; John Peirce, past president GaLTT, current president AFoCC.

In early July when Doane and I sailed to Gabriola, we met six directors of the Gabriola Lands and Trails Trust (GaLTT) at a picnic table in the local campground at Silva Bay. They regaled us with the story of the conservation of the 707 Community Park and the ITC's fourth nature reserve on the island, the Elder Cedar (S'ul-hween X'pey) Nature Reserve.

Rob Brockley, the current president, and John, Tom, Norm, Anne, and Kerry, five past presidents of the GaLTT, felt to me like an extended family, all veterans in the conservation movement. They seemed so relaxed with each other, laughing and correcting each other's memories and comments. A couple of the men reminded me of John Scull—one of my mentors and the instigator of many conservation and restoration projects around the Cowichan area. All displayed a quiet but firm dedication to the challenges of land stewardship and conservation. The two women were equally remarkable with their creative ideas and perseverance in protecting nature for itself, and helping people access its recreational elements and beauty via an expanding trail network.

Kerry Marcus, GaLTT's founding president, described herself as a trails advocate and equestrian. A retired federal fisheries manager, she led off with her perspective on the conditions when GaLTT was conceived in 2003.

> I had enough time personally to do something in the community, so I put my name forward for the local parks and recreation advisory committee (POSAC). With less than 2 percent of the island protected, we wanted to create an entity that could do fundraising and hold lands. We got talking about that in general terms when Ron Holmes of the POSAC pointed out a fantastic piece of land for sale. But we couldn't do it in the timeframe, and so it sold, which cemented for us the fact that we needed to be ready to go ahead, as the opportunities came up. In 2004 the founding members gathered and we registered as a society, had our first AGM, and elected our first board.

There was a conservancy already working on the island. The Gabriola Land Conservancy (GLC) had a slightly different focus than GaLTT, whose mandate focused on creating trails, environmental protection, and conservation. The prior GLC had two strong leaders, Leigh Anne Milman and David Boehm. Kerry remarked that "they did amazing work. Leigh Anne was like a bull terrier, and got stuff done." The two organizations realized their priorities were different and originally maintained two separate organizations.

Kerry explained that the original Gabriola Land Conservancy was instrumental in acquiring the 65.36 hectare (~162 acre) Elder Cedar (S'ul-hween X'pey) Nature Reserve. The property contains some of the last remaining mature forest stands on the island with veteran Douglas-fir trees and several freshwater wetlands and riparian areas. The GLC had been working for over twenty years to designate this Crown land area for conservation and recreation through a unique provincial government free Crown Land Grant transfer program.

The resulting Elder Cedar (S'ul-hween X'pey) Nature Reserve was granted to the Islands Trust Conservancy (ITC) in 2006, with an added conservation covenant co-held by GaLTT and the Nanaimo and Area Land Trust (NALT).

A Conservation Covenant is a written legal agreement between a property owner and a government body or one or more land trust organizations designated by the Surveyor General, that sets out specific restrictions or requirements that the landowner will uphold to ensure conservation of all or parts of the land. It is registered on title under Section 219 of the *Land Title Act* and "runs with the land" in perpetuity (it continues to exist on title after the property is sold or transferred, binding future owners).

The ITC describes the significance of the name, S'ul-hween X'pey, in their management plan. "To recognize the rich First Nations history embedded within the site, the Islands Trust Conservancy with the assistance of Snuneymuxw linguist and Elder Dr. Ellen White, named the Reserve 'S'ul-hween X'pey' which directly translates to 'elder cedar.' However, this name has a deeper meaning as it possesses connotations of unseen ancestors and guardians."[7] Spared from much of the logging that has occurred on Gabriola Island, these 65 hectares may well have guardians looking over this forest.

The current president, Rob Brockley, explained that every year the ITC gives a management contract to GaLTT for maintenance work on the property. This type of partnership is a common theme on the islands today, as the local conservancies are on the island, already familiar with the property and its management needs. Often, as in this case, the local land trust initiated and then partnered with the ITC during the acquisition of the area. Rob added that, now that the area is finally protected, GaLTT is considered a continuation of the Gabriola Land Conservancy. He said that Leigh Anne Milman (GLC's founder) was given a lifetime membership with GaLTT.

According to Rob, GaLTT has developed strong, collaborative, and respectful relationships with the Regional District of Nanaimo, the Islands Trust Conservancy, and BC Parks over the past several years. "They appreciate our efforts and know GaLTT will deliver what we promise."

Rob told me that they are also committed to developing respectful and meaningful relationships with the Snuneymuxw First Nation. Rob added that indications from the Snuneymuxw are that they too are interested in a respectful relationship with the community.

This eroding sandstone in Gabriola's Silva Bay is a common sight, called honeycomb weathering.

In 2006, GALTT endorsed a major project—a density transfer of inland forest land, now called the 707 Community Park. The density transfer process creates parkland or other community amenities by trading residential density from elsewhere.

Kerry Marcus, the founding president who was involved in the project, explained how the deal was done:

> It was a big piece of land—707 acres. GALTT had talked to landowners who had forestry-zoned land that might be transferred to park. At that time, landowner Mike Jenks came cautiously to meet with us, and we explained how the density transfer process would work with the official community plan. He asked if he made one of these applications would we support it. GALTT's major role was to convince Jenks that the application could work and, secondly, we had a list of trusted GALTT members and supporters, enough to go ahead. The density transfer process had not been exercised before on Gabriola, and it was poorly understood.
>
> The rezoning application was contentious as many were suspicious of the outcome. With GALTT's strong support and our ability to encourage those who supported the idea to actually come out to meetings, the rezoning application was approved, resulting in an increased number of lots for the new owner, Centre Stage holdings, on their 300 acres of view property, in exchange for 707 acres of forest land for park.

Rob said, "After the dust finally settled after many years, the Regional District of Nanaimo (RDN) owns close to 1,050 acres of the original Weldwood land as the 707 Community Park. It is the largest community park in the regional district and is larger than Vancouver's Stanley Park."

As a result, in 2021, 12 percent of the island has been protected—the vast majority acquired through density transfer. Rob explained, "Just last year the RDN acquired 400 acres through the density transfer process. The reality is with the cost of land these days, that offers the best opportunity to acquire parkland, but the downside is it results in more development. That's a balance, but GALTT feels if the parkland is valuable enough, and trail connections are involved, the balance is often worth it."

Rob sought out Gabriola in 2010 as he was transitioning into retirement. With a background in forest research, he was familiar with trail maintenance and some of the challenges of acquiring and managing lands for conservation purposes.

GALTT's dual focus is to create trails and conserve land. They feel that trails get people out in nature, which helps them first appreciate and then support the protection of land. Some people think those two mandates conflict with each other, but GALTT feels that they complements eachother.

Their first trail was the Yogi Trail, in Cox Community Park, a 40.4 hectare (100 acre) community park near the ferry terminal. It needed a bridge, a trail rerouting and a new connector trail, outlined in the RDN's Management Plan. From 2004 through to 2005, the Nanaimo Regional District built the bridge and approved the plan for GALTT's first trail.

The next past president to speak that day in the campground was Tom Cameron. He came to Gabriola from Alberta in 2000. As I later learned, so did three of the other past presidents. Tom managed the Parks and Wildlife Ventures program, a form of land trust.

> My background is plant ecology, and my initial love is conservation. There is a real frontier in working with small lots. Every lot that remains undeveloped results in environmental benefits, and vice-versa as every lot developed has an environmental impact. As I worked with the Alberta Sport and Wildlife Federation, I pushed money to trail organizations, including the Trail Net (all uses—snowmobiles, ATVs, skiing) a coming together for a unified trail. Coming to Gabriola, I came with trails fresh on my mind, and I think I was the instigator of better trail signage. People were afraid to use 707 lands because they were afraid they'd get lost, and did get lost. I wanted to make signage to be useful, rather than meaningless, such as—a trail to nowhere, type of thing. So the signage helped to get them around and out of the park. I think GALTT has done remarkable work, having not owned the land.

Tom's colleague Norm Harburn was another past president in this circle of interviewees. Norm managed the Alberta Sports, Recreation and Wildlife Parks Foundation. He also worked with the Calgary Parks Foundation, involving private citizens and garnering their financial support for acquisitions. He commented that the new BC Parks Foundation is doing the same thing. Norm, like the others, was retired and looking for something useful to do when he came to Gabriola Island. He shared an interest in the trails work and had experience trail clearing. Tom and Norm had also raised millions of dollars for conservation together in Alberta, so it was easy for the two to work together here on Gabriola. At this point in our discussion, they all laughed, remarking that "progressive" ideas were coming from Alberta.

Tom added, "It's no coincidence that the presidents here have all been public servants. We are experienced as administrators, and that explains why we are hesitant to own land. He said, "If we can find someone better qualified to own land, why would we do it ourselves? We have been strongly in favour of working with the Islands Trust Conservancy, the Regional District of Nanaimo, and the BC Parks Foundation."

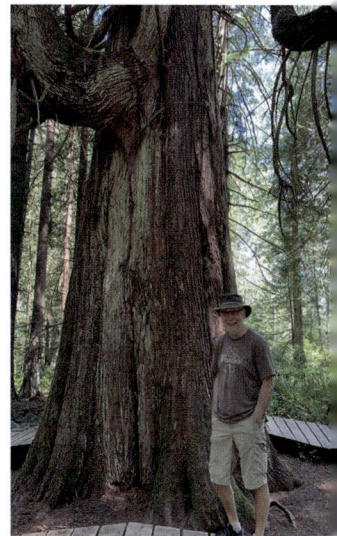

Rob Brockley, current president, in front of large cedar on the boardwalk GaLTT built.

The Islands Trust Conservancy gives GALTT a service contract to help with managing ITC's three Nature Reserves. The focus at the Elder Cedar (S'ul-hween X'pey) Nature Reserve has been to create boardwalks to protect wet soils from further degradation and to stop people from trail braiding—stepping around the wet sections. After our interview, Rob took me on a hike through this very popular nature reserve, proudly showing me the large old growth trees with the boardwalks surrounding and protecting them.

Norm commented that such boardwalks not only protect roots, but they open areas to more multi-use options. A few trails restrict horses and bicycles, but most are designated as multi-use.

Tom explained further the challenges of creating multi-use trails:

Doane and I enjoyed a walk through Gabriola's many trails and shorelines.

I've advocated for higher trail standards. Very few of our trails are built to multi-use trail standards. The ones that have been built to the higher standard, such as Cox Park, cost more money. We've been averse to using machinery, but sometimes one needs to do more initial damage and end up with a long term trail. Old logging roads are the best trails. We have an old population here, and some are advocating for strollers, walkers, etc.

Tom, who is a member of a local bike group, noted the support from the mountain bike community.

I'm a member of one of the mountain bike associations and get their emails, so I know they are working on trails all the time. They look at the trail differently than we do. Their motives are different, yet they also want to connect the trails to the community. They help by using handsaws. Sometimes they don't even tell us! They have enough confidence to open their eyes to more than their own interests, so they accept our priorities too. This shared trail user aspect helps us be more and more connected. We've been lucky so far as there are few motorcycles on the trails.

There are challenges with e-bikes on multi-use trails, Kerry added. "From a horse's perspective, you can hear a motorcycle coming, unlike a speeding e-bike!"

Anne Landry, the next director to provide her perspectives, worked for Parks Canada her whole career. In the fall of 2011 she came to Gabriola, partly due to knowing Duane West, another former GALTT board member who also had a career with Parks Canada. (Duane subsequently moved to Lasqueti Island, where he sits on the board of the Lasqueti Island Nature Conservancy.) "A quirky thing here," Anne explained, "is many of us had connections together through previous work with Parks Canada."

Anne noted that improving accessibility for those with mobility restrictions is a current project for GALTT. Through Facebook, they learned that people with mobility restrictions wanted to get to the parks, but couldn't. So they started a pilot project, at one of the local provincial parks, improving a trail and making a picnic table and outhouse more accessible for wheelchairs." Anne added, "We'd like to help get people to the water. Wheelchair access is important for recreational access and serves a variety of users."

Rob expressed pride in the 80 kilometres (50 miles) of trail they have on the island today. "We've almost completed the Descanso to Drumbeg trail system. You can basically walk the entire length of the island now on trails, or quiet rural roads." Rob explained that GALTT is still largely known within the Gabriola community primarily as a trails organization, but their new strategic plan focuses more on conservation efforts.

Anne, now the chair of the conservation committee, explained, "We are changing our focus so people think of us more as a traditional conservation land trust. However, we don't apologize for our trails work."

GALTT has recently advocated for and contributed money toward the purchase of two properties by the regional district. The most recent was the purchase of a small piece adjacent to the 707 Community Park, which was a remainder parcel from the most recent density transfer process.

"It had high ecological values, and it was a catchment for nearby Coats Marsh, an important wetland, now a regional park." Rob explained, "We lobbied the RDN to purchase that remainder piece and contributed a significant amount to the purchase."

Rob added, "We also worked with the RDN and the Mudge Island Land Trust Association, led by a local, Jack Schick, to purchase a piece of land at the northern end of Mudge Island." This organization's main objective was to protect this small property overlooking Dodd Narrows, and once they achieved it, they donated the rest of their funds to GALTT and folded.

Both the Mudge Island Land Trust and the Gabriola Land Conservancy turned their funding over to GALTT when their own work and projects were completed.

Anne remarked that GALTT has a policy to work with groups with like-minded objectives, including stewardship groups like the Gabriola Streamkeepers. GALTT signed a memorandum of understanding with them setting out the terms of their partnership. Anne told me that the Nanaimo and Area Land Trust (NALT) mentored them early on, being open to phone calls and meetings in their early days before they had charitable tax status.

She added that the Land Trust Alliance of BC's Seminar Series has really helped them to come together and share ideas, bumping up their expertise. "The most memorable one was a number of years ago when a whole bunch of us went to a seminar on covenants with the Nature Conservancy of Canada. We came home looking like deer in the headlights—oh this is a serious thing."

This hard working volunteer board was aware that they might move farther and faster with paid staff. Anne described how they currently operate as an organization.

We have no office, no phone number, and no paid staff. We do our communications through our website and Facebook page, printed materials, and personal contact like the local farmers' market, and community events. We have reflected on this from time to time, as we realize we would move faster with paid staff, but that comes with other obligations. We just hired someone under contract for the first time as the coordinator of our new Nature Stewards program, which is focused on encouraging private landholders to conserve natural habitat and augment it through other stewardship actions, such as bird boxes. We've got some funding through RDN and ITC this year, but we're using a lot of our own reserve funds.

Their membership fees and donations are a main source of income, raising around $25,000 a year. A new fundraising committee is now set up for land acquisition. Norm said that GALTT will be doing more of this in the years ahead. They agreed that helping people set up bequests in their wills is an area that they haven't worked on much, but could proactively take on with this new committee.

GALTT has made a colourful map of their trails which they regularly update and sell around the island. Anne told me that the sea stars on the map show some of the most popular public shore accesses. There are over one hundred public shore accesses on Gabriola, about half of which have been developed with trails.

Anne remarked that, "a general principle is to get along with our neighbours. For example, GALTT always informs neighbouring property owners before building a new shore access trail. Some people are more receptive than others. One needs to determine how essential a trail is overall, and sometimes choosing which battles are worth fighting."

Anne agreed with Tom that one of their biggest challenges is how to protect small lots. Anne described the challenges of working with small lots and with Treaty lands:

On Gabriola we have more small lots than many other islands, making covenants more challenging to establish. We are encouraging landholders to take personal action to conserve natural habitat through our new Nature Stewards program. Something we've done is produce this Trails Map, which shows the trails and nature reserves and parks. It has been a great way to get the message out. Sold for five dollars, it has been a great source of funding. Park land is coloured green. The lands coloured in blue are currently managed by the federal or provincial government, and they are all slated for treaty. The Snuneymuxw First Nation has a Douglas Treaty from 1854, and the lands shown in blue on the map are being held for the Snuneymuxw. The trails on those lands have little signage and we do minimal trail work out of respect for the treaty process. The distinctions on the map help show that there isn't as much parkland on Gabriola as many people think. The relationships with First Nations are going to have major implications on the island and everywhere. We recognize that First Nations have limited capacity, especially with about 1,000 acres of the island in this Treaty land status). This is a significant well forested area (about 10 percent of the island) but outside the OCP. Thus, anything could happen there.

The last past-president of GALTT to speak was a large distinctive-looking man, John Peirce. He explained that his father started two land trusts in Massachusetts. Then, when John moved to Calgary, he helped create Nose Hill Park, which he asserted is the largest municipal park in Canada. I said that I recall that park, having grown up in Calgary myself. Hilarity broke out—another Albertan.

John continued, "in 2000 I was on the board of both GLC and GALTT, which I tried to bring together. By the time I got involved in GALTT, I felt there was a mechanism needed to get more trails. So my principal time on the board has been with that, and helping with succession planning. I came up with the concept of trail licenses. I used the Trans Canada Trail as a model, plus we used the trail license agreement of the Squamish Regional District as well. There is a video on trail licenses on their website. Unlike conservation covenants, they aren't attached to the property title."

I learned that three of these past directors have established trail licenses on their own property. John explained that when he sells his property, he wants the trail and its license to be part of the terms of the sale. John added that they currently have nineteen trail licenses which provide important links, such as connecting neighbourhoods together, linking to other trails, and providing alternate access to parkland and beaches. Rob added that they have also built several trails on Ministry of Transportation undeveloped rights-of-way and on undeveloped shore accesses to get people to the water.

John Peirce is currently the president of American Friends of Canadian Conservation (AFOCC or American Friends), an American charity whose goals are to work with American owners of land in Canada. He explained that he worked on the first AFOCC arrangement with an American woman with land on the island, Sally Robinson. "She has been coming to Gabriola for fifty to sixty years. She owns 22 acres overlooking Gabriola Passage. She had lots of discussions with Leigh Anne Milman trying to learn how to protect it. They had talked about using the Natural Area Protection Tax Exemption Program (NAPTEP) through the ITC, but Sally needed an individual approach, not a boiler plate approach.[8] She is a bound and determined person, and she wanted her own method. So ITC suggested she talk with American Friends."

Through AFOCC, John was able to work with Sally to create Robinson Woods, which is the name of her property. She now has a registered conservation covenant on title which restricts future development. John explained:

She gave up the right to build two houses, as well as protecting all the land. The value of the covenant as a tax deduction was hundreds of thousands of dollars. Sally supported the concept of trails, so her negotiating point was "I'm going to get the trails in first, and you must agree to have them maintained." The trails went in and now GALTT monitors the covenants and maintains the trails. As the first AFOCC covenant in BC, it became a benchmark for the St. John Point property on Mayne

These Garry oaks tower over the "puzzle rocks" in Gabriola Passage. This weathered sandstone has what geologists call horizontal bedding layers cut by vertical fractures with just a bit of tafoni or honeycomb weathering.

Island. I feel that I have brought new ideas, and helped link to American Friends, where I now sit on the board as president.

In 2021 there were seven conservation covenants registered on private land in the Gabriola Island Trust Area. GALTT co-holds two and manages a third.

Tom remarked, "A covenant on a small lot is so much work and the cost is prohibitive. The cost of these lots is astounding. Some go for as much as $700,000! The Gabriola ecosystem suffers at this threshold. The key is protecting a bigger piece and taking responsibility for doing it. It's not all up to governments."

John Peirce added that the AFOCC also accepts cash donations by American landowners to Canadian land trusts and like organizations. "For example, if people want to give money to Ducks Unlimited Canada, they can give it to American Friends and vice versa. In total we have helped over $16 million US coming north with links through organizations such as the Seattle Foundation. This included Halibut Island (recently protected by TLC The Land Conservancy). A regular donation comes from someone who works for Microsoft that goes to the Comox Valley Land Trust. The recent acquisition of Halibut Island and funds to the Comox Valley Land Trust via Microsoft have all been channeled through the AFOCC."

With their new Nature Stewardship program, they are expanding their areas of work. "We have broadened the kinds of things we've been involved with—trails, trail licenses, covenants. Now we are adding removal of invasive species and restoration as a conservation issue," Anne explained. "At Drumbeg Provincial Park there has been a huge multi-year community effort to get rid of Scotch broom, and through BC Parks we've recently received funding to start restoration work."

These rare wetlands in the Elder Cedar (S'ul-hween X'pey) Nature Reserve offer habitat for amphibians and birds, and some relief for people in the heat of summer.

Kerry Marcus described their more recent restoration idea—a native plant depot. "This new idea came to fruition recently. There is so much development, clearing land, etc. We set it up where volunteers come in and salvage native plants if landholders are willing, before they develop their lot. Plants go to the native plant depot, a simple set up with a few pallets. People can take plants for use on their own properties. No money changes hands. It's fun to let ideas grow. Because one or two people are really keen, these ideas can come to pass."

I found this group's work to steward and protect lands on their island so inspiring! They are working in so many different and creative ways near to a bustling metropolis to protect nature. Their camaraderie was obvious, as they were frequently adding to each other's stories, interrupting, and laughing together often, while deftly managing these very successful semi-urban trails and land trust.

The GALTT group of presidents expressed apprehension about protecting more than their current 12 percent, with the expense of small lots and with many of the larger undeveloped parcels part of the treaty process. Anne reported that there are 490 undeveloped lots on Gabriola. Rob remarked that there needs to be self-responsibility at an individual level, which is why he feels the new Nature Stewards program is so important.

They also noted the common difficulty in attracting young people to their organization's board because so many are surviving on multiple jobs. However, on Gabriola, they do have a couple under fifty-year-olds on the board now. These retired, volunteer directors have initiated and generously led this organization from 2 percent to 12 percent land protection on Gabriola. They want to mentor others and pass on the torch.

John brought up the need for financial contributions from the public. He mentioned the Canadian government's Nature Legacy Initiative, a funding program for acquiring lands. Recently extended to 2026, it requires a 1.5:1 financial match in order to apply for the $118 million over four years set aside for the program. With the matching funds requirement, there is substantial need for private donations to access this program, and of course, to help pay for the administrative requirements of maintaining a charitable society.

After my crewmate Doane and I bid farewell to this group of keen elders, Rob, the current president, took us to the Elder Cedar (S'ul-hween X'pey) Nature Reserve. The size and extent of this protected forest was substantial, with the boardwalks ringing the larger cedars. Their massive arms and roots grew out of a healthy wetland, filled with light dappled ferns and skunk cabbage. Only healthy wetlands sustain this large plant, reportedly used by Indigenous people for coughs and headaches. In the 1800s, it was used to form the drug dracontium.[9] With its repugnant aromatic response to leaf damage, it is a rare plant to find on these typically drier islands. We passed many other walkers while we were there, and one group asked us for directions, as some of the trails lead off to the unmarked Treaty lands. I could see that the popularity of the nature reserve offered an essential link to this beautiful forest and a shady oasis in summer for Gabriola islanders.

With the pressures of a more suburban island, this land trust works creatively to help protect natural areas for wildlife and for people. These fun and hard working GALTT folks said that taking responsibility for doing this type of work is essential.

This tombolo is part of Saturnina Island, accessible at lower tides. We rowed out to see the entire island, which was protected by the BC Parks Foundation only days before.

Nearby Saturnina and Link Island—Protected in 2021 and 2022

We only had the later afternoon left before my crewmate Doane had to catch a bus to Parksville and leave me to make the next leg of my journey alone. Luckily, the waters were calm, so we got in the dinghy and headed across a short pass to Saturnina Island, which had just been purchased by the BC Parks Foundation. The GALTT directors had mentioned that the island was on their list of priorities for protected islets around Gabriola. We were excited that the newly formed BC Parks Foundation had purchased it, announcing its protection within days of our trip. The island will be leased to the Islands Trust Conservancy and managed as a Nature Reserve. GALTT plans to be involved in its management and has already begun the task of removing small patches of invasive plants.

As Doane and I drew up to this small island in my dinghy I had identified with my charts, we saw some kayakers enjoying the unique tombolo which reaches out to the Strait of Georgia, with its arching wavelike arm protecting their sun bathing bodies. This unique geological feature is created from the south easters that pummel the straights in winter. We heard an eagle call, then saw it high above in a Douglas-fir tree, safely protected from chain saws. The undeveloped Saturnina Island was in stark contrast with the neighbouring islet, which was full of the sounds of cheerful kids and the

The great blue heron, sighted frequently in each bay, has a long beak which allows it to deftly eat fish, frogs and rodents.
MYLES CLARKE

sight of beach toys below the large houses typically found now on these isolated islands. We walked the flat, hard sandstone beach that characterizes this area, and looked up to the forested upland area, where KEEP OFF signs announced its prior history of private land ownership. But for now, we enjoyed the beach and gentle ocean sounds of waves, gulls, and our own oars as we made our way back to my sailboat for dinner.

Mudge and Link Islands

On my return trip a few weeks later, I passed the neighbouring Mudge Island, where GALTT worked with Jack Schick and the Mudge Island group to conserve the land on the north end of the island which borders Dodd Narrows. Next door to Mudge Island is Link Island, which has been lovingly owned by an American family since the 1960s. Shortly before Betty Swift passed away in 2021, she left instructions that the entire island be gifted to the Islands Trust Conservancy so that the island's natural habitat would be protected forever.

Link Island has the added protection of a conservation covenant held by the Gabriola Land and Trails Trust and the nearby Nanaimo and Area Land Trust. And, indicative of the new connections between land trusts and Indigenous people, the Islands Trust Conservancy is initiating conversations with neighbouring First Nations about its management over time.

The Swift family's dream is that Link Island will become a location for climate change research. Swift left instructions that her children and grandchildren be allowed to use the island for the duration of their lives. This arrangement is called a "life estate" which allows for permitted uses by the family of the donor.

Here is a woman and her family from Seattle willing to give away the $3.73 million value of this 21.24 hectare (52.5 acre) island. "This gift is about the future," said Barbara Swift, Betty Swift's daughter. "It is a gift for us all."

CHAPTER TWO

THETIS ISLAND

Women Leading the Way

*"Taking action with others is an antidote
to climate and environmental grief."*

ANN ERIKSSON
Thetis Island Nature Conservancy (THINC)

LEAVING GABRIOLA NEAR SLACK TIDE I headed south through Dodd Narrows. I made a brief stopover in Whalebone Passage, between Ruxton and Pylades Islands. I watched excitedly as eight Harlequin ducks and a couple of pigeon guillemots cavorted between the rocks and the splashing waters of the rising tide.

A couple of months earlier, in June, I had participated in a nesting survey on Sea Egg Rocks, west of Lasqueti Island, of glaucous-winged gulls, black oystercatchers, and the pelagic and double-crested cormorants. These local gulls, cormorants, and oystercatchers build their nests on remote and isolated rocks or islets. Pigeon guillemots, residents all year here, nest on the cliffs. The gulls build nests of grasses, forbs, lichens, mosses, and twigs. When we counted them, some barely had anything under their speckled blue eggs. Oystercatchers build thin nests of mussel, limpet, and clam shells. The pelagic and double-crested cormorants build large stick nests. Double-crested cormorants only nest in the Salish Sea, with one known exception.[1] The intelligence and tenacity of these sea birds to lay eggs and raise babies in remote locations, safe from human and other predators, didn't surprise me. Birds are far smarter than we realize.

I relaxed, enjoying the seabirds and their play. But then I remembered that a southeast wind was coming, so I left this protected anchorage and headed off south to my next stop—Thetis Island.

As the southeast winds picked up, I motor-sailed into the rising seas. A few hours later, I set my anchor in Clam Bay, which lies between Thetis Island and the recently renamed Penelakut Island. This popular stopping point is a fairly open, shallow bay. Between the two islands lies a slender pass opening to a channel dredged first in 1905 to allow the fishing fleet through at high tide. A fascinating thesis written by David Lewis Rozen on place names of the Hul'qumi'num note that this tidal area between Clam Bay and Telegraph Harbour was called "shéts'ewelh," meaning "dragging [canoe] in between," likely derived from the previous state of tidal flats of mud and sand.[2] Locals now call it The Cut. I learned recently that because these two islands were once thought of as one island, Thetis is now also referred to as the "Thetis side of Penelakut Island."

Glaucous-winged gulls are the most common gulls found around the Salish Sea, nesting on remote rocks in spring.

By now, it was late afternoon, so after arranging an interview for the morning with Ann Eriksson, one of the founding directors of the Thetis Island Nature Conservancy (THINC), I got in my dinghy and paddled around. As I neared the Penelakut Island shore, I saw numerous great blue herons feeding among the gulls along the edges of the low tide. I was surprised at the number of birds feeding there, but then I saw some eelgrass and guessed why the shoreline attracted such healthy life.

I had met Ann previously when she was the Gulf Islands Regional Coordinator with SeaChange Marine Conservation Society. This organization, founded by Nikki Wright, has been working with islanders mapping eelgrass beds, transplanting eelgrass to nearshore bays, and recently the society arranged to pick up debris from the sea floor around some of the islands. Eelgrass is a tall ribbon-like sea plant that traps sediment, stabilizes the substrate, sequesters carbon, and reduces the force of wave energy, reducing coastal erosion. This nondescript tall grass-like plant forms the base of a highly productive marine food web, providing a nursery for young salmon and a home to hundreds of marine creatures. As climate change raises sea levels, increased winds and wave action will continue to erode shorelines. Unfortunately, many people who live on the waterfront add large rocks and other forms of bulkheads thinking they are protecting their homes. This has proven to make the problem worse, increasing erosion as waves dig into and undermine the shoreline below. SeaChange and their partners offer shoreline restoration workshops which provide alternative ideas to help buffer the increased sea levels and wave action that waterfront owners face.[3]

In the morning, I got in my dinghy and headed through The Cut to meet Ann and two other women who had taken the protection of nature on Thetis Island into their own hands.

Ann Eriksson is a biologist and writer of adult fiction and ecological literacy non-fiction books for younger readers. She and her husband, Gary Geddes, a renowned poet, teacher, and editor, welcomed me to their waterfront home in The Cut. Like Ann, Gary puts his passion on the line, telling me he was recently arrested at the old growth logging protest in Fairy Creek on Vancouver Island.

Ann, who was raised in the prairies, first discovered the Gulf Islands in 1974 while on her way to an exchange program in New Zealand with a friend. While waiting in Vancouver for their flight to Auckland, the two girls took an excursion to Victoria aboard a BC Ferry. While transiting Active Pass, Ann looked over to Galiano Island and announced that she wanted to live there. Eight years later, she did just that. She lived on Galiano for ten years before moving to Victoria where she raised two children and earned a degree in biology with a minor in environmental studies. She started writing in 2000, combining her interests in ecology and social issues. I had recently loved reading her 2010 novel, *Falling from Grace*, about a woman who pursued entomological research in the canopy of Canada's West Coast ancient forests. There she meets the protesters who come to bring attention to the old growth logging going on all around her.

Ann and her husband Gary moved full time to Thetis Island in 2010. Knowing small communities are volunteer run, she joined a community garden group, out of which grew the Thetis Island Nature Conservancy. At the time, Thetis was the only Southern Gulf Island with ferry service that didn't have an active conservancy. Ann related how the Thetis Island Nature Conservancy got started:

> We thought, let's just give it a whirl and expand our educational offerings from gardens to nature. We created a society and were about to have our first community meeting when someone came forward and said that a large property on Burchell Hill was for sale and that we needed to protect it. The price was over half a million dollars. We were just a little group, and the idea was terrifying, but we decided to try. That was the beginning of lots of fundraising, which in time proved successful for the purchase of the Fairyslipper Forest Nature Reserve, now owned by the Islands Trust Conservancy. We were short quite a lot near the end, and the Cowichan Community Land Trust came in at the last minute and contributed enough to complete the acquisition.

Ann drove me in her electric car to the 16.6 hectare (41 acre) Fairyslipper Forest Nature Reserve. Named after the beautiful fairyslipper orchid (*Calypso bulbosa*) which blooms there in the spring, the reserve is situated within Canada's smallest and most at-risk biogeoclimatic zone—the Coastal Douglas-fir.[4] A handsome wooden kiosk built out of locally milled wood and constructed by volunteers graces the trailhead. It houses a triptych information panel designed by a local graphic designer. It describes, with beautiful drawings, the species at risk that are known to live in the reserve: peacock vinyl and silver crackers lichen and Ozette coralroot. The at-risk red-legged frog and Pacific sideband snail also have their homes in the forest.

As we walked along a trail, built by local volunteers and a group of children from Penelakut, through maturing second-growth, I noticed many large old veteran Douglas-fir, western redcedar, western hemlock, and arbutus trees. Ann reminded me of a phone call she made to my husband, Gordon Scott, when these two conservation campaigns first got started. With over thirteen years of experience as conservation director for a Washington State land trust, he assured her that once one area is protected, other landowners will come forward to discuss options for protecting their land. Gordon worked in conservation in Washington State, first as a planner for Whatcom County, then for the Lummi Nation. Today he is the president of the Lasqueti Island Nature Conservancy. Ann met him at several land trust conferences over the years, and sought him out for advice.

Ann paused beside a particularly large, old veteran Douglas-fir. "This land has become a beloved place in the community for locals and visitors. You see vehicles in the parking lot every day. We manage it for the Islands Trust Conservancy. We maintain the trail, try to keep invasive species such as Scotch broom and English holly under control, and have installed nest boxes for western screech owls."

Ann later took me to The Portal, a former Anglican church camp, which was purchased by the Porter family for the community's use for nature education, conservation, and sustainability purposes. THINC has been operating nature education

The beautiful fairyslipper orchid, *Calypso bulbosa*, the namesake of the Fairyslipper Forest Nature Reserve on Thetis Island. MARCIE WELSH

programs since 2016 out of an old camp craft shack on the property, now known as the Nature House.

Ann explained,

> Students hired under Canada Summer Jobs run programs for us at the Nature House each summer. We offer other nature education events throughout the year. Along with nature reserve management activities, we participate in several community science initiatives including forage fish monitoring, the Western Screech Owl nest box program, the Community Bat program and Purple Martin Recovery program. Most of the work is carried out by volunteers, but in 2021 we were fortunate to hire a year-round, part-time education and stewardship coordinator, which has allowed us to add new activities in sustainability, community food security, and landowner outreach. Keeping the funds flowing through donations and grants is a big challenge for a small organization.

Ann told me that THINC's funding comes from donations, memberships, fundraising, and a small contract with the Islands Trust Conservancy for management of the nature reserves. These are augmented with grants from Canada Summer Jobs and the BC Community Gaming Branch. THINC has also been successful in securing one-time grants from foundations such as the Gosling Foundation, the McLean Foundation, and the Sitka Foundation. I was impressed with this diversity of funding support in such a short time.

I toured the Nature House, where THINC also has its office and maintains a pollinator garden. The old building was crammed full of colourful nature displays: a humpback whale made out of recycled plastic bottles, a bat cave, a giant bee hive, a salt water aquarium and touch tank, and a library of donated books.

Afterwards, we sat down outside on a picnic table, overlooking Stuart Channel, with two of THINC's other directors, Maureen Loiselle and Laurel March.

Laurel, a board member and philanthropic landowner on the island, started the conversation. "The reality is there's so much more that needs to be done. The number of people who are interested in conservation is pathetically small. Human beings are so self-absorbed and have lost their connection with nature." Laurel pointed out that the Nature House and THINC's educational programs help students of all ages appreciate and understand the uniqueness and rarity of this, the most endangered ecosystem in BC—the Coastal Douglas-fir zone.

It was not until she became involved with THINC that Laurel realized how small and special the CDF zone truly was. She explained the challenges on Thetis Island. "Our culture has so much attachment to private property rights. This precious area we live in is 90 percent privately owned. It is unique in its diversity and number of endangered species it contains, but it is also so important that we protect it because, unlike most of the province, there is very little land that is publicly held."

Maureen Loiselle, a resident of Thetis for over thirty-five years, added, "people don't understand the real values. We have to educate people about where we live, especially the newcomers who are still scraping all the understory away. When we started to fundraise for the acquisition of Fairyslipper Forest, I heard people say, 'there's

The Nature House includes a touch tank aquarium and other displays, such as these of feathers and native species plants.

nothing but trees on Thetis. Why do you want to protect more?' A recent clear-cut in the harbour opened up a few people's minds."

Maureen laughed as she told me, "even our husbands said, they'll never do it, and now they have to swallow their words." She went on to say, "Sometimes, in these small communities, funding things like sports centres and community halls is easier. It took us three years to raise $500,000 to protect land for all the islanders. The new community centre got grants and donations right away. Fundraising for Fairyslipper was a collaborative effort. We called everybody in the phone book."

Ann added, "Fairyslipper was a huge community effort with more than half the funds coming from local donations. In celebration, we danced and ate cake together."

The third founder of the Thetis Conservancy I met that day is Laurel March. She grew up in Vancouver and told me she has always loved trees. She described her family's role in THINC's successful acquisition project on Moore Hill.

The founding ThINC directors the author met: Ann Eriksson, Maureen Loiselle, and Laurel March.

I first visited Thetis because my mother's cousin had been searching for property in the Gulf Islands. He learned of acreages for sale on Thetis in 1989. On a soggy day he came to check out a 52-acre Moore Hill property but found it too rugged, and determined he should return to investigate the adjoining lots. My mother and I came along on his second mission. We were totally supportive of his purchasing the lot with the glorious, varied shoreline we were all enamoured with. Not wanting to have people drive through this lot to access the two lots over, he also purchased the adjacent lots (they were very cheap at the time!). Mum and I were so taken with Thetis that we thought we should see the 52 acres our cousin had initially rejected.

The next visit to Thetis found us all on the magical ridge of Moore Hill walking through open forest with views to either side. My first instinct was that this property had to be protected. We put in an offer, but to our disappointment, a woman had visited the previous day and her offer had been accepted. We then turned our attention to the lot on the other side of our cousin's, which we collectively purchased, much to the delight of our cousin, who now had assembled 52 acres!

Fast forward to 2014, my mother and I acquired our cousin's Thetis properties from his estate, and I have moved to Thetis and joined the board of THINC. We became actively engaged with our partners the Islands Trust Conservancy and the Cowichan Community Land Trust in an effort to acquire 40 acres on Burchell Hill to create the island's first publicly accessible nature reserve. We had until 2017 to raise $500,000 and I knew that most of the money would have to be raised locally. In 2015 we learned through our ITC partners that the woman who purchased the 52 acres on Moore Hill had approached them about the possibility of protecting her property. Realizing that my long-standing dream of seeing 100 acres on Moore Hill preserved might be ultimately achievable, I decided to contact her to let her know of our shared interest. I spoke of protecting my own property and indicated I might in the future be in a position to help her ensure that her property was preserved. She was adamant that her property was not for sale. A few months later her situation changed and she called in a panic needing to sell her property.

I indicated as a first step, before it could be considered for conservation, an appraisal would be required. She got back to me within weeks with an appraisal of $1 million. I encouraged her to contact the Islands Trust Conservancy. They are a wonderful partner to THINC. They submitted an application to the Habitat Stewardship Program seeking assistance over two years for both the Moore Hill and Burchell Hill projects. While the program officer had been excited by the scope of the two Hills Projects, in the end, funding was only provided for Moore Hill in 2016. The owner made a contribution through the Ecological Gifts Program, and my family contributed the balance, with both areas being put into the ownership of ITC.

The tenacity of this woman and her philanthropic family's ability to contribute to these local campaigns is a fascinating story. With the determination and hard work of these initial women directors, THINC has accomplished a great deal since their founding. They have helped to create a strong conservation ethic on the island, protected two nature reserves, and built trails on the Fairyslipper Forest Nature Reserve.

THINC continues with nature education and community science programs and manages the recently-created People's Apothecary Garden, a medicinal plant garden located on private land but open to the public. The board has gone through many changes of directors. Community support has remained steadfast. THINC has more than sixty members, which is a lot on a small island like Thetis with a population of 379 people. In 2022, THINC launched a Nature Stewards Program working with private landowners to protect and restore biodiversity on their property. Ann said, "It's part of the global initiative to protect at least 30 percent of the planet by 2030. We're at about 5 percent now, so we have a long way to go. We're thrilled to have Elders and other Knowledge Holders from Penelakut on our working group and participating in cultural site visits as part of the program." It takes a whole community to rise to the needed calls to restore our relations with the natural world.

I was truly impressed with the extensive work of this fairly new organization. Ann took me back to my dinghy in The Cut. On parting, she told me about a recent talk she heard by Richard Hebda, who said he follows the Indigenous land acknowledgement with an acknowledgement to nature. Richard had been the curator (in botany and earth history) at the Royal British Columbia Museum for thirty-eight years and is a passionate researcher, professor, and speaker on vegetation and climate history in BC. I thought about this as I rowed back to Clam Bay and my sailboat. As gulls and a bald eagle flew above me, I counted over ten great blue herons feeding along the muddy low-tide edge of the beach on Penelakut Island. The amazing diversity of life, just here along the shoreline is miraculous. Giant birds feed on tiny fish protected and nurtured by an underwater garden of eelgrass full of untold numbers of aquatic species.

I looked north to Thetis Island where Andy Lamb and his wife Virginia live. Now retired, in his working days Andy was the chief collector and education coordinator at the Vancouver Aquarium and fish culturist with Fisheries and Oceans Canada. His

ThINC directors at Moore Hill Nature Reserve in 2020.
GARY GEDDES

bestselling 2005 book, *Marine Life of the Pacific Northwest: A Photographic Encyclopedia of Invertebrates, Seaweeds and Selected Fishes*, is a treasure and contains an extensive collection of the many fascinating marine creatures living in the Salish Sea. Ann told me he is one of THINC's most ardent volunteers, as he organizes an annual sea star count and is famous for his intertidal walks. In the bay out in front of his home, I noticed a mooring buoy Ann had told me about. It is an innovative new bottom friendly mooring that was installed by SeaChange to replace Andy's old mooring and chain, which can drag on the sea floor at low tide and destroy areas of eelgrass beds. SeaChange is one of the first to trial these new bottom friendly mooring systems. They have installed them at Ford Cove on Hornby Island and Kwilákm (Deep/Mannion Bay) on Bowen Island.[5]

As dusk set in, I heard the call and response of two crews of seven Penelakut paddlers. Then I looked out the hatch and saw them paddling—strong and focused. As one called, the others responded by lifting their paddles over to the other side. The rhythmic beauty of their oars matched the sounds of the waves hitting my own craft's hull. Twice they paddled around the bay, past each modern yacht, calling out when abreast of our recreational vessels, such a contrast to the simple, plain canoes they paddled.

The Penelakut people, with a population of 1,001 registered Penelakut Community members, are split into half on-reserve and half off-reserve. Their reserves are in four locations: Galiano's northern tip, Tsussie on Vancouver Island, Tent Island, and Penelakut Island.

After an evening meal and paddle around, I went to bed. Then in the middle of the night I awoke to sounds of drumming and chanting. It continued for hours until its rhythm lulled me back to sleep. A few days later I learned that more than 160 unmarked graves that may hold the bodies of Indigenous children had been found on Penelakut Island, previously known as Kuper Island, and the former site of one of Canada's most notorious residential schools.[6]

I awoke in the morning and recalled the night's chanting. I felt like I was amidst a sea change in our cultural world. With this disturbing new knowledge of some of the impacts from the settler rush to colonize the Salish Sea, I blessed the neighbouring Penelakut Tribe. I hoped that they would be able to find some reconciliation with the world of conservation.

Ann and Laurel had left me with a final story about a recent trip they made to Penelakut Island. Thetis islanders had been invited to visit Penelakut to celebrate the opening of a new trail built by local youth. One of the Penelakut women told Laurel how grateful she was to walk the trails and learn about the plants she saw along the way. These recent contacts and fledgling relationships between Indigenous communities and land trusts is a positive progression today.

As I lifted up my own anchor and chain, I considered my own impacts, as I headed out to my old home port on Salt Spring Island.

Bald eaglet, calling for food—a wake-up call. MYLES CLARKE

CHAPTER THREE

SALT SPRING ISLAND

Protests, Fundraising, and Generous Donations

"It took major fundraising, and it took some of us taking off our clothes for calendars, websites, and horseback rides down Howe Street."

MURRAY REISS

I AWOKE TO THE SOUND OF A MOTOR. Peeking out my portlight window, I saw Sauv going by in a powerboat. I sold Sauv my previous wooden sailboat when I left the island years ago. Opening the hatch, I was greeted by the familiar sight of Salt Spring Island's Mount Maxwell and Burgoyne Bay. My senses were in rapture as I heard the *awk-awk-awk* of a great blue heron as it flew over and landed at the head of the bay, joining another five herons seeking food in the tidal waters of the estuary, now a provincial park.

After twelve years living on Lasqueti Island, further north, what a joy it was to be here again, in the calmer waters of the Southern Gulf Islands. Looking north toward Maple Bay, I listened to the chirping purple martins at the dock, the trilling belted kingfishers, and then I saw an osprey! What an amazing place—still very much alive and full of the mystery and diversity of life.

In 2021, on my return to the bay where I had once moored my sailboat, I saw again the familiar slopes of Mount Maxwell with its Garry oak and giant Douglas-firs welcoming me back. The day I arrived, Houseboat Steve, a live-aboard who had been in the bay for over thirty years, came over to say hello. His yellow and white two-storey houseboat was still there, along with a pair of endangered barn swallows nesting under its eves and rufous hummingbirds buzzing back and forth. The night before I endured the sounds of two gulls screeching at his windows. Now that the entire area is protected as a park, he told me about the increasing visitors, some with dogs that people let roam on the beach, against the provincial park's signage prohibiting dogs off leash. He was particularly disgruntled about a visiting boater who had allowed his dogs to kill some river otters who had been trapped on shore. One of the island's many characters, he cared about and knew intimately the otters, birds, and marine life of the bay.

Belted kingfishers, loudly calling, drew my eye. Here I counted nine great blue herons feeding on shore at the low tide line. They were flying into nearby trees, and I wondered if they were setting up a new nesting colony. A great blue heron nesting colony existed across the island at Walker Hook in 2008, but the birds had abandoned the area due to a combination of eagle predation and an adjoining new human development. With hopes of seeing a new heron colony develop, I was reminded of

Mount Maxwell from my boat in Burgoyne Bay.

the resilience of nature, given half a chance, and the growing conservation ethic that has propelled Salt Spring Island's incredible conservation achievements.

Some of the biggest changes on the islands in the Salish Sea in the last fifty years have occurred on Salt Spring. With its three ferries, the island draws a transient working population and more tourists than other islands. It has a hospital and several doctors. It has the largest population of any island—the 2021 census counted 11,635 residents, a 10.2 percent increase from 2016. Many wealthy people have moved to Salt Spring as the burgeoning Vancouver and Victoria populations have spilled over to the next island "paradise." The artist community has exploded, and with it a different type of community from the back-to-the land island I and many others sought when I first moved here in the '80s.

The Formation of the Salt Spring Island Conservancy

Maureen Milburn is one the island's local heroes for her work in conservation. With six other women, she started the Salt Spring Island Conservancy (SSIC) in 1994, motivated to do something about the lands on the island that were being cleared and developed.

Maureen told me that the Conservancy's formation came out of several streams. To their horror, MacMillan Bloedel sold 1,214 hectares (3,000 acres) of the island, very cheaply, to a local of disrepute who came in and logged it. Maureen said it was traumatic, with MacMillan Bloedel originally offering to save some areas for park land, in return for tremendous development. Islanders lost that area, but it motivated these women to come up with ideas to stop it ever happening again.

The second stream came from a landowner, Martin Williams, who offered some of his land as a donation, and the rest at a reduced price in order to conserve it. Maureen and Fiona Flook, another of the founding women, went to the Saturday market, raising money so they could purchase the property in partnership with the Islands Trust. However, Martin wasn't satisfied with the option of the land going to the regional government because they could not promise to protect it in perpetuity. He wanted to have a local organization protect his land, forever.

This is one of the reasons for working with a local conservancy or land trust. They will ask another land trust to register a conservation covenant on their acquired properties, creating a legal agreement on title promising to protect it in perpetuity—by a second organization. Local governments and especially the provincial government will rarely make that promise in writing.

Fiona Flook, the second founding woman of the SSI Conservancy I interviewed, said her catalyst for joining the Conservancy was from being part of a Crown Lands Use Coalition (CLUC).[1] The Coalition was formed because the Province was downsizing its Crown land holdings and selling off small parcels. Salt Spring Island had a few parcels of Crown land for sale, with rumours of another golf course in the offing. They formed a coalition of community groups, including the Chamber of Commerce and other local businesses. Fiona explained, "A few of us went out with hand held compasses, before geographic positioning systems (GPS), and walked around and found the corner pins. We looked at these Crown lands and said, wouldn't it be nice to save this."

When they were at the market, they spread out her maps of the island showing the precious Crown lands that were undeveloped, still primarily intact. Through this Crown Lands Use Coalition they applied for a Free Crown Land grant, a program that was set up for a time by the Province. Several of these Crown land lots were eventually added to the Mount Erskine Park. Fiona remarked, "We've saved a lot of trees on Salt Spring over the years. I felt that the island could get overpopulated quickly."

Maureen and Fiona, together with another five women—Ann Richardson, Nancy Braithwaite, Heather Martin, Ailsa Pearse, and Mallory Pred—could see the threats and challenges that were coming and decided to do something that had rarely been done before—form a land trust to acquire and protect lands forever. Maureen told me, "Sometimes you just have luck. We got lucky. The group of people just worked. People can do so much when they come together."

They headed over to Galiano Island to visit the fledgling conservancy already started there. Ken Millard of the Galiano Conservancy showed them around, described their founding constitution, and generally encouraged their neighbouring island to form a land trust, so that they too could own land, manage it, and protect it themselves. Although Galiano's purposes were more related to protecting land for community use, and practicing sustainable forestry, the SSIC's founding women decided to focus on land conservation for habitat protection, specifically.

During their early years, the Conservancy housed itself in Maureen and her husband Sam Lightman's home. Here they kept the records and started their own newsletter, *The Acorn*. Sam ran the communications for their first campaign, putting something informative in the local paper, the *Gulf Islands Driftwood*, every week. Sam was a communication professional, so he was ideal as the first editor of *The Acorn*.

The Mill Farm

The new Conservancy quickly became involved in a very dramatic campaign to conserve a piece of land that was owned collectively by ten partners. Like a bad marriage, over time things were not turning out as planned for this group of landowners. The

The Founding Directors of the Salt Spring Island Conservancy, known as the Founding Mothers, from left: Fiona Flook, Alisa Pearse, Nancy Braithwaite, Heather Martin, Maureen Milburn, Ann Richardson, and Mallory Pred. SALT SPRING ISLAND CONSERVANCY

Mill Farm is an area on the southwest side of the island with rare stands of old growth trees. With the zoning at third reading, two of the owners repudiated the group's internal bylaws. Bob Twaites, one of the "children of the divorce," told me that, "with the help of Ian Clement, a very generous lawyer who donated his time, we attempted to reconstitute the group's bylaws in a legally binding form." Sadly, despite many extensions to give the group time to reform, the two aggrieved most-recent purchasers went to court, because they had no way to sell, use, or enjoy their shares. All owners would be compelled to sell through the *Partition Act*. This is similar to a legal settlement for people co-owning a home when they can no longer live together. Bob suggested that the Salt Spring Conservancy bid to buy the lands.

By now the Conservancy had acquired legal status. So, back to the market they went to raise more money, this time for the ~65 hectare (160 acre) Mill Farm. Because they decided to take pledges, in case the deal didn't go through, they were sitting with money promised but nothing to take to the courthouse. Maureen explained how the drama unfolded:

> We had a snap decision by the court that it would be heard on Wednesday. They phoned me on the Friday before, and said "you have to turn up in court on Wednesday and your money has to be in the provincial government coffers by Monday." We were sitting with hundreds of pledges, from $50 to $500, but we couldn't get them in time. So I thought, oh my god, what are we going to do? Okay we need to put in $100,000 by Monday. All we need is ten people with $10,000, and call them and ask them to lend it to us. I got the list, and the first person I called was Gary Holman. He said don't worry, I'll lend you the money. I thought this is fantastic. The next person I called had a ton of money, I told the story to them and explained this is just a loan. This person turned me down. I thought, Oh, no, this is going to be hard. Then the phone rang, and a local woman, Gay Alkoff said, "Maureen, I understand you need $100,000. Come over this afternoon, and we'll lend it you." And we went over, and she and her husband said, "We just want to give you the money," and that was it! We had the money for court.[2] Before Monday, someone else gave us an extra $50,000, "in case you need it."

A second bidder was a Washington State logging company. They had the capacity to increase their offer to win title to the land, but the new Conservancy didn't. Bob offered to put his own share into the young Conservancy's hands, but a surprising turn of events transpired. The owners all stood up in court and said they would take the lower bid. And the judge? Justice Alan McEachern said, "This isn't a democracy, but I'm inclined to accept the slightly lower offer." That was wonderful. Maureen said that the heroes on that day were the landowners, who accepted the lower offer.

The Conservancy worked with a number of other partners on the campaign to protect the Mill Farm including the Capital Regional District (CRD). Through diligent research, they learned that the CRD had a Parks & Recreation Reserve and realized that it had significant conservation provisions. They approached the chair and their local representative and joined forces.[3] In the end, the CRD took title to the land because the young Conservancy was concerned about long-term management.

The Mill Farm campaign had high media profile and it served to educate and energize the community toward land preservation. The money they had raised went to the Mill Farm purchase. Maureen finished her story by saying, "The outpouring of support was exceptional and the success of the campaign was an antidote to the unfortunate loss of MacMillan Bloedel lands. As an island we came to understand that we could work together to achieve great things in land conservation, and this set an example for future conservation successes on the island."

Salt Spring Water Preservation Society

Before the founding of the Conservancy, a group of people on the island united to protect watersheds. The Salt Spring Water Preservation Society's (sswps) mandate is to protect sources of drinking water, to educate islanders, and to research water resources. Potable water is supplied to many islanders under regional water authorities. The North Salt Spring Water Improvement District was a major player. Bob Twaites, who was also involved in the sswps, told me, "Tom Gossett and the sswps proposed that only electric motors be allowed on St. Mary Lake," the largest lake and a primary water source for much of the island. They were challenged in court on that, and lost, first at a provincial level. Then the Society's counsel, Jack Woodward, fought it all the way to the Supreme Court of Canada and won, leading to hundreds of lakes across the country being protected through this type of legislation.

Another challenge came along with a large development planned for Channel Ridge, an area on the west side of the island which forms a large part of the watershed for St. Mary Lake. Lindholm Development had big plans for a large village, almost a city, and asked for double density in exchange for giving up areas at the top of the ridge to protect the watershed. The plan went to the Islands Trust for approval. The Salt Spring Water Preservation Society, while not wanting the extra densities proposed, was willing to accept that the land on the watershed side of the ridge would be left and covenanted, rather than developed. But, as Bob explains, before the deal was complete,

> The developers brought in logging equipment and logged the top of the ridge. Jack Woodward, often a hero for ssi Water Preservation Society, jumped up and got an injunction to stop the logging. Mr. Lindholm was furious, and when the injunction was served in court, he went into the courtroom, had a heart attack, and died. The land was subject to an agreement now. One can't benefit from an agreement and then change it—such as logging to provide views for future residences along the ridge. The land was promised as a natural barrier and was not to be mucked with. We spent a lot of time going there and ensuring that the logging wasn't continuing. In the end, we preserved 273 acres, a lot on a steep slope, visible from the St. Mary Road, as that deal settled.

In order to enhance its protected status, subsequently, sswps registered a conservation covenant on the watershed lands, co-held by the Salt Spring Island Conservancy and TLC The Land Conservancy of BC.

There have been a lot of amazingly dedicated people on Salt Spring Island, and those in the sswps, including Bob Twaites, Tom Gosset, and Ian Clement were to save yet another of the island's main water supplies—Maxwell Lake.

View from the top of Mount Maxwell (Hwmat'etsum) looking into Sansum Narrows, showing the forested slopes of Mount Bruce, at risk of logging in 1999.

After spending the night tied to my old mooring, I went into Ganges to interview a few more Salt Spring Island conservationists the next morning. There at the historic Mahon Memorial Hall, a local fibre art show portrayed the beauty and degradation of nature through twenty stunning fibre art hangings. True to its artistic reputation, the show moved me to tears, feeling both humanity's care and intimacy and its blind willfulness. As I was leaving, I bumped into two seasoned islanders I had known from my Salt Spring Island days—Peter Lamb and Jean Gelwicks. Over lunch we discussed the evolution of the Salt Spring Island Conservancy, the larger Salish Sea, and conservation today.

Jean and Peter had been early board members of the Salt Spring Island Conservancy. Peter had also served as a Salt Spring Island Local Trustee for a few years. Having worked in the energy sector in Ontario as a young man, he knew first-hand the destructive power of the oil industry. Peter wrote *The Islands Trust Story* in 2009 in celebration of its thirty-fifth-year anniversary.[4] This thirty-two page booklet summarizes the various stages of this unique regional government's authority, including its associated land trust, the Islands Trust Conservancy (formerly called the Islands Trust Fund).

Rather than subsidizing and supporting the fossil fuel industry, Peter believes that the preserve and protect government mandate needs to be expanded into other regions. Recognizing corporate powers, he thinks we need senior government intervention—legislation and laws that would prohibit environmental destruction. He lamented that current governments campaigned with promises to stop the continued cutting of old growth which they are still allowing, while subsidizing the fossil fuel industry, liquefied natural gas (LNG), and devastating pipelines.

In 2010, Peter helped to establish Transition Salt Spring, a group focusing on finding solutions to the looming changes to our climate. He conveyed a frustration that is all too familiar, and the reason that many people work for their local land trust to acquire or covenant lands to protect them. He noted the couple's personal actions: they drive an electric car, ride electric bikes, have rooftop solar panels, and a heat pump. They rarely travel by air.

Jean Gelwicks explained that as a young girl she had lived in Arlington, Virginia, near a forest and field with a stream running through it. She spent much of her time getting down, close to nature, and being in wonder of it all. She has carried this passion for nature into her adult life, leaving a legacy early education program that has resulted in adults who now protect what she taught them to see, understand, and value.

Jean reflected on the youth education program, Stewards in Training, that she and a few others led when she was with the Salt Spring Island Conservancy. The program began with one grade and then, year by year, grew to where it now includes kindergarten to grade seven. "Over the first eight years in school on Salt Spring Island, students visit different locations to learn about all the ecosystems on the island, having fun, and hopefully learning to take care of it." She and a few other Conservancy volunteers started, first in the classroom, teaching them about what they would see, then out they went into island ecosystems to explore and be mesmerized by the fascinating creatures they saw. Then exhausted, but excited, the kids returned back to their classrooms to review what they had seen. This program is ongoing with all students, including home-schooled students.

Garry oaks in Burgoyne Bay Park. These Garry oaks are part of the large Garry oak woodland which flanks the west side of Mount Maxwell (Hwmat'etsum).

Although Jean didn't give herself much credit for this successful program, others did. Bob Weeden, another past Conservancy director and lifelong conservationist applauded her incredible creativity and determination to help young people learn and care for nature around them. Bob highlighted one particular memory. When I interviewed Bob at Burgoyne Bay, he said, "Being managers of pieces of land with trails, salamanders, and creeks, we could offer the children real experiences. I remember being on a few of these tours, and taking an individual child and following their questions along the trail. They got so interested, and it was so exciting to have that interest. It's like food for the soul."

The Conservation of Mount Maxwell (Hwmat'etsum) Watershed and Burgoyne Bay

While living on Salt Spring Island in 1999, I took a trip up the Sechelt Inlet on a friend's converted fish boat. As he led us through the tumultuous Skookumchuck Narrows and Sechelt Rapids, I faced backwards in trepidation as it wasn't quite slack tide. Safely through, I sighed with relief as we travelled further, hoping to find some wilderness in the Narrows and Salmon Inlets. As we turned into Salmon Inlet we were shocked to see a clear cut mountainside, ringed with logging roads and denuded hillsides. How could this kind of outright desecration be legal? Would any returning salmon survive the destruction of the watershed leading to its named inlet?

On our return home, as we rounded the north end of Salt Spring Island, along Stuart Channel and past Vesuvius, the densely forested western slopes of Salt Spring's Mount Maxwell (Hwmat'etsum) came into view. I felt gloriously happy as I gazed at the wholeness and beauty of the forests all along the edges of my home bay. I took photo after photo of the dappled Garry oak slopes, as we headed into our anchorage in Burgoyne Bay (Xwaaqw'um).

The next day I learned that two business men from Vancouver had bought 2,023.4 hectares (5,000 acres) of the south end of Salt Spring Island. With this purchase, 10 percent of the island—the entirety of the forests surrounding the bay and beyond—was now in their hands.

Once home, I put the photos together into a collage and mailed it off to a friend at the BC Conservation Data Centre. A short time later she called to say that the extent of the intact Garry oak woodlands evidenced by these photos helped determine that it was the largest in Canada! This added to the ecological inventory that had been done three years prior to the new owners taking possession of the lands. The South and West Salt Spring Conservation Partnership had established that "the new company's purchase encompassed" the highest concentration of sensitive ecosystems and rare and endangered species in the region.[5] A conservation battle was on.

Mount Maxwell's Baynes Peak is one of the highest peaks on the Southern Gulf islands, overlooking the bay and channels that connect over to Vancouver Island. Its dragon shaped peak became an early provincial park in 1938—so early that it still has some of the largest old growth Douglas-fir trees in the Gulf Islands. This majestic mountain's peak is significant in several ways.

There are many huge rocks that sit precariously on Mount Maxwell's western flanks, creating large caves within. A big earthquake affected the area approximately three hundred years ago, confirmed by the age of the trees on the mountain. As a result, soils were exposed and seeds took root in this perfect growing condition. Interestingly, very similar huge rocks stand singly in fields across the water in the Cowichan Valley.

In Chinese culture, a mountain is associated with either a dragon or a tiger. Dragons are "powerful and benevolent symbols in Chinese culture, with supposed control over watery phenomenon, e.g., summoning rain during a drought."[6] Along with the big trees surrounding the top, Mount Maxwell's flatter eastern slope includes Maxwell Lake. Its watershed and connected streams go down to form Blackburn Lake, another source of drinking water on the island, unprotected from development up to the late '90s.

The history of protests on Salt Spring goes back to 1964. At that time, Weldwood was buying lands on many of the Gulf Islands. They purchased ~300 hectares (743 acres) of south Salt Spring Island, from a coal company that held title—Canadian Collieries. An anti-logging protest developed when they began clear-cutting, which started out peaceful enough, but eventually led to damage to some of their equipment. This was later condemned by island organizations.[7]

Then, in the early '90s, MacMillan Bloedel sold their 1,214 hectares (3,000 acres) to a local logger, leading to one of the primary reasons for the founding of the Salt Spring Island Conservancy. These lands were also clear cut. For an island community in the '70s and '80s with small farms, orchards, a couple of schools, the village of Ganges, and a growing tourism economy, these logging operations and loss of forest lands were starting to generate a lot of community angst.

This large arbutus is among the largest in the province, situated in front of one of several huge conglomerate and sandstone rocks that tumbled down Mt. Maxwell

Private Managed Forest land is a land classification established in 1988 by the BC Assessment Authority to encourage landowners to manage their lands for long-term forest production under the *Private Managed Forest Land Act.* Its historical origins go back to the E&N Railway construction grants given in 1884 by the Crown to private landowners including forestry companies. Private Forest Land is not under the authority of the Islands Trust, causing lack of protection throughout the islands.

Bavaria's eleventh prince, Johann von Thurn und Taxis, owned 2,023 hectares (5,000 acres) of Salt Spring Island from 1962 to 1999. Thurn und Taxis was from a wealthy aristocratic family who made their money in early postal services. He invested heavily in BC after the Second World War. He formed the Texada Logging Company, which owned the largest area of Private Managed Forest land on the island.

Having lived on the Texada Logging Company property in one of its five houses in the mid-nineties, I viewed the company as a friendly owner with an on-island manager overseeing selective logging and house rentals to islanders surrounding Burgoyne Bay. Some logging was done during this tenure, with plans to cut a third of its timber every twenty years.[8] There was a small dock and boom boat moving logs below the house I rented at the end of the road, which also led to a small public dock.

In 1996, four levels of government, local conservation organizations including TLC The Land Conservancy of BC, Salt Spring Island Conservancy, and the Water Preservation Society met with the intention of securing large land holdings for conservation in the south and west of Salt Spring, including Prince Thurn und Taxis's landholdings. This was one tenth of the island, and adjacent to large Crown parcels. The South and West Salt Spring Conservation Partnership (SWSCP) met for three years up until the sale of the land to developers in 1999.[9]

Members of the South and West Salt Spring Island Conservation Partnership: TLC The Land Conservancy of BC, the Capital Regional District Parks, BC Parks, the Salt Spring Island Conservancy, the Salt Spring Water Preservation Society, the Islands Trust Fund, the Nature Conservancy of Canada, the Habitat Acquisition Trust, the Salt Spring Island Local Trust Committee, several landowners with an interest in conservation covenants, and the Salt Spring Island Parks, Arts, and Recreation Commission.

With the prince's passing in 1990, the heirs found that they couldn't sustain the debts that had been incurred. The land was then purchased in 1999 by two Vancouver developers, Rob MacDonald and Derek Trethewey, naming their company the Texada Land Corporation. Their interests were large-scale logging and real estate development, including fancy estates on the slopes of Mount Maxwell.

The community moved into action, holding a welcome protest breakfast for the new owners to discuss their plans—as the company started to log. This all ran counter to the last three years of community planning to purchase the lands from the previous owner.

Although the Islands Trust was regulating land use, with their preserve and protect mandate on the Gulf Islands, they still had no jurisdiction over lands in the Forest Land Reserve, which some of these forests were in. And the logging had begun in earnest, with three to five acres being cut a day!

Three separate campaigns took shape. The protection through purchase of the Mount Maxwell watershed happened simultaneously with a campaign to acquire the larger area surrounding the entire Burgoyne Bay. A third focus was affinity groups, some who held protests to stop the active clear cutting that was going on.

When the previous owners, Texada Logging Company, had title, Bob Twaites explained to me by phone that through the visionary actions of Tom Gossett, the Salt

Spring Water Preservation Society (sswps) made an offer to purchase the watershed lands. "We made an Agreement to Purchase the watershed, while we tried to raise the money to buy the area, but that offer languished. People weren't excited about the campaign as they didn't perceive the danger to the lands at that time. Then, when the land changed hands, we weren't able to exercise that Agreement and we switched to a new campaign."

The ssi Conservancy and the Water Preservation Society worked together to raise funds so the upper lands of the watershed could be held by the North Salt Spring Water District. Bob of the sswps explained, "Money was tight, and we were trying to raise money for an on-island thing. We had raised quite a bit before, but the plan was to invest a certain amount which would make the deal too sweet for North Salt Spring Waterworks to not want to buy it. It was a brilliant plan, as the water district had the ability to borrow, and we had willing donors, and interests in caring for the land."

With other groups on the island working to raise the money to buy some of the forest land slated for development, the community got very busy. Having the future protection of the lands around the bay so close to my heart, I was directly involved in the campaign from the beginning.

I called Briony Penn, a personal friend, then on the board of TLC The Land Conservancy of BC. She and I agreed that the campaign needed someone local to head it up. We called Elizabeth White, a recent arrival on the island who had some experience with green business. She agreed to take on the job as fundraising lead, as long as she wasn't paid! Elizabeth got going quickly, chairing our weekly meetings and preparing an appeal portfolio which outlined the campaign, the amount needed to raise, the ecosystems and habitats at risk, maps of the area, and an appeal that in the end inspired donors from all over the world!

We held weekly meetings to devise ideas and plans to buy both areas. Confirmation that the Garry oak woodlands were the largest in Canada, and that the forested area was the largest expanse of contiguous Douglas-fir ecosystem left in the Southern Gulf Islands, became key campaign messages. But raising the money to buy the land was not the only focus. Many people chose protest and community activism to bring attention to the destruction happening on the island and the ineffectiveness of the Islands Trust to stop it, without being given legal authority by the Province to effect their mandate.

Jack Little wrote an extensive description of the protests and campaign in *BC Studies*. He hit on the key point about private property rights, particularly how landowners with large lands can severely reduce species at risk and areas with endangered ecosystems, with no laws to stop it. "Relatively small though the area in question on Salt Spring was, by attracting widespread public attention the campaign to protect that land did demonstrate how a local community could unite to challenge the right of a privately owned company to damage an exceptionally scenic and ecologically important environment."[10]

To Salt Spring islanders though, the area was not that small—10 percent of the island. We opened an office in downtown Ganges, so we could post information about the land, the campaign, and offer a meeting place in a central location. Various community initiatives were created through affinity groups, each group being independent, yet with a common goal of protecting the land. Some affinity groups chose direct action at key points where the logging was taking place.

The phenomenal Elizabeth White in 2001, who led the local fund-raising campaign to conserve the lands. TAMAR GRIGGS

Salt Spring Women Preserve and Protect—intrepid nude women in front of logging truck, from the calendar. HOWARD FRY

Reviewing Jack Little's recent article, I was reminded of the two years of intense community action and the sheer number of people involved, sometimes risking so much. I felt ineffective and numb, as I was stuck in the office doing my provincial Land Trust Alliance work, a single parent with a teenage daughter at the local school. Up on Mount Bruce and Mount Tuam people camped out and protested for months. After the company clear cut areas near the Buddhist monastery on Mount Tuam, some folks pounded crosses in along the road for every loaded logging truck that went by. Some stood in front of the trucks, and wheelchair user Sally Sunshine chained herself to a loaded logging truck. Others gathered around campfires, sang songs, and united together to try to stop the logging. I recall one fellow I knew who was arrested, eventually jailed for months, losing the custody of his own children for a time, in defense of the forests. Another woman in Ganges chained herself right under a logging truck once it was stopped by other protesters.

The island seemed on fire during this time—the fire of anger, despair, revenge, and community kinship. Some staunch private landowners objected to the protests, being outside the law, while the company's strategic lawsuits against public participation (SLAPP) lawsuits drew hundreds to Victoria to defend the actions of the protesters. These same SLAPP suits were used on Galiano and Denman Islands by logging companies intent on using personal threats to thwart the protests.

The company tried to counter the bad press, calling several community meetings, agreeing to negotiate for certain areas, building fish ladders along a creek they had trashed, printing full page descriptions of their plans, while the mortgages they had taken out to buy the lands were being paid with the sale of the trees being cut.

There were several actions in Victoria at the legislature. Along with gumboot dancers, a large banner reading Unchain the Trust was held by local politician Gary Holman and others—scientists who knew that what was being done on our little island was a reflection of the lack of political will to enact laws that would protect these at-risk ecosystems on private lands.

Briony Penn, a member of the South and West Salt Spring Conservation Alliance at the time, said, "In September 2000, after four years of meetings, research, inter-agency cooperation and community effort, a proposal was developed. This was signed by representatives from the Capital Regional District, the Islands Trust, and representatives from provincial and federal government to the Pacific Marine Heritage Legacy Fund (PMHLF)."

> In 1995, the British Columbia government entered into an agreement with the federal government to commit $30 million to the Pacific Marine Heritage Legacy Fund (PMHL) to match the federal government's commitment of $30 million. In the end, lands were traded instead (see Saturna Island). The PMHL Fund was for land acquisition for parks—originally in the Gulf Islands but later it expanded as far as Denman and Savary Islands.

Another event that brought international attention was the creation of the Salt Spring 2001 nude calendar. It raised $100,000! A professional photographer, Howard

Fry, created a twelve-month calendar designed with scenes of naked local women in nature, meeting for tea, hiding behind trees, and doing the many things that this community actually did to raise attention, donors, media, and the money to contribute to its protection. Ruth Tarasoff and Andrea Collins spearheaded this part of the campaign and selected the watershed as the portion that these funds would go toward.[11]

Other events raised more money. A rock concert at the Commodore Ballroom in Vancouver was held with local Randy Bachman headlining the event. Having watched art auctions raise quite a bit of money before, I and a few others organized the Where Art Meets Nature Art auction, which expanded into a fortnight of evening presentations with local and guest speakers, including Robert Bateman, Bristol Foster, David Suzuki, and others.

Then, the first small successful sale of 19.4 hectares (48 acres) of the land adjoining Maxwell Lake was purchased by Mike Larmour of the North Salt Spring Waterworks.[12]

The CRD was heading the negotiations for the rest of the land at the time, which they eventually withdrew from because they said the company was asking three to five times the appraised values for the land. As the company was ever increasing their sale price during negotiations, in chilly January of 2001 a group of us went to Vancouver to protest outside the offices of the developers. The media portrayed Briony as Lady Godiva, who with other women, marched in front of the developers' offices, on a horse—topless. The company, chagrined, came back to the negotiating table.

All these protests and media events were fine, but with no legal jurisdiction to stop the logging, we needed to buy the land—the work of a land trust. The price tag was huge—around $20 million at 2000 year rates. TLC The Land Conservancy of BC led the first wave of fundraising. They gave charitable receipts for the first $850,000 raised—enough to resume negotiations. Bill Turner, Chair of TLC at the time, brought in some big players: the Province of BC and the Nature Trust of BC. More appraisals were done and discussions ensued.

A film *"Ah... the Money, the Money, the Money"*—*The Battle for Saltspring* was made through the National Film Board by Mort Ransen. The title is based on a quote from one of the two developers, who came to a community hosted gathering early on, and in answer to a young child's question, "Why are you logging these forests?" he turned and said, "It's the money, honey." This film shows the incredible dedication and earnestness of so many Salt Spring Island people to stop what we all saw as incredible desecration to a community and to the forests, as logging truck after logging truck cleared trees, bushes, stream beds along with the birds, bees—everything in their way—as negotiations were going on.

Continued fundraising through music festivals, T-shirt sales, and many private donations kept rolling in.

Less than two years after these developers bought the lands, and after many hectares of land were stripped of their climate mitigating trees, we won the protection of just over half of the land they had purchased. They still made a nice profit on the sale of the lands, on top of the sale of the timber they cut, but the development corporation's plans to strip and flip the area were foiled by the determination of Salt Spring's tenacious community, many thousands of donors to the campaign, and the work of several land trusts in collaboration with other agencies.

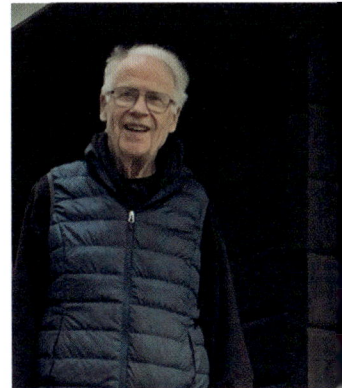

Bill Turner, with TLC The Land Conservancy of BC at the time, helped initiate the campaign and the negotiations to acquire the land.

After the dust settled, most of the forests surrounding the bay became part of the new Burgoyne Bay Provincial Park. The Nature Trust of BC became the owner of the Garry oak woodlands along the north shore of the bay, and the watersheds up at the top were bought by the North Salt Spring Island Water Authority.[13] The Salt Spring Island Conservancy spent long hours drafting a covenant to protect the 106.4 hectares (263 acres) of the watershed, and today the entire area surrounding the bay is conserved.

Land trust organizations could become authorized legal holders of Conservation Covenants after 1994, under Section 219 of the *Land Title Act*. A conservation covenant remains on the title after the land is sold or transferred, binding future owners of the land to its terms.[15] It is a powerful way to protect all or a portion of a property that has a significant natural area, such as around streams, wetlands, or an area of forest. Maureen told me that the SSIC registered the first conservation covenant held by a land trust over a watershed in BC.

It seems apropos that Mount Maxwell is known by the Cowichan as Hwmat'et-sum, or "bent over place," connected to origin stories about the relationship of humans to the land. The Salt Spring community sacrificed much of their time, reputations, money, and passion to conserve this land. In the end, it was legally protected through the partnerships of land trusts in tandem with government and many people—working locally to protect what impacts us all—globally. The campaign in all its forms reflects a burgeoning ethic of conservation, new collective partnerships, and the rolling over to a new century.

The Stqeeye' Learning Society has been building relationships with BC Parks, Salt Spring naturalists, organizations, businesses and the larger community to bring Indigenous priorities back to the land since 2014. Xwaaqw'um (Burgoyne Bay Provincial Park) is located in the heart of Quw'utsun (Cowichan) Territory. The Stqeeye' Learning Society is an Indigenous-led, non-profit organization based on Salt Spring Island that supports relationship building and reconciliation through traditional ecological restoration and land-based education programs.

Final ownership of the lands went to:

Province of BC: 13.4 million, CRD Parks: 1.5 million, TLC/SSI Appeal (public donations): 1 million for 665 hectares (1643.251 acres) around Burgoyne Bay—up slopes of Mount Sullivan, Mount Tuam, and Bruce Peak.

The Nature Trust of BC: $3.5 million for 282 hectare (686 acres) area of prime Garry oak meadow from Forest Renewal BC's private forest biodiversity program.

North Salt Spring Water District: $1.14 million 127 hectares (317.5 acres) for Maxwell Lake community watershed purchased with funds from community donations, SSWPS, and SSIC.[14]

First Staff, Educational Events, and More Lands Conserved

The founding women and others in the Conservancy were so busy doing the work of trying to protect these places before they were privately bought and developed that not a lot of work had been done developing the Salt Spring Island Conservancy as an organization. To remedy this, the directors took a leap. They received a grant of $105,000 which allowed them to hire staff and open an office. Karen Hudson became the first executive director. The Salt Spring Island Conservancy's first office was down the hall from the Land Trust Alliance of BC, which I was coordinating by then. I can still hear the sounds of her uproarious laughter travelling way down to the end of the hall. She is a vibrant woman, full of ideas, energy, and inspiration. Her extensive background included climbing up nuclear power plants and posting banner drops about their dangers. She told me how she came to work for the Conservancy.

> In September 1999, I had just moved to Salt Spring. November 3 I got message that they had started logging the Texada lands. I remember having a conversation in my car with my daughter. Even at three-and-a-half she said, "Mom we can't let them cut those trees down." I was invited to a community meeting, and we sat around in a big circle, and everybody talked about what part of this huge area that they would start working on. That was a big moment for me. A couple of months later, I saw the notice that SSIC was going to hire their first executive director. Through this group, I got to know a number of people, so that was a great introduction to them.

Karen grew the organization from a budget of barely $20,000 a year to 1 million—in two years! Initially she worked to acquire grants from the Habitat Stewardship Program. In the first year, they were awarded $500,000 and the next year—a million! When Karen started, the Conservancy had a database of 250 supporters; in five years it went to 1,000. This was a result of hosting monthly events on natural history topics that drew in the larger island. These educational talks ranged from owls to water catchment, bringing in a diverse group of people. Karen said, "that was where we got most of those new members. The directors and volunteers would bring in these great speakers from across BC and offer them a weekend in their home on Salt Spring Island."

As noted earlier, the SSIC focused on protecting the watershed of the Texada lands with the local Water Preservation Society. Karen recalled a culminating event and concert at the Farmer's Institute that raised $35,000 for the watershed. "Andrea Collins came in with two cheques for $100,000 each! I remember thinking, all the founders are here. We were all standing there, and at that moment we felt that it was actually going to happen. We felt successful. Those are little things that could easily get lost."

The Conservancy's grants enabled them to hire biologists who met with landowners, documenting endangered species, arranging conservation agreements, which in time grew to legally binding conservation covenants, and then to outright donations of land.

Species at Risk are rated into three large categories. Federally, they are Endangered (Facing imminent extirpation or extinction), Threatened (Likely to become endangered if limiting factors are not reversed), and Of Concern. Provincially, though there is still has no species at risk legislation: they are rated Red, Blue and Yellow. For more information on specific species see The BC Species and Ecosystem Explorer.[17]

Manzanita Ridge and Mount Erskine

Karen told me about a particular donor who really made a difference. Martin Williams lived on the north end of Salt Spring. He had a vision of protecting the whole area around Mount Erskine. He owned some lands on the south side of the top of the mountain with coastal Douglas-fir habitat and rare Arbutus-Hairy Manzanita ecosystems. In 2003 he donated some of his land, 49.3 hectares (19.95 acres), to the ssi Conservancy, while the Conservancy raised the rest of the property's costs. (This is often called a bargain or conservation sale.)

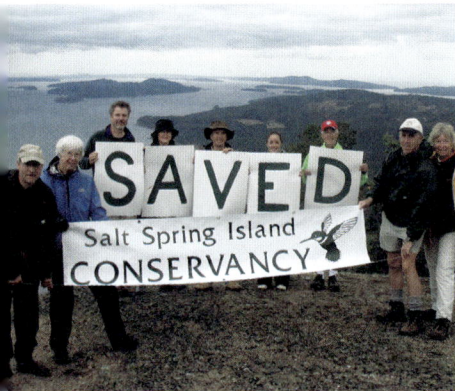

Group on the top of Mount Erskine in celebration of its protection. From left: hiker, Margaret Spencer, Ashley Hilliard, Wendy Hilliard, three hikers, Peter Lamb, and Jean Gelwicks.

"In the beginning, it was a small area with one person's vision to have it protected," Karen said. "By being so generous to donate a whole chunk, a campaign was made possible to fund the rest." This became the Manzanita Ridge Reserve owned by ssic. It is protected by a conservation covenant held jointly by the Islands Trust Conservancy and the Salt Spring Island Local Trust Committee. The Manzanita Ridge Reserve became the start of a larger Mount Erskine project.

The top of Mount Erskine features high cliffs and astounding views. The area is full of trails, which up to 2004 were often used by hikers, without realizing they were on private land. Charles Kahn, who was with the Trail and Nature Club at the time, had been in contact with the owner about taking people on hikes in the area. When the owner was thinking of selling the property, she approached Charles. He then talked to Peter Lamb, then the president of the ssi Conservancy, to see if they would get involved in fundraising and holding title to the land.

Peter told me, "There wasn't any development planned, but we were concerned about more development on the top of the mountain. We did have land adjoining it, so we started an intensive fundraising drive." Within six months, they succeeded in raising the $625,000 needed to purchase the top ~40 hectares (100 acres). Peter said, "It was a challenge, but we knew we had good support, because a lot of people knew about Mount Erskine and the trails, and we told them if we don't protect it, you won't be able to hike up there. We had approached bc Parks about them participating, and they did contribute matching funds. At the same time, the Conservancy was very concerned about taking on the management responsibility of 100 acres. So we purchased the land in 2005 and gave bc Parks a 99-year lease."[16] They now manage 107 hectares (164.5 acres), which includes this ~40 hectares (100 acres), plus the adjoining Crown lands.

Even with the extensive trail network, the area is relatively undisturbed because no road leads into it, and the terrain is rugged. As well as having the red-listed arbutus/hairy manzanita plants, it is within the Coastal Western Hemlock Biogeoclimatic

Zone (CWH), unusual in the Southern Gulf Islands, with Douglas-fir as the dominant tree species.

Martin's dream of seeing the whole area conserved started with an earlier land donation. In 1976 Dr. J. H. Fisher gifted the Province of BC 22.46 hectares (55.57 acres) on the northwest slopes of Mount Erskine for a park and greenbelt area. The title to the reserve was then transferred to the Islands Trust Conservancy in 1996. Now called the Lower Mount Erskine Nature Reserve, it has steeply sloping forested areas and rocky bluffs and outcroppings. It is part of the well-used trail network leading to the summit of Mount Erskine. Lower Mount Erskine Nature Reserve, along with the adjacent Mount Erskine Provincial Park and Manzanita Ridge Nature Reserve now make a large, contiguous natural area totaling 150 hectares (372 acres).

Personal Land Donations and an Eco Home Tour

Karen described a surprise land donation which came from Cordula Vogt and her mother. "I remember going to Cordula's house, which was a modest home. She had a daughter, yet she chose to honour her late husband and donate this property. Its 29.1 hectares (74 acres) was named after her husband. It was so inspiring and surprising, as she, an ordinary person, gifted a huge amount, in her husband's memory."

This is the area where the Conservancy started running the school program. Karen explained, "Every year the kids went to this property and learned about nature. I remember helping with the set-up, the children going to the stations, and the people who helped. At a different site, on Ford Lake, Robert Bateman set up an easel and taught children how to paint. It became more than just a protected area; it became an educational resource for the community."

When Karen first came to the island she was interested in green building ideas—a sustainable approach to construction that produces buildings that have less impact on the environment. She took note of the various homes and buildings that were unique, such as straw bale, rammed earth, and those that used alternative building materials to our dwindling wood supplies. Karen explained that she saw significant land was being cleared for large homes and hurting watersheds. So she created an Eco Home Tour as an education event and fundraiser for the Conservancy. "Part of the requirement to be on the tour was having a small footprint, use of other materials, and showcasing how to preserve water areas on a property and generally how to develop with nature. We knew that educating landowners to steward their properties and live with nature, instead of clearing whole areas off, not to mention water catchment ideas, would be of interest." The Home Tours raised $25,000 a year for the SSI Conservancy, and the idea of them spread to other organizations and islands, catching a wave of green building.

In 2004 the Conservancy celebrated ten successful years, and by 2008 they bid farewell to its first executive director. The Conservancy's staff had grown to include an executive director, two biologists, and an office coordinator. That same year, the organization received an anonymous donation of 7.2 hectares (17.8 acres) on the north end of the island, which became the North View Nature Reserve. Although some

SSI Passive solar house with rain-water catchment and active solar on carport. TRANSITION SALT SPRING

portions of the reserve were clear-cut prior to its donation, these areas were cleared of Scotch Broom and replanted with native species.

Another nature reserve was created in 2011 through a blend of business interests, donations from the widow of the owner and from the community, and a couple of significant grants. Alvin Indridson's widow was settling the estate of her husband, when her realtor contacted the Conservancy. Alvin had mentioned during his lifetime that he wanted to preserve this ~128 hectares (316 acres) of land, which is a significant size within both the Coastal Douglas-fir and the dry maritime Coastal Western Hemlock zone ecosystems. The property included forest and meadow areas, a small lake, streams, and small wetlands. When the project started in 2009, Ashley Hilliard, a lawyer and president of the Conservancy at the time, with the second executive director, Linda Gilkeson, worked to put the acquisition pieces together. He told me that one of the surprising elements in the project was a grant they received from Shaw Communications.

Ashley had personally set out to improve his own internet service when he bought his own property at the south end of the island. Through support from the South Salt Spring Ratepayers, he was able to secure stable internet for the south island and a donation from Shaw's community granting program. He explained, "It was an innovative structure and some last minute major grants that put us over the top. The surprise was it was simply a contact I had made along with the South Salt Spring Ratepayers, to a contact with Shaw Cable."

Blackburn Lake, SSIC Builds Its Own Office

For a local island land trust, the next stage was a big leap. By 2013, the Salt Spring Island Conservancy had acquired six nature reserves themselves. Another five nature reserves had been conserved on Salt Spring over the years by the regional Islands Trust Conservancy.

Christine Torgrimson, the third executive director for the Conservancy, hailed from Montana. A visionary soul, she helped establish a land trust—the Montana Land Reliance. She also worked for years from Salt Spring on a cross border coalition—the Yellowstone to Yukon Conservation Initiative, which set out to create a corridor of protected areas which would conserve intact habitats for species to migrate across the continent.

Simon Henson

Indridson Nature Reserve

This reserve was a partial donation by the estate and family of Alvin Indridson. It was purchased with major financial assistance from the Nature Conservancy of Canada with funding from the federal government, Shaw Communications, and other organizations and private individuals. The acquisition was a partial donation through the federal Ecological Gifts Program.

Christine is an avid yoga practitioner, so while she attended the Salt Spring Yoga Centre she looked over at the neighbouring lake and golf course and thought, "Wouldn't it be nice to protect that." Once hired on at the Conservancy, she visited the new golf course owner and told him if he ever wanted to sell, the Conservancy could fundraise to buy it. Others had approached him, but a pivotal moment came when the golfer-owner from Victoria walked into the SSIC office one day and said, "I'm going to sell."

Off they went on another fundraising drive with the owner giving a partial donation on the purchase. The Conservancy's seventh nature reserve was initially 13 hectares (32.6 acres) situated at Blackburn Lake. It was purchased in 2013, thanks to the generous support of the landowner and many donors. This was the third watershed area the Conservancy would protect (in addition to the Maxwell and St. Mary Lake covenants). Blackburn Lake is one of the island's seven major lakes and integral to the Cusheon Lake watershed, a potable water supply. Christine said, "Blackburn is really loved by the community and really important to watershed health. It was not just a nature protection initiative, but really important for community health. When we fundraised for it, our tagline was, 'for the water, for the wildlife, and for people.'"

The next year a neighbouring landowner who owned 2.3 hectares (5.8 acres) came in to talk to the Conservancy about her land. "It was so amazing," Christine told me. "She came in with her financial advisor, wanting to know what the options were. What tax benefits could come from a partial or whole donation? She wanted to memorialize her husband, who had passed on, but anonymously. She listened to me talk about what was possible, and why it was important to protect the forested area south of the nature reserve. She said, 'Let me think about this for a minute.' She sat quietly and then said, 'I'd like to donate it.'" This generous gift of land added key habitat to the nature reserve for northern red-legged frogs, a blue-listed species at risk, who go into the forest to hibernate in the winter. Christine told me this was a highlight of her time with the Conservancy. "Those are incredible moments. The generosity and people's love for certain places on the island was a really powerful testament to human goodness."

Christine wasn't finished with this initiative to protect the lake and wetlands around it. "I kept bugging the landowner we'd bought the initial acreage from to sell us some more of the land, particularly around the frontage of his parcel. We wanted to protect the wetlands, a little spring near the lake, and the stream outlet leading to Cusheon Lake. He agreed to let us add another seven acres to the reserve. We negotiated that through the purchase of a *profit à prendre* and a subsequent boundary adjustment."[18]

The first 13 hectares (32 acres) of the Blackburn Nature Reserve were acquired thanks to many donors, the Habitat Stewardship Program, Islands Trust Conservancy, and the Salt Spring Island Foundation. In subsequent years, the reserve was expanded to 18.4 hectares (45.5 acres).

Between 2014 and 2017, about half a million dollars were invested in significant wetland and stream restoration in the reserve—one of the most highly disturbed areas on the island. Well over a dozen wetland areas were restored around the lakeshore, as well as several upland areas and four stream bank areas.

Thanks to funders like the National Wetland Conservation Fund, World Wildlife Fund, Habitat Conservation Trust Foundation, Wildlife Habitat Canada, and the Vancouver Foundation.

CHRISTINE TORGRIMSON

Now the Blackburn Lake Reserve is 18.5 hectares (45.6 acres), encompassing over two-thirds of the Blackburn lakeshore and including all the streams entering and leaving the lake. If that isn't enough of an accomplishment, more was to come.

Christine explained, "During that time an exciting thing happened. On Christmas eve in 2013, I got a knock on the office door, where I was doing some painting. A friend was standing there and said, 'I want to talk to you about Blackburn.' I moved the painting gear off the table. We sat down, and he said, 'I'd like to donate a building on the Blackburn Reserve, to provide an office and meeting space for the Conservancy. I'm willing to donate the costs to cover an energy efficient building, and I've been researching designs and potential builders.'" What an amazing opportunity for the Conservancy!

In June 2015, the Salt Spring Island Conservancy celebrated the opening of its beautiful new building at the north end of the Blackburn Lake Nature Reserve. This area had been one of the golf course's greens, so it was heavily impacted by human use over the years. Since that time, activities at Blackburn Lake Nature Reserve have included major wetlands restoration and establishment of a native plant nursery. As well, they hold the Stewards in Training programs here and arts and nature events. In recent years, the Conservancy constructed a demonstration Garry oak ecosystem area, so people could come to the nature reserve and learn about this endangered ecological community and obtain plants for their own property's restoration.

The Salt Spring Island Conservancy was able to build an office thanks to a generous donor. DEBRA COBON

Not long after the building was complete, Christine told me, barn swallows started nesting on the building. She's often seen peregrine falcons there too, who nest up higher in the Mount Belcher area and fly up to hunt over the open areas of the Blackburn Reserve. Other endangered species they've seen there include great blue heron, several bat species, especially the little brown bat. Christine said, "There is a beaver population on the reserve, doing their own amazing restoration work. The Conservancy has wildlife cams, and through them we've seen baby beavers at night."

Howard Horel Nature Reserve

Howard Horel was part of an old, established island family. He had a saw mill, loved the land and Salt Spring Island, and was a conscientious forester. Christine described what happened when he died in 2015 and some of his land was later offered to the Conservancy.

Howard always wanted to protect some part of his family's land. Not long after he died, his heirs approached Christine about the land. "I worked with them on a partial purchase and donation agreement. This allowed them to keep 20 acres of the 82 acre parcel, through a Section 99 subdivision." (This section is available for governments and land trusts that allows for subdivision without the usual access road requirement.) "In 2018, the Horel family's 62 acres were donated to the Conservancy. It's an important part of the upper Fulford Creek watershed, right near Ford Lake." Christine added, "When it was acquired, it increased a connected area to about 300 acres with varying levels of protection, including two nature reserves, a CRD park, and Crown land."

The Evolution of Salt Spring Island Conservancy, a Community-Based Land Trust

With the increase in wealth from Vancouver and Victoria spilling over to the islands, the gap between the rich and poor has deepened. The population has increased 10 percent since 2006 to almost 12,000. With all this, the cost of buying lands for conservation and housing has risen exponentially.

Bob Weeden, one of the first men to join the all-women board, came to Salt Spring from Alaska where he helped found an environmental advocacy society and fought for protection of caribou and birds as well as for Indigenous rights. He fought against a large dam that would impact salmon and plans to detonate an atomic bomb as an experiment. Working with this kind of watchdog organization can achieve great goals, but it can also feel tiring over time. When Bob was invited to join the board of the SSIC, he thought, "It's small in size, compared to hundreds of millions of acres I fought for, but that is abstract. When someone says 'that piece of protected ground goes from the shoreline up to the top of Mount Maxwell,' I can get to know that. It's more intimate, fun and involving in a nice way. I was happy to be part of a positive, intimate group—rather than fighting against things."

Bob commented on the rising costs of acquiring land. "There have been several land purchase possibilities recently, in the several millions of dollars, for fewer acreages. With it comes more partners for fundraising and more money spent on fundraising. The Mill Farm was only $600–700 thousand for a large acreage! That's inconceivable now."

The educational work that the Conservancy has done over the years has really had a positive impact, Bob explained. "The effect of educating 400–500 students, which shows up years later in individuals whose lives were changed because of that small contact, is huge. Many went on to college, to study environmental engineering for example. But I do think that in the long run conservation withstands fads. With climate change, the land is still there and it's there for old or new species."

Christine gave me an example of the education program's longevity. "I was at the Conservancy booth at the Fall Fair, and a young couple came up in their early twenties. They told me, 'we grew up on SSI and we'll never forget the Conservancy. We were in the school program, and we got to lick a slug—it's seared in our memory.'"

The Conservancy now has its fourth executive director since its founding twenty-five years ago. Penny Barnes is a biologist whose family settled in the islands in the Salish Sea. "I always felt bonded to the Gulf Islands. Becoming involved in the Conservancy was an opportunity to help preserve the environment I fell in love with when I was about eight. I felt I could really make a difference, if I applied myself. And secondly it is a way to give to the community—for my love of the island."

Penny summarized the diversity of ways the Conservancy has conserved and protected lands on ssi as of 2022.

> In addition to completing acquisitions and protecting land through conservation covenants, one of the things we are good at is community outreach. We have 806 acres in Nature Reserves and another 798 acres are in conservation covenants, including the Mount Maxwell watershed, for a total of 1,604 acres. Through stewardship agreements, we have protected another 1,476 acres. These involve reaching out to landowners and talking about how to restore and enhance land as habitat. A lot of people on Salt Spring know what species at risk are; there's no need to explain that. The school education program ensures that every child can have a day in nature. Our program's grants help educate the young and bring a lot of people to the nature reserves where we provide educational signage and workshops. This helps with covenant and acquisition goals. We've been around for twenty-seven years. People know us. They know what we can achieve.

Helping young people and new landowners connect with and relate to nature is key to changing our mindset, so we can work with the natural ecosystems and cycles that support life. On Salt Spring, the landowner stewardship program has helped people understand their lands, make plans for their own homes, gardens, and steward it for the long term. Penny told me that in 2022 alone this program added 45.7 hectares (113 acres) to their total lands protected, with a diversity of habitats. "In addition to walking the land with the landowners, we produce a report for them that speaks to their properties: the invasive plants, the ecosystems, and we give them a few free plants from our nursery that suit their property. We have no shortage of sign-ups." She explained that sometimes the program is a first step to a covenant, or a landholder will put their land into a bequest. "This just happened last week. Someone made a bequest—the Conservancy will be in their will." Not only can people donate money to support a conservation land trust in a will, but they can also leave their land as a legacy for the future.

Cash Bequests for Conservation

In January of 2021, just before I started my journey to the islands, I heard about the passing of one of the Conservancy's founders, Nancy Braithwaite. Originally living in Sansum Narrows with her husband, Roy, she moved to Trincomali Heights where she later registered a conservation covenant over her land. She named it Ruffed Grouse Covenant after the yellow-listed bird she loved to hear drumming in the spring.

Over her life, she supported philanthropy by quietly giving large sums of money to several conservancies, including some for the recent acquisition of Reginald Hill on Salt Spring by the Nature Conservancy of Canada. In her will she donated $12 million to the Victoria Foundation and the Salt Spring Island Foundation, which will be held in a special fund for conservation and ecojustice. She was an only child with a father who invested in banks and reinvested the money; thus she was able to give significant bequests.

Bequests of cash in a person's will are a great way to help a land trust or conservation organization with its work. Another founder of SSIC and the Land Trust Alliance of BC, Ann Richardson, left her entire estate to the local Salt Spring Island Conservancy.

Another generous philanthropist from Salt Spring is Susan Bloom. Susan's generosity has helped with the most recent acquisition of areas on Salt Spring's Reginald Hill on the south end near Fulford Harbour.[19] She also donated a significant amount through a bequest in her will to the Victoria Foundation, called the Cereus Fund.[20]

The Victoria Foundation made a recent grant from that fund to the Islands Trust Conservancy's Opportunity Fund. Many land trusts in the Salish Sea apply to the ITC's Opportunity Fund for appraisals or surveys to help landowners defray costs for registering a conservation covenant or making a partial donation of their land.

Makaroff Reserve—A Very Generous Family Donates Some of Their Lands

Some of the highest land values are associated with waterfront lots. When landowners acquired land in the early part of the twentieth century, both the cost of purchasing it and the annual taxes were much less.

Doctors Robert and Shauna Makaroff bought 129.5 hectares (320 acres) of land on Salt Spring in 1973—one upland lot and five waterfront lots. Their daughter Joan told me that in 1976 the adjoining property was sold to a logging company, who then started to clear cut a beautiful area that had never been logged. Her parents were horrified by this. They mortgaged other lands they had in order to buy as much of the adjoining property as possible, ending up with another 28.3 hectares (70 acres). They included in their piece as many of the big Douglas-fir trees as they could. On this land they registered a restrictive covenant with the CRD that ensured it wouldn't be logged.

In 2007 two members of the Conservancy's Acquisition Committee began talking with the Makaroffs about a possible donation of their land. Joan said, "Although they had been talking with the Conservancy periodically between 2007 and 2011, a number of factors delayed their decision on when and how to proceed with covenants or a donation of the land."

After their parents died in 2012, Joan and her three sisters decided they would honour their wishes to protect much of the land by donating three of the five lots that go down to the water. "My parents were quite interested in protecting the area. They were concerned that it should be kept as a natural area, as they were really concerned with increasing development." Joan said, "My parents never looked at this land as an investment commodity. They looked at it as wilderness. We also feel that way."

The donated 37 hectares (91 acres) extend to the water on the southwest side of the island, near to the Mill Farm Regional Park. Full of Douglas-fir, cedar, arbutus, Garry oak, and small streams and wetlands, it has significant marine shoreline and nine provincially or federally listed species at risk. Karen exclaimed, "Think on today's market what three waterfront lots would cost. The SSIC could never buy that."

In 2022 these generous daughters donated a fourth of the five waterfront lots. Joan explained, "The other thing that really makes it possible is the federal government's Ecological Gifts Program.[21] It's a good incentive, though you're still donating. Donors are not required to pay capital gains on the donated property, and if the financial situation allows, you can offset part of the capital gain on other buildings or areas—or offset your income tax. It's great to have that program."

Joan had some advice for others considering donating land for conservation. "If you're planning on doing something like that, you need to be clear about what your goals are. What's important to you? The SSIC was an informative sounding board for my parents when they were deciding how they might protect the land. They suggested different scenarios—donating, or putting conservation covenants on the land, but they did not push for anything in particular. They took the time to build a relationship in a very respectful way."

Joan told me the family are now discussing what will happen with their descendants—their kids and grandkids. They are thinking about further donations and covenants, looking for tools to protect the land they still have, while being able to live there and enjoy it.

DESPITE SALT SPRING ISLAND'S large and growing population, I still find that there are areas where I get lost—in a wave of beauty and diversity that connects and grounds me—to this place, like no other on the planet. The Garry oaks on the hills of Burgoyne Bay are a magic garden, its hillsides covered in glorious purple camas, and white death camas. Blue-eyed Mary's that emerge from the mosses that caress the dry soils. The spring gold flower and purple satinflower make surprising entrances into the field, and then the luscious fawn or Easter lily rises up to awaken us to spring, new growth, and the promise of hope. There are so many people willing to do whatever they can to conserve natural areas they love, so many ways to conserve this precious earth. On Salt Spring Island, many people who really cared about the land did something that will last—for all of us, for wildlife, and for the future.

After a long day of talking with inspiring defenders of the land, I returned to my boat, which I've often felt was like a womb—my place of coming back to my own source. Letting the days' events simply settle, I went inside to get a drink, then sat in the cockpit, with my back against the cabin. The water's lapping against the hull gave me a sense of ease—with the rhythmic sound of moving water. The sun was the biggest sauve—as it warmed my face and body—massaging me with healing warmth. Then it was over the side for a dip into the cold invigorating waters of the Salish Sea. The next island I was to visit would offer strong medicine for the rest of the journey ahead.

The Makaroffs donated three of five beautiful lots that go down to the water on Salt Spring Island. SALT SPRING ISLAND CONSERVANCY

With increased land values, some of these conservation tools can really help. The federal government's Ecological Gifts Program offers a 100 percent capital gain deduction for gifting ecologically significant land to a land trust or government agency for perpetual protection. A conservation covenant can also be registered through the Ecological Gifts Program.

CHAPTER FOUR

NORTH AND SOUTH PENDER ISLANDS

A Coming-of-Age for the Community and the Land Trust Movement

"As it began to go forward, it had a magic of its own. We were in the right place at the right time."

LAURENCE PITT

Pender Islands Conservancy

LEAVING BURGOYNE BAY WAS LIKE PULLING TEETH. I longed to stay and bathe in the Douglas-fir forests and Garry Oak woodland we had protected over twenty years ago. But I needed to get to my next destination, the Pender Islands. This was one of the first communities to take action themselves to conserve a very special place of ecological importance.

At Cowichan Bay I picked up my new crewmate, Heather Crawford, a friend from the Caribbean who wanted a chance to sail around the Southern Gulf Islands. We headed south through Sansum Narrows, a narrow channel between Cowichan and Salt Spring island. Today the waters were calm, typical of the Southern Gulf Islands in summer.

As we entered the Narrows, we watched with trepidation as a beautiful northern flicker was attacked by two bald eagles, each chasing it into the sea. When it came up, the other one chased it down again. I had never seen this type of predation so close before. In past years I had often seen a pair of eagles standing on the rocks on the Salt Spring side of the channel—acting like sentinels of the pass. We were propelled through the Narrows with the falling tide; I didn't see the outcome of the flicker attack, and I didn't really want to either, so I steered the boat through the Narrows with the current threatening to take us aside.

As we continued south, I reminisced with Heather about past sailings through the channel. Mount Tzouhalem arched up on the Cowichan side. We steered past Burial Island amidst the fast running water of the Narrows and then passed Musgrave Landing, where I'd sometimes stopped overnight to set a crab trap or two. Just up the road from the Landing was the Mill Farm, the first area protected on Salt Spring by the newly formed Salt Spring Island Conservancy.

The lower hills of Mount Tuam came into focus just as we rounded the south end of Salt Spring. Passing Fulford Harbour abeam of small Russell Island, we encountered a light wind; so we raised the sails. After three hours making little headway, we pulled them down again, started up the outboard, and headed for Prevost Island. After six hours in the sun, we were ready to get into some shade and anchor after a

James Bay is the outer bay of Prevost Island, part of the Gulf Island National Park Reserve.

six-hour trip. I had often come from Salt Spring Island to Prevost for an overnight getaway—anchoring in one of the many north facing bays. Today we headed to my favourite—James Bay, facing north up Trincomali Channel.

Prevost Island, like several other smaller islands such as Link and Saturnina, having been owned for decades by only a few families, so they were still largely undeveloped. Thanks in part to these families' recreational or small farming activities on these remote islands, their relatively small footprint left the area as a prime site for conservation. This site on Prevost Island is now a part of the Gulf Island National Park Reserve. It includes coastal Douglas-fir forests, including large maples and an old orchard.

The next day we hauled up the anchor and made the short trip from Prevost Island to Otter Bay on North Pender Island. As we passed the Otter Bay ferry terminal and then the busy marina, we made our way to a small, quiet cove within the larger bay, Hayashi Cove. Typical of the islands I'd visited so far, we saw two herons in the bay. One was perched atop a purple martin nest box and, nearby, several purpler martins were flying around. Later I learned that the boxes were installed on the pilings by the local Naturalist's Club, who joined forces with the Pender Islands Conservancy Association (PICA).

The purple martins are a conservation success story around the shorelines in the Salish Sea. The purple martins' natural nesting habitat has been lost, "throughout their original breeding range on coastal lowlands around the Georgia Basin... due to timber harvest, fire prevention, snag removal, burned timber salvage and agricultural and urban development."[1] Thanks to the BC Purple Martin Stewardship and Recovery Program, many individuals and organizations, including PICA, installed nest boxes on abandoned old pilings and public and private docks. Thankfully, the BC purple martin population has increased from a low of five breeding pairs in 1985 to over a 1,200 nesting pairs in 2018. There are still a few known cases of these large swallows nesting in natural snag cavities of older trees or abandoned non-creosoted pilings, but primarily, it has been the intentional installation of these nest boxes that have led them back from the brink of extinction.[2]

We counted forty-four Canada geese in the bay. The now common Canada geese have been increasing by over 7 percent each year in the last 50 years.[3] Prior to the '80s, Canada geese were rare in around Vancouver Island and the Gulf Islands, especially during their spring breeding times. The cause of the increase is twofold. During the 1970s and '80s Canada geese were introduced to the coast from various locations across Canada as a game bird.[4] An example, from nearby Sidney Island reports that fifty geese were introduced in 1986 then, eleven years later, in 1997, three hundred were recorded on the island. Unfortunately, the proliferation of lawns, golf courses, and urban and semi-urban parks offer Canada geese reliable food sources. With their increasing numbers, many people are concerned about their impacts on natural habitats such as estuaries and Garry oak meadows.

The cackling goose, the shorter and far less common goose, isn't doing as well in BC. Most people don't know the difference between them, but the cackling goose has a stubbier bill, a more rounded head, and shorter neck. However, neither species can be harvested except as noted under the *Migratory Birds Convention Act*.[5]

I counted more geese on the Penders than on any other island. With lawns flanking the fairly new tourist accommodations near the Otter Bay marina, and the availability of eelgrass in some of the coves and bays around North Pender, it was no surprise these primarily now-hybrid geese were here in large numbers. Conserving and restoring natural habitat, such as native trees, including snags that offer nesting cavities for swallows and owls, and retaining understory near the shorelines is needed to help the native birds and amphibians survive.

Heather and I rowed our dinghy over to the cove's Gulf Islands National Park Reserve dock and swam in the warm waters. The reflection of the beach mirrored in the waters, with areas in shadow like on the land, reminded me of a Carol Evans painting. I was looking forward to meeting a couple of the Pender Islands Conservancy's directors in the morning to learn more about areas on Pender this small community had conserved primarily on their own, nearly thirty years ago.

IN THE '70S PENDER, BOWEN, little Mudge Island, and Salt Spring faced a population boom that threatened the natural and cultural features that people were moving here to enjoy. BC Ferries started travelling to the islands in the '60s, drawing tourists and developers in droves. In previous decades, regional districts had overseen land use planning, but these distant government bodies on Vancouver Island paid little attention to overdevelopment on the Gulf Islands.

On Pender, the Magic Lake development, the largest at the time in BC, was on the market. A 242.8 hectare (600 acre) subdivision with an original 1,200-lot plan was up for approval. In response to citizen outcry, the Province enacted a 4 hectare (10 acre) minimum lot size freeze on subdivisions for the islands in 1969. The Capital Regional District, responsible for the Southern Gulf Islands, studied their options. They considered conservation areas, park acquisitions, "and a controversial option to link islands with bridges and highways. A local federal MP proposes a National Trust for the islands and an International Joint Commission considers a proposal to designate the Gulf Islands, the San Juan Islands and Point Roberts as an international park—an alarming prospect for the government and for many islanders."[6]

In 1974, after an all-parties committee of the Legislature agreed that the Gulf Islands needed protecting, the Province of BC enacted a separate regional body to regulate development and protect the 470 islands in the region—the Islands Trust.

Purple martins migrate from the Salish Sea to Brazil.
MYLES CLARKE

The object [mandate] of the Trust is to preserve and protect the Trust Area and its unique amenities and environment for the benefit of the residents of the Trust Area and of British Columbia in cooperation with municipalities, regional districts, improvement districts, other persons and organizations and the government of British Columbia.[7]

This new regional government now had the powers to regulate development through approval of each island's official community plans. The Islands Trust would then write the bylaws that put into law the aspirations of the community's plans. However, it wasn't until 1990 that the Islands Trust Fund (now Conservancy) was created, which had the authority to own and covenant lands in order to protect them.

In response to a proposed sale of a 4 acre lot to pay for the Magic Lakes Estates' sewer and water repairs, the Pender Island Conservancy Association (PICA) was formed in 1992.[8] With development encroaching on the at-risk coastal Douglas-fir forests and wildlife habitats, the Pender Island community was alarmed by yet another "taking" for this large development.

On North Pender Island, meeting initially over the Magic Lakes Estate's impacts on yet another piece of land, the founding directors of the Pender Island Conservancy and their members decided that a land trust or conservancy was urgently needed. With a local base, the society could raise funds for both conservation areas and recreational parks and be responsive to local needs. Their constitution included research, education, conservation, and involvement in land use decision-making purposes.[9]

Medicine Beach

The story of Pender Islander's successful conservation of threatened places starts with Medicine Beach. It was the first protected place on the Gulf Islands, conserved by local islanders and a newly formed conservation land trust. The sheer number of people involved, their creative ideas, their determination, and their ability to bring in a multitude of sources to help them raise $500,000 to protect a property which to them had immense ecological significance—in little more than six months—is incredible! The cost and effort seemed beyond the reach of such a small community in 1993, but these people had perseverance and optimism.

The 8.09 hectare (20 acre) Medicine Beach property is at the head of Bedwell Harbour, which lies between North and South Pender Island. The brackish marsh and beach is a quarter of the property and the rest is high bank waterfront.

Medicine Beach is known by the W̱SÁNEĆ First Nations as E,HO,. With an extensive archaeological midden that stretches along the shoreline, it has a long history of use as the historical location of a summer village site of the W̱SÁNEĆ people.[10]

For the people of the Pender Islands at the time, it had its own strong medicine. Dr. Don Williams led the fundraising committee of ten who worked tirelessly for six months to secure the property owned at the time by the Atkins family. Everyone I talked with about this project stressed that the wetland and beach were key to its attraction. Don described it as a marsh jewel. He and Karl Hamson, another member of the committee and one of the early directors of PICA, explained why the community would want to protect it.

According to Dr. Don (as he is affectionately known on the Penders), "The impetus was that we were a wild place with at least one drinking establishment. There was a pub on South Pender—long before Poet's Cove and Browning Harbour. It was a pretty wild place on the weekends. I used to be the doctor, so I spent a lot of Saturday nights sewing up people. Amongst the conversations Karl and I had was we don't need another pub. That was a bit of a conversation between 'them' (those who wanted to buy the Atkins property and set up a marina) and 'us.'"

Shelley Easthope was one of the initiators of the campaign to protect Medicine Beach. LYLE HAMER

Shelley Easthope, from the family who built the famous Easthope marine engines, was in the "us" camp. She spent her life near the ocean, with a close connection to the land her family owned above Medicine Beach. "We had a lot of respect for the land, the fish, and especially to the marshland. We were steeped in how important it was. A lot of people don't see that, and when you live close to it, you know that."

The landowners, the Atkins family, had been steeped in the marsh's importance, having bought it from previous owners who were also protective of its significant attributes.

Mimi Nordby, whose grandmother owned a home in 1946, described in a letter to Shelley dated November 2005, the history and importance of the place. Mimi wrote to Shelley her appreciation for being in tune with her own feelings about the Medicine Beach area, after reading a book of stories and poetry that Shelley had published:

My first impression of Medicine Beach was this wonderful long trek down through the woods, because I was little and the roads were very narrow in this area, opening onto what we still see today but no houses, no boat shed, large slabs of slate littered all over the area below "the teeth" and an ancient skeleton of a Model A or T car, right at the end of the road. I had hours of fun driving that car to every imaginable place. We spent practically our entire time in the summers on the beach, we would play on the midden, in the swamp (as we called it) although we did not venture in the water part . . . The first place, after opening the cabin up, was down to the beach, claim it once again, sit for hours, just being. I quite often never knew which way to sit . . . looking out towards south Pender looking at Dead Man's Island (as we called it) or looking into the marsh . . . The pull of emotion and longing for this place is so strong! . . . Mrs. Seymour told my grandmother she was constantly chasing people off the little "deadman's Island" looking for artifacts . . . She in turn sold to Mr. & Mrs. Voicey, they in turn were also protective of the marsh and surrounding property. Mr. and Mrs. Voicey were retired when they bought and as they aged sold to Ken Watters. I think as each owner sold they must have instilled in the buyer the importance of the place, although it was subdivided and the lots towards the canal were sold. Mr. Watters sold to Atkins and the rest, thank heavens, is history. My aunt, during the Vander Zalm years tried to get the marsh under the government's protection. Premier Vander Zalm thanked her for enquiring but stated the Province of BC unfortunately had enough sanctuaries or something to that effect.

I liked your analogy of circles. To me, Medicine Beach and Bedwell Harbour are like a circle. If I sit on the beach, the marsh behind me, the "arms" of the land out to the gap, all are encircling me. I also have had the thought, now it is in our care, we are, with ourselves and homes, encircling it protectively.

For eight years the Atkins family approached the Islands Trust with hopes that they could protect it and subdivide off a portion for themselves, Shelley explained. The trustees at the time said it wasn't possible, so she and Karl Hamson were asked to look at the land to see what could be done.

Shelley explained how things got started:

We got an appraisal to get a price, a valuation of the land first, as without that we didn't know what we were talking about. The assessor walked it and said how beautiful it was and suggested, why don't you buy the whole thing. Karl and I sat in the parking lot, had a beer, and said yeah, why don't we. So Karl took it to a general meeting of the Conservancy, and they voted on it and passed it as something they were willing to undertake. Then we had to look at the nuts and bolts, and later we found out it hadn't been done before—this kind of community partnership.

An artist in the community, Corre Mott (Alice), and calligrapher Pamela Brooks designed T-shirts and started silk screening them, and Lynne Wells and I started selling them at the market every week that summer. We told people why it was important and raised a bit of funds. At that point, a new Conservancy board were evaluating whether they wanted to do it or not, but we kept going, as we were determined we would do it no matter what. In September, a new board said yes they would go for it, and needed a fundraising committee. A lot of people got involved at that point in the whole activity and the whole community got behind it.

Medicine Beach
with Brackish Marsh
behind on North
Pender Island.
KEVIN OKE

David Spalding and his wife, Andrea, were founding board members of the Pender Island Conservancy. They had lived on Pender Island for more than thirty years. A professional writer, naturalist, and paleontologist, David told me he made a life-long voluntary commitment to nature conservation. His vocation included writing a book on west coast whales, histories of dinosaur research around the world, and several other books about the Southern Gulf Islands. David and Andrea were integral to bringing key people together to start the fundraising efforts to save Medicine Beach. They even composed a song about it. David replaced himself on the new board that fall, bringing in another key islander, Lawrence Pitt, to help with the task. Lawrence described the experience:

I became a director on the Conservancy board and volunteered to take the file. I came up with a strategy. I met with the two brothers in the family, who had a significant print operation in Vancouver. The valuation of the property was $500,000. There was also a road access down to the water, an emergency barge access, which would always be permanent. A lot of the interest in that support was focused on wetland conservation. I was deputy chief of fire fighters and they would tease me about raising half a million for frogs. People recognized the value and rarity. We had a committee, and I sweet talked Dr. Don to be the front guy. Everybody loved the doctor, so he was our fundraising icon in the community.

Shelley recalled a day that the new fundraising committee met with the Atkins over lunch. The matriarch of the family said, "They had been approached multiple times while they held the land, by someone wanting to purchase it to turn it into a marina. Because that's what happens on this type of land on these islands." Shelley explained that the family knew how precious it was because development, especially of sites on the waterfront, was happening everywhere.

The fundraising committee was the key to the project's success. Dr. Don Williams described them as real optimists, each with a job based on their skills and interests. Those whose profession was writing, editorials, and university people were the writing division. Some brought muffins to the meeting. Two or three would go give a talk at one of the clubs to answer questions. They brought in a professional fundraiser who advised them to make the campaign short—they decided on six months. They brainstormed about how to get the community to come up with the needed funds.

Dr. Don explained their communication plan and next steps. "We talked big about the total package of half a million. That helped, as everyone thought that was daunting. It became clear that we needed a biological survey." Jan Kirkby, a biologist who lives on Pender, did an initial assessment of the marsh including identifying the different ecosystems and species she found in this rare place where freshwater and saltwater meet, with a cattail marsh at the back.

The Islands Trust Conservancy's 2018 management plan describes these ecological communities. "There are ten red and blue Provincially listed ecological communities that have been identified on the property and the tidal marsh (s1- red) is of special significance because these ecosystems are extremely rare on the Gulf Islands. There are 11 red and blue Provincially listed species that have been noted on the property including five birds, one bat, one dragonfly, and four plants. The Sanctuary is home to many other mammals including eight bat species and the sandy beach is an important spawning area for Surf Smelt."[11]

Don Williams reiterated the values of the marsh.

> The biologists were starting to see that these wet marshes were not just valuable for the ecology, but also in recycling hazardous things—natural filters of metals and other nasty things we are putting into the environment. That got people's attention in the early press releases.
>
> One interesting thing is there was no internet or computers. It was all done by hand and writing. There was developing the story, the narrative of how fragile an environment it was, why it was such an interesting challenge. It's a very unique piece of land, with southeasters blowing straight down that bay. The berm was partial salt water, with fresh water running out of it. There are two kinds of rails there—the Sora and the Virginia Rail. My grandson goes down there and calls them, and they call back. He is an ornithologist.

Lawrence Pitt, the link between the fundraising committee and PICA, wrote many of the formal grant applications. He said that the community had raised funds for decades for things, but this was the first eye popping amount. He described how they brought in local donations.

> As it began to go forward, it had a magic of its own. We were in the right place at the right time. It was so gratifying to pull that off. The whole community got really active. Dr. Don devised this idea—a list of deep pockets on the island, and we would go and visit them. Our initial idea was they would bone up. It sort of worked, but the community was doing it at smaller scales—but one bigger donor, Ursula Poepel, and a local pharmacist stepped up with ten thousand each, so that really catalyzed a lot of energy. Another donor I recall was Mae Moore (singer/ songwriter). Her father donated his boat, one he had built and loved. But at the time he was in the last stages of cancer and had very little energy. When we went to say hi to thank him for it, his eyes just lit up. Dr. Don and myself and the father

Medicine Beach Marsh. DAVID A.E. SPALDING

were outside talking boats. Mae Moore and her mother were saying come in out of the rain. And he said, "In a bit, we're talking boats." Don was a boater too. It really helped to galvanize the community.

This was happening at the same time as the purchase of Jedediah Island. They learned that a landowner could get a tax receipt for reducing the price, equivalent to donating it for conservation. Laurence told me during our telephone interview that the family made the biggest donation of $127,000 making it feasible to raise the rest. Laurence said, "The first big chunk came from the Nature Conservancy of Canada and Wildlife Habitat Canada for $60,000. Once we knew we could publicize that, we could get the community active in thinking about how we could do it." Thanks to Laurence and Don Williams and many visits to Victoria, they secured a grant of $78,000 from the BC Habitat Conservation Trust Fund (HCTF). It took less than six months—and time was of the essence for the family.

Don Williams described some of the details of the events and individual meetings that resulted in hard won donations toward the purchase.

> We worked hard all winter. We wrote to all the foundations. We got every community club on the island to put on one event, and each of the board members put on one event Groups such as the Girl Guides put on a fantastic dinner evening. The committee members turned out in tuxedos for the fancy dinner. All these little events turned into a huge amount of public interest and support. The Lions Club—all the clubs donated. These events really caught the attention of people with deep pockets, and we would go see them personally. There was a guy who built downtown, George Coates, who owned a coal mine in Alberta. He said, you're going to fail, but OK I'll take you on. I'll make a donation. Come back in May, after winter, and we'll see how you've done. I will then donate a sizeable chunk. One old timer said, "What the hell do you want that swamp for? I thought these are just things we can build on"—curmudgeons, answer their questions and sharpen our approach. We did and Coates paid up.

The Fundraising Crew turned out for the fancy dinner theatre event to raise the funds for Medicine Beach. From left: Dr. Don Williams, Therese Williams, Doreen Ball, Shelley Easthope, Adrian Schamburger, Angela Southward, Thierry Keruzore (our chef), Lawrence Pitt. SOLSTICE ACTOR

An entire community got behind the protection of a relatively small 8.09 hectares (20 acres) of land! Because this was the first conservation acquisition initiated by locals, as early as 1993, it was a coming of age for the land trust community on the islands. They were self-organized at first, then they worked with the local Conservancy in the end. To raise additional funds for the acquisition, artists donated their watercolour paintings of the wildlife of the marsh. They hosted a Home, Garden, and Points of Interest tour, and a barn dance. Lawrence described the barn dance. "They had a huge potluck dinner, the fire department had a big bonfire for the youngsters, the folks from the realty office headed up the bar, and a fabulous bluegrass band entertained the seven hundred people who showed up. We raised $18,000 that night, from an island population of 1,100 people."

The community rallied behind the campaign, consolidating new friendships, having a great time while raising the funds. Doreen Ball described the first event. "Karl Hamson's first Medicine Beach fundraiser barn dance was a real hoot. Cars were parked in the sheep pasture. Holly Arntzen and friends played. Pat Sundahl sat at her treadle sewing machine and made a down quilt throughout the dance, sold tickets for it, and presented it to the winner at the end of the night. James Barber put on a fancy $100 a plate dinner for fifty at Stanley Point. Angela Southward organized a dinner theatre event, where the fundraising committee turned out in fancy clothes and tuxedos." Doreen described the '90s and early 2000s as a Renaissance time when "the stars had lined up and there was an assemblage of people living here with just the right backgrounds and skills to do whatever was needed to save several parcels of land."

I recall the stunning map created by Michelle Marsden of Medicine Beach which was published in *Giving the Land a Voice, Mapping our Home Places*. Doug Stanley did watercolours and small paintings. Kevin Oke did a beautiful poster, which is still being sold by the local Conservancy in its new storefront office today. Lawrence Pitt described the culminating events which ended with—of course—a big celebration!

> At the end, we had a big event at Clam Bay Farm. We had a stage and music, food, and dancing. And the premier, Mike Harcourt, came and brought the cheque over from his minister. We said, "we're just short of the total amount that we need." The amount missing was 58 dollars. This was just the amount the local Brownies had raised the weekend before. So the Brownies put us over the top and it was a done deal. It was the right time—a coming of age of this community setting the stage for future stuff.

Today, Medicine Beach is protected for its wildlife and ecological values and is still a beloved area for Pender islanders. The marsh is partially fenced, with beautiful illustrated educational signage outside near a parking area. The forested area has a trail and stairs. The beach is still accessible with the road coming down to the parking area. The Pender Island Conservancy and local islanders did the work of raising the funds, and then passed the title to the Islands Trust Fund (Conservancy), who now own the property while PICA manages and monitors it.

Many smaller island land trusts in the Salish Sea pass on the ownership of these conserved areas to the Islands Trust Conservancy, who are able to hold the property without having to pay taxes. The local conservancy then doesn't have to pay the annual liability insurance either. And to be sure that the property is protected forever, the Nature Conservancy of Canada and Habitat Acquisition Trust (in Victoria) co-hold a conservation covenant on Medicine Beach which is registered on title.

Brooks Point Regional Park

Pender islanders did not stop with Medicine Beach. They moved on to another acquisition project on South Pender Island where Haro Strait meets Boundary Pass, looking over to the US/Canada border. The day I walked from Brooks to nearby Gowlland Point, the turbulent seas were filled with hundreds of marine birds. I could see and feel the raw energy of the ocean, here in Boundary Pass with its rich and fragile marine life, on the edge with humanity.

This acquisition occurred in three stages. Allan and Betty Brooks, well-known naturalists, owned Brooks Point in the '70s. Through the '90s, the couple tried in vain

View of Gowlland Point from Brooks Point. Both Points were protected and became a Capital Regional park. DAVID GREER

to get various levels of government to purchase the land so it could be protected in perpetuity. Paul Petrie, who lived next door and became a leader in the campaign to protect it, treasured Brooks Point as an ecological gem. Allan and Betty allowed their neighbours, Paul and his wife Monica, and their other neighbours, John and Eve Smith, to access the point, which was an excellent location to view orcas. Allan even allowed John and Eve to pasture their two rescued Orkney ponies on the point. Paul described Eve Smith as an environmentalist, feminist, and socialist whose dad had settled on Samuel Island, an island north of Saturna. He saw her as a mentor to many of the young adults who came to Pender in the 1970s. She gave them an appreciation for protecting land.

In 1995 Allan expressed concern about the taxes going up and was thinking of selling Brooks Point. Jan Kirkby, who had helped with Medicine Beach and later worked for the BC Data Conservation Centre, arranged for a formal appraisal which set the value of Allan's three lots at just over $760,000. Allan agreed to donate one of the three lots if the community could raise the remaining $540,000 to protect the Point.

Paul gathered support from local neighbours and formed the Friends of Brooks Point (FOBP). This local group was instrumental in the property's protection. Paul explained, "It was a snowy late November afternoon when Allan, Betty, Jan, and I met at the golf course café where the agreement was reached to acquire the Point with their help and blessing. They had a ferry to catch and a long drive ahead to Black Creek. We agreed to come up with 70 percent of the appraised value, and Allan agreed to donate the remaining 30 percent. We needed an organization with charitable status to raise funds. I went to PICA in 1996, and they consented to manage the donation account and provide charitable receipts if the Friends of Brooks Point would coordinate the fundraising."

Thanks to CRD Parks director, Lloyd Rushton, the Capital Regional District (CRD) got involved early. With a promise of $200,000 from the CRD, the community again held fundraising events to find the remaining $354,000. It took two and a half years. Paul told me, "The Islands Trust Fund (now Conservancy) was one of the first donors and Victoria's Habitat Acquisition Trust came in with a very timely $5,000 donation after a rather 'dry' fundraising period. That donation reenergized our team who met at the Whalewych's farmhouse every other Sunday morning to plan upcoming fundraising activities. With an agreement to make this a regional park, and a final $50,000 contribution from the Nature Conservancy of Canada, the acquisition was completed. Paul added, "Lloyd Rushton and I travelled to Black Creek near Campbell River to present Allan Brooks with a recognition plaque in appreciation of his contribution." These very generous landowners donated a significant portion of the value of the land to protect an area they loved and knew was significant to islanders.

Susan Taylor created a Disappearing Line Map around the time that the first phase, Brooks Point, was acquired. Featured in *Islands in the Salish Sea: A Community Atlas*, the map reveals what is normally hidden by the sea's tideline:

A continuum of native species from ocean bottom through intertidal zone to terrestrial zone and on up to the treetops... Rare too is the stretch of native grasses, where the meadow of the bluff adjoins dense thickets of salmonberry, leading to a tall mixed forest of Douglas-fir and Grand fir. The open grasslands host delicate native wildflowers in the spring and are habitat for several species of endangered birds. The point provides valuable habitat for migratory birds on their way to their breeding or wintering grounds: up to 105 bird species have been recorded there, including five provincially endangered and nine threatened species. In addition, many marine mammals can be observed from Brooks Point, including otters, seals, porpoises and sea lions. Orcas often frequent the area to rest in the nearby shallows.

Phase two of what became Brooks Point Regional Park was Gowlland Point. The point includes a navigational light and one of the largest stands of chocolate lilies on the coast. The Capital Regional District acquired the 0.9 hectare (2.2 acre) property in 2000 for $286 thousand, with a 30 percent contribution from TLC The Land Conservancy of BC.

Phase three was the ~1 hectare (2.6 acre) parcel between the two points. This was a challenging accomplishment for the community and the Regional District. First, the district agreed to take out a loan, based on an agreement from another organization that promised to raise funds for it. When that money didn't come through, the Regional District wanted to subdivide off a piece to pay off the loan they had secured. The Pender community, and especially PICA and FOBP, made the community aware of the possible subdivision, and again raised enough money from the community along with a grant from the national Habitat Stewardship Program for Species at Risk. The acquisition was completed in early 2014.

Because there were three phases, and so many groups involved, the CRD established a seven-member Management Plan Advisory Group "to provide ongoing advice regarding the park management plan." A consolidated covenant is being negotiated under the leadership of the Islands Trust Conservancy and the Victoria land trust—Habitat Acquisition Trust. Paul said after the consolidated covenant is complete, "PICA and the FOBP will advocate additional protective measures in consultation with the covenant holders and CRD Parks to more fully protect this ecologically sensitive land."[12]

Working with the Regional District and their conservation partners, Habitat Acquisition Trust and the Islands Trust Conservancy, these two small community groups, PICA and the FOBP, conserved what is now an outstanding shoreline and coastal bluff park. Brooks Point Regional Park could only have happened thanks to these stalwart individuals and all the generous donors who contributed to this campaign.

The Pender Islands Conservancy Today

On a bench inside the Gulf Islands National Park Reserve I interviewed Graham Boffey, a long-time Pender Island Conservancy director. Graham immigrated from England, where as a toxicologist, he was involved in research projects on the metabolism of food additives and pesticides. When he moved to BC, and was working in

The chocolate lilies (*Fritillaria affinis*) that bloom en masse on Gowlland Point in May are one of the most dense concentrations anywhere in the Southern Gulf Islands. Smaller scatterings of chocolate lilies also bloom on Brooks Point. DAVID GREER

the Kamloops hospital, he got involved in a joint research project with Agriculture Canada on tick paralysis. It wasn't a far leap for me to connect his interests linking pesticides and insect research to environmental protection. Graham explained:

> I came to Pender from the Interior. The Islands Trust concept was a new idea to me. I've always been concerned about protection of the environment. This [Islands Trust] concept was a good one, and fit in with what I was thinking. Then when I initially came here I got involved in the CRD Parks and Recreation Commission on the island. After I stepped down from that, I bumped into Sylvia Pincott, and she said you've got plenty of time on your hands, why not get involved in the Conservancy. I joined and have been on the board for ten years, the president for a significant amount of that time. I've always been impressed with the Conservancy.
>
> Currently, I'm chair of the Stewardship Committee, and I supervise it on behalf of PICA and the Islands Trust Conservancy. My other interest is to help establish conservation covenants. PICA has about twenty, with two in progress at the moment, mostly held jointly with ITC.

Sylvia Pincott and Barrie Morrison were foundational to the organization's success. Early Conservancy founders, they helped establish conservation covenants as an effective tool to protect private land on the island. Barrie Morrison created a memorial fund when his wife died years ago, for islanders who wanted a covenant, but needed help with the financial costs, such as paying for a survey that must be done if the covenant protects only part of the property. The Islands Trust Conservancy now handles the fund on behalf of the family.

A conservation covenant enables a landowner to protect specified areas of their property in perpetuity. In some cases, such as when a conservancy/land trust owns the land, the entire property can have a conservation covenant registered on title. It might indicate that everything within the area covenanted is to be left as is, without human intervention. In some cases restoration is allowed, with review by the conservation group. With over twenty conservation covenants registered on titles on Pender Island in 2022, it is clear that some landowners here are dedicated to protecting their land—beyond their time of ownership.

Graham also told me about the many new programs that the Pender Conservancy has undertaken. "In conjunction with the Parks Commission in 2010, we did a wetland and stream mapping project finding GPS locations of the streams and ponds on the island. The results were sent to the Islands Trust."

He listed more of their educational and stewardship programs: an annual beach clean-up; a raptor nest location project; a Hope Bay Salmon Stream Restoration project; and an ongoing eelgrass planting project with the SeaChange Marine Conservation Society. In 2007 and 2008 they began workshops on building bat and Purple Martin boxes and on planning for the annual broom pull. Graham told me Ursula Poepel, a pharmacist on Pender and treasurer for many years, was so addicted to broom removal that they called her Broom Hilda. Like all land trusts, the Conservancy also offers educational presentations on topics related to flora and fauna and conservation science.

Areas can be protected by a land trust independently, or through a partnership that leads to a park acquisition. Future development can be limited through a conservation covenant on private land. However, actions from neighbours, invasive species,

Sylvia Pincott and Keith Pincott at Brooks Point. The cabin behind has been removed and the area restored. PAUL PETRIE

and the changing climate can still impact a conserved area, so long term monitoring and management are needed.

Pender and nearby Saturna islanders have a strong interest in marine protected areas, being on the edge of the inside, more protected waters, and the outer Georgia and Haro Straits. Graham told me that Sara Steil and Honore Brownie were early directors who were fanatical about marine protection. PICA today is involved in several marine protection projects, often in partnership with Mayne and Saturna islanders.

Graham was not the only one I interviewed who wanted PICA to do more advocacy around marine protection and tree protection with various government agencies. Graham voiced his fears about the growing impacts in the marine world, which are shared with many others:

> One day I checked and sixteen freighters were anchored from Cowichan Bay to the US border. That concerns me, and the destruction of eelgrass and kelp beds from anchors. The other concern is oil spills. We've had occasions over the years when freighters between us and Saturna were dragging anchors. I'm also concerned if the Trans Mountain Pipeline continues to go ahead with huge freighters.
>
> Tree cutting is another issue, because the Islands Trust don't seem to have the powers to control that. There have been a number of lots on the island where the owner comes in and clear-cuts the whole thing on an ocean front lot. We need to keep as many trees as we can.

The Pender Islands Conservancy has evolved since they started thirty years ago, from a fledgling community group of volunteers to a sophisticated land trust that acquires and protects land with its many partners. Today PICA has a part time biologist on staff with many summer students. Graham introduced me to Elizabeth Miles, the current president, who took me in her hybrid car to see the Conservancy's new Hope Bay office and storefront. As we were driving there she said, "As I look around at all the changes from development here, and the impacts of climate change, there's only one thing to do: work to protect as much as we can and help educate the youth about the importance of nature." When we arrived at Hope Bay she pointed to the Pender Island Conservancy's new handmade sign and storefront Nature Centre.

The four young summer students inside the Nature Centre greeted us with big smiles. "We are counting forage fish, having outdoor camps, and bringing the next generation along," two very enthusiastic young students described their summer programs, focused on helping Pender youth become more aware of the importance of nature. Their summer program includes week-long camps on intertidal and forest ecology. These young university students excitedly told me they found some forage fish eggs at Medicine Beach and Brooks Point, in addition to ones found earlier at Hamilton Beach and Browning Beach, which, they explained, are heavily used areas. In addition to forage fish surveys, these keen students also make posters and presentation materials which they take to the Saturday Market. They include photos and text about the different bats, Purple Martins, and non-native European wall lizards now found on the island. These posters were creatively displayed at the Nature House, along with T-shirts, cups, and other paraphernalia that bring in a bit of funding support.

After driving around with Elizabeth, we came back to the dock at Hayashi Cove where I'd left my dinghy. The dock is managed by the Gulf Island National Park

Pender Island Conservancy's store and office at Hope Bay.

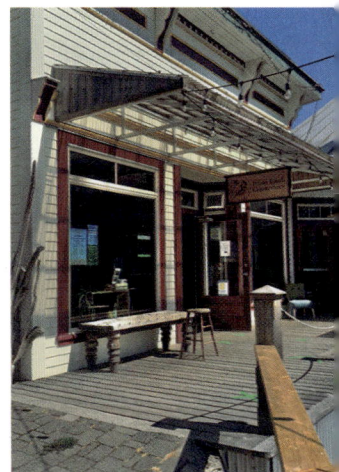

Reserve (GINPR). Here on North Pender Island the national park is a significant size, with trails and a small office between Roe Islet and Ella Bay. In 2015, the joint federal/provincial Pacific Marine Heritage Legacy program bought several properties in this area, including the nearby Turner property, off of Shingle Bay where a herring processing smelter had been located. Don Williams told me that, historically, the boats that came into Shingle Bay were ballasted with bricks, which were then dropped off and loaded up with herring oil.

How abundant it must have been in this area, with names like Roe Islet, Roe Lake, and Shingle Bay, the former site of the industrial fish plant. Our lack of knowledge about natural history and a commercial industry have almost decimated these forage fish over the past twenty years. We tend to think that the Salish Sea's most abundant fish were salmon, but archeologist Dana Lepofsky shatters that myth. "From 1000s of years ago, the archaeological sites in the Salish Sea are dominated by herring bones. In most sites, herring bones make up 60–100 percent of all archaeological fish bones."[13]

Tla'amin Elder Charlie Bob put it this way. "The depletion of herring from over-fishing" was just like taking our home away." Not only were herring the source of Indigenous people's sustenance, these small herring and other forage fish are still the foundational feed for most marine birds and coastal mammals as well. The Pender Island Conservancy, like many other conservancies today, are identifying forage fish spawning beaches and helping locals understand that driving on these beaches or hauling logs across them can destroy the young eggs.

At the cove, Heather and I could see a lot of green seaweed at the outer end of the bay, and there was a strong smell. I wondered if it was from the die-off in late June or something else. My eyes moved to the water closer inshore. Reflections from the water and small waves lapping the shore under the skirts of the maple, cedar, and firs draped over the bay sent ripples of bliss through me. I had one more person to interview to add to this story of conservation on Pender Island.

Raincoast Conservation Foundation

In 2020 the Pender Conservancy started working with a new partner. Raincoast Conservation Foundation (RCF) is a province-wide organization whose two founding leaders, Misty MacDuffee and Chris Genovali, both live on North Pender. Misty met me in her small A-frame house on North Pender. With lightning speed, she told me about how RCF started moving beyond issues-oriented work, such as saving the Fraser River salmon, to working as a conservation land trust. After participating in a Pender Earth meeting several years ago, Misty met Shauna Doll, who had a grant for six months forestry work. They teamed up together and created a Gulf Islands Forest Program. Misty said, "she's been indispensable ever since."

> Living in the Trust Area for as long as I have, I know that the Trust is failing in its duty to preserve and protect. We're watching the Coastal Douglas-fir zone just get hammered, considering 99 percent of the original forest is gone. And the second growth forest is being converted to other land uses. We're ravaging this ecosystem, and the region. Our Gulf Islands Forest Program started by trying to update the bylaws so they could actually implement what they are mandated to do. But the trees are still falling, and the pressures are mounting. And it became obvious that the Islands Trust is not going to act in a time frame that is relevant to the climate

The 5.2 hectare (13 acre) Flycatcher Forest was acquired in 2022 by the Raincoast Conservation Foundation and the Pender Island Conservancy Association.
ALEX HARRIS

or the biodiversity crisis and the only response is to start buying land. And so that's when we started talking with folks at the Conservancy.

They started with a 5.26 hectare (13 acre) acquisition project called S,DÁYES, the Flycatcher Forest, which abuts onto a large forest that Misty said is some of the best habitat left on the island. In about four months they raised $400,000—very impressive for two small organizations. Misty explained that some national and other funds they considered came with a stipulation that you've got to give public access. Because they wanted it managed for the ecosystem, rather than human recreation, they didn't accept any regional district or other government money for the Flycatcher Forest project. "It doesn't mean we're going to exclude people—there's a beautiful wetland there, it's got great birds, but we're not making a trail through the woods."

At Medicine Beach, there was a conscious decision to keep the public out of the marsh, which was achieved by putting a fence around it. Several of the original fundraising committee people I talked with stressed how important it was to them that it be protected for the wildlife and not for people to impact it. Some were disappointed when the upland forested part was developed with a trail and stairs.

Raincoast then looked to a bigger vision, identifying properties that connect to areas already protected, areas that still had a lot of biodiversity and tree cover.

We were actually looking at another acquisition when two more properties came up on the radar, and that's when we had to let go of the one we were looking at. The opportunity with the Kingfisher Forest took precedence. Now we've secured a purchase option and made a down payment/deposit of just under $200,000, in a year and a half we need to find two million. It's an amazing property. It doesn't quite connect with the national park, as there's a property in between. It's waterfront, upland forest, and includes a wetland and a pond. So we got a good deal, but if we hadn't, it was going to be developed for luxury homes. It's within what's left of the Coastal Douglas fir zone. It's a big acquisition, 45 acres on the ocean, and it abuts Plumper Sound. We are doing this, and I don't know where the money is going to come from.

Since I interviewed Misty, Raincoast, and the Pender Island Conservancy raised the over $2 million needed to protect this 18 hectare (45 acre) property now called KELÁ_EKE Kingfisher Forest. KELÁ_EKE is the original SENĆOŦEN name for Razor

Point that means the place where the kingfisher is. Along with over five hundred individual donors, and a number of anonymous foundations, the project was made possible by the Government of Canada through the Natural Heritage Conservation Program, part of Canada's Nature Fund. Support was also provided by the Sitka Foundation, McLean Foundation, Islands Trust Conservancy Opportunity Fund, and Greater Victoria Savings Credit Union Legacy Foundation.

This type of perseverance is what it takes to conserve land. Misty told me how she got into caring for the environment, from her childhood days living in Ontario.

> I remember being in high school in grade ten or eleven and learning about acid rain. We had a biologist from the Ministry come in and talk about what was happening to the lakes in Ontario. The pH was so low that there wasn't a lot of living organisms in those lakes. They were dying and dead from acid rain. One morning, the biologist said they were going out monitoring and as they were putting their boat in, they saw a grandfather taking out his grandson to go fishing. They had all their tackle, and he said, it's going to be great. The biologist didn't have the heart to tell him that there were no fish in the lake. I've never forgotten that. When I was even younger, I learned the moths were changing from dominant white phase to the black, because the soot covering the trees after the industrial revolution meant the predators were taking the white moths and leaving the black moths. So it was everything from natural selection to the human footprint.

Misty expressed sentiments I was starting to hear from many of the Southern Gulf islanders where I traveled that summer. Pender Island's natural ecosystems are under significant threat, with a large and increasing population, and many who have deep pockets—with the means to greatly impact the lands and surrounding ocean. Misty explained the situation from her viewpoint.

> These islands are under so much pressure now, and it's a new form of pressure from people with a lot of money. They can do whatever they want to do. Before you would be constrained in having a massive impact on a piece of land simply because the cost of doing so would be prohibitive. That is now out the door. If there's granite or bedrock in the way, you just blast it out. If you're worried about water, you just drill a well or put in a desalination system. If you want to go as close as you can to the shoreline, but you're worried about stability—you armour that shoreline. All of these things have a massive footprint on an ecosystem that is already under so much climate pressure, and struggling to maintain species. So everywhere you turn you see the human footprint. In the Islands Trust area, 90 percent of land is privately owned. So private land acquisition is the only way we're going to set aside large tracts of land in the coastal Douglas-fir ecosystems.

Indigenous History and Connections

Paul Petrie and Raincoast Conservation Foundation are now working on bringing Indigenous people together on the Penders, Mayne, and Saturna to reconnect with these islands. Paul described some of the history in the area and how these organizations are raising awareness both for current islanders and for the W̱SÁNEĆ people who once counted these islands as part of their territory. Paul described for me some of this work.

These islands have rich Indigenous history. The w̱sáneć First Nation, because of the *Indian Act*, was broken up into four different band councils, which were separated. So reserve lands are managed by different band councils. When land was taken away, they set up little postage stamp [sized] reserves—except for on Saturna.

I work closely with the w̱sáneć First Nation through the Brentwood Bay head office. There is a process underway, partly funded by the Real Estate Foundation, partnering with Raincoast Conservation Foundation, doing a series of five videos around the three islands—the Penders, Mayne, and Saturna. Using a 56-foot [17-metre] research vessel, they bring youth and elders to the islands and take videos, reconnecting them with their territory. They also had a climate action project bringing both islanders and w̱sáneć people together jointly to compare traditional ecological knowledge with climate science. Given the impact of colonization and displacement of Indigenous people from their homeland, I would like to see more Indigenous protected land and have First Nations involved in stewardship of that land.

As I left the Pender islands, I considered the amazing work of this community, along with this thirty year old Conservancy and the Raincoast Conservation Foundation. I feel so grateful to these wonderful people who worked so hard for many years, initiating some of the first locally-driven campaigns to protect lands on the islands! A few of these founders have passed on, but they left a legacy of conservation lands for the future. I really enjoyed meeting the enthusiastic youth on the island who are jumping into the field and educating islanders about the amazing species found here and the need for their protection.

I considered the next island on my journey, Saturna. I was about to meet people who had spent decades raising awareness and resisting similar challenges from human impacts on their shared ocean channels. With over 50 percent of Saturna Island in the Gulf Islands National Park Reserve, I wondered how it was connecting the land and sea.

Recently acquired by Raincoast Conservation Foundation and the Pender Island Conservancy, KELÁ_EKE Kingfisher Forest on the shoreline includes a wetland and pond.
ALEX HARRIS

CHAPTER FIVE

SATURNA ISLAND AND THE GULF ISLANDS NATIONAL PARK RESERVE
Connecting the Land and Sea

*"The future can be too scary to contemplate. We all have beloved
friends and children. It's up to each of us to create a vibrant
creative life, and it doesn't mean you hide your head in the sand."*
PRISCILLA EWBANK

FROM A KNOLL ON SATURNA ISLAND'S EAST POINT, I reveled in the raucous sounds of golden-coloured Steller and darker California sea lions. I watched fascinated as these giant marine mammals lugged themselves up onto Boiling Reef. The island's rich marine life is a result of the nutrient rich turbulent waters created by the tides, the swift currents, and the Fraser River. These waters attract marine mammals—southern resident orcas, transient orcas, humpback whales, minke whales, seals, porpoises, dolphins—in staggering numbers. The bald eagles, cormorants, oyster-catchers, river otters, and ravens were all within sight of each other, some claiming the same rock and the same fish. I felt right in the midst of the phenomenal Salish Sea.

This spectacular scene was marred by the fog, or was it smoke—the Big Smoke—the city of Vancouver in the distance. Although Saturna Island feels remote, it is within a major transportation corridor, surrounded by a population of eight million people. Saturna Island, with its southern shores facing Boundary Pass, is the furthest south and east island on the Canadian side of the Salish Sea. As the Saturna Island Marine Research and Education Society (SIMRES) has aptly phrased, "this is an ideal place to study the convergence of wildlife and humanity."

The island is also known as Tekteksen, a name in the SENĆOŦEN language meaning "long nose" which refers to this peninsula at its very eastern point. In many ways Saturna is unique because it is in the geographic centre of the entire Salish Sea, reaching from Read Island in the north to Lummi Island and Bellingham in Washington State. Conservation efforts on the island focus both on the rich marine environment that surrounds the islands and its at-risk terrestrial environment.

Saturna Island has a relatively small population with 465 residents recorded in the 2021 census. In the same period, Lasqueti, my home island, had slightly more with 498 residents. However, Saturna attracts many more visitors, being part of the more popular Southern Gulf Islands and accessible by a car ferry. The island is also the home of an estimated 37 species of marine mammals and more than 3,400 species of birds, fish, and invertebrates.[14] The small human population and extensive area of undeveloped lands in the most at-risk Coastal Douglas-fir zone in BC were the

impetus to locate the largest area of the Gulf Islands National Park Reserve (GINPR) on Saturna Island. With several small regional parks, and two recent private land acquisitions by the Nature Trust of BC, over 50 percent of the island is now within a park or protected area.

I visited Saturna by ferry in the spring of 2023. As we neared the terminal at Lyall Harbour, I saw two huge freighters anchored out in Plumper Sound. The freighters are a sore point among islanders. As mentioned in the Pender chapter, the communities on the Penders, Saturna, Mayne, and up the coast to Nanaimo, have been objecting for years to the increase in anchored freighters waiting for up to several months to be directed into Vancouver's harbour. In addition to being an eyesore, these large, parked ships create light and noise pollution, anchors drag—disrupting kelp beds and damaging the habitats on the bottom—and spill fuel and waste water, although illegal, into the surrounding ocean with all its sensitive marine life. I turned my attention back to shore deciding to focus on the positive actions of the islanders I was about to meet.

PRISCILLA EWBANK ARRIVED on the island in 1970. She explained during our interview in her wonderful hand hewn home, that she came young and fresh out of university with a landed immigrant card. "I knew I was home when I stepped off the *Mayne Queen* and walked up the road past the Saturna Community Hall and into my new island life." Initially she was attracted to the island's stunning physical beauty and enthralling biodiversity. Over time, however, she became just as drawn to the island's vibrant social and activist community. The Heritage Community Hall and the annual Saturna Lamb Barbecue have been mainstays in her life. This tiny community, off the beaten track, grew skilled in charting its own path.

Priscilla spoke at length about how work on their official community plan in the '80s fostered positive community dialogue. These discussions focused on limiting growth and balancing fee simple ownership, recognizing common amenities and needs for common services. It also led to the creation of two large land co-ops complete with cluster housing. These initiatives helped keep several natural areas intact.

When faced with a school closure due to low enrollment in 2008, the community responded by establishing the Saturna Ecological Education Centre. It serves grades nine to twelve students. The goal was a residence based, outdoor ecologically focused education program. A local architect, Richard Blagborne, designed the building. His inclusion of an off-grid alternative energy system supported the school's ecological goals. Thanks to ecologically minded educators (the superintendent of the district and a local teacher) it was opened in 2011, with an outdoor curriculum that was ahead of its time. Under School District 64's authority, the kids complete the mandated curriculum for the last two years of high school. The students live in sleeping cabins through the week. The school's common building offers a warm meeting space and classroom. It began the year in 2023 with a full registration of twelve students.

The school project coincided with another innovative community initiative. In 2009 another collective environmental education and heritage project involved salvaging and restoring a heritage lighthouse, the Fog Alarm Building (the FAB), at East Point (Tekteksen). Assisted by federal agencies and scientific researchers, the community converted the old lighthouse into an information centre, showcasing local marine biodiversity and island history. Run by the Heritage Committee of the Saturna Community Club, they acquired grants and student help. Then they started to design their first installation about the history of humans and orcas. This featured the evolving scientific understanding and relationships between whales and people.

This led to one of the most seminal events on Saturna Island—the 2013 Whale Symposium. The conference brought together leading scientists and long standing whale researchers from the 1950s to discuss the trends and potential impacts on the southern resident killer whales and other whales in the Strait of Georgia. Richard, who coordinated the project with another eighty volunteers, told me during our interview that the months he spent restoring the Fog Alarm Building at East Point made him realize it was an astounding site. "Being at this central apex of the Salish Sea, you saw lots of natural wonders, the orcas, eagles, owls, and sea lions, yet you could lift your eyes and see Cherry Point, the refinery, and ships going by. What it revealed to me was this is a fascinating place for science, being right on the boundary."

All these conservation and educational initiatives drew on island volunteers. Priscilla credits Richard Blagborne as the driving force in all of these projects. "Richard was a major organizing force, providing inspiration and vision for the Saturna Island Ecological Education Centre, the Fog Alarm Building at East Point Park, and the Whale Symposium." She highlighted his "warm laugh and his wonderful liking for people. He is deeply interested in conservation and renewal and can imagine and fulfill what he sets out to do personally and with community involvement and backing." Saturna was lucky to be able to draw on Richard's professional background in architectural design, exhibition planning, programming, and project management.

"Through all of these conservation actions and educational initiatives," Priscilla explained, "Saturna residents have learned first-hand that community strength comes from working together." The community has taken powerful steps to conserve the island and its surrounding marine archipelago.

The Gulf Islands National Park Reserve

Early in the '70s, there was a push to create a series of natural heritage sites across Canada. Parks Canada wished to create a national park in the Georgia Basin/Gulf Islands due to its being in the unrepresented at-risk Coastal Douglas-fir zone. In the Canadian context, the Salish Sea (known as the Georgia Basin then) is one of the busiest marine areas in Canada, being a hub to Vancouver, Victoria, and Seattle, with an international flavour and a huge population. However, only two percent of publicly owned park land was protected at the time. Sadly, the political and social climate wasn't right for a national park here in the '70s.

Between the '70s and '90s conservationists recognized that protected areas needed to be large enough to sustain whole ecosystems. Secondly, they determined that some natural areas needed to be free of human intervention. This spawned specific objectives, such as that low impact recreation should occur in designated areas in national parks.

Twenty-five years later, in the mid '90s, a lot of things changed. Following the creation of Gwaii Haanas National Park Reserve and Haida Heritage Site (South Moresby), Nahanni National Park Reserve, and Kluane National Park and Reserve, the Province of BC agreed to the creation of a national park in the Georgia Basin.

The federal and provincial governments came to a unique and far sighted agreement—to create the Gulf Islands National Park Reserve (GINPR). They worked together to establish the GINPR with the Pacific Marine Heritage Legacy Fund (PMHL) established at $60 million: $30 million to acquire land and another $30 million to create additional provincial parks. The Province initially agreed to provide funding, but after an election (and in order to honour the agreement) they gifted provincial lands to the network instead, resulting in an enlarged land base including chains of islets.

Kelp and kelp forests are habitat for many species, including small forage fish shown here. Kelp has been lost around many of the islands and is being closely monitored on Saturna, where it is still abundant in some locations. MAUREEN WELTON

Thanks to the same cultural and political climate that led to the creation of land trusts on the islands in the '90s a new Gulf Island National Park Reserve was avidly supported by landowners and other conservationists. Everybody was excited about it, as the Gulf Islands were so poorly protected at the time. Today, with the price of land increasing astronomically, this was clearly a far-sighted conservation vision which has left a significant legacy.

Bill Henwood from Parks Canada and Mel Turner from BC Parks were charged with identifying the lands to be purchased, initially from Sidney to Denman Island. They presented them to a steering committee that included the federal and provincial governments and the regional government—the Islands Trust.

Ultimately, the boundary went through Active Pass—south, excluding Galiano and Salt Spring islands. It included areas on Mayne, Saturna, Pender, and other smaller islands, such as Cabbage, Portland, Isle-de-Lis, D'Arcy, and Prevost—all within a large polygon. Bill told me that Tom Lee, the Parks Canada chief executive officer (CEO) at the time, was the brains behind it all, along with Jake Maslyn, who was the assistant deputy minister for BC Parks.

I met Bill Henwood in the mid '90s on Salt Spring when he was working with islanders on a potential Gulf Island Marine Protected Area. He is a rare individual, disarming and kind—the perfect man for talking with landowners about the conservation options they might consider for the new national park.

Bill told me that establishing the GINPR were "the best years of my career. We had fun, and it was very rewarding. The Gulf Islands are lucky, as many landowners saw the only alternative was to sell their larger property to developers. And we came along and gave them another option. People just loved the idea that we could purchase it, keep it intact, and make it part of a national park. Especially on Pender and Saturna, those parcels would otherwise have been developed."

Bill's provincial counterpart, Mel Turner, was the regional director for Conservation at the time. In my interview with him, he had much to say about his joint work with Bill. "As soon as Bill and I were announced as the 60 million dollar men, every realtor was after us. In some cases people approached us with the idea of selling. Some people we had approached before, so we knew many of the owners. I've always been impressed with the care a lot of these private owners took of their property. They were in such good condition that they could be acquired for park purposes. In contrast there were a lot of properties that were subdivided into small lots, like on Pender."

Mel was familiar with the Province's priority list, prepared ten years earlier. He had already investigated many of the sites. "We knew the properties we'd like to acquire. It was a matter of whether the people wanted to sell." Mel has over thirty years of experience, having been involved in the establishment of over one hundred parks. He said that the Province had expropriated Mount Seymour Park many years ago, but that didn't go well. This reflects a guiding principle for many land trusts who only work with willing landowners.

The Province had various system plans over the years, identifying a whole series of areas they thought would make good provincial parks. The list was based on natural and cultural values and gaps the parks agency was trying to fill. Every year there was a land acquisition budget. If a property became available, and it filled the goals of the *Park Act*—recreational opportunities, or representation of at risk biogeoclimatic zones, or important historical areas—it could be acquired. For the Gulf Island National Park Reserve the subzones and site associations were also considered, as they were trying to make sure there was a complete representation of the Coastal Douglas-fir and drier Coastal Western Hemlock zones. Mel explained that the list could be leveraged with adjacent Crown land, adding better representation of species and recreational areas and a combination of all of those.

He laughingly described his job as "drifting around in a boat and telling Ian to buy this." Ian Atherton, who was the negotiator on the acquisitions for the GINPR and many other provincial parks, has been key to the successful transfer of many private lands into park status. Of course, with any job, there's the highlights, and then there's the nuts and bolts. The Province traded significant Crown lands in the process, but overall it was all about buying areas with relatively intact ecosystems.

From Saturna Island the Washington coast and its iconic Mount Baker are clearly seen behind the CCGS Sir Wilfrid Laurier Canadian Coast Guard ship.
MARTIN WALE

Provincial Parks Added to the Gulf Island National Park Reserve (GINPR)

- Cabbage Island
- Isle-de-Lis
- McDonald
- Prior Centennial
- Winter Cove
- Beaumont
- D'Arcy Island
- Princess Margaret
- Sidney Spit

Ecological Reserves Added to the GINPR

- Saturna Island
- Brackman Island

According to a sign in James Bay, the area off Prevost Island I had anchored in the night before I went to the Pender Islands, it had been purchased as part of the GINPR through a partial donation from the previous owners. Large maples, Douglas-fir, Garry oaks and western red cedar surround a dilapidated orchard, with a small sign that tells visitors to enjoy the fruits, if they are in season and ripe. There are a few walk-in camp sites on Prevost Island, primarily available for kayakers. The issues of mixing recreation and conservation were debated during the time of the acquisitions and are still hotly debated today.

I also talked with Wayne Bourque, the planner working for Parks Canada during the time of the acquisitions. He described to me some of the issues at the time of its creation.

Boat Passage between Saturna Island's Winter Cove and Samuel Island is only navigable by small boats at high tide. Winter Cove is now part of the Gulf Island National Park Reserve. MARTIN WALE

Trying to convince people that the Gulf Islands weren't going to be overwhelmed by tourists was a difficult sell. There were hiking opportunities, boating opportunities, but basically they were weekend, or week long boating opportunities. This is not an extended area—it's limited in scope. At the same time, various recreation groups were saying, how about another campground? Some of that has been accommodated since its establishment. When you listen to all the people who want to speak up and say something, not everybody gets what they want. Some are just beyond any conservation value: they were overharvested, too small, too fragmented. Many people were disappointed. Some wanted to leave a commemoration—and then found their land was not the kind sought after.

The other thing was everybody loves a park, but not in your backyard. Why did you buy that property? I didn't think it had any value. You get into discussions like, "No bald eagles nest there," but habitat is important to other species and the functioning of the ecosystem. You see a much greater education process going on. We saw it increasing because people were asking questions. "Why are you doing that?" One of the funny stories is about having your pet on a leash. "Oh, there's a park warden, I'll put the dog on a leash." There was an enforcement presence, but they weren't doing it for the best reason. There's also a huge education program needed. "Why do I even need to put a dog on a leash?" You have to answer the questions and educate people about the purposes of a functioning ecosystem, rather than species-centered.

If you explain the conservation value, that sometimes creates an aha moment. People were afraid we were going to create another Banff. But the Gulf Islands have their own scenery, tourism, and ecosystem values. I've travelled around the world, and I don't think you could find a better sailing area.

On Saturna, there were formal presentations and facilitated workshops to discuss the community impact of a national park. Parks Canada was clear from the outset that they needed community support to site a large park on the island. Several individuals and families facilitated the park's creation by selling their private land holdings to Parks Canada, seeing this as a way to protect their holdings for future generations. Parks Canada then invited Nuu-chah-nulth Elder, Ron Hamilton to serve as the first park superintendent of the GINPR, as he had with Haida Gwaii, to co-establish Gwaii Haanas National Park Reserve.

The GINPR was formally established in 2003. One of the defining aspects of the park on Saturna is that it was created in an established community. Around this time, Saturna islanders created the Saturna Island Parks Liaison Committee to serve as a vehicle to resolve issues around fire, water, tourists, transportation, and park management.

Tourism has become more of a problem than the planners initially thought, especially after the pandemic brought so many people to the islands to live and play. Many of the larger national parks in Canada and the US are over capacity. Further, especially provincially, there seems to be a politically driven move from conservation for ecological protection to developing parks for recreation and economic gain, adding even more stress to these protected areas.

After Ron Hamilton retired, Wayne Bourque became the second Park Superintendent. In fact, he was the park superintendent when Parks Canada was hit with a $29 million budget cut in one year during the Prime Minister Harper era. He had a tough job because he had to protect the funds allocated to purchasing lands. To continue to achieve their acquisition goals, he helped negotiate the no-cost transfer of Environment Canada and Transport Canada lands on Saturna.

The cuts to Parks staff included, especially, its scientists. It also reduced the maintenance and management of things like trails and invasive species control. Local societies picked up some of the slack, but it has been a slow crawl back. Now more than ever, local citizen science and charitable land trusts are doing the work once allocated to the public purse. Thankfully, these organizations are also acquiring more ecologically intact lands and helping to manage and restore parks and other natural areas.

Restoring lands that have had been impacted by human development or invasive species is only one of many concerns that managers of conservation lands and national and provincial parks must consider.

The Gulf Islands National Park Reserve on Saturna Island with feral goats on the hillside.

The Gulf Islands National Park Reserve and Indigenous Partnerships

Relationships and agreements with the Indigenous peoples, whose traditional territory parks and protected areas include, are another significant obligation. There are 146 hectares (360 acres) of lands designated as Indian Reserve #7 on Saturna, under the management of the Tsawout First Nation and the Tseycum First Nation. The entire GINPR is within many First Nation's traditional territories, which includes the w̱SÁNEĆ Nations who are part of the Douglas Treaties. However, the Gulf Islands were never relinquished under the Douglas Treaties, and are part of ongoing Indigenous Title negotiations.

The GINPR's interim management guidelines set out some initial goals to "develop cooperative relationships and working arrangements with Coast Salish First Nations to ensure that their interests are reflected in the management of the national park reserve, to respect their unique history and current use, and to ensure that the activities that they may carry out in the national park reserve are managed in a cooperative fashion."[2] A full management plan for the GINPR is still under development.

In the meantime, Kate Humble, current superintendent for the GINPR, explained to me during our interview that Parks Canada has been working with an Indigenous Management Board. This board includes eleven Nations, including the w̱SÁNEĆ people—Tsartlip First Nation, Tseycum First Nation, Tsawout First Nation, and Pauquachin First Nation, plus five others from the Cowichan (Quw'utsun) Nation: Penelakut Tribe, Halalt First Nation—Lyackson First Nation, Cowichan Tribes, Stz'uminus First Nation, as well as the Snuneymuxw First Nation and Malahat First Nation.

The GINPR is gradually moving into management planning for a comprehensive agreement with nations represented at the Indigenous Management Board: at minimum they would like a Cooperative Agreement which allows for consultation on planning, management, and operations of a National Park Reserve, but the minister responsible for Parks has final decision making authority. However, Kate explained that a potential goal for the future is to create a Co-Management Agreement where decisions are made by consensus of the whole board. At this point, Gwaii Haanas National Park Reserve and Thaidene Nëné National Park Reserve are the only national parks working through this type of consensus based Co-Management Agreement, though the agreement at Nahanni National Park Reserve comes close.[3]

Options for participation with First Nations include: economic opportunities; protection of historical, cultural, or spiritually significant sites; interpretation of historic use; protection of traditional knowledge; traditional, sustainable resource harvesting rights; and other cultural rights.[17]

Kate, the current superintendent, explained to me, "Relationships on the ground are very close, mostly driven by First Nations' priorities, so significant consultation is already happening." As an example, she told me about the Beaumont Marine Park site on South Pender Island, which is now closed to overnight camping because the area is located in a culturally and ecologically sensitive location. The site is still open to daytime users, as well as the permitted use of mooring buoys. Kate told me that Parks Canada and the Nations represented by the members of the Indigenous Management Board are working together to find a new camping location, reviewing potential sites to replace the one at Beaumont.

On Sidney Island (where half the island is part of the GINPR) the w̱SÁNEĆ First Nations brought concerns about the impacts to vegetation by invasive fallow deer to the attention of Parks Canada. The Sidney Island Ecological Restoration Project brings together Parks Canada, the w̱SÁNEĆ community, the Pauquachin First Nation, the Province of BC, and the Islands Trust Conservancy to restore the forest, manage fallow and black-tailed deer and plant bulbs and medicinal plants on Sidney Island.[18] In addition to management of black-tailed deer, and forest restoration, Sidney islanders have removed over 15,000 fallow deer over the last thirty years.[19]

Members of the historic Quw'utsun Nations and the W̱SÁNEĆ Nations and the National Park are working in partnership on another project to restore two sea garden locations on Russell Island in Fulford Harbour, off of Salt Spring Island.[20]

During the lowest tides of the year in July 2022, I joined my community on Lasqueti Island and our Indigenous neighbours as we explored amazing low-tide zones. A whole world opens up as rocks turn to circles, and ancient faces appear in our minds. Rocks aligned along the mid- to low-tide line are meant to capture and rear clams. Lower down one might find a large ring of rocks with a small opening—wuχoθen (fish traps) that could have fed a community, which become obvious once you see them.[21] Rediscovery and restoration of sea gardens is exciting both for Indigenous people and residents as we come together to learn about, document, and celebrate this place based mariculture. As the ceremony's facilitator, Bill White, said, this coming together "in a good way, not a hard way" is already creating community, reconciliation, and adaptation in our changing world.

Mount Fisher Bluff was acquired in 2022 by the Nature Trust of BC. ALBERT NORMANDIN

Recent Conservation on Mount Warburton Pike

Two conservation areas on Saturna Island have recently been acquired by the Nature Trust of BC (NTBC). Jasper Lament, a biologist and Vancouver native, joined NTBC as its chief executive officer in 2012. After years of working in the US and with Ducks Unlimited on wetland conservation, he is now back here in BC leading the oldest province-wide land trust.

The first acquisition NTBC completed on Saturna was the Money Creek conservation area. During my interview with Jasper, he told me the owners made a significant donation through the Ecological Gifts Program and NTBC raised the rest of the funds to purchase these 58.1 hectares (143.5 acres) of sensitive land adjacent to the GINPR. An often essential match for other charitable donations is the federal government's Land Trust Conservation Fund, which requires a 1.5:1 match ratio.[22]

The second area that NTBC acquired right next door is called Mount Fisher Bluffs. This property leads up to and includes areas of Mount Warburton Pike, the highest peak in the Gulf Islands after Mount Maxwell on Salt Spring. These 31.2 hectares (77.2 acres) have both the endangered Garry oak and Douglas-fir ecosystems, including warm golden grasslands, rocky bluffs, and the forested ridge, which offers extensive views of the Gulf Islands and over to the San Juan Islands in Washington State. Like some other conservation acquisitions, this project required a subdivision, requiring appraisals and surveys.

Priscilla took me to see these high mountain properties, adjacent to some of the National Park Reserve lands. The area's outstanding view with extensive golden grasslands along the slopes was like no other I'd seen on the islands. I noticed feral goats grazing lower down on the bluffs. Priscilla told me that landowners on Saturna are very concerned about feral goats and conversations are underway with Parks Canada over how to manage the herd. Mayne Island's fallow deer and Lasqueti's feral sheep are herbivores (plant eating ungulates) that have considerable impact on the islands. Feral animals are a released domestic species. Without control from predators, they can easily put the ecosystems they inhabit out of balance. They disrupt the ecological communities of native species and even ecosystem processes through their consumption of food, occupation of habitat space, and exclusion of otherwise dominant vegetation types.[23] It's also a social challenge because people find it hard to recognize the impacts of these feral animals. And of course, they are cute, especially when they are young. These are one of many issues that need careful consideration as we learn to understand the sometimes complex relationships between ourselves and the many species who share the lands and waters of the Salish Sea and the larger world.

Over the years, many noted scientists have commented on the ecology of Saturna. Ian McTaggart Cowan and Barry Crooks took the lead in the early years. More recently, Harvey Janszen collected over 3,000 vascular plant specimens, mostly from the Southern Gulf Islands. He also curated comprehensive species checklists documenting the flora of the Southern Gulf Islands, Saanich Peninsula, San Juan Islands, and various other localities throughout the Salish Sea.

Harvey's dataset establishes a critical baseline record of the regional flora: a vital resource for understanding future ecological change in these communities.

Most importantly though, the long-term conservation of these places is the essential first step in protecting nature for the future. These conservation areas not only store (rather than emit) carbon in the soils, plants, and forests, but they also expand connectivity to neighbouring lands, which allows for habitats to be more diverse and species to move across and stabilize.

Richard Hebda, a familiar ecologist on the south coast, suggests that conserving larger areas is a key strategy in this time of changing climates. "Small isolated parcels tend to be subject to a higher risk of accidental events such as fires, than large, well-connected parcels. There is also a well demonstrated tendency for the loss of species from small areas compared to larger ones. In general, ecosystems on the entire landscape will need an adaptation strategy for the future."[24]

These huge Douglas-fir trees in the Gulf Islands National Park Reserve on Saturna Island provide shade, habitat, and store immense amounts of carbon.

Valuing Nature in an Era of Climate Change

Biomass and soils, the living carbon of ecosystems, remove and store carbon dioxide from the atmosphere naturally. Adapting to and reducing the degree of climate warming demands more than reducing or replacing the use of ancient carbon, namely fossil fuels, for energy. One of the essential life support services provided by ecosystems is the protection of the climate through carbon cycling. We suggest that "Carbon Stewardship" is an important concept that needs to be incorporated into policies and planning for climate change. This includes protecting the carbon stored in natural and semi-natural ecosystems.

SARA J. WILSON AND RICHARD J. HEBDA, *Mitigating and Adapting to Climate Change through the Conservation of Nature*[25]

Marine Protection around the Southern Gulf Islands

Protecting marine areas and species requires a different approach from typical land conservation. We can't buy the ocean, nor conserve its ecosystems and species directly or easily. With Saturna Island's extensive and diverse marine life, its proximity to eight million humans and their impacts, a changing climate, and the intersection of land and sea, these are significant challenges.

The Salish Sea is an area of high biological diversity with 190 large and small estuaries critical for salmon rearing, staging, and migration in addition to the Fraser River. Five of these rank in the top ten estuaries in British Columbia for their ecological value.[26] The Gulf Islands have been designated as an area of national importance for its ecology, wildlife and human communities. The creation of the Gulf Island National Park Reserve in 2003 reinforces the unique importance of this area. The connections between land and sea—both a mystical and ecological dynamic—is what draws us to the islands in the Salish Sea.

Saturna, adjacent Tumbo Island, and the Pender Islands, are within a very unique marine area with deep sea channels and swift currents next to a major shipping channel—Boundary Pass. To the south live our neighbours in the San Juan Islands, and directly east across the Strait is the mainland of Washington State—all within the Salish Sea. This inland sea spans the international border between Canada and the United States. With very different political and legislative laws, the islands in the Canadian Salish Sea face their own particular challenges in protecting the living species and ecosystems along its lands and waters. The outflow of the Fraser, and the inflow of the Strait of Juan da Fuca and the waters from Puget Sound all meet at Saturna Island.

In the spring of 2023, I met three local Saturna islanders who are focused on marine protection, through research and education. Susie Washington Smyth welcomed me to her waterfront home on Saturna Island. Because of Susie's background in science, education, and environmental policy and regulation, she served on the board of the Nature Conservancy of Canada for six years and on the board of the Islands Trust Fund (Conservancy) for another six years. Susie arrived on Saturna with an extensive environmental management background that allows her to understand science yet still be able to understand differing perspectives. Now retired, she continues to volunteer on projects related to the protection of wildlife in the Salish Sea.

Susie introduced me to Maureen Welton and Martin Wale, two of the founders and directors of the Saturna Island Marine Research and Education Society (SIMRES). Maureen Welton has a background in graphic design. One of the founders of SIMRES, she described herself to me simply as a concerned citizen. Taking a seat in Susie's ocean view home, Maureen said, "Problems in the ocean transfer to the land and everywhere in between." She explained further that birds are a direct link between them—whether it is the migrating warblers and turkey vultures who come from as far away as South America in the spring, or the seabirds like the harlequin ducks and buffleheads who leave the ocean to go inland to nest. Maureen is also the local Christmas Bird Count coordinator on the island and leads the local bird group started in the '70s by Harvey Janszen. She mentioned that recently they had seen mountain bluebirds and golden eagles along with other anomalies here on the edge of the Salish Sea.

Maureen described the gathering on Saturna Island in 2012 that brought her into SIMRES. "We had a community meeting about the national park's creation on the island, jobs and housing, considering the challenges of keeping young people on the island. From that meeting SIMRES was formed, growing out of an interest in the environment and protecting species and the ecology." She explained that SIMRES also works on terrestrial issues, such as removing invasive species, as they are part of the Parks Canada Liaison Committee. But their primary focus is marine research and education.

Martin Wale is currently the volunteer president and CEO of SIMRES. He is a United Kingdom trained physician recruited to Canada to work with Island Health and the Ministry of Health. Now semi-retired, he continues to do executive coaching. He knows how volunteers can only carry so much responsibility and many burn out. He explained that such work has been a life-long passion. Like Maureen, he cares immensely about marine life and all that connects with it.

Maureen and Martin recounted that "In 2014, Richard Blagborne, one of our island residents, initiated a whale conference on Saturna. It was the fiftieth anniversary of Moby Doll, captured at East Point off of Saturna Island for the Vancouver Aquarium. This was the first orca captured on the West Coast.[27] The aquarium wanted to build a whale sculpture, but they didn't know the dimensions. They commissioned an artist/harpoonist to capture an orca so they could then make this sculpture." Maureen added, "They had no success until the day they were leaving, when the J-pod came by. They harpooned a youngster, but it didn't die."

They towed the young whale to Vancouver, and it swam along with its mother following. Then it was kept in an enclosure at Jericho Beach. Thousands came to see this "killer" whale that up until that time, fifty years ago, was considered a Moby Dick sort of monster, a human killing creature. Not long after, it died, possibly from a skin disease or from damage made by the harpoon and additional gun shots used to try to kill it.[28]

However, this captured whale changed how humans relate to whales. With the interactions between Moby Doll and his visitors (it was determined after naming that the whale was male), including the very man who captured him, people saw that the whales' behaviours showed a deep bonding between their kin. They learned what these orcas ate, and that they were highly intelligent. Thus began the scientific study of the three sub-species we know today—transients, offshore, and residents.

When all the whale researchers in the field came to Saturna for this 2014 conference, it became the impetus for people to realize their island is an unusual place. "This is where it all started," Susie said. "We realized there is something unique about this area and that we are in the middle of the Salish Sea. Bill Austin, who started the Shaw Marine Centre in Sidney, identified that we have some of the richest biota in and around the Salish Sea."

Whale research advanced from seeing killer whales to recognizing an intelligent marine mammal from the capture of Moby Doll on Saturna Island in 1965. MAUREEN WELTON

During our interview, Martin described some of the successful SIMRES projects. In collaboration with Professor Ruth Joy of Simon Fraser University, two of her master's students have come annually to Saturna to undertake fieldwork on whales and vessels in and around the waters of East Point. Martin also mentioned other SIMRES projects including eelgrass studies, sea star counts, collaboration with Parks Canada regarding the marine environment, and broom eradication on park lands.

SIMRES installed hydrophones to provide a live underwater soundscape in Boundary Pass. This feed comes from an array of four hydrophones positioned at Cliffside and Monarch Head on Saturna Island.

SIMRES recently mounted an infrared camera at Cliffside, soon to be augmented by a second unit and radar, courtesy of Fisheries and Oceans Canada.

Building on her interest in whale research, Susie started the Southern Gulf Islands Whale Sighting Network (SGIWSN), which is closely affiliated with SIMRES. SGIWSN currently includes over seventy trained citizen scientist volunteers from Saturna, Pender, and Mayne who record their sightings using Ocean Wise's provincial tracking system, the Whale Report. Additionally these reports and related photographs are document on the website—spyhopper.ca. This creative and illustrative site was developed by Lucy Quayle, a graduate student from Simon Fraser University who is currently under contract with Fisheries and Oceans to compare hydrophone and citizen science data.

Martin added that, thanks to donations from individual donors, they now have hydrophones recording cetaceans twenty-four/seven in Boundary Pass. You could be lucky enough to hear different cetaceans from the recordings made by these hydrophones located at the pass from SIMRES website—live![29]

"The whale sighting network is hand in glove with SIMRES," Martin stated. "We have presented the data on whales to the federal government over three years," he added. "Initially they only barely listened, but by the third year, they not only accepted our data, but now they use it for internal planning."

Martin described an all too common problem for conservation: lack of funding and volunteer assistance, a consistent challenge. Programs like the federal government's Habitat Stewardship Program (HSP) only funds projects for three to four years. He sighed, "After that, they want something new—but that doesn't help with long term data collection and research." Unfortunately, their four year grant to do this data collection has now run out, but they are continuing to collaborate with a regional coast group. Working with a BC hydrophone network, SIMRES is now synchronizing equipment and practices from the north and central coast.

"Misinformation is another challenge that SIMRES works to challenge," Martin explained. "For example, the whale watching groups believe in sustainable whale watching. However, when a whale is sighted, there will be at least six, sometimes ten whale watching boats in attendance, from the US and Canada, following the whales for hours. The Southern Gulf Islands Whale Sighting Network is recording the number of boats and the number of whales, as part of our assessment of the Interim Sanctuary Zones, with the hope that they can change some of these behaviours." They gave me a sad example from last year when a mother humpback with a new calf were followed by six boats, day after day, for multiple days.

Susie noted the serious decline of southern resident killer whales (orcas), kelp beds, and of course the salmon. "When the federal government created the mitigation measures for Roberts Bank Two," she added, "they needed to demonstrate that they were doing something to protect the southern resident killer whales. So they put a Sanctuary Zone by Saturna because they knew the southern resident killer whales have been seen here, and over on Pender." Interim Sanctuary Zones prevent vessel traffic but so far are only in place from June 1, 2023, until November 30, 2023, with some exceptions.

Maureen, who lives along the Saturna Sanctuary Zone for the southern resident orcas, recently took note of another issue. A keen observer, she noticed that the kelp seemed healthy on the east side of the island, between Saturna and Tumbo Island,

but that it was dwindling substantially on the Boundary Pass side of the island. It turns out that, "this problem has been happening all over the world, from California's Santa Monica Bay, San Francisco, Gwaii Haanas, Norway, and Tasmania." Maureen explained that the largest known barrens in the Salish Sea has been found near East Point, in the Interim Sanctuary Zone.

Several years ago, SIMRES started doing kelp surveys based on methodology developed and led by the Mayne Island Conservancy. Using an underwater remote viewing unit (ROV) and professional divers, several sea urchin barrens have been discovered along Saturna's Cliffside shoreline.

Maureen proposed that the sea urchin imbalance could be caused by the cascading effect of sea star wasting disease, which started appearing along the entire coast in 2013. Sunflower stars, which are a main predator of sea urchins, have been decimated in the last few years due to this disease. "Another likely suspect in this sea urchin imbalance," Maureen explained, "is warming oceans due to climate change."

This small organization with its keen board of directors has collected essential data and continue to advance science for the protection of marine species—all linked to the health of the Salish Sea. Run by concerned citizens, their data is now considered the source of essential knowledge on what is happening around the Canadian islands in the southern Salish Sea.

Martin described Maureen as a perfect example of a concerned citizen who has been asking questions, recruiting experts to help discover and collect data, which then informs science. In time, with considerable advocacy and numerous reputable scientific presentations, politicians may consider the ramifications of the industrial projects they have been approving in the Salish Sea.

Understandably, another of the islanders' biggest concerns is the federally approved second tanker terminal in Tsawwassen—Roberts Bank Terminal Two. These passionate Saturna Island people are not about to give up.

Martin explained that with the support of surrounding island communities, the whale watching network has been collecting and presenting verified data to national and international audiences. At the recent International Marine Protected Areas Congress (IMPAC5) in Vancouver, this small group, with the help of an English production company, created an installation called *Critical Distance*. They designed a virtual reality experience of whales echolocating to find food and to communicate, amid the deafening sounds of oil and "natural" gas tankers, container ships, and the increasing commercial tourist boats out to get their own glimpse of the wild beings who have no say in the matter.

The data available from this citizen science group and many others including the Raincoast Conservation Foundation clearly reveal the dire impacts from commercial expansions in the Salish Sea. The scientific methods and data presented to the national Cohen Commission of Inquiry into the Decline of Sockeye Salmon in the Fraser River revealed that the numerous Atlantic salmon fish farms are affecting sockeye travelling past these farms in the northern Salish Sea, while those who travel south and don't pass the fish farms are in much greater abundance. The Commission recommended limiting commercial expansion and taking a precautionary approach.

Sea urchins have increased since the demise of their primary predator the sea otter and the more recent demise of another primary predator, the sunflower star. Sea urchins are now impacting the holdfasts of kelp, leaving sea urchin barrens in some areas. MAUREEN WELTON

The continuing submissions for more industrial expansion such as the Robert's Bank Container Port "shows action of a political nature—denial and suppression of an inconvenient fact. In legal terms, it is known as willful blindness, also characterized in some circumstances as gross negligence."[30]

Hopefully the increase of salmon where the fish farms have been removed, and the growing concerns about the health of the Fraser River and the larger Salish Sea, will provide a change in course.

Over dinner in her beautiful waterfront home facing Tumbo Island, Susie outlined the depth of the struggle. Her husband had worked in the Canadian Foreign Service for years and later became the president of the Canadian Petroleum Association. "The oil and gas industry is the sacred cow of Canada," she explained. "It's like guns in America. We can't talk about it."

She expressed her disappointment about the Interim Sanctuary zones because, "no in-depth science had been done, and if there was, the public sure didn't see it. In fact, when challenged the federal officials fell back on the precautionary principle."[31] Fisheries and Oceans Canada states that "the precautionary principle recognizes that in the absence of scientific certainty, conservation measures can and should be taken when there is knowledge of a risk of serious or irreversible harm to the environment and/or resources using best available information."[32] Susie exclaimed, "that principle can be counted on if you have baseline data from which further actions can be measured, but it is useless if there is nothing to measure." As Susie put it, "there is limited

The Gulf Island National Park Reserve looking to Boundary Pass.

evidence-based decision making for any of the mitigation measures for the whales. In fact, the container ships, tankers, ferries, and the whales travel in the same area." Maureen and Martin agreed with Susie on this point. They expressed a desire for year round protected areas and vessel slowdowns in Boundary Pass.

In his interview with me, Martin explained that "Fisheries and Oceans are now asking us to present our data at government meetings because they now have confidence in our methodology and rigorous care, and because they believe it. It's the most accurate and up-to-date data that exists. So I think that's pretty exciting and a great affirmation. It speaks volumes to the contribution which citizen science can make. It's a huge step that our data is now accepted—this is pretty exciting."

Susie and other islanders have had some great success in stopping projects that would impact the Salish Sea. Back in 2000, BC Hydro and Duke Energy wanted to build a natural gas pipeline that would travel from Washington State to Vancouver Island.[33] Not surprisingly, she helped organize several communities to come together and intervene as the GSX Concerned Citizens Coalition. They wrote to the federal government and explained why this project had regional and local significance and should be subject to a full Environmental Impact Assessment. Having previously worked for seven years on the *Environmental Assessment Act*, she knew how the process worked. After two hearings, one approval, and four years, the project was eventually cancelled. Messy as it was, this is an example of how citizen science and advocacy can work.

Surprisingly, a new marine park came out of the cancelling of this project. Gordon Scott, the conservation director at the Whatcom Land Trust at the time, had been following the path of BC Hydro buying property and easements across Washington for the project. He explained how it ended up as the Point Whitehorn Marine Reserve:

When I read that the project was stopped, I asked a BC Hydro representative what they were going to do with their property on Cherry Point, in Washington State. I learned that it was going to be put up as a surplus property. One of my board members mentioned it to a state senator who mentioned it to the governor, who talked to the premier. The governor asked if they can help, and I said "we want to buy it." So we got a grant from the Washington State Department of Ecology, we made a bid to BC Hydro, they accepted it, and we ended up buying the BC Hydro property where the pipeline was going to go underwater to Vancouver Island. We then traded it to the Trillium Corporation, for the Point Whitehorn Property, which is now the Point Whitehorn Marine Reserve.[34]

These islanders and their organizations have had a significant impact on both science and political advocacy. As the coordinator of the Whale Sighting Network, Susie had some advice for young scientists. "It's not enough to measure change; you have to be able to speak to it." In making this point, Susie echoed something I've heard from other scientists about communicating the results of their work to the general public and to government. "Young people working in the sciences need to pitch their science as a means for change. We don't need to exaggerate. The facts speak for themselves. We need to learn how to speak in a way both to the general public and to government—from the classroom to the voting booth."

The SIMRES website shares astonishing close-up photos of sea life around the island.[35] The regional whale sighting network Spyhopper plays live recordings of the whales and other sounds from the hydrophones they have installed.[36]

Beyond their research, they also have a dynamic educational program. SeaTalks, which started in 2014, offering a series of six to eight talks a year about topics which Maureen explained are, "Top of mind, current, in the news, and of interest to people. They are well attended, and the experts who lead them help teach everyone about the environment."

The Saturna Island Marine Research and Education Society has created a community of people interested in and passionate about the marine environment and especially cetaceans—the apex species, "because if they are healthy, the ocean is healthy." Maureen added, "to me the most exciting thing about living here is that there has been growth in the number of people who are willing to take action to make sure the environment they live in is protected and sustainable."

Saturna's population has increased 31 percent in the past five years. With these increases in population and the intensifying impacts of climate change, the dedicated and passionate people I met during my conservation journey are building a living arch over these challenging times into the future.

Priscilla Ewbank, who has been an historical force for Saturna island and its conservation, pointed to a path forward in these times of change.

I have a grandchild on the way. With my large biological background—the future can be too scary to contemplate. We all have beloved friends and children. It's up to

Orcas "spyhopping" off of Saturna Island. MAUREEN WELTON

each of us to create a vibrant creative life, and it doesn't mean you hide your head in the sand. It means that you find the most fruitful and giving way to be the best way humans can live—kind, humorous, thoughtful and compassionate. I work to be one of those people and to align myself with people like that. I find a great variety of kids coming up. So I am always seeking to show or to be a part of this bountiful and astounding world we live in and to show respect and trust and complete enjoyment. This is the life I live close to nature. I don't know what happened, but I ended up being able to live in this Salish Sea area. It is very inspiring and astoundingly beautiful.

As I was leaving Saturna, Priscilla pulled out a copy of the *Saturna Island Artistic Community Map* from the Islands in the Salish Sea Community Mapping Project. Priscilla told me, "On Saturna, the community actively discussed what special places needed to be included." Finalized in 2005, she told me, "we've sold our map at the store consistently ever since. We have it on cards. People love it. We give them to honour departing islanders who have contributed to the health and happiness of the community."

As I contemplated these remarkable, dedicated, and skilled islanders, I made my way back to the Pender Islands, where my sailing journey recommenced to a much more populated island, Mayne, the home of several long-serving conservation friends and mentors.

Seals hanging around the kelp beds. MAUREEN WELTON

CHAPTER SIX

MAYNE ISLAND
Conservation across Borders

*"After the first decade of awareness raising, holding
great events on natural history, we went in and bought
St. John Point, for the community and the region."*
MICHAEL DUNN

ON A STILL SULTRY JULY MORNING Heather and I pulled up anchor and headed out of Otter Bay, past the boutique cottages next to the marina and the ferry terminal toward nearby Mayne Island. The ocean had a silver grey mirror like sheen, with no wind, so we had to use the motor. As we transited Navy Channel, we heard a shrill bird call, and looked up to see an osprey flying high above with a bird in its claws. Suddenly it dropped its prey, and two eagles swooped down and one snatched its prize. I needed to have eagle eyes and pay attention too—as I spied the rocks off a long shelf off Dinner Point, I headed to port (veering left) to avoid a reef jutting out from the Mayne Island shore.

As we rounded the point and headed into Dinner Bay, we saw more urban styled homes, close-set with docks along the shoreline. With so many docks and moorings around, there was little room for anchoring, so we decided to use one of the vacant moorings. Normally, this practice is verboten, but I felt this was a better choice as we were only there for the day, and it would eliminate any impacts from anchoring in the eelgrass bed. Little did I know then that we were anchored in one of the busiest bays on the island. I was yet to see the fascinating, less developed bays and shorelines around Mayne Island where intact kelp beds and sublime forests of arching arbutus and Douglas-fir trees gnarled their protective branches over the Salish Sea.

Like Pender, half a century ago this bay had a herring saltery. At the head of the bay was another sign of past history, the location of the former farm of the Adachi family—one of the Japanese-Canadian families forcibly removed and dispossessed from Mayne Island after Canada declared all people of Japanese descent "Enemy Aliens" in 1942. The Dinner Bay Community Park and the Japanese Memorial Garden provide recreational, community, and historical gathering places for visitors and residents. Similar to a few other islands, the Mayne Island Parks and Recreation Commission, a local committee under the Capital Regional District, manages this community park.

Once safely tied to a mooring, I rowed to shore and walked up to this local community park to meet with two of the Mayne Island Conservancy's dedicated volunteer directors. I was really looking forward to reconnecting with these two esteemed conservationists I had worked with in the past, founders of the Mayne Island Conservancy (MIC), Helen O'Brien and Michael Dunn.

Today, the island is starting to take on the name SḰŦAḴ in recognition of its deep history of W̱SÁNEĆ people's occupation. Located on the Mayne Island side of Active Pass, Helen Point and its peninsula are a reserve of the Tsartlip, a W̱SÁNEĆ First Nation. As described by Paul Petrie in the Pender Island chapter, the settler communities on Mayne, Pender, and the Saturna islands have been reaching out and reconnecting with the Indigenous people who once knew and cared for these islands and the habitats and behaviours of the wildlife that are now being conserved by locals.

Mayne Island's population has jumped 37 percent since 2016, with the 2021 census recording 1,304 residents. Many of the islands have seen intense increases in recreational homes, in addition to full-time resident homes in the past ten to fifteen years. The increase in buildings, though, reveals that of 1,292 buildings, only 706 are full-time residents. Fortunately, the Mayne Island Conservancy (MIC) has been working directly with new property owners on the island since 2003.

The pandemic is one source of the increased populations on the Salish Sea islands. Most new owners are seeking a quieter, rural lifestyle—or a second home to escape to. Disturbingly, especially on the Southern Gulf Islands, this has brought a widening economic divide. An urban mindset has also arrived, with the human tendency to change things—cutting trees, adding exotic species, redesigning things to reflect the comfort and familiarity of an older home. There appears to be little regard for the perspective advocated by architect Christopher Alexander. In his seminal book, *Pattern Language*, he recommends contemplating "place," waiting through all four seasons before designing a home or landscaping. This approach offers people time to understand the seasonal changes surrounding their new home before setting out to develop it.

Mount Parke

Originally formed to protect a specific area, the Mayne Island Conservancy started out as the Friends of Mount Parke. Helen, one of the founding directors, is a tall gregarious woman with the stamina of a twenty-year-old! This suits her, as her background is in oral storytelling and children's literature. She told me it wasn't long after she arrived on the island in 1998 that a couple of people approached her for help to protect a piece of commercially-zoned land in the middle of Miner's Bay, off Active Pass. She and some friends got busy raising awareness about the need for its protection. Through a small tax levy, they raised the funds to turn this threatened piece of land into a community park.

Emboldened by their early success, Helen, and Ann Johnston, along with several other visionary leaders on the island, decided to take these kinds of conservation campaigns into their own hands—working with whomever would take an interest. Next they focused on protecting an undeveloped area around Mount Parke, the highest mountain located in the centre of the island. At that time, only a small section of the ridge—21 hectares (52 acres)—was designated as a CRD community park. Its primary focus is parks for people, including hiking and developing trails and, in some cases, supplying barbecue areas and recreational games like I saw at the head of Dinner Bay. This difference between the purposes and uses of a community park and a nature reserve or conservation area are important. Both have their different uses and values.

Michael Dunn and Helen O'Brien are two of the key founders of the Mayne Island Conservancy.

View from Mount Parke, an area that MIC worked for years to protect and is now a CRD park.

In 2003 the Friends of Mount Parke formed to protect the whole ridge and make it accessible to the public. The area is ecologically sensitive; with south facing ridges and cliffs, it is home to species not found on other parts of the island. When Helen took me there in the spring, turkey vultures, bald eagles, and common ravens soared in the updrafts, plunging within feet of us to land in large trees.

Back in 2003, the owners were logging the property, and Mayne islanders objected especially as the mountainsides went directly down to the village. The Friends of Mount Parke met with the owner, had several appraisals done, and raised one third of the ridge's value to acquire it. Helen told me that Ann Johnston, her mentor, was instrumental in organizing events and tracking the funds. Several offers later, the owner ceased logging, but hung onto the title, with hopes that the land would increase in value over time. The directors then put the project aside and chose to expand their focus to the larger island.

At this time, a naturalist group was already active on the island. Started by Michael Dunn in the '90s, their work included the Christmas Bird Count, Oceans Day celebrations, beach clean-ups, and establishing the Active Pass Important Bird Area (IBA).

Michael joined Helen and the Friends of Mount Parke. They spent their first decade raising awareness of natural systems. From that came a merging of the natural history club and the Conservancy. Through site visits or "Walkabouts" for new land-owners, they started a program that has become such a success that it has spawned similar ones across the region. Michael explained how it began. "They are curious about what's on their property. The realtors know about us. They recommend, 'oh go talk to the Conservancy—about the trees, etc.'"

As Helen explained, "We put out a publication, *Tread Lightly*, in a welcome pack-age that covered all sorts of things, and in that we mentioned the Walkabout. Before we had paid staff, I was doing it, then Michael took it on, just to walk with them and listen. We have a certain amount of land formally protected. And we have prob-ably double that under a stewardship lens, where people owning the land are acting responsibly, maintaining the land, and finding it exciting when they see the changes happening. The Walkabout program we call the Gateway—into more formal protec-tion, looking at the long view."

Michael added, "We put it out there to private property owners, particularly new owners. They come to us knowing that we do free ecological assessments of properties. We walk around with them. They tell us their dreams. We tell them what we see, and discuss any issues they might want to look at. If they have invasive plants, or if it's been heavily logged, we suggest how to restore it. We have a native plant nursery, so we can supply plant stock. People are working to do ecological stewardship and still live here."

Another islander, Ron Pither, owned Veralaya Farms on Mayne Island at the time. He described himself as a forester/farmer and small mill owner. Ron galloped ahead of the formation of many land trusts on the islands with his now forty-year-old regional conservation/activist organization called West Coast Islands' Stewardship and Conservancy Society. A pioneer in the field, he helped with the founding of the Denman Conservancy, Conservancy Hornby Island, Quadra Island Conservancy, and the province-wide Land Trust Alliance of BC. Living on the island during their first effort to protect Mount Parke, he called Ann a brilliant woman, "like a dog on a bone, keeping data, volunteer hours, and tracking donations."

In the late '90s many Mayne islanders were in Ron's words, "a conservative lot." Islanders knew about Galiano Island Conservancy's court case from a SLAPP suit activated by MacMillan Bloedel. The details were vague, but emotions were strong, thus the Mayne Island community was at first hostile to the word "conservancy" especially to not be like Galiano. Thanks to the careful communications of people like Michael and Helen, the Friends of Mount Parke were confident enough to change their name to the Mayne Island Conservancy in 2005.

Mayne Island Conservancy Founders and Staff

Ron explained, "Michael Dunn and Helen O'Brien are phenomenal ambassadors. They got into a slow education, were very temperate and took caring steps by discussing process and providing positive messages, but it was a hard battle. Some people became conservative Conservancy people."

Michael Dunn had professional experience in the field of wildlife conservation, working for the federal government's Canadian Wildlife Service during the latter part of his career. He managed three funds from different programs: one for protecting wetlands; the Georgia Basin ecosystems at-risk fund; and a third for buying private lands for conservation, knowing there wasn't a lot of public land available. Similar to the Gabriola Island founder's story, he brought this professional experience to the Mayne Island Conservancy.

"I was involved with the federal government putting money into eligible projects, such as for closing the gap at the end of a deal. Also having federal funds as part of an acquisition helped bring in other contributors. There were significant ones, such as Salt Spring Island's campaign to protect the Texada lands (Burgoyne Bay). There was a $50,000 gap with only weeks to the closing date. Another was in Sooke, at Ayum Creek, and Sooke Potholes. That was a three million dollar one that we went in on. Protecting and conserving nature has been my passion. I retired and just continued on doing this work as a volunteer."

Since Helen's previous cohort, Ann Johnston, had passed on, she remarked, "Aren't we lucky to have Michael here now!"

Michael inspired me with his natural history and mapping skills. In 1994 I brought Michael and a few others together on the Southern Gulf Islands for a workshop on identifying and mapping natural features on one's own property. After the workshops, we created a how-to manual, depicting base map and survey techniques, inventory features, sources of information, and an introduction to community mapping: creating a bioregional map atlas. Named by Ron Pither, *Giving the Land a Voice, Mapping Our Home Places*, the book includes many of the beautiful maps islanders created.

Dedicated to teaching more of this kind of ecological literacy, Michael and his future wife, Jessica, founded the Gulf Islands Centre for Ecological Learning in 2002.[1] With the support of School District 64 (Gulf Islands), the Centre started on Mayne Island. It soon expanded to offer programs and learning experiences on other islands, to help nurture "eco-literate" citizens through children's summer camps, school programs, and adult and family events.

Michael's own nature education had taken root during his early years in Victoria. He told me it all started with two naturalist uncles, who provided inspiration and a keen interest. In his school years, scientists took his nature discoveries seriously.

> All the people at the Royal BC Museum (it was the Natural History Museum then) were my mentors. There were lots of formaldehyde critters, which were housed in one wing of the Legislature. All the people there, including Clifford Carl, the director of the museum then, were helpful. Our elementary school is just down the road, so we'd walk in after school, check the stuff out. We'd have jars. He'd open his office, and we'd come in. He would identify the bugs. Then there were the geologists just across the road. We would go in with all our "diamonds" and "gold" that we thought we'd found. And they would identify our samples for us, saying, "This is a good rock," and tell us what it was. To me this knowledge was always available and accessible. In hindsight, I see now it was a privilege.

The MIC has a native plant nursery at Michael and Jessica's house.

The native plant nursery at Michael and Jessica's place has been in operation since 2011. They grow about 35 species for a total number of 600 to 800 native plants, primarily shrubs and trees to use in local restoration projects. Two thirds are used for restoration in public parks and one third they sell to private landholders.

The term "landholder" is used by many land trusts to help people recognize that one doesn't "own" land; rather one "holds" it for a while, before passing it on. This is a different way of thinking about the land. We are only here temporarily and our impacts reach far beyond our own land stewardship.

Rob Underhill, a biologist now working for MIC, explained further. "The Walkabout program is a strong educational tool for people. Some engage in small-scale habitat restoration following our consultation. We continue our site visits to help them by lending tools and materials."

Helen added that the program has helped not only recent residents understand the specific nature of the island's ecology, but it has also brought in new donors and directors, fulfilling a bigger picture.

Malcolm Inglis joined the Conservancy's board after one of these Walkabouts. "We were the first people the local Conservancy did this kind of consultation with. We had just bought our property, and it was covered with broom. We just walked around with a bunch of lovely people from Galiano Conservancy and the Mayne

Conservancy. We have 16 acres, mostly wooded, which we walked through. It was such a wonderful experience. I felt like I'd found my people. So I was really well disposed toward working with the Conservancy once they approached me." Later, Malcolm became the board's president.

Generally early board members, all volunteer, are willing to put in time for specific projects, especially raising funds to acquire land for conservation. But often the day-to-day work of keeping track of things burns out volunteers hard and fast. Helen told me that Ann, from her early years as a director, was insistent that they hire people. They hired Leanna Boyer as their first biologist/executive director.

Leanna's early work focused on eelgrass and kelp mapping. In recent years more people have recognized the importance and extent of these marine plants and their relationships, especially around the West Coast.[2] Unfortunately, kelp forests have been reduced significantly around areas of the coast because of sea urchins, bottom dwellers who are voracious grazers on it. The sea urchins once were the main food diet of sea otters. With the hunting and then almost total extinction of sea otters around the coast in the early twentieth century, the cascading effect of over hunting one species is still being felt today by what scientists are calling sea urchin deserts. Certainly around my home on Lasqueti Island, we have lost the kelp beds that once nurtured and protected the abundant salmon in the Salish Sea.

It was a joy to see these floating kelp bulb heads on my walk along St. John Point in early April. Seals love to hide in these kelp forests, tricking people with their kelp head similarity.

Thanks to Leanna's early inspiration, this work of mapping priority eelgrass and kelp beds is ongoing. The Mayne Island Conservancy now models the techniques used by divers across the islands.

Rob Underhill was lucky enough to find a job with MIC shortly after he received his degree in biology from the University of Victoria. Rob described his surprising transition to living and working on Mayne Island after a short stint with Parks Canada at Fort Rodd Hill.

A wonderfully healthy kelp bed exists along St. John Point. SHARI WHITE

> I went from a well-funded office at Fort Rodd hill overlooking Fisgard Lighthouse to a 6-foot-by-6-foot shack in Leanna Boyer's garden, with chickens outside. It was a shock between the two work environments. I thought, "what just happened to my career." I had no experience with the non-profit sector and the great work they have done and continue to do. Over time I came to appreciate living in the small community, and have made great connections on Mayne Island. When my partner and I were expecting our first child, we decided to fully commit to the island, and purchased a house in 2016. Now I can't imagine making a different choice. I love the community and MIC is the best employer I've ever had. I have worked in a lot of different industries, but I feel lucky now, and appreciate it so much. Now we have a different office as the organization has grown a lot over the last ten to eleven years.

Today, Rob does most of the Walkabouts with landholders. By 2021 they completed 138 consultations on 433 hectares (1,070 acres).[3] Michael explained that new opportunities came up from just this type of awareness raising. Doing stewardship work could lead to a covenant or acquisition. "But first we needed things in place—designation by BC Land Title to hold Section 219 covenants, and Section 218—a statutory right of way (to enter the land and monitor the covenant)—and then becoming an eligible recipient of Environment and Climate Change Canada's Ecological Gift program.[4] We already had charitable status. All those markers to take on land trust authority were an effort, but we completed them. We were getting prepared for the opportunity. In 2016 came the big opportunity—with the start of the St. John Point campaign."

St. John Point

This ~26 hectare (64 acre) peninsula on the south end of Mayne Island is known as ȾÁ,WEN by the Coast Salish First Nations. Situated within the coastal Douglas-fir ecological community, it contains many endangered and threatened species, including the four largest natural vegetation communities which are red-listed—federally listed as endangered. As with the Mount Parke project, the owners had allowed people to walk on the footpaths that wind through the forest and along the shores of their property, and the owners allowed kayakers to land on St. John Point's two gravel beaches.

St. John Point on Mayne with arbutus and Seaside Juniper looking to Saturna island.

The property was owned by the Eddy family, who had bought it in the mid '50s. In 2015, the three Eddy brothers considered selling. Their citizenship crossed borders—one was Canadian and the other two were American. The brothers started worrying about the future of the land with its joint ownership and the Canadian capital gains taxes they would have to pay when they sold.

One of the brothers lives in Washington State, which is home to the American Friends of Canadian Conservation (AFOCC, American Friends). As mentioned in the Gabriola chapter, this US 501(c) organization was set up to help Americans who sell land to a conservation organization in Canada so that they can receive a US income tax deduction for a charitable donation. The founding of this cross-border organization has allowed generous landowners like the Eddys to leave a legacy of conserved land in just this type of situation. The US brother contacted this cross-border organization about a possible conservation sale of their Mayne Island property, and discussions began.

The American Friends then contacted MIC, and they proceeded to draft an agreement to work together. The local Conservancy assisted with developing the purchase process, price, and agreement to donate it as an Ecological Gift. The American Friends were to hold the American brothers' two thirds interest in the property and MIC would hold the one third interest of the Canadian brother, once the deal was closed. Their goal was to raise $3.6 million (of the appraised $4.5 million) within eleven months. The goal for this small community was $2 million.

In an amazingly short time frame, nine-and-a-half months, and with a population of only one thousand, they raised the needed funds to purchase the land. I asked how they managed to raise so much money in such a short time. "We had a multifaceted approach," Michael said, "and built a community 'ownership' of the campaign and the outcome." Their goal: to bring the land back into the commons of the island.

St. John Point Fundraising Campaign Elements

- We contacted one-on-one some key resident donors who we felt would support this acquisition. An initial anonymous donation of $1 million set the tone!
- We launched the campaign with a "big reveal event" where we announced the project, the conditions, and the target for our community campaign. We started from a very strong position, as we were almost halfway there.
- A local chef offered five international meals for about 16 in a lovely private home (raising $20,000).
- We took community members on scheduled walking tours of the property offering tea along the way.
- We invited our regional arts community to create original works of art inspired by St. John Point. "Artists on the Point" produced stunning images which were donated to the Conservancy and then auctioned at a community auction ($40,000).
- We continued the one on one campaign with selected donors and raised a further $400,000.
- Local businesses and restaurants offered benefit concerts, special meals, and various community businesses had tip jars for the campaign.
- Presence at the weekly summer markets brought in donations.
- The rest of the island's $2 million goal was raised from individuals in the community, including children (selling kindling, using their allowance).

The Mayne Island Conservancy also wrote fundraising proposals to government agencies and foundations. Successful foundation applications raised over $300,000. Then the two partner organizations, MIC and AFOCC, brought in the Capital Regional District Parks to close the deal.

Michael explained how the transaction became a Capital Regional District (CRD) Park:

> The transaction ended up as a transfer of the interests of both the Mayne Island Conservancy and the American Friends to the CRD. At the time of closing both MIC and AFOCC held title, but before transfer to the CRD occurred, a conservation covenant in favour of MIC and registration of an Ecological Gift had to occur. Once these cleared, the title was then transferred to the CRD. The transfer of the AFOCC interest was to a governmental conservation organization whose primary purpose was the protection of the property in perpetuity. In addition, having both a covenant and an Ecological Gift registered further ensured that the ecological values found on this property were going to be protected. All of this met the AFOCC requirements of the IRS with regard to flow through transactions.

The Ecological Gifts Program (EGP) is another form of long-term insurance, or protection, that the property will be held in conservation perpetually. This federal government income tax incentive program gives owners of land in Canada a 100 percent capital gains deduction for the donation of significant ecological land to a designated recipient (land trust or government agency). This also applies to a bargain sale or split receipt for selling the land at a significantly reduced price, usually a minimum of 20 percent of its value. If one is to sell or pass on land to a family member, this program can enable the landholder to keep some of the land in the family, rather than sell it to pay the costly capital gains tax.

When Helen and I walked along the St. John's Point peninsula on a rainy April day, a year and a half after my initial sailing trip, I noticed the floating heads from the kelp, a welcome sight as these large plants are not only habitat for so many marine creatures, they are also a part of the blue carbon bank that is becoming more and more important with climate change.[5] All along this shoreline I saw several sea birds—common loons, common mergansers, and buffleheads—chasing each other like young kids. The peninsula is lined with huge arbutus weaving their way around the firs. At the end of the point, a series of juniper trees bravely face the southerly winds and sun. A glorious view of Saturna Island faced us, while small Lizard Island sat in front of Samuel Island to the west. We went back along the middle trail, which is much wider than the shoreline trail, making the area accessible to people with mobility challenges. At the end of the peninsula was a flat beach where we found a dog owner throwing sticks from the beach into the water.

This regional park is now a wonderful legacy from the Eddy brothers and the many donors who contributed to its purchase. The Mayne Island Conservancy completed a multitude of documents transferring the property through the American Friend's beneficial tax process into the hands of the CRD. This conservation project has been featured at national conservation gatherings as an example of how land trusts can work with willing American owners of Canadian land to leave a legacy for the future, while receiving their own personal tax benefits.

Given all this volunteer leadership and effort, and multiple donations from the community and the foundations, I asked Helen why the Conservancy didn't want to own the land themselves. She responded with a similar sentiment I heard on other islands. "It's not a written policy, but we feel in our hearts that we don't want to own land, but future boards may want to."

Land trusts on small islands are primarily directed by a board of volunteers who dedicate an inordinate amount of their lives to campaigns such as this one. However, for long term protection, management and oversight is essential, even if the land is primarily left alone. Sometimes invasive plants need to be removed. Sometimes trees fall down from a neighbouring property. Salt Spring has a much larger population, able to support their larger land trust with management and restoration projects. For long-term permanent protection, smaller land trusts often register the title of a property with a larger conservation organization that has a larger member base and deeper pockets to manage the land.

The Gabriola Island Land and Trails Trust mentioned this same rationale for transferring properties they have worked to protect to a larger conservancy, in their case, the Islands Trust Conservancy. Here on Mayne, MIC has transferred St. John's Point to the Capital Regional District. Two other conservation land trusts working

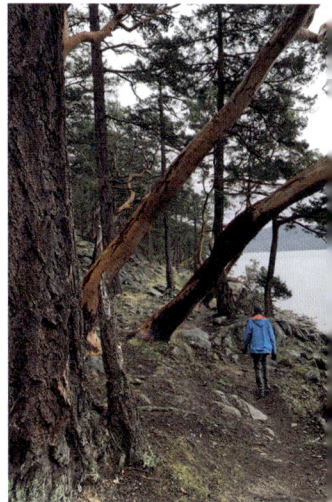

Helen O'Brien walking the trail along the now protected CRD Park at St. John Point.

in BC can also accept transfer of lands protected by the local community: NCC, the Nature Conservancy of Canada and NTBC, the Nature Trust of BC.

Most of these local land trusts do the hard work of raising the funds, rallying their community's support, and facilitating agreements with willing sellers. And at a time when property values are sky rocketing, and less and less land is available that still has ecological integrity, the work of local land trusts is essential—and performed by what I can only describe as local heroes!

Mount Parke—Expanded at Last

In 2020 the Conservancy had a surprising turn of events. The Capital Regional District (CRD) informed them that Mount Parke's owner was now willing to sell the ridge. Because of MIC's earlier interest in this property, the CRD asked them if they could raise some funds to assist in the purchase. With a $50,000 contribution from MIC, the additional ~47.8 hectares (118 acres) were added to the park. Having become so successful through their recent St. John's Point campaign, they were able to transfer this amount from a dedicated CAMAS fund (Conservation, Acquisition, Management, and Stewardship).

On a walk along the trails of Mount Parke in early April, I marveled at its extensive size, with the highest point in the centre of the island. At the top, the expansive and numerous viewscapes scan from Prevost Island, next to Salt Spring Island, to Samuel Island near Saturna, and beyond to the San Juan islands. The well-maintained trails lead up to several viewpoints, such as the Halladay viewpoint, named after one of three Mayne Island Parks and Recreation commissioners who helped make it a park. Also at the top, beside the park, is a private property with a federal communications tower.

Sadly, I spotted the invasive Scotch broom on the trail. Even this plant's tips had been eaten by deer, including the feral fallow deer which are plentiful here. The ridge is largely forested with plants in the Douglas-fir/arbutus subzone, with large firs, arbutus, cedar, alders, and a few Garry oaks. Salal, huckleberry, and Oregon grape filled in much of the understory. These native shrubs were not abundant, but hopefully a few of the spring flowers noted on the sign at the top would appear later in the spring: larkspur, satinflower, spring gold, sea blush, Hooker's onion, and chocolate lily.

Word on the island explains that a half century ago, a farmer had been licensed to keep these exotic deer, but they could not maintain their operations. When falling trees took out the fence, the deer escaped to move across the island, eating the under-story while expanding their numbers exponentially. MIC has recently committed to advocate for management of these invasive deer.

Edith Point

Along Mayne's southeast shores, lies a long, skinny peninsula leading to Edith Point. Because the peninsula has restricted access for deer, this 35 hectare peninsula is lush with vegetation. Consequently, its 3.5 kilometres of undeveloped shoreline provides extensive habitat for an abundance of bird species. Its mature forests with a few old growth veterans includes a rare, old shore pine forest with spectacular views of the Salish Sea and Coast range into Washington.

The Graves family owned the point for almost thirty years. The family consulted with Michael over fifteen years about how to leave a conservation legacy of at least

part of the property. Then in 2018 they asked MIC to help them find a conservation solution for the property. "They were aging and wanted to complete something while they were alive. MIC completed a baseline report for the family as a foundational document to show funding partners interested in the property." The baseline report not only established the ecological rationale for conserving Edith Point, it also helped the landowners understand the significance of the property they wanted to sell.

"Through a study carried out by the Mayne Island Conservancy we learned a great deal about the ecological value of the land and wanted to officially preserve the land we have been stewarding for the past thirty years," said one of the owners, Don Graves.[6]

The baseline report is a biological survey of the land. In addition to describing the Douglas-fir veterans and shore pine trees on the property, the report also revealed that it contains pockets of coastal meadow, and a small wetland. Biologists have documented over 170 species of vascular plants, including the rare seaside juniper, growing on the rocky bluffs along the south shore.

Rob Underhill, the Conservancy's biologist, told me that for years Don and Betty Ann Graves provided public access to a large section of their two lots. Other than the house site at the far end, the two lots were undeveloped, thus preserving one of the more pristine ecosystems on Mayne Island.

Michael described the transaction's trajectory.

The Graves wanted to sell the majority of the property for conservation but still keep their house and have access to the property guaranteed. I spent about two years discussing this project with other organizations who would be interested. The Nature Conservancy of Canada (NCC) and the Islands Trust Conservancy agreed to participate in the purchase. The NCC already had identified this property as a priority acquisition for them, and they were willing to purchase the larger of the two lots that make up the total property. The ITC and MIC would partner and work to purchase the smaller lot and undertake a Section 99 subdivision to remove the house site from the conservation area. A registered easement was also placed on both lots to allow access to the house site property at the end of the point. The three agencies created a working Memorandum of Understanding (MOU) and the Nature Conservancy of Canada (NCC) became the lead working with the owners. The owners opted to only work with the NCC and asked that the title of both lots be registered to the NCC as well.

The agreement for sale was signed—the owners would donate an Ecological Gift of 50 percent of the fair market value and settle for a cash purchase for the rest (in the order of just over $4 million). All the funds raised were through private or family trust donors. The owners also insisted that MIC would have a role in the long term management of the property. The NCC and MIC had a working agreement for that purpose setting out the roles and responsibilities of the parties post purchase. In addition, MIC committed to contributing funds by a low-key fundraising request to specific donors. In ten days, MIC was able to contribute and raise just over $550,000.

The NCC provided the remainder of the funds for the purchase. In August 2022 the Graves family finalized their land donation through the Ecological Gifts Program. The family will continue to own a private 3 hectare (7.5 acre) parcel surrounding their home at the end of the point, and the rest of this ecologically significant property will be conserved in perpetuity.

During my second trip to the island in April, my husband Gordon and I walked along a trail out to Edith Point. This spectacular peninsula has long views across the strait to Mount Baker and other snow-capped mountains. We walked along the sandstone shoreline. In the first small, deep arm of the bay we saw an unusual sight: a seal was swimming upside down in the water for over ten minutes. It looked to me like it was having a gay old time, twisting up for breath or snatching some delicious fishy treat and then diving back down into the shallow waters of the slim embayment. Gordon thought it might be sick. We turned and walked down the trail to the next point, and looked out to see the seal staring back at us, its head in its usual upright position.

As we walked the maintained trail through the salal toward the point, we stopped short of the small area set aside for the home of this generous family who conserved the rest of the peninsula for the future. We saw two cormorants swimming with their necks raised high above the flat calm waters, two eagles soaring and calling to each other with their strange cry, and one gull chasing one of them madly. Had it taken its chick? Then, just barely, we heard the first spring bird calls I'd heard on Mayne—possibly a chickadee or a wren along the trail. Thankfully, this peninsula, cut off from the fallow deer, is an extraordinary refuge! We saw huge arbutus trees jutting up at crazy diagonal angles above and between the firs—small new shore pines growing all along the shoreline path, and giant cedars, greeting us at every turn of the trail.

I wondered how such a conservative island could raise over two million dollars in such a short time, coming from their early days of reticence. Michael gave it some context. "After the first decade of awareness raising, holding great events on natural history, we went in and bought St. John Point, for the community and the region. That really changed people's perspectives. Now we've gone from a lot of hesitancy to one of the core groups on the island."

Mayne Island Conservancy Today

The Mayne Island directors I interviewed all said that the conservation of Edith Point and St. John Point were their most concrete successes. "However, you could draw circles around the habitats that we feel we have helped through the Landholder Stewardship Program," asserted Rob. The program has made a difference by motivating

The protection of the peninsula at Edith Point, Mayne Island, took over fifteen years.

people to take action as land stewards and by giving them the knowledge and tools needed. And, the program brings in new donors and directors and even some bequests.

I spoke with Malcolm Inglis, the president of MIC at the time, by phone. He told me that the protection of St. John Point was their most successful achievement over the past twenty years. He added that protecting this property brought the evolution of the Conservancy to a new level. "We became much more professional through all that process work. We built our communications skills, we became a lot more visible, and we built a strong constituency here on the island who supports our efforts to protect land."

Michael added that registering the conservation covenant on the title of St. John Point, now owned by CRD Parks, is another notable success. The CRD has only one other covenant, on Pender Island at Brooks Point. However, years later, it is still being negotiated. Michael explained the problem. "They had to designate it as a conservation area through their own policy, so that restricts what they can do internally. Some of their day-to-day activities we wouldn't consider acceptable, but we had good communications, so we knew that a lot of stuff wouldn't go sideways, while we are here."

Once an organization acquires land, they must determine how to manage it. Levels of protection can vary from an area that is closed or restricted to the public, right through to areas which are open to the public for recreation. The protection of the habitats and species within these conservation sites varies depending on the levels of public access and the type of organization that holds the title. The management plans that typically follow the formal protection of a site sets out their long term goals, any restoration or management plans, and their uses. These range from national parks, such as the Gulf Island National Park Reserve, to a community park with its primary purpose of providing a neighbourhood park for play and recreation.

MIC's long-time president Malcom remarked that the threats are increasing. Mayne's recent population growth, the largest in BC, has had some real impacts on the island's ecosystems. "All of us are disconcerted about the way people come in and have this urban sensibility that they try to apply to their property. They strip it down, and they come with a lot of money. Then they plant new gardens and other trees. But there's also lots of young people, with respect for the land, with small kids. We started doing more education through our website, and through the community's monthly publication, *The Mayne Liner*. We ran a series on how to live with a light footprint on Mayne Island. We're trying to get the message out about how you can develop without stripping it." Symptomatic of the growing number of people on the island, Malcolm added that the Walkabout or Stewardship Program has also boomed in the last few years.

Thanks to the work of the local Conservancy over the past twenty years, Mayne Island has three new conservation areas and residents are much better educated about how to care for the land they are stewarding.

The vast majority of wetlands and wet forests on Mayne were cleared and drained for agriculture in the late 1800s and early 1900s. The local Conservancy has done some extensive wetland restoration at Hedgerow Farm. After they installed a weir and deer fencing, they observed re-flooding of a portion of a hayfield that was formerly a wetland. Changes at the site occurred rapidly. Wetland plants such as sedges and rushes expanded to fill areas once dominated by exotic grasses. Bird species such as red-winged blackbirds, barn swallows, and violet-green swallows began feasting on the dragonflies and other insects thriving in the shallow waters. Pacific chorus frogs found the site, and now great blue herons hunt in the shallows. Occasionally the distinctive breeding call of the Wilson's snipe can be heard. The restoration of this site signals another successful avenue that the Conservancy has followed thanks to their stalwart volunteer directors, and the staff and contractors they are increasingly adding to their fold.

In addition to providing plants, tools, and information to help landholders, the MIC also holds public speaking events and workshops, publishes articles in the local newspaper, and updates their extensive website. Recently, Rob has found grants to support his once a week classes on nature-based education in the local school.

The protection and restoration of land on Mayne Island is an ongoing challenge. Overabundant deer impact the extent to which natural ecosystems can recover on their own. "And it's not just a matter of solving soil compaction; everything we plant has to be within a fence. It makes restoration projects expensive and difficult to maintain," Rob explained.

Malcolm told me they started advocating to reduce the fallow deer in the last few years. MIC has been asking the provincial government to take action and educate islanders about the impacts on the understory from the deer, especially the fallow, feral ones. "They are the single biggest threat to our local ecology. New people come and think that what they see is natural. And it's not. The forest understory has been decimated. We've lost so many ground nesting birds, native flowers, even the arbutus are threatened with extinction. I don't think there are any young arbutus outside of fences. Education is needed and it will join with our advocacy on this issue in the future."

Michael noted that he hadn't seen the grouse and pheasants that used to be plentiful on the island in over five years. He added that it's hard to face the social pressures. "Bambi is cute, but there are many songbirds who no longer sing here." The big picture reveals that food plants eaten by one species are often at the expense of other species on these islands. Without predators such as cougars, and in some areas bears, no longer around, it's a particular challenge.

Rob described some of their marine work. Since 2009 three local divers have measured the extent of eelgrass in all of Mayne Island's larger bays. Overall, over the last thirteen years the data from these annual dives shows a 41 percent decrease in the area the eelgrass covers. "Unfortunately, it is one thing to observe negative changes, and another to prevent them," Rob lamented. "On the marine side of things, the tools we have and level of understanding is insufficient. The pattern of drainage and ditching and vegetation cover removal—those types of changes affect the way surface water flows across the island. In a heavy rainfall event, erosion is much more severe than historical patterns show if vegetation were left intact."

I thought about the busy Dinner Bay shoreline where divers found significant loss of eelgrass.

I learned that a 57 percent reduction in the extent of eelgrass in Dinner Bay was measured in the last thirteen years. Loss of eelgrass is one of the many impacts from development on the Gulf Islands. It worries Rob. "As the moored boats move back and forth in the wind and current, the heavy chain drags along the bottom, creating a circle on the seabed where no eelgrass grows." Thankfully, many mariners are now

Healthy salal, a native shrub with summer berries, is essential for many songbirds seen here at Edith Point Mayne Island.

using rope instead of chain on their moorings, and with the new bottom friendly floats that keep the line off the bottom, the impacts can be reduced substantially.

Another cause of the eelgrass loss, Rob suggested, is reduced light and erosion from shoreline development. "Retaining vegetation along shorelines and waterways is the best way to reduce erosion. When surface water is drained and directed into ditches, it typically moves faster and in greater volume, increasing its erosion potential and retaining suspended sediments." He suggested, "when possible, allow water to slow down, and spread out like it would naturally in an undeveloped ecosystem."

MIC is a small local organization saving land and building a scientific record of the marine habitats around this popular island and, Malcolm championed, they provide economic benefits too. "We now have two full-time employees as of last year. Most people on the island don't realize what an economic force we are. We bring in a lot of external money through grants and so on. We provide professional jobs with benefits. It's stable employment for skilled people. We bring in one to two students every summer and spend a lot on deer fencing and other supplies, and we put on a lot of events, putting money into the economy."

They all seemed so proud that the Conservancy has evolved enough to be able to support two families on the island and to offer additional work for students in summer. Given our society's change of direction from resource extraction to restoration and conservation, it is great to hear employment in the field is expanding, especially for young people.

One of the memorable conversations I had with these Mayne Island Conservancy people was with their outgoing president, Malcolm. He told me, "I've grown so much in this organization. My working life was in info tech and in the corporate world. I never really felt like it was a good fit for me. But I did a lot of training in the end of my working life, working with people. Since I came here I've applied it lots, in public meetings and so on, being the president. I've really been able to apply those learnings, build my own personal skills, values, and sense of self. I'm approaching seventy-five, and I still feel like I'm learning. It's so inspiring to work with all the good people here and be part of this great organization. I feel quite humble working with these very accomplished people."

During our sailing journey to Mayne in the summer of 2021, Heather and I explored the Japanese Memorial Garden at the head of Dinner Bay, honouring the Japanese residents who were forced to leave their island home.[7] The removal of Japanese residents during the Second World War significantly impacted the social and economic dynamics on many of these Southern Gulf Islands.

With reconciliation and Indigenous-led conservation now coming to the fore, MIC has created an Indigenous Relations Committee. Working with several other organizations on the island, they have designed an Ethnobotany Garden. The chair of the committee, Jennifer Iredale, outlined the project.

> Similar to the Japanese Gardens, this garden has been conceived as a means of commemorating and honouring the Indigenous people who have cared for this land since time immemorial. Interpretive signage is planned to educate visitors about native plants and their traditional W̱SÁNEĆ uses in both English and SENĆOŦEN. The project will include an outdoor Indigenous art exhibit with murals, carved poles, and sculptures on the same property. Information will be shared about the W̱SÁNEĆ worldview

in which the natural world takes care of humans, which engenders humanity's responsibility to care for the natural world.

The Ethnobotany Garden will join the Japanese Garden on Mayne Island in years to come, as islanders, like people everywhere, acknowledge and face past injustices and begin to find different ways forward toward reconciliation.

Michael and Helen, among the dedicated co-founders of this very busy land trust, both expressed hope that the younger generation will become active stewards of the islands. Helen remarked that some new people moving to the islands are starting gardens and trying to live more sustainably. Michael agrees, "When you see the light in their eyes, how they behave in their lives—that's where my hope is. I see a lot of hope in the world right now. It just has to coalesce into a bigger movement. Lots of great things are happening. I focus on things that are doable and have positive outcomes."

I was uplifted by these inspiring people who have dedicated so much time and energy to protecting land, doing research, and educating people about their surrounding marine environment. With the support of many people on the island, the Mayne Island Conservancy has been able to create new protected areas and parks, hire young professionals, and help landholders steward their own lands.

With nature reserves and new parks increasing all over the islands, I too hope the next generation will enjoy and learn from the amazing diversity and life force of nature and help to protect and conserve it. In turn they will likely teach their children about caring for the biodiversity and health of the islands and the larger Earth.

As I left Mayne Island, I turned my boat and my attention toward the next island in my conservation journey. I was about to meet a number of energetic and knowledgeable young people, taking on the leadership of one of the very first land trusts on the islands—the indomitable Galiano Conservancy Association.

Mount Parke on Mayne Island looking over to the Penders.

CHAPTER SEVEN

GALIANO ISLAND
Saving It from the Corporations

*"There was so much we did to build the
community and save it from the corporations."*
BETH THEISSEN,
daughter of Ken and Linda Millard, Galiano Island

A SLIGHT BREEZE PROPELLED US TO PUT UP THE SAILS and head for Galiano Island. As we passed the chaotic waters of Active Pass, we dodged fancy yachts and the big BC Ferries. Their wakes caused my small sailboat to rock wildly from side to side as these large vessels passed by.

I felt a surge of nostalgia as I surveyed Galiano's shoreline. I had lived here for a year in the early '90s. As we turned to starboard past Phillimore Point, I was so excited that I cheerfully sang the refrain I had written back then, "Sweet Home Galiano!" As we pulled into Montague Harbour (Sum'nuw) I saw that much had changed. Sum'nuw is a Hul'q'umi'num' name meaning "the encircling place."[1] We wove our way past the bathing suit clad, recreational boaters with their paddle boards and motorized dinghies in a harbour now filled with anchored boats, moorings, and docks.

We headed to the harbour's commercial dock, where I found some of the boats there ~4.5 metres (15 feet) wide, with huge three-storey cabins and dinghies aft with 20 horsepower motors. Our small sailboat, leading my wooden dinghy with oars, was modest by comparison. What a change from the days of small inflatables and wooden skiffs. I was taken aback by these changes in the harbour, but I was here to learn more about the efforts and successes of Galiano islanders, the epitome of local heroes and the home of the first land trust on the islands. After we tied up at the dock, I found a nest full of four small barn swallows calling for food, right there on a small shed, oblivious to the noise of the large yachts at the gas dock. This was a welcome sight.

The Active Pass area between Mayne and Galiano Islands is an exciting place—for birds, fish, whales, and people. It has been officially designated as an Important Bird Area (IBA) since the '80s. The tumultuous upwellings from the ocean bottom create very strong currents and whirlpools at all but slack tide. As many as ten eagle nests have been recorded in the Pass, and Pacific loon, Brandt's cormorant, and Bonaparte's gull all visit here during their migrations. The passage of orcas, seals, sea lions, and lately humpback whales can often be seen by the people who also pass through on BC Ferries—in 2022, 17.9 million passengers! The Mayne and Galiano Island Conservancies are co-caretakers of this IBA, providing signage, stewardship, and education about the area and the need to protect the shorelines on either side of the pass. As a result, many residents record the birds and other wildlife they see. But, as with the islands themselves, recreational activities of tourists and new arrivals of residents make one wonder how these wild beings will survive into the future.

This busy pass has been popular for thousands of years. Oral histories and archaeological research conducted at Georgeson Bay on Galiano and Helen Point on Mayne tell us that "Indigenous peoples have traveled through Active Pass on their seasonal rounds and lived along the shoreline of the Pass for at least 5,000 years."[2] Newer archaeological evidence will likely go back much farther. Recent evidence has revealed that people were living on Lasqueti Island for more than 7,000 years, Haida Gwaii for more than 13,000 years,[3] and up the coast at Triquet Island for more than 14,000 years![4] The Southern Gulf Islands lie within the traditional territories of the Hul'qumi'num Treaty Group (HTG), Tsawwassen First Nation, and the W̱SÁNEĆ (or Saanich) First Nations.

In the Hul'qumi'num' language the name of Active Pass is Sqthaqa'lh, which means "bigger passage or entrance," in contrast to Sqtheq ("narrows"), which is the name for Porlier Pass at the north end of Galiano. There is a story in Hul'qumi'num' oral tradition about Xeel's, the "Transformer," who stepped across to Vancouver Island from Washington State on a mythic journey and left his giant footprint (Shxixnetun) along the Galiano shoreline of Active Pass.[5]

One of the earliest locally driven and privately held conservation lands on the islands, the Bluffs along Active Pass today is a stunning 138.65 hectares (342 acres). HENNY SCHNARE

Bluffs Park

When I first came to Galiano in the mid-nineties, my friend Haidee took me up to the Bluffs on the north side of Active Pass. This has been a cherished place on the island for generations. Its high viewpoint atop the steep cliffs, rising 120 metres from the sea to the lookout, has a fantastic view of Active Pass and beyond to Mayne, Saturna, and the State of Washington. I learned from my long-time land trust colleague, Ron Pither, that the Bluff's forest, steep cliffs, and rocky outcrops formed the earliest Nature Conservancy Area on the islands, preserved by a generous landowner and the fundraising efforts of members of the Galiano community in 1948!

In the late '30s the Bluffs was owned in two sections by Mr. and Mrs. Max Enke. Being a very popular area for islanders, they offered ~5.6 hectares (14 acres) of one of their sections and ~32.4 hectares (80 acres) of another for $1,000. One of the founders of the Galiano Club, Paul Scoones, spearheaded the purchase of the lands and, through donations from a number of philanthropists, the money was raised. Unfortunately, before the property was transferred, during a business trip to Belgium in 1939, Max Enke was held as an enemy alien and spent the next six years in prisoner of war camps. When he returned to Canada in 1946, the family generously gave the adjoining section to the Galiano community, under the ownership of the Galiano Club "to be held in trust in perpetuity as a park."[6]

One of the earliest locally driven and privately held conservation lands on the islands, the Bluffs today is a stunning 138.65 hectares (342 acres).

The original deed allowed for selective logging on one area of the property as a prior agreement was in place. Some of the trees were used for the island's first fire hall and hydro poles. Thirty years later, the Galiano Club updated its Deed of Trust to clarify the lands use as "solely and irrevocably as a Nature Conservancy Area, as defined under the *Park Act*."[7] The updated Deed of Trust also set aside $8,000 for its long-term management. These types of funds today are referred to as endowment funds. Interest generated can be used to cover costs associated with the property. The Club's representative told me that "to date the costs have exceeded any interest generated, and the Galiano Club has undertaken fundraising initiatives to address the shortfall." On this property these costs have included legal reviews, surveys, developing management plans, and recently, a reconstructed Japanese Pit Kiln. Like on Mayne island, there was a small Japanese community who lived on the bluffs, and they made their own charcoal.[8]

The Bluffs' 2020 management plan points out:

> The definition of recreational use has broadened and the natural ecosystem within the Bluffs has become much more precious... with over 500 documented species, including 12 species of conservation concern. More than a quarter of Galiano's remaining old-growth coastal Douglas-fir forest is protected within the Bluffs, as well as a considerable extent of the island's diverse Garry Oak woodland and rock outcrop communities... As the integrity and extent of these ecosystems continues to be diminished by human activity, the need for protection and stewardship of our remaining natural areas becomes all the more critical... The high conservation priority placed on the Coastal Douglas fir [sic] forest places the natural heritage of the Bluffs into perspective as both a local legacy and gift of global ecological significance.[9]

Although the Galiano Club is a service organization, whose primary purposes are not conservation, their recently approved 2020 management plan clearly shows that its directors and the club have committed themselves to the island's long-term protection using legal and financial tools familiar to the land trust community today.

Adjacent to the Bluffs is Matthews Point Regional Park, held by the Capital Regional District, with trails leading between them. With careful and light use by the public, these two community parks offer a refuge for the fascinating marine life and precious terrestrial ecosystems that make up the biodiversity of the islands in the Salish Sea.

Galiano's Forestry and Conservation Pathway

From 1960 to 1992 MacMillan Bloedel (MacBlo) owned 60 percent of Galiano Island. How the community on Galiano worked to purchase and protect many of these lands is a seminal story.

Loren Wilkinson, a kind, soft-spoken man and former professor, was my main guide around the island that summer. He picked me up at Montague Harbour and took me up island in one of the first hybrid electric cars. Here was yet another Conservancy director ahead of the crowd, picking me up in a hybrid that had early, push-button style controls. He described the community's protection of many areas of the island for nature and for people as a "major triumph for a small community's ability to direct its future."

The Vancouver Coal Company purchased ~3,356 hectares (8,294 acres) of Galiano's ~5,665.6 hectares (14,000 acres) in 1888 for a dollar an acre.[10] That was just after BC entered Confederation to become Canada's sixth province in 1871. The terms

This historical aerial photo shows the clear-cuts on Galiano Island that led to the founding of the Galiano Conservancy Association. CLEAR-CUT ALTERNATIVES, KEN MILLARD

"to join the Dominion depended on the construction of a trans-continental railway" among other items.[11] Roughly two million acres of land were privatized for the railway and taken with no compensation for the Hul'qumi'num people. The bid to build the line was given to coal baron Robert Dunsmuir's company, who built the Esquimalt and Nanaimo (E&N) Railway on Vancouver Island.[12] Trees were needed to shore up underground coal mining tunnels. The Galiano lands were transferred several times. Then in 1960 the lands on Galiano were transferred again and became part of MacBlo's holdings as Tree Farm 19, part of the East Vancouver Island District with its office in Chemainus.[13] For thirty years, the company practiced industrial tree farm logging—creating big clear-cuts on a small Gulf Island.

The north end of Galiano was once home to a number of Penelakut people. Ronaldo Norden, an outstanding artist/engraver, lived on Galiano from the '70s to the early 2000s. He saw the transition of MacBlo from a "big daddy" type of neighbour to a distant corporation making decisions that didn't include the community in which they worked. He told me, "There were two sets of squatters at the very north end at Coon Bay—the workers' families from Chemainus, which the company allowed, and then when they left, in fall and winter, the hippies came and the company turned a blind eye. I made an etching of a couple of the cabins." Ronaldo told me "the Chamber of Commerce asked MacBlo to get the squatters and everything out. They put up eviction notices on the cabins. There was no protest, and one day the bulldozers came in, and squash—all gone. You live with the sleeping giant—the giant would allow you to take windfall firewood, or allow you to walk through their lands. But these corporations have to deal with the locals. They also owned Mount Galiano and Mount Sutil at that time."

Etching of two cabins at Coon Bay where two sets of squatters lived—the workers' families from Chemainus and the hippies. RONALDO NORDEN

But times changed. Galiano is only a forty-five minute ferry ride from Vancouver. MacBlo started developing plans for a resort and casino at the north end.

Gary Moore and his wife Barbara lived next to Coon Bay. "I was called to action by the chainsaws," he said. "I could hear them 600 feet from my house. A poster at the North End Community Hall brought eighty people to an impromptu meeting, and we decided to go down and talk to the loggers. So we went down and talked to the loggers, who suggested we get BC Parks involved."

"We had so much energy. MacBlo sold 4,500 acres on Salt Spring Island to land developers, which got rezoned right away. With the strip and flip thing going on over there, taking land out of forest land (industrial forest) and turning it into residential at the signing of a sales contract! We saw that coming, and had the impetus to get ready," Gary explained.

Risa Smith was a recent PhD graduate in ecology in the late '80s and lived on Galiano. She told me that MacBlo started logging toward the north end—at Coon Bay. "It had a beautiful beach and forest. There was a big demonstration. They had to stop logging." She got involved in trying to conserve some of the MacBlo lands, and was to become one of the founding board members of the Galiano Conservancy. (On the board of the Islands Trust Conservancy in 2022, she also works as a climate scientist with the International Union for the Conservation of Nature as co-chair of protected areas/climate change advocacy.) With such international acclaim today, the island was lucky to have her during these early years.

In 1972 representatives from MacMillan Bloedel gathered with the community at the hall. During this large public meeting their representatives described their vision—they would sell 1,200 lots, in one half and one third acres—citing the need for more population, more stores, and services.[14] This was shortly after the Magic Lake subdivision on Pender was being put through. Despite the 10 acre (4.04 hectare) freeze the Province had now implemented, these forest lands, which were then under Managed Forest Lands status, were about to be sold in small lots.

Luckily, the regional director for the Outer Gulf Islands was Jim Campbell of Saturna Island. He heard that the company wanted to put 1,000 houses up on Mount Galiano. This was the jewel in the crown for Galiano, and MacBlo's plans of creating one-quarter and one-third acre lots on Mount Galiano's slopes overlooking Active Pass drew panic. He chartered a plane and got some government people to fly around saying, "Hey, take a look at this. We need to protect this!"

At a public meeting, Campbell announced to the people of Galiano: "Future planning is up to the people of Galiano. 'If you want three lots to the acre,'… 'It is my job to get it for you. If you don't want that, then I must stop it for you!… You can thank God for M&B [MacMillan Bloedel]. It was only through their outrageous proposals that we got the approval of the Capital Regional District of the principle that the people have the right to decide the pattern of their own development."[15]

So with Campbell's urging the first official community plan (OCP) on Galiano was developed. The new OCP created different zones. "In this first Community Plan, the forest had two designations, 'Wilderness,' and 'Wilderness/Forest.' In those days, forestry was not considered a land use but an extraction like mining, controlled by the provincial government.[16] To give the forest a use in the local bylaw, it was permitted one residence to a parcel, which would have been a District Lot of about 65 hectares (160 acres). So long as the land remained in Tree Farm, however, this provision did not apply.

This early official community plan's (OCP) preamble, especially items 1 and 5, which remain today, are a reflection of most of the island residents' shared goals and mirrors some of the purposes of the newly forming Islands Trust:

1) The people of Galiano Island, being mindful of the pressures from a growing West Coast population, and a demonstrated desire of many to find relief from the urban congestion and associated tension through a rural atmosphere, and being aware of the physical limitations of Galiano Island to accept uncontrolled population increase without degradation of the rural way of life and damage to the ecological system, deem it desirable to create a Community Plan to deal with these issues.

5) As the present generation inherited these islands in a relatively preserved state so this Plan attempts to perpetuate this state and preserve the unique environment for all future generations.

As described in the Salt Spring Island chapter of this book, in 1974, shortly after this first OCP was drafted, the provincial government created the unique local government authority—the Islands Trust—with a mandate "to preserve and protect the Trust Area and its unique amenities and environment for the benefit of the residents of the Trust Area and of British Columbia in cooperation."

Some of the soon to be founders of the Galiano Conservancy Association deemed this transition from forestry to residential development a betrayal.

Carolyn Canfield, who moved to Galiano in 1987, was in search of a quiet rural life as she had been involved in some conservation vs. development struggles in her previous home near Ottawa. "When I arrived, I was aware of the Islands Trust and the kind of people who were involved in local government. They weren't the young hippie arrivals from the '70s. These were retired people, who most often had administrative, business, or military experience—veterans who were highly respected."

She explained that the company had a muddled relationship with islanders. "In 1972 a road was put through from north to south, about the same time as the telephone and electric power ran alongside it. This happened late, compared to other communities. MacBlo allowed for these roads and power lines to go through, but still there was no road allowance. Any time there's a subdivision, there has to be a road dedication. But MacBlo was not an ordinary landowner, but an institution—kind of big daddy—doing some logging on the island."

Loren Wilkinson, who lived on the island, felt the transition in land use was deceptive. Like many others who went on to found land trusts on the islands, Loren and his family had been arrested in Clayoquot. "The irony of the situation was Mac-Blo owns their forest lands outright on Galiano—zoned and intended for forestry. They were trying to take it out of forestry and use it for real estate, using every legal means they could. In Clayoquot Sound it was not their land, but Crown land, and they were using every legal means to turn it into forestry, whereas on Galiano they were trying to take it out. My wife, my daughter, and I were some of the first people arrested at Clayoquot Sound."

Ken Millard, a central figure in the founding of the Galiano Conservancy, put it succinctly: "The conversion of excellent forestland to real estate development goes beyond Dunsmuir and the E&N land grant . . . What is now happening all over Vancouver Island began on Galiano in the 1970s. The public subsidizes logging companies for decades with preferential taxes, then these same companies try to develop the land and make a killing on real estate."[17]

Geoff Gaylor, another founding director of the soon to be Galiano Conservancy, explained that they went to many meetings with foresters, including the forest manager in Chemainus, and tried to talk the company into doing the remaining logging in a more environmentally sustainable manner—not clear-cutting. "Then all of a sudden MacBlo stepped in with a different department, marketing the lands—yet they started clear cutting like crazy. They took off over one thousand logging truck loads off in that last year—and later sold it all."

Carolyn Canfield described her perceptions about the actions of MacMillan Bloedel, or MB, as many islanders refer to the company:

> So when I arrived MB was upping its intimidation tactic, to accelerate logging. MB had made a decision that they wanted to use the land on Galiano for property development. The greatest money was for development. A destination resort, casino—these things they mentioned. But what became apparent, only after the lawsuit, was MB wanted to accelerate logging to create a backlash in the community, where they could then say, you won't let us cut trees, you tree huggers (like Clayoquot). You won't

let us cut down our forest timber, the only remaining use is for development, and you can't stop us because you don't have zoning that covers us. They used this tactic of accelerating clear-cuts in plain view of the public roads to create panic and persuade the community that development was a good thing, modernization. This was done on the Sunshine Coast, and similarly on Cortes island. People from the Real Estate division were saying "This is progress. People in the city will help you start a library." You wanted to vomit, the Island was full of retired UBC professors. People's private libraries beat the pants off that. The idea that a rural community would embrace big city conveniences was so not the island culture. The character of Galiano was absolutely distinct from other islands, because the dominant land use was forestry.[18]

The company's ideas about which areas they would develop and subdivide include many of the conservation lands on Galiano today: Coon Bay (Dioniso Provincial Point Park), Galiano Mountain (Mount Galiano Park), a section of Sutil Mountain (Sutil Mountain Reserve), and two large waterfront areas north of Retreat Cove (Bodega Ridge Provincial Park). In 1987, an informal, local group was formed to try to work with MacBlo. Clear-Cut Alternatives, (CCA) goals were to encourage community involvement in the forest issues and to educate themselves and islanders about other options. They brought in professionals and experts in the fields of both forestry and conservation. These guests included Bob Nixon, editor of *Forest Planning Canada*; Bert Brink, Nature Trust of BC; Phil Haddock, retired professor of forestry at the University of British Columbia (UBC); Cameron Young, author of *The Forests of British Columbia*; and William Rees of UBC on Planning for the Future.

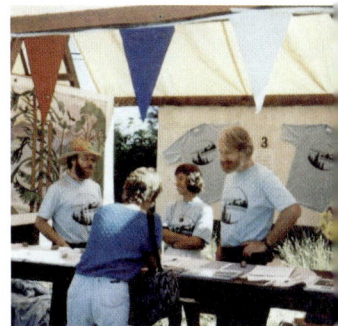

Clear-Cut Alternatives booth, 1988. From left, Gary Moore, Dawn Christian, and Ken Millard.

Another group, which came shortly after, was the Galiano Forest and Land Use Council, which was developed as a tripartite public forum. Based on the Bruntland Commission's recommendations, it including company, community, and elected representatives. The community representatives were voted in and included those who were soon to become the founders of the new Galiano Conservancy Association—Ken Millard, Geoff Gaylor, and Gary Moore. The larger group discussed alternative forestry models and a community purchase of some of the lands. Geoff told me he, Gary, and Ken, especially, attended many meetings as part of this council, including going to Chemainus to meet with MacMillan Bloedel's general manager.

Geoff told me that they suggested that the community could buy the lands. "We saw that in order for good forestry to be practiced on the island, it would have to be practiced by us, therefore it was a good idea to buy half from MacBlo." Clear-Cut Alternatives and some of the Council's discussions were based on creating better forest stewardship, which went beyond timber objectives and jobs for their employees.

However, neither CCA nor the Land Use Council succeeded in convincing the company of logging differently, or waiting for the community to come up with an amount to buy all the MacBlo lands that the company would accept. They wanted residential use values, instead of the forestry use values that the lands had been purchased and taxed on for decades.

What has become clear to me, talking with many people on the island and reading the background material, including a legal review of the situation, is that the company not only wanted the largest profits from the land, but it was at the expense of a community that was becoming divided over every sale. Margaret Griffiths explains much in her publication, *The Story of Galiano Island, Across 30 Important Years.*[19] She was personally sued by MacBlo as an island trustee. Sheila Anderson, who became a Galiano trustee later, explained that MacBlo was promoting the sale of these "investment in paradise" lots based on the idea that forest lands could become residential or even commercial given time and a few underhanded tactics.

Sheila describes the ramifications, up to today, of selling these lands without overall consideration of the island as a community, which needed watersheds protected, roads that accessed "lands beyond" that were open to access for fire protection, and access to other areas of the island.

> The idea was in order for them to gain a residential right they would have to rezone. The argument was the island was not prepared to suddenly be developed. Our *Land Use Bylaw* didn't have preparation for half the island to be developed. Nothing had been done, because we had been told that MB [MacMillan Bloedel] was there for the long term. Those trustees, Dianne and Margaret, put in initial forest bylaws that made it clear that these forest lots don't have residential rights. A few were sold prior, which were marginal and in awkward places. They were given F2 zoning, which did allow a dwelling. They had been removed from Managed Forest Land status and were very steep, not accessible for logging. These were kept separate from the whole big tree farm that all at once MB took out. They should have been told to dedicate the road, giving road dedication to the Province. So we're left with land locked properties with no road access. This made it more challenging, but they knew they had no residential right—in the sale's disclosure. But that didn't stop them from whining—it was the community's fault. In some cases a purchaser would get other buyers and not tell them there was no residential zoning.[22]

Dionisio Point Park

Several people from the Land Use Council took some BC Parks representatives to see if they would purchase any of the four district lots up at Coon Bay. This brought them a local alternative. Ian Atherton, BC Parks acquisition staff in those days, explained to me that Dionisio Provincial Park was purchased as four parcels: two upland parcels MacBlo said they would donate and the other two waterfront sections they wanted a commercial value for as they planned a destination resort there. Ian reviewed the properties and found there were several archeological reports on Dionisio Point, with precise locations for middens, which was very unusual at that time. So they had to reconsider and accept a rural recreational value.

Dionisio Provincial Park, which includes Coon Bay, has more recent Indigenous history and connections than these middens. I went to Dionisio Park, which is right on Porlier Pass, both by land and water. A friend of mine who has Indigenous ancestry took me in his refurbished fishing boat to visit his cousin, who was supposed to be on another small fishing boat on a float in the Pass. We did met this cousin, the next day over in Chemainus, where the main office of the Lyackson First Nation is located.

The Lyackson people today hold one third of Valdes Island, which is directly across Porlier Pass from Galiano, in reserve status. A portion of the headlands at the top of Galiano Island is dedicated as Reserve for the Penelakut—29.1 hectares (72 acres)—remnants of land once the territory of Indigenous people. Both the Lyackson and the Penelakut people are part of the larger Hul'qumi'num Treaty

Group, who along with the Chemainus First Nation, Cowichan Tribes, Halalt First Nation, and Lake Cowichan First Nation share the language and original territory from the entrance of Juan du Fuca Strait to Cape Mudge at the south end of Quadra Island. Today, members of the Penelakut Tribe are working with the Galiano Conservancy on several projects.

Dionisio Provincial Park still feels secluded—a wild, hidden gem. The fast flowing tidal currents of Porlier Pass create an astounding intertidal life visible at low tide. Sea stars, nudibranchs, chitons, and swimming scallops are just beyond the sandstone shelves, pebble and sand beaches, and colourful wildflower meadows. When I visited the area by land, it was by car to the end of a long road, which felt so isolated from the rest of the island. This was the private property from which I accessed the park and was where I first met Gary and his wife, Barbara, many years ago. Today Dionisio Provincial Park has marine only walk-in camp sites with adjoining lands in private forest land ownership.

Dionisio Provincial Park and sea lions, which were traditionally harvested by the Penelukut people in this location. GARY MOORE

Galiano Conservancy Association's Formation

Gary explained, "The three of us (Gary, Ken Millard, and Geoff Gaylor) with support of the community, openly explored how land trusts could help us. We talked with Bert Brink of the Nature Trust of BC and also four other organizations including a Scottish Nature Conservancy. Bill Paterson, one of our supporters at the time, knew this group personally because he supported them financially."

Unlike many of the other island land trusts, in 1989 the Galiano Conservancy was being formed with both sustainable community and conservation goals. According to Geoff, when the group called a meeting to announce and form the new land trust, it was attended by over 250 people. On June 21, 1989, the Galiano Conservancy Association was founded to "preserve, protect, and enhance the quality of Galiano's human and natural environment."

Almost everyone in the field of conservation, and especially on the islands, knows of Ken Millard, one of the most inspirational and generous figures in the land trust movement in BC. Ken was a mentor for several other island land trusts too. He and his wife, Linda, were instrumental in the formation of the first land trust on the islands, the Galiano Conservancy Association (GCA). Ken, as a physicist and violin maker, had energy and abilities so diverse and so focused that his story is important and unique.

Ken Millard was perhaps the most highly regarded baroque violin bow maker in the world—internationally renowned. Because of a life-threatening allergy he developed to the dense tropical woods he used, he was forced to stop making baroque violin bows. He turned all his energy from bow making to the Conservancy. Risa Smith, another co-founder of GCA, described him as fearless, willing to take risks in the face of formidable challenges, in pursuit of what he perceived as the greater good.

Loren was a very good friend of the Millard family. "He seemed gentle but beneath the surface there was steel," Loren said, "and people soon found out that Ken had an unwavering commitment to land stewardship."

I met Ken at a multi-island workshop on Galiano in the early '90. He seemed to me a mild man, suited to his luthier background, but I could tell he held his cards close, with immense knowledge and confidence.

He worked since GCA's inception for twenty-six years, voluntarily, with a deep commitment to conservation, restoration, and education. The early successes of the GCA were fundamentally due to the unwavering dedication of Ken and his wife, Linda. His vision was for a corridor of conserved areas across the island, which would help the Galiano community sustain themselves into the future. The reality has now far surpassed even his expansive vision.

In 1990 the new Galiano Conservancy Association put together a proposal to buy all of MacMillan Bloedel's lands—60 percent of the island.

Carolyn Canfield is a confident woman who has little fear of powerful players. With the Conservancy formed, they considered the possibility of a community-owned forest. They talked to a lot of people and talked about the capacity of the community. Carolyn explained what they discussed.

> What financial plan could be supported by the community that would allow us to hold half the island. We, with (Mike Hoebel—chair of our meetings) came up with three forms of land use—conservation, community housing, and selective logging— to be conducted as a model for other locations hand in hand with Herb Hammond, at a non-industrial scale. This would be done at a modest level of development so the damaged ecosystems and groundwater would remain intact. We thought that we would be able to develop partnerships that would assist in making this financially possible. There needed to be a willing seller.

Risa described their conundrum. "When we got started, over the years one person, Ken, was the most persistent, eventually against buying the MacBlo land, but then for it. Ken kept it going. He was the soul of the organization."

With Gary, Ken, Carolyn, Geoff, Risa, and a few others, they put together a proposal to buy all of MacBlo's lands. Carolyn explained, "Our proposal was for one third development, one third park, one third selective logging. We talked with Mel Couvelier, an MLA for Saanich and the Islands and also the finance minister at the time, and he came on-side about it."

Geoff described to me their initial negotiations to buy it all:

> We figured if we could raise 10 million... But in the meantime, MB did their own assessment at 20 million. Eight of us bought a share in MB and went to their AGM at the Hotel Vancouver. We all made a speech. We said, you are trying to spoil our island. All this was recorded by the CBC. At the end of the meeting, Jimmy Pattison, one of their directors, comes over and says "I'd like to help you deal with this." So, he said, "I'd like to meet with you three at my office and see what can be done to make this work." That week his daughter was kidnapped, so we thought he wouldn't meet us. But the meeting was on, and we went into his office (which was a whole building on West Georgia) where we met with him for forty-five minutes. We went through our proposal, and he says, "You guys have got to put some money on the table. They won't listen unless you have money behind you." So we went back and got ten people to agree to a $100,000 loan each. We have a million—end of story.

Except it wasn't. The company wanted to have the lands evaluated as real estate, even though it had been purchased and managed as industrial forest land, a value much lower. MacMillan Bloedel decided they were going to sell it all. The community was given six months, then another two months, to see if they could come up with a proposal. They wanted $20 million for the whole thing.

Risa explained to me some of the awkward questions the community struggled with. "There was a big movement to purchase it. People pledged money. We had Vancity [Credit Union] behind us. Then it became apparent that we wouldn't be able to buy it all, and they wouldn't sell it to us as it was part of a private forest land district—the East Coast of Vancouver Island. They didn't want the precedent of the community buying. So a small group said we should buy it piece by piece. At the same time, Geoff Scudder and I did an insect study to show how important Bodega Ridge was ecologically—from the sea to the mountain. We worried that it too would be logged. The GCA was not supportive of buying little pieces—we had a vision for the whole island, not bits."

Bodega Ridge Park

The Conservancy directors wanted to protect some land—not just to save the ecological functioning of a place—but for the community to access generally. Gary said, "We kept an airplane pilot busy taking people to the bay to try to figure out how to protect it. It was a major campaign. We had so much energy." Some directors took John Eisenhauer and a few other delegates from the Nature Conservancy of Canada (NCC) on a tour to see other areas of importance to the community. Bodega Ridge is in the centre of the island. The ridge itself is 328 metres high above sea level, along a cliff edge. There is forest land at the top of the ridge, which then goes down a cliff to Trincomali Channel.

Turkey vultures, bald eagles, and falcons all enjoy flying around Bodega Ridge's 328-metre high ridge. MYLES CLARKE

The acquisition of what today is Bodega Ridge Park was a complex joining of three different district lots of ~69.8 hectares (170 acres) each which had originally been purchased from MacBlo. One lot had been purchased by a logger from Salt Spring who threatened to clear-cut it. With that in mind, it was purchased again by a group of individuals including Robert Bateman, Rene Marlow, and Bill Paterson. Another section was owned by the North Galiano Community Association, who had plans to subdivide it. The third was purchased by a group of local islanders calling themselves the Leap of Faith Corporation. These islanders included Gary Moore, Geoff Gaylor, Loren Wilkinson, and a few others. They were willing to take a personal risk to acquire it, in hopes that a deal could be struck to move these lots into conservation. According to Loren, Ken was influential in getting large and small donors to guarantee to buy it, if it couldn't be purchased by NCC. "The operation we put together was to not only purchase one of those lots, but then to get NCC involved and have them purchase from each of the three different entities with the national funding scale available to them. In the end they turned it over to BC Parks. This is one of the best examples of a story of a multiple partner campaign that really worked."

Today, the Bodega Ridge Park is nearly 400 hectares (988 acres). At the top one sees spectacular views of Trincomali Channel, Salt Spring Island, and over to Vancouver Island. The forest leading up to the ridge is nesting habitat for bald eagles, peregrine falcons, and turkey vultures and below the sandstone formations at the water's edge can be found large wildflower populations. I love the unique small manzanita bushes, which I found on the ridge and have rarely seen on other islands. The hairy manzanita bush generally grows on sunny, high rocky ledges and looks like mini arbutus trees. They have white or pink flowers that bloom in late winter and offer their blackish-red berries to hungry birds.

Loren told me that one of the most important things that resulted from this package of acquisitions was it led to the purchase and preservation of important key areas of natural habitat. "Another piece was Laughlin Lake, which we purchased, and a big chunk of the headwaters of the watershed that flows into Cable Bay—the Great Beaver Swamp. This spawned a time of both amazing philanthropy and community mobilization, and deep division."

Mount Galiano—Galiano Club Nature Protection Area

Then in 1991, shortly after MacMillan Bloedel started selling their land, a group of people on the island decided to go ahead and purchase one of the favourite hiking and viewpoint areas on the southern end of the island. "Mt. Galiano should belong to the people of Galiano to be preserved in trust forever. A group of concerned citizens obtained an option on the property, the Galiano Club spearheaded a massive, whirlwind community-wide fundraising drive, and through the lowering of the price by MacMillan Bloedel, the option deadline was met and Mount Galiano was bought."[21]

Similar to the Bluff Park Nature Protection Area, Mount Galiano was put into trust by the Galiano Club, under the terms of the *Park Act*, "to be retained in its natural condition for the preservation of its ecological environment and scenic features."[22] Similar to the Bluffs Park, the Deed of Trust for Mount Galiano included an endowment for its long term management. Shortly after it was acquired, a trail was put in to reach the top of this, the highest point on the island. The 84 hectare (34 acre) Mount Galiano Nature Protection area is a second growth Douglas-fir forest, with a small area of Garry oak trees planted by the Garry Oak Meadow Preservation Society after it was acquired.

The Private Forest Lands

MacMillan Bloedel still had lots of land to sell. According to Gary Moore, "The forestry lands were put on the real estate market with a disclosure statement that they did not carry a residential use. However, they were marketed by MacBlo's real estate division (and after purchase initially taxed) at residential prices."

Carolyn Canfield, deeply involved with the Conservancy in its early years, explained the basis of the conflict due to the sale of these Managed Forest Lands to individual "forest lot owners." MacMillan Bloedel's private forest lands were in the Managed Forest Land (MFL) category, designated with no residential use. They were outside of the Islands Trust's 1988 zoning maps, which is consistent with the provincial legislation. The *Managed Forest Act* allows private forest lot owners to be outside of municipal jurisdictions. Once land is taken out of Managed Forest, it comes under municipal laws, and on the islands under the *Islands Trust Act* and local zoning. Many of the purchasers, however, were speculating that they could have residences on their forest lots. These zoning issues created tension on the island for years after.

My friend Ronaldo and his wife, Annie, eventually left the island they had loved. He told me, "Disillusionment set in for many, like how can they get away with this land flip, while we little guys follow the laws, pay our taxes, and be honest? For many it was a rapid loss of innocence."

The Lawsuits

In a move that further divided the community, MacBlo decided that both the Islands Trust and the new Galiano Conservancy were conspiring to reduce the value of the lands they were selling. This resulted in a civic lawsuit overseen by a single judge which at first MacMillan Bloedel won, but then a year later was overturned. The Sierra Legal Defense donated their time and arguments to overturn the original case in the BC Supreme Court with the second court case determining that the zoning of Galiano Island's OCP was valid.

In her reasons for judgement, Madam Justice Southin stated that "once land is developed, undoing the development, if it is harmful to the public interest or what some people perceive to be the public interest, is next to impossible. I have said 'this downzoning' because it was implemented pursuant to both s. 963(1) of the *Municipal Act* and s. 3 of the *Islands Trust Act*. If there were no s. 3 of the *Islands Trust Act*, I might be of a different opinion but s. 3 is not a mere piety. To put it another way, these by-laws were enacted for the purposes or the objects of s. 3 as well as for the health and welfare of the inhabitants of Galiano Island. They therefore had a lawful purpose."[23]

A cartoon demonstrating how some people felt in 1995. RONALDO NORDEN 1995

This paragraph has been used many times over the years as conservation-minded islanders throughout the Islands Trust Area have taken legal action to defend precious lands and waters from harmful actions.

But by August 1995, most of the lands on Galiano had been sold to individuals. After extensive deliberations, the Islands Trust offered the forest zoned owners a variance—donate 75 percent of their property to the community, as a woodlot or for conservation—and they would designate 25 percent of their lands in 5 acre (2.2 hectare) residential zoning.[24]

One thing that conservation land trusts do today is purchase insurance to protect themselves against this type of liability. It's one thing to volunteer one's time, and in many cases, professional experience to a cause, but to have to defend oneself against a SLAPP suit is untenable. Unfortunately, insurance is part of the cost of running a successful land trust. Many donors often balk at the 8 percent administrative item found in many budgets, but it helps cover these real and essential costs of protecting land, and the volunteers and staff that run these charitable organizations.

When MacBlo sold quarter section parcels to a diversified collection of new owners it created a division on the island that still exists today. Bowie Keefer, who ended up buying one of the private forest lots created, described the trajectory that moved the community forward: "MB sold out to stump bag loggers, who came in and cut two Stanley parks worth of forest. When they finished they sold out and left, leaving the other forest owners who largely share the same environmental values as other islanders. Clear-cut logging has not happened since the turn of the millennium." Bowie added, "The striking thing going back thirty years ago is it was a checkerboard of clear cuts, which are now green with new forest and farm land."

Anger about logging, the lower sale prices of forest lands, the residential restrictions, and fear of subdivisions led to an extended land use conflict. However, at the time of my interviews, Bowie Keefer, a forest lot owner, and Keith Erickson, formerly with the Conservancy, commented that positive things are now happening. Both Bowie and Keith related that the new Ecoforestry Society is drawing in many of the forest lot owners and there is a growing awareness about the landowner stewardship ethic needed to protect water and biodiversity as well as consideration of actions needed to reduce wildfire risks, which are increasing with climate change.

Mount Sutil—Galiano Conservancy and the Nature Conservancy of Canada

Shortly after the Galiano Conservancy was formed, one of the first areas that the group identified as important ecologically was Mount Sutil. The owner of an FM radio station in Vancouver purchased the top of the mountain in case they needed a transmitter antenna in the future. Geoff told me they learned that the owner was retiring, so someone suggested, "Why don't you go talk with him?" Carolyn, Ken, and Geoff, directors on the board, met with the owner and told him the story of trying to save things. They again took John Eisenhauer, from NCC, to see this sensitive mountain top, a beautiful Garry oak ecosystem which is an ecological community ranked at risk today. With NCC, the Galiano Conservancy was able to raise the funds to acquire the 17 hectare (42 acre) summit in 1990 for the price of $42,000. In 2002 the title was placed in Galiano Conservancy's name only. Due to its fragility and high ecological values with many species at risk, access is only allowed through permission of adjacent landowners. The successful acquisition of Mount Sutil was soon followed by a second, larger project.

Mt. Sutil's Garry oak hillside. GCA

Pebble Beach Reserve

Ken Millard identified a 62 hectare (154 acre) parcel of land which could provide the connecting link between two Crown land parcels located at the west side of the island at Retreat Cove, on the east coast facing Georgia Strait. District Lot 63 was owned by BC Tel, but he knew they weren't interested in the land. They only wanted a 1 metre (3 foot) right-of-way to protect the cable that crossed the island at this location. Ken with his quiet, yet confident, approach convinced them in 1998 to sell it to GCA for a fairly cheap price, $430,000. "It was formerly MacBlo land, brutally logged, and reforested as a tree farm plantation." Loren explained, "the forest even had Napalm sprayed on it." It is next to a piece of Crown land of almost the same size, which though selectively logged, is a beautiful forest. The BC Tel property, combined with the Crown lands on either side, came to be called the Pebble Beach Reserve. The property was purchased by GCA with money raised from the community, the Nature Conservancy of Canada, and the Pacific Marine Heritage Legacy Fund.

Although the Conservancy has been in contact with the Province about acquiring these Crown lands, it is unknown what will happen, as today many of the Crown lands, at least on the islands, are being held for potential Indigenous reconciliation.

The Galiano Conservancy received funding from Forest Renewal BC to develop a restoration plan for District Lot 63 in 2001. The GCA's original goal was to restore the property to a healthy forest through an innovative restoration plan. Ken brought in Herb Hammond, a BC professional forester known for his restoration work, called ecoforestry, to help with the project through his company, Silva Forest Foundation out of Salmo. Together they developed a plan and with numerous volunteers and some paid employees, they pulled over plantation trees to their root balls, re-erected old snags, and redistributed woody debris. This restoration project became a well-known case study, and people from all over the world came to see what was going on here. Thus, and perhaps most importantly, it became the first of many educational projects for the GCA.

I first met both Ken and Keith, who became the Conservancy's first executive director, on the Pebble Beach Reserve at a workshop. I was impressed with these people who were so dedicated to re-establishing a forest on this cleared—and what seemed to me like a wrecked land—by hand! Ken was up a tree, seemingly held there by ropes, and Keith was describing some of the techniques to the gathered group. They even had standing dead logs planted upside down! It seemed confusing to a neophyte like me, but their enthusiasm and determination was infectious.

On my walk through there in 2022, I could barely believe that this was the same forest I had seen at least twenty years before. The adjacent Crown land didn't seem that much different to this piece now, and as I walked with Loren, he proudly showed me the understory, with its lush red huckleberries, arching white ocean spray blossoms, and protective boughs of cedar, fir, and hemlock. I felt held in the arms of Mother Nature, with her ability to heal—to restore a world once desecrated.

Eric Higgs, a professor of ecological restoration at the University of Victoria (UVIC), said he took great interest in the project when he came to Galiano for a conference of the BC Society for Ecological Restoration. He told me even though he was the chair of an international restoration society, he had never seen these techniques before. He was astounded at the restoration work being done on the property by the GCA.

It was the early days of restoration. They were not working from a recipe book. They brought together a diverse group. Ken called in favours from Herb Hammond, an ecoforester, and a number of people in the community. I felt that it was rooted in the community. It was a devastated piece of property. It was a MacBlo testing site for new techniques. It was scarified, had non-genetically local tree species brought in. Ken and his colleagues used different treatments. They sometimes cropped the tree to spark new growth, and also pulled trees over. And he was using complex pulleys, because he was a physicist, he was using big come-alongs [a hand-operated winch] and chains and hauled the tree over, leaving the root mass standing up, which creates a different topography. The tree would expire slowly and become a haven for birds. It was fascinating to me. I'd never seen someone take down a live tree. It made a ton of sense: wind throw is an important dynamic in coastal forest systems—it's natural and creates openings and gaps. All of this was done without fossil fuels, by hand. And the forest was quiet while they were at work. I thought, wow this is a one-off crazy thing, but they kept going, continuing their innovation around restoration and marine work.

Eric has been bringing his students to Galiano ever since to show them the restoration processes at work here. An arrangement with the Conservancy set the stage for Eric's students and some of his colleagues in other universities to do further research on restoration techniques. Some come for up to six months work, doing

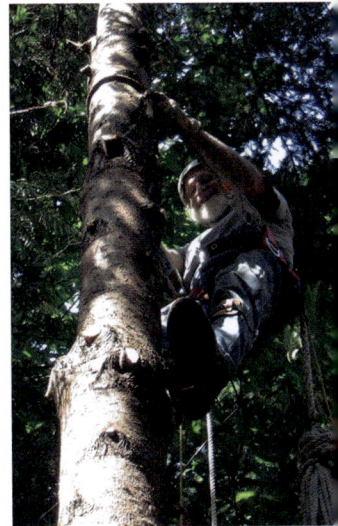

Ken Millard in 2004, climbing a plantation Douglas-fir tree to top it by hand, letting light into the forest understory below to promote vegetation growth and diversity. KEITH ERICKSON

internships or applied research on the property, which they dovetail with the management activities that GCA is doing. People have come from Germany in particular, from a Technical University out of Munich, usually as part of their practicum training as part of their degree.

Eventually, it became a restored forest, a place for international scientific study, and it introduced a young man to the significance of using Geographic Information Systems (GIS) mapping for conservation.

Keith Erickson, a graduate of UBC's forestry program, saw a job opening to write a management plan for District Lot 63—the Pebble Beach Reserve. Hired as a summer student in 1998, he created the plan and fell in love with the land and the community. He worked with another Galiano islander, Meg Holden, who had done her graduate thesis on mapping work and using GIS. Together they used Galiano as a case study and model.

Between 2000 and 2003, the Conservancy worked on air photo interpretation and ground truthing, leading to a Galiano Island Landscape Classification system with a series of open houses and community reviews and an engaging UP-CLOSE workshop series. These included experts in forest and Garry oak ecosystems, marine and foreshore ecosystems, freshwater aquatic ecosystems, and landscape connectivity.

Keith summarized the need for and use of this type of local GIS work.

At the time, land use plans or conservation plans, and the generation of mapping and information to support them, were top-down initiatives controlled by government, national organizations, or large corporations (this is still somewhat true today). By creating GIS and mapping capacity at a local, grassroots level, we were able to achieve a level of information that was far more detailed and accurate than anything else available. We were able to engage our local community in its creation so that there was trust and buy-in for the product. We then could use the information to identify and galvanize community held values and to support community based planning.

Keith's GIS experience was sought by other community-based land trusts. Citizen science (as it is called today) and locally generated maps are empowering tools for conservation, land use decision making, provision of emergency services, and private land stewardship.

Kids Educational Programs

The ecological restoration and management that the Conservancy was doing on the Pebble Beach Reserve led to new directions. Keith Erickson, then the executive director, explained that they started seeing the value of engaging the local community and beyond. They had kids and youth doing hands-on kinds of work on the land and learning new things. The GCA started a broader educational program, bringing kids over from the lower mainland and Greater Victoria to learn on Galiano Conservancy sites, Crown lands, and other private properties where permission was given for nature education. These kids' programs were initially run voluntarily by Barbara Moore, Gary's wife, an experienced program coordinator through the Elderhostel program. They started with the Galiano Community School to develop some of the ideas. But they soon expanded to invite urban schools where the kids needed these types of outings for their own relief from the city and for their own ecoliteracy. There is a marine element to this program as well. Barbara explained the benefits. "The colours of sea stars, the slimy texture of a sea cucumber, the deceptive beauty of an anemone—nothing in *Finding Nemo* or *SpongeBob* has prepared them for the reality which may be a bit daunting and much more exciting than cartoons."

The Conservancy arranged to have a floating nature house at Montague Harbour Marine Park from May to October. With summer staff, they hosted over 4,000 visitors a year, "engaging them in conversations about marine life and environmental issues, and conducting interpretative programs." Barbara added, "This hands on 'please touch' approach keeps all ages engaged for hours. Simply watching creatures interact up close is fascinating."

"It became apparent quickly that what would make a more powerful experience would be if they could stay for multiple days and have a more immersive experience." Keith explained, "Through that lens we were looking for a property to purchase that would fulfill our goals of protecting Galiano's ecology and sensitive areas, as well as providing a place where large groups of kids could come for multiple days—a camp."

Laughlin Lake

Laughlin Lake, the largest lake on Galiano Island, provides a connecting link between Bodega Ridge Park and the Pebble Beach Reserve. The 27 hectare property was purchased in 2000 from a court ordered sale for $148,900.[25] The smaller area of the lake was colonized by beavers, disturbed by a major road and gravel extraction over the years. The Conservancy and the community have been doing ongoing restoration on the site, ensuring that its wetland areas remain healthy habitat for native species.

Kids exploring sea life at Montague Harbour. GALIANO CONSERVANCY ASSOCIATION

Great Beaver Swamp

The headwaters of the Beaver Creek watershed were created by a beaver dam as early as 1888.[26] This large wetland adjoins the Crown land next to the Pebble Beach Reserve. The Beaver Creek Swamp provides a valuable habitat for birds and amphibians and is a regular watering hole for black-tailed deer, river otter, mink, and other mammals. The 18.1 hectare (45 acre) parcel was purchased in 2003 for $185,000. A boundary adjustment ensured that the all of the wetland was protected. It is the source of Beaver Creek which flows northeast to the Conservancy's newest conservation area at Cable Bay on the Georgia Straight side of Galiano Island.

Millard Learning Centre

Ken Millard had a vision to tie together the natural features of land through an assembly of areas—protecting watersheds and forests. Gary Moore explained, "As early as 1993, GCA directors began to promote the idea of the present Mid-Island Protected Areas Network, by proposing designation of a continuous tract of some 924 hectares from sea level to sea level across the island."

Many of the people who helped bring the Millard Learning Centre to fruition with their new sign. GALIANO CONSERVANCY ASSOCIATION

Eric Higgs, the UVIC restoration professor who first visited the GCA's reforested lands, said, "Islands find you as much as you find them. We had a strange and wonderful option to buy piece of land in 2008. Not long after, both my wife and I, and our daughter, were drawn into the Conservancy." Eric worked extensively with the GCA directors to help bring this vision of a mid-island conservation corridor to reality.

The mid-island property that was finally found was one of the largest undeveloped pieces left on the island, with beautiful Douglas-fir forest and wetlands, which also fit the vision of bringing large groups over for educational excursions. The adjoining property (which was later acquired by the Islands Trust Conservancy) would create a link between this property, the Great Beaver Swamp, and the Pebble Beach Reserve further north. The acquisition would fulfill the dream that Ken had envisioned for a large mid-island conservation corridor. The property was 76 hectares (188 acres) and included a mile of waterfront. It would offer multi-faceted opportunities. Its foundation was the protection of wildlife and biodiversity. Such a large property would also offer educational opportunities, recreation, and restoration potential. It was a critical area that offered outstanding potential to conserve a large area of Galiano's land, linking its terrestrial areas to the Salish Sea on both sides of the island.

The owner wanted to sell for a $4 million price tag. A few years of at least one failed partnership and a shortage of large donors created an impasse—for a while.

"The idea went on ice." Keith told me, "A few years later, the first iteration of the federal government's Natural Areas Conservation Program (NACP) partnership with the Nature Conservancy of Canada came up, granting money to 'other qualified organizations' (local land trusts). It was open for funding 50 percent of the cost of acquiring significant land, with a one to one ratio required for matching funds. This was new and not that many organizations out there were ready to go. So that gave us the impetus to start renegotiating with the landowner, but we had to get 50 percent. We went to the membership and decided to go for it. We applied for that program and were successful. We made it happen in 2012."

However, its acquisition took a hard toll on many of the directors and the staff they had now added to the mix. They raised one million dollars on top of the two million dollars that the federal fund covered, but they were left with a one million dollar debt for several years. Keith explained how it impacted the organization moving forward.

We ended up carrying almost crippling debt for years. And it was debilitating, as it took away from our work. We couldn't take on other projects, and to find people who would donate money for something that had already happened was next to impossible. We ended up getting bailed out by an unexpected "bluebird" donation from someone who donated her house and waterfront property to the Conservancy. She had originally donated it to house some of the international interns, but we told her we need the money. We're in debt, so we sold it on the market and were able to pay off all our debt and build an office. So we got lucky in the end, but had that not happened, honestly we might still be saddled with that debt... The biggest lesson learned there is not going into debt. I'm a much more conservative person now as a result, because I had to live the five years after that every day, being slowly more and more demoralized by being not able to pay it off. But it forced our organization to become much more professional, more organized.

Keith told me that Ken dedicated himself to paying off that debt for the last few years of his life.

They succeeded in the end to acquire the money to pay the debt, but not before Ken Millard, now tired and very stressed over it, cut a couple trees on his property, came into his home, lay down, and expired. It was September 27, 2015, and a lunar eclipse was happening. Loren explained that this was significant as "Ken was a cosmic figure." His determination to have a core of land across the island—a mid-island protected area of different habitats—was realized. In his honour, the Millard Learning Centre was named.

My guide on Galiano, Loren Wilkinson, in the kitchen of the Millard Learning Centre.

Eric explained some of the temporary fall out, and the bounce back that happened after. "When Ken died we lost a massive sixty hours a week for free volunteer, plus Linda, Ken's wife too. How could we make a go of it without that huge support? The Giving Circle [an annual donation campaign] came a little bit to the rescue. People were generous. It was the biggest transformation. It was hard work, as development is all about relationship building. They connected us with a donor who was willing to gift her property to the Conservancy, and that paid off the debt and allowed us to create the offices, with no more rent. It was paid off in 2017."

The Giving Circle program encouraged people to be generous and unrestrictive with their monthly or annual gifts, providing a stable source of funding that can be used where it is needed most. Other fundraising efforts included a planned giving program, a property acquisition fund, plus a musical walk-along event to support underprivileged children to attend their programs. They hired and trained staff in a development (fundraising) capacity, so they were not working as volunteers. They made connections and expanded their partnerships with other land trusts, for example, the Islands Trust Conservancy and the Nature Trust of BC.

At the same time Keith Erickson, now fully taking on the role of executive director of the Conservancy, began to pick up the pieces from their lost leader. The development of the Learning Centre property began. The Conservancy built an office on site, funded by grants and some of the "bluebird" funds. The building has a solar system, which is grid-tied (connected to the main electricity grid), using and demonstrating solar power and alternate energy systems. A classroom and a kitchen building were provided by the Silva Forest Foundation in Salmo. This they disassembled, loaded into a semi-trailer truck, and rebuilt on the Centre land. They created a little campsite around it, and the entire complex now accommodates up to thirty to forty students in tents, with a commercial kitchen facility, and a beautiful timber

The classroom provides space for workshops, meetings, and even for drying some of the herbs from the native plant nursery.

framed classroom. "We have forest gardens, including a permaculture food forest, and the forage forest (which we created in partnership with local First Nations)." Keith said, "It's a brilliant piece of land with so much opportunity for collaboration and demonstration of how we can live sustainably. I feel that this is the GCA's biggest achievement."

Vanilla Leaf Nature Reserve

The bridging property between the Millard Learning Centre and the Great Beaver Swamp is a 40.5 hectare (100 acre) property that was owned by a private landowner as part of a larger property they had bought from MacMillan Bloedel. The acquisition of this property would complete the protection of the Great Beaver Swamp wetland complex, and of perhaps greater importance, its acquisition would connect and complete a mid-island conservation corridor. Because the property needed to be subdivided off of a larger property, the GCA brought in the Islands Trust Conservancy (ITC). The ITC was able to complete the subdivision of this land without a road through a Section 99 subdivison, which at that time only government agencies were able to do.

The Vanilla Leaf Nature Reserve was purchased in 2013 by the Islands Trust Conservancy (ITC) with funding from the Natural Areas Conservation Program's grant funds, the GCA, and the Galiano community. The owners allowed for the subdivision of this 40.5 hectare (100 acre) property from the rest of their lands in order to complete the conservation of the Great Beaver Swamp and the Mid-Island Protected Area Network. Keith Erickson provided the ecological inventory, data, and mapping for the property's management plan. After the purchase was complete, the GCA registered a conservation covenant on the Vanilla Leaf Nature Reserve and acted as the land stewardship partner.

The ITC owns several other nature reserves on the island, including the Trincomali Nature Reserve.

With the acquisition of the Millard Learning Centre and the Vanilla Leaf Nature Reserve, the dream of a Mid-Island Protected Area Network was realized, linking the

Trincomali Nature Sanctuary, Millard Learning Centre, Vanilla Leaf Lands, Great Beaver Swamp Nature Reserve, Pebble Beach Nature Reserve, Laughlin Lake Nature Reserve, and Bodega Ridge Provincial Park.

The evolution of the Galiano Conservancy has shown how challenging it can be to transition from an organization with a strong leader, to one that has strength and capacity through a multi-staff and board committee approach. However, with the incredible success of these conservation acquisitions, and the current state of the GCA's programs, its evolution is clearly phenomenal.

Risa told me, "Ken ran everything himself, and a lot of organizations start like that. He was an absolutely amazing human being, but you can't have one person doing everything. When he passed away everything was in his head. I was on the board at that time. I always wanted to hire an executive director. There is not one model. There can be a committee process where different board members are responsible for things (education, land management) so not one person is responsible for everything. There is always someone who puts the most into it, and incredible people can get burned out."

Almost everyone I talked with from Galiano said that going into debt was the biggest mistake and lesson that they learned. It is very difficult to raise money for a property that has been already purchased for conservation—whether it is a case like this, where some debts are left to pay off, or for its future management.

My guide on the island, Loren, remarked at how surprised and pleased he was to see the Conservancy grow and expand after Ken's passing. As I look around at the land trust community, including my own organization on Lasqueti, it's clear that this is one of the biggest challenges. Financial support for conservation organizations, including their administrative and operational capacity, is essential to sustain these land trusts in their work to protect natural areas, without burning out their dedicated volunteer directors.

Galiano Conservancy Association Today

Chessi Miltner grew up on the island. He told me that he met Keith Erickson playing soccer. Once he got involved with the Conservancy, he was mentored by Keith. He was initially a volunteer director on the board, and later he was hired as the second executive director.

Today, the GCA has up to nine year-round staff who run their diverse programs. Typically their staff includes the ED, and program coordinators in the areas of development, conservation and climate action, sustainable food systems, restoration, and education. GCA operates the Education and Sustainable Food Systems programs as social enterprises, recovering some costs through program and rental fees, and sales of the plants and foods that they grow on site at the Learning Centre. However, they remain heavily reliant on grants and donations. Chessi outlined a bit more about the staff and their funders. "Usually we have interns and summer students [seasonal staff]. Funding comes from grants, memberships, plus an annual donation appeal we call the Giving Circle, where supporters donate at different levels annually or monthly. These funds are unrestricted, so they are available for salaries or other expenses. Wage subsidies and project grants allow us to keep a full house."

"As a living laboratory," Chessi explained, "the Millard Learning Centre allows us to pursue all our goals: environmental education, restoration, renewable energy, sustainable food production, and wildlife conservation, all in the same place at the same time, open to the public where both this active and passive learning happens."

Loren proudly showed me the beautiful sign made by a remarkable woodcarver, Arnim Rodeck, that welcomes people to the site of the Millard Learning Centre. "Look at the map. Together with other pieces, we have protected amazing pieces of land, crossing the island, with a couple watersheds. Without rating the three: preservation of key areas through purchase; restoring it through activity to a more natural habitat; and using the land as an educational basis (which is now our biggest activity). It's an awesome achievement."

During my 2021 visit to the island, Loren took me to the native plant and forage nursery. "There are both edibles and native plants here," he explained, "and lots of local people buy them. We sell regularly. During COVID, our sales went up as everyone was working in their gardens. It's not quite paying for itself—we still depend on grants. We get general agriculture grants and restoration grants, and we purchase some plants for our own restoration work."

At the nursery, I met Cedana Bourne, the Sustainable Foods Systems coordinator. She coordinates the Food Forest, the Nursery, and the GCA's tea company Forest Garden Tea. The herbs are harvested on site and dried from the rafters in the classroom—where it's warm and dry—blended, packaged, and sold to local businesses

The extensive conservation corridor of the Mid-Island Protected Area Network on Galiano Island.

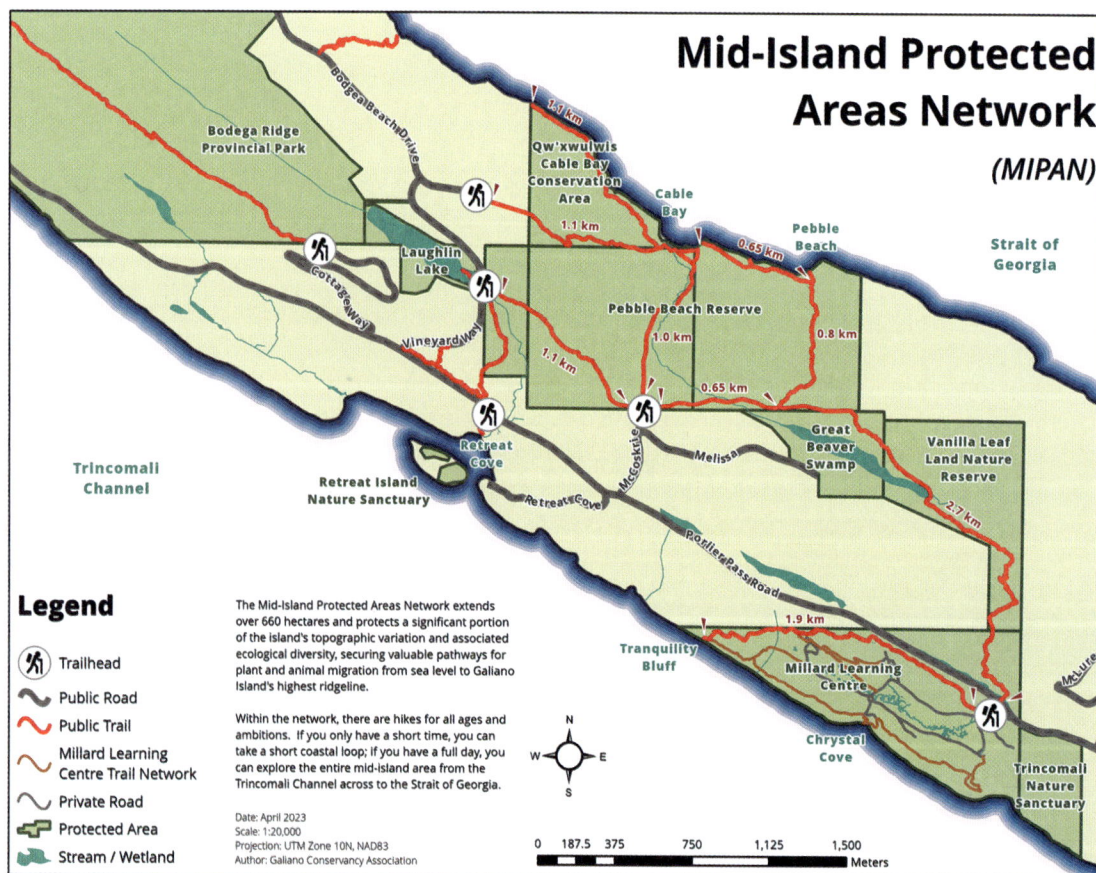

in the GCA office and at the Saturday market. The Food Forest is where they grow edible plants, such as garlic and berry plants. Cedana told me "I'm always looking for greens and things that aren't brassicas, to help maintain a good garden rotation and avoiding issues like club root." Cedana, a Registered Holistic Nutritionist and herbalist, teaches classes on the site as well.

Another innovative restoration project the GCA has taken on involves a small section of logged land within the Millard Learning Centre. The land, previously owned by a local logger, had many cedars which Loren told me were used to build houses on the island. Only one "grandmother" tree was left standing in this area. This land, now called the Nuts'a'maat Forage Forest, is being restored with Adam Huggins, a student of Eric's and now the restoration coordinator, using ecocultural restoration. Nuts'a'maat means "working together with one heart, one mind" in the Hul'qumi'num' language. It is a collaboration between the Galiano Conservancy (GCA), Access to Media Education Society (AMES), members of the Penelakut Tribe, and the Galiano community. In conjunction with Penelakut Elders, they have worked together to restore and plant native and forage food plants on the site. Then in the last few years, the GCA worked with Karen and Richard Charlie and a handful of other Penelakut families to facilitate traditional hunting of deer at the MLC, and offer Feed the People workshops, where Indigenous Knowledge Keepers teach participants how to skin and process deer for food.

Adam shared his perceptions that this type of restoration and reconciliation involves deconstructing—slowing down. Not asking what to do, but rather what does it mean? What is our relationship with the natural world, while learning this hand in hand with Indigenous people.

IN 2020, THE GCA STARTED a new project—the acquisition of the Cable Bay property, adding even more to the mid-island network. The property, District Lot 64, came up for sale for about $2 million. Partnering with the provincial land trust, the Nature Trust of BC, the Galiano Conservancy worked to raise funds for these 26.5 hectares (65.5 acres) of ecologically diverse coastal Douglas-fir forest with over 1 kilometre of pristine sandstone beach and rocky shoreline at Cable Bay. A favourite spot for islanders and visitors alike, it is one of the most important biodiversity hotspots on Galiano's Strait of Georgia shoreline. It has long been a site for resting and finding rejuvenation, both by the resident and overwintering birds and by the Indigenous people who waited out storms here before crossing the Strait to the mainland. It abuts the Pebble Beach Reserve, with a creek that emerges from the Great Beaver Swamp, within the neighbouring protected areas. The Nature Trust of BC is now on title, and the GCA is the land steward. This latest acquisition now connects 500 hectares (1,250 acres) of protected coastal Douglas-fir habitats.

As I headed back to Montague, I considered the amazing legacy of these founding directors and the outstanding work of the Conservancy today. I had lost my crew as Heather had to return to Lasqueti to attend an event on neighbouring Texada Island to celebrate work that Living Oceans had done with residents, cleaning up the many bays and shorelines around the Salish Sea earlier that spring. I accompanied Heather to the ferry via the Magic Bus, which travels between the harbour and the Hummingbird Pub, where she walked to the ferry.

After I returned, I made my way over to the permanent moorings around Montague Harbour Marine Provincial Park. As I began to pull up my anchor so I could go over, another rower came to check on me. This was the only other person I had seen in the busy harbour that didn't have an engine on their dinghy. I noted that his generous offer of help matched his human powered skiff.

I had taught my daughter to swim in the mid '90s when I was living on Galiano. Today the bay is filled with families and swimmers, enjoying the sandy isthmus that runs along Gray Peninsula. I walked around to the end of the park and noted the salal and Oregon grape berries I had made into jam one year, and the wild asparagus that I had learned to eat as part of the summer plants that the islands in the Salish Sea offer. I saw a bald eagle from this viewpoint, plus six pigeon guillemots, with their flashing white epaulets on their jet black feathers. These year-round birds nest on cliffs, along with the purple martins who now nest in the human-made homes, some I had seen at a private dock near the marina. I also saw fourteen geese, crows, and a squirrel chattering away. Later I saw a great blue heron. I also talked with the BC Parks contractor about my 10:00 AM observation of five people digging and collecting clams. It turns out this is legal on the outside, as long as the people have a license. I was surprised, as I would have thought the idea is to protect nature in a provincial park, including the intertidal creatures!

The Galiano Conservancy Association worked with the Nature Trust of BC to raise the funds to acquire the newest property within the Mid-Island Protected Network. ALBERT NORMANDIN

Conservation Covenants and Land Donations to the GCA

The Galiano Conservancy holds conservation covenants over lands owned by private landowners. Chessi explained that in turn, other land trusts have placed conservation covenants on some GCA properties. Taking a conservative and careful approach to legal agreements, he remarked that they abide by the standards set by the Canadian Land Trust Alliance for land trusts when entering into Conservation Agreements.[27]

Like other land trusts and conservancies, the GCA works with landowners to design and register conservation covenants, when they want to protect their land beyond their own ownership. Chessi gave me one example from a Finlay Lake property. "In 2001, Marjorie McClelland placed a conservation covenant on the Finlay Lake property. It was her desire that this area be protected in its natural state. In 2014, Marjorie's estate donated the land to the Galiano Conservancy. This 6.9 hectare (17 acre) parcel of land contains one of the larger wetlands on Galiano.[28] It is also home to beaver and a number of species of dragonfly which are at risk and the red-listed red-legged frog."

Retreat Island, off the west side of Galiano, was owned by Jillian and Robin Ridington in the mid-nineties. Jillian and Robin, a producer and radio documentary producer, have been documenting the Dane-Zaa speaking people of the Peace River region, now the Doig River First Nation and Blueberry River First Nations, for over thirty years.[29] Strong supporters of the GCA, they placed a conservation covenant on half the island they stewarded. Then in 1999, just before they were to sell and move on, they donated this half to the Conservancy.

I met Jillian and Robin many years ago and had a tour of their home nestled in the forest on Retreat Island. They built their home so that outside the island one doesn't really see it. Today I realize these ethnographers had a percipient relationship with nature. Their daughter is a scientific observer and videographer. Her great photos and video of hatching moon snails is on the Galiano Conservancy's website.

Bowie Keefer was one of the forest landowners who put a sustainable forestry covenant on 20.2 hectares (50 acres) of the 68.7 hectares (170 acres) he bought from MacMillan Bloedel. Now, he is involved in the Galiano Ecoforestry Association, building a bridge between islanders and the forest lot owners. He believes that building trails on private lands between the protected areas, creating a network between the provincial and regional parks and conservation areas, unencumbered by no trespassing signs, would bring islanders more into a "right to roam" kind of culture that is common in European countries.

A sustainable forestry covenant has different priorities than a conservation covenant. The Islands Trust allowed the sustainable forestry covenant under Galiano's official community plan to provide an avenue for forest lot owners to build a house on their forestry-zoned lands by registering this type of covenant on the property. The idea is that even though forestry is an allowed use on the land, the covenant is designed to result in no net loss in forest cover.

After spending a couple of days at Montague, I headed up past Parker Island (which shelters the northwest side of Montague Harbour) toward Retreat Cove. I was looking forward to meeting Ken and Linda Millard's daughter, Beth Thiessen, up the western shore of Galiano in a small bay with a public dock.

While waiting for Beth, I noticed lots of swallows flying, both the migrating barn swallows and the familiar violet-green swallows. It was great to see the numbers of uncommon, larger, cinnamon-coloured barn swallows with their steel-grey breasts and forked tails. This a yellow-listed species I see far less frequently now than the blue-listed purple martins. Here too were the familiar martin boxes installed at the dock. The turkey vultures were soaring above and the juncos were happily flying from tree to tree. A baby seal was crying through the night and rubbing itself against my keel—no sign of the mom. Things felt pretty good here, though signs on both sides of the road said KEEP OUT. There is a much quieter feeling here mid-island, yet I heard sirens and a back-up warning sound.

Beth came down to talk with me on my boat. She mentioned that even though the community had worked so hard to protect areas from development, the sounds of busy construction and the two-year timeline to get a construction contractor on Galiano confirmed that development is still on full throttle here on the Southern Gulf Islands. Montague is busy, yet the houses around the bay still seemed relatively small and unobtrusive.

Beth took me to see Ken and Linda's residence, an unobtrusive 9.7 hectare (24 acre) site. She took me to the workshop that had been Ken's, revealing stacks of exotic wood and partial bows still lining the inside of the building. She also showed me cartons of files. She said that her mom, Linda, kept every single publication or newspaper article she found and filed it away. Beth told me that Linda, an archivist, welcomed everyone who came into the office and asked how she could help. When Linda first started building the library at the Conservancy, she would read all the books and write up something about them. Every issue of the local magazine the

Active Page would come out with an article that Linda Millard put in. Beth told me that Linda lives with her sister in Vancouver now.

My guide while I spent a few days on Galiano in July 2021, Loren Wilkinson, has been looking for answers to how to live sustainably in place, most of his life. Coming from a Christian perspective, he suggests, "What we call nature is Creation, and we have a particular relationship/responsibility to it—not domination. How do we relate to a place? How can we be at home, and yet have a human presence in a natural culture that's bigger than us, and yet have a distinctive place in it. The Land Trust movement is an answer to—how do we be responsible people in a place?"

When I interviewed Carolyn Canfield, she mentioned this idea of the land trust movement fulfilling some of the puzzle. "It's astonishing for me to look back at where the Conservancy is now, and see how close that is to what we were originally imagining." She recalled going to an early meeting of the Land Trust Alliance in the US. "The land trust movement had really taken off in the US, and there were lots of examples of trade-offs with conservation and semi-protected land, and some housing, and all kinds of legal structures to protect land over time and prevent encroachment on conservation lands. There were some legal structures that didn't apply in BC, but it gave us the idea—this could happen here."

People on Galiano are working to heal the early years of conflict with corporations and their capitalistic profit-based values. They are working toward a new ethic of community and sustainability that is needed everywhere. They are forging a path forward with willing donors and sellers, partnering with other land trusts. My friend Ronaldo, who now lives on Lasqueti, told me that he thinks the Galiano Conservancy today is a model for land trusts across the country, considering the diverse ways they have worked to conserve, restore, and educate people about how we can live with yet protect nature.

The Trincomali Nature Reserve is protected by the Islands Trust Conservancy and forms part of the Mid-Island Protected Area Network. It is an important cormorant nesting site.

Coastal Bluff Protection—Tricomali Nature Sanctuary

As I left Retreat Cove, I headed even further north to another public dock at the north end of Galiano Island. The seal I first heard and then saw in Retreat Cove was rubbing itself against my keel all through the night, and then wrapping its tail around my outboard prop, calling to its mother, I assume. Then after ensuring it didn't get caught in my prop as I left the dock, I saw it raise its head as it slipped back from following me out of the bay as I left.

During this transit, I counted twenty cormorants tightly perched along the cliffs while passing the Trincomali Nature Sanctuary. The Islands Trust Conservancy and the Land Conservancy of BC purchased the property in February 2001. At the south end of Galiano's Mid-Island Protected Area Network, the property had been logged by MacBlo, and then purchased by a series of forestry landowners. This 12 hectare waterfront parcel was created when a larger lot to the north was subdivided through a section 99 subdivision. The Nature Sanctuary includes a small spring, some young forest, and high cliffs. The sandstone of the coastal bluffs is cracked, faulted, and eroded providing nesting habitat for a significant colony of both double-crested and pelagic cormorants. The red-listed peregrine falcon and blue-listed olive-sided fly-catcher have also been sighted repeatedly here.

Valdes Island/Le'eyesun Conservancy—A Budding Land Trust

Once I passed the Coastal Bluffs, I found the dock just south of Porlier Pass, also known as skthak or skthok071h—meaning "narrows" or "little narrows."[30] Here I met with Dan White from the Valdes Island Conservancy. A water taxi driver and a diver, Dan bought one of the seventy-five three-acre lots that were initially leased and later sold by a developer from Vancouver. Many of these cabins are still leased, with only six to ten full time residents; the rest are filled with primarily summer visitors.

Dan told me about the Valdes Island Conservancy's founding in 2007. "Years ago at a Valdes Day, there was discussion and formation of the Conservancy to protect areas from development. One third of the island is First Nation, and half is forestry (MacMillan Bloedel, now Mosaic)." Dan told me there has been no active logging for some time. "It was a lot busier in the '50s and '60s than now, because of the logging and fishing. Now it's tourists and vacationers."

More recently, Le'eyesun/Valdes's Crown land was transferred to the ten First Nations in the Hul'qumi'num group. The Lyackson First Nation website states, "Valdes Island is the centre of the Lyackson community and our Nation finally has full control over this territory of ours. Some of us live here, while others regularly visit, or stay here for the summer."[31] Dan told me that Lyackson means tip of the Douglas-fir tree. I learned from Rozen's *Place Names of the Island Halkomelem* that Porlier Pass was known in the early twentieth century as the Cowichan Gap, and it was an important site for harvesting sea mammals, including sea lions, dolphins, and porpoise.[32]

Dan is vice-chair of this small eighty member Conservancy, chaired by Marja de Jong Westman. Dan told me the Conservancy was established to help protect the existing biological and cultural communities of the island. The Conservancy works with many partners, including the Lyackson First Nation and the Galiano Conservancy Association. With the GCA this small Conservancy has been researching the efficacy of Rockfish Conservation Areas and marine life. Marja is an instructor and the coordinator of the department of biology at Capilano University. She organizes the annual two-day bio-blitzes on Valdes Island. A third director, Doug Campbell, chairs the relation committee for the Lyackson. He is a retired Federal Court of Canada judge. This small Conservancy installs and monitors purple martin nest boxes, holds annual bat counts, and removes invasive plants.

As I left Dan and the turbulent waters of Porlier Pass, I considered this connection between the islands. This creation story not only links these islands, but it also sets them firmly in the Coastal Douglas-fir zone that is so familiar to me. I headed to De Courcy Island's marine provincial park for the night.

De Courcy to Saysutshun (Newcastle Island)

On the morning of my departure from De Courcy Island, I waited inside Stuart Channel while a tug and log boom crept through Dodd Narrows. Seeing that some people are still removing the habitats of species at risk and the carbon capturing trees, I became even more determined to focus on sharing these stories of how we can protect what is still standing. Once cleared, I followed, hoping I was still in time for the slack tide. Once through the Narrows, I was forced to turn to avoid a few logs that were let go in Northumberland Channel. Then I noticed cormorants swimming all around in the water, and more ducks than I'd seen the whole trip.

A bit further on I noticed the high cliffs on Gabriola Island. But wait, what were all these cormorants doing flying around out here among the tankers, tugs, and log booms all along both sides of Northumberland Channel? Looking east, I saw the Gabriola cliffs, white with the sign of cormorant nests. There were cormorants in the hundreds! I edged closer to see if there were any babies in the midst, amazed at the sheer numbers of these black sentinels of the coast. I was enthralled by nature's abundance and tenacity.

Cormorants and babies in a sandstone cave. TRUDY CHATWIN

FROM HERE I WENT ON TO Newcastle Island, now named Saysutshun, a marine park officially renamed in 2021 and now managed by the Snuneymuxw First Nation. This was an indication of the many new relationships between Indigenous communities, BC Parks, and conservation groups in BC. As I found my way into Mark Bay at the south end of Saysutshun, a kind Kiwi helped me locate an empty mooring. The bay was fuller than I'd ever seen it, but of course it had been twelve years since I'd last been there. The mooring cost $14, courtesy of Pacific Yachting and the Marine Parks Forever Society. Here was another group protecting the bay from dragging anchors. Since 1962, the Marine Parks Forever Society had contributed to several coastal conservation acquisition campaigns including Jedediah Island, Squitty Bay on Lasqueti Island, and recently an expanded marine provincial park up Princess Louisa Inlet. They have also raised funds essential to ongoing management of the parks. This was yet another reminder of the generosity and kindness of those committed to protecting nature.

Saysutshun (Newcastle Island) has a history that mirrors much of the coast of BC. Bill Merilee's fascinating historical review of the history of Newcastle Island mirrors that of many of the islands I'd just visited.[33] The Snuneymuxw had several villages on the island, with herring a staple food source filling the channel and bays between Newcastle and Protection islands. The island's trees were a source for canoes and houses and burial boxes. In the nineteenth century, coal was mined from the island and all around Nanaimo. Then sandstone was cut and sold from the island's smooth shores. Over four herring salteries were run by Japanese people along the inside shores. Then in 1930, the Canadian Pacific Railway purchased the island for $30,000 and Vancouverites and Victorians came for picnics aboard the Princess ships. The Pavilion, still standing, had bands and formal dances to amuse visiting guests. This set the stage for the eventual purchase of the island by the people of Nanaimo for $150,000 (less its mineral rights) and the Province accepted it as a park for $1 in 1960. This was one year after Montague on Galiano was established in 1959—the first marine park in BC.

During my stop on Saysutshun Island, I spotted forty Canada geese, nine black oystercatchers and eight sandpipers, along with the usual robins and juncos. As I walked the shoreline trail I saw some killdeer or semipalmated plovers in a wetland area. This serene scene was interrupted by a raccoon, running at high speed down the trail and off to the beach.

I left Saysutshun later that morning, heading for home—the island in the middle of the Salish Sea. Passing Hudson Rocks, I saw both cormorants and gulls sitting on the rocks. Michael Rodway's newest book, *Seabird Colonies of British Columbia, Part 4: Salish Sea*, indicates that cormorant nesting sites overall have plummeted, especially off Hudson's Rock just north of Nanaimo, described as a colony of concern.[34] Last count was over 100 double-breasted cormorant nests and 67 pelagic cormorant nests. However, none have been counted since 2001. In contrast, the Gabriola cliffs I viewed on my way home had high counts in 2022. Trudy Chatwin and her friends from Protection Island and Simon Fraser University counted 205 double-crested cormorant nests and 90 pelagic cormorant nests that year. They did a count by kayak in 2023 and found 154 double-crested cormorant nests and 86 pelagic cormorant nests—a dwindling number. I didn't realize that devoted people were voluntarily counting nests until I had been asked to help. Trudy is a retired endangered species biologist who worked for the Province. Another dedicated islander, she was involved in the protection of land in Gwaii Haanas.

As I motored home to Squitty Bay, I had lots of time to reflect on the growth and extensive work of the community land trusts and others I had met on my journey to the Southern Gulf Islands. With again no wind, my outboard motor carried me over the flat mirror-like waters of the Salish Sea, back home that very hot, dry summer of 2021. Reflecting on all the wonderful, dedicated people I'd met, I felt exhilarated. Even though, like me, almost everyone said that they often felt despair over the dwindling forests, wildlife, and natural areas, they were raising their heads and hearts, taking their islands' futures into their own hands. Little did I know that my future journey to the Northern Gulf Islands would lead me to meet even more defenders of nature on land and in the ocean—some literally through the courts!

Herring spawn off Denman and Hornby Islands. REBECCA BENJAMIN CAREY

CHAPTER EIGHT

HORNBY ISLAND
Hillsides and Herring

*"When I come home on the ferry in winter to Hornby, the whole side
of the island is dark. I heave a big sigh of relief—we saved it!"*

JAN BEVAN,
past director, Conservancy Hornby Island

THE MEDITERRANEAN LIKE SANDY BEACHES, flower filled Garry oak meadows, and stately Douglas-fir forests have drawn both residents and countless visitors to Hornby Island. The conservation of these beautiful forests, meadows, and beaches, now protected as extensive parks, has not been easy. Today, the island's popularity is both an economic driver and a significant challenge to its ecological and social integrity.

As a sailor I was drawn to the large, open southeast anchorage at Tribune Bay. Its shallow, warm ocean water and sandy beaches are irresistible to thousands of other visitors who come by boat and ferry each year. The shoreline is rimmed with golden coloured grassy bluffs and enchanting Garry oaks, the only native oak species in the province, with its associated ecological community—rated critically imperiled in BC. From Tribune Bay heading southwest are surprisingly long shallow waters, sandstone ledges, and rocky conglomerate shorelines that lead out to Norris Rocks and Heron Rocks, aptly named for one of the area's abundant marine bird species. Evocative open caves and sandstone ledges then lead north up Lambert Channel between Hornby and Denman islands toward Ford Cove.

The marine area from Flora Islet in the southeast to Heron Rocks on the southwestern shores and around to Ford Cove are habitat for an amazing diversity of seventy bird species, including the red-listed western grebe, Brandt's cormorant, common murre, and marbled murrelet.[1] Adding to the birds, both humpback whales and orcas often pass through, and sea lions (Steller and California) winter around the island. Off Flora Islet, the bluntnose sixgill sharks, a federal species of concern, had congregated in the summer months in the past. According to Anna Zielinski, one of my guides on Hornby, they have not been seen in recent years because no one has been monitoring on Flora Island recently, However, the abundance of seabirds and sea mammals that congregate here in spring is still a stunning reminder of nature's magnificence!

The herring run in Lambert Channel and around Denman and Hornby Islands is one of the largest, in terms of number of fish, from Mexico to Alaska. Being the last of five commercial runs on the inside protected coastal waters, the herring draw much of this amazing diversity of life. The frenzy of ducks, eagles, sea lions, and human fisherfolk greet the dwindling runs each March.

Prior to the arrival of European colonists, Hornby Island was within the territory of the Pentlatch, K'ómoks, Qualicum, Shíshálh, and Tla'amin people. The island's numerous archaeological and petroglyph sites support oral histories of long term occupation by Indigenous people. The island is becoming known as Ja-dai-aich, meaning "the outer island." The Shingle Spit ferry landing sits on what was once a prominent village site.[2] The Garry oak meadows at what is now Helliwell Park offered easy access to dietary staples such as camas, chocolate lily, and wild onions, in addition to harvesting of deer and berries.[3] The Tla'amin Nation, across the Salish Sea near Powell River, have regained their plant gathering rights in a shared area protocol. Two Guardian Poles were raised in recent years, in Helliwell Park, and on neighbouring Fillongley Park on Denman Island. According to a couple of local people I interviewed on Hornby Island, this was a major ceremonial event that many local residents describe as a transformative awakening to Indigenous culture.

In the late nineteenth and twentieth centuries, Hornby Island's economy was based on logging, farming, and fishing, like most of the Gulf Islands. Only thirty-two settler families were known to live on the island at the turn of the century. By the '60s that lifestyle changed toward today's arts and crafts economy, with some people farming, and many others who provide services to residents and tourists.[4]

On a summer day in 2021 while moored at Tribune Bay, I rowed to the park to do some yoga. I met two summer park wardens driving a wheelbarrow filled with bags of garbage. When I asked what is the biggest threat to the ecology of the parks, they responded unanimously with "overcapacity." For the August long weekend in 2021 they recorded 1,200 cars on the park's counter, and another 107 boats in the bay. Based on these numbers, they estimated that around 3,000 people a day come to this island of 1,225 residents. In road races to cross Denman Island, there are four sailing waits in summer to Hornby, so the ferry just ends up doing constant runs, abandoning their regular schedule. I asked these two young wardens what they thought could be a solution. They suggested, "local ferry passes, plus reservations. Then you might not get people camping on the side of the roads or on the beaches because they found there was nowhere to stay." I noticed giant water tanks along the island's roads, apparently for additional fire protection. With no body of water larger than a farm pond, and increased visitor use, islanders are very water conscious.

On two separate trips, I learned about the history and collective efforts of the local people who have worked for over thirty years to conserve Hornby Island's diverse and rare ecology. Today close to 36 percent of the island is protected through parks, other protected areas, and conservation covenants, thanks to the hard work of many people, especially the past directors and members of Conservancy Hornby Island (CHI).

The early history of provincial park lands on Hornby starts with Helliwell Park. Located at the far southeast end of the island, it includes endangered Garry oak woodlands and meadows and a rare old growth Douglas-fir stand atop a high sea bluff. Helliwell Park was created in 1966 when John Helliwell donated his land to BC Parks. The Province added the much larger marine component to the park in 1992, and then they added Flora Islet in 1996 through the Pacific Marine Heritage Legacy Fund.

Tribune Bay Park was jointly purchased by the Devonian Foundation and the Province, and was established as a Provincial Park in 1978. The former lodge and

Hornby, and surrounding areas from Comox to Nanaimo, is the last of five former commercial herring spawn fisheries in the Salish Sea, occurring in the early spring. Herring once made up a primary food source for Indigenous people. Today the Department of Fisheries and Oceans (DFO) states herring supplies 68 percent of Chinook salmon diet, 61 percent Coho, and 71 percent of ling cod diet— which in turn is the main food of the endangered resident orcas. REBECCA BENJAMIN CAREY

related buildings and facilities are located on the eastern side of the park. Its 95 hectares (235 acres) of Douglas-fir forest rimming the unusual white sand beach are visited by thousands annually. About 70 percent of the park is forest and about 30 percent is grassland, resulting from former cultivation (directly behind the beach). The forest is a second-growth mixture of Douglas-fir, western red cedar, grand fir, western hemlock, and bigleaf maple. Surface water is limited to a small pond in the forest and an intermittent stream on the south edge of the grassland, near the shore.

Along Tribune Bay a small, private 6.35 hectare (15.7 acre) forested in-holding parcel borders the existing park. Along the road from the Hornby Island Co-op to the beach at Tribune is a private campground, which has been in operation for decades. Both properties have recently been purchased by BC Parks.

When I talked with Tony Law by phone, he told me that he worked for twenty years looking after Tribune Bay and Helliwell Parks as an employee of the successive companies that had the Parks Facility Operation contract. Being familiar with several BC Parks supervisors, he encouraged acquisition of these two adjacent sites. Tony told me that he spoke with both owners of the two properties and BC Parks encouraging them to discuss conservation options. He added that years later, "as a Trustee, I drafted letters sent by the Local Trust Committee to BC Parks supporting their acquisition. In the fall of 2021, BC Parks acquired the private campground and the adjoining piece of private land, as part of BC Parks recreation and park infrastructure goals."

Helliwell and Tribune Bay Parks are gems in the Salish Sea. The sandstone shores reveal multiple tidal shelves at low tide. Overhanging arbutus, Garry oaks, and Douglas-fir trees drape the foreshore in shapes and sizes that stimulate some of the artistic creativity the island is known for. The endangered Taylor's checkerspot butterfly is also found here, as well as on Denman Island.

Early Formation of Conservancy Hornby Island

On my 2023 trip, I met five Hornby Island residents who were involved in the early years of Conservancy Hornby Island (CHI). These dedicated individuals spent decades working to bring their island community together, advocating for ecological protection. Their initial formation came out of resisting logging and several new developments that impinged on natural areas of ecological importance on their island. Not unlike other land trusts in the Salish Sea, CHI's early history had significant challenges, which over time developed into a series of conservation success stories.

Anna Zielinski, a renowned Canadian abstract artist, introduced me to several early directors of CHI. Anna moved with her husband Bob to Hornby Island in 1972. With her red hair, freckles, and medium stature, she might easily be passed by, but she is a formidable force, highly respected for her keen environmental ethic, patience, and persistence.

Through Anna, I met Tom Knott, who gathered together the founding board.[5] Tom moved from the US to Vancouver and became involved with food co-ops and recycling. He told me that he initially took a trip to Hornby with friends and, feeling the spirit and power of the land pull on his heart, he decided to move. Thirteen years later, in September 1988, he came to steward his own bit of land

Tribune Bay in summer, filled with residents and tourists alike.

on the island. Becoming involved in the community quickly, Tom soon became the president of the Hornby Island Residents and Ratepayers Association (HIRRA).

Raven's Development of the Sandstone Strata

Tom was a treasure trove of stories. In my interview with him, he told me about a 40.47 hectare (100 acre) property which was owned by a company that had plans to parcel out 10 acre lots for executives. It was then sold to Raven Lumber who made an application for a bare land strata development. Preliminary plans were approved, with small lots on the waterfront and a large area of common lands. However, Tom explained, "the application was altered on submission to the Ministry of Highways. The 88 acre parcel was no longer common land, but was legally attached to Lot 1 of the waterfront lots, and the only common land was the access road. This was quite naturally seen as a deceptive betrayal by the community on Raven's part." With rapid clearing of trees and a change from common land to a road, many islanders were angry. Tom explained how this issue spawned the Conservancy.

"The strata council approached HIRRA, a number of islanders expressed outrage, and as president I felt I had a responsibility to the community to get involved. I was glad too, on my own account." HIRRA and the owners of the Raven Lumber met a couple of times. As Tom explained, the situation became heated.

They started logging, and a group of activists went in and tried to disrupt things. Those who were outraged gathered into an ongoing picket, but the cutting continued and the first loads of logs began moving out. The protest then shifted from harassment to an attempt to stop the cutting by moving into the fall zone, the area into which cut trees were landing. The faller working the job was horribly traumatized by how close he had come to dropping a tree on a man carrying his child. When I got to the site (how fast vital information could spread pre-internet!) he was locked in his truck with the engine on, heater full on, shaking and doing everything he could to keep himself from sobbing. The most violent protesters were banging on the windows. Of course the job site was shut down and stayed shut until the management company got an injunction to stop the protesters.

A few days later, I got a call from the company to tell me they were coming up to serve the injunction. They wanted to meet with me first. So we met, two managers and a small group of us from the island, across the road on a mossy clearing in the sun. Once again, word spread that something of significance was happening over at the Raven lands! Bikes, cars, even a young couple with a stroller full of kids started appearing, wanting to speak, needing to tell how they felt, all speaking respectfully. The management left to have a private talk, then came back and proposed that they finish falling in the block that they had laid out and the injunction would only be served if there was any more disruption to their work. I objected. "After what we've heard here, I can't go back to the community and say we've agreed to continued logging." After they talked with the contractor, they came back and said they would clean up what had been cut, with no new cutting. Raven kept their side of the bargain.

Out of this came the suggestion to form a conservancy by one of the island trustees, John Fletcher. Tom said, "As we explored the possibility, the need got clearer and clearer. Our recent success in stopping the logging on the Raven lands lifted everyone's spirits."

Sheila McDonnell, who was on the founding board said, "A lot of the founders were involved in Clayoquot, so there was a growing awareness of old growth needing protection. Tom brought us all together into a circle, in reaction to the Raven land, which they were logging." By now it should be no surprise that it was with the help of Ron Pither that these initial founders prepared their constitution and bylaws, adapting their collective needs and desires to form Conservancy Hornby Island (CHI). CHI was founded in 1991 with multiple purposes of stewardship, preservation, education, and research.[6]

They tried to raise funds to acquire some of the threatened lands, but Tom concluded, "After all this talk about a purchase, we could never pull the money together. A positive end came recently though, as one of the things we wanted was a community garden. The latest purchasers have set that up on the former Raven land. Now it's a beautiful garden working quite well."

The Thousand Oaks

These were trying times. Just as this issue subsided, CHI had another battle with a different land development project. It concerned a very large property stretching between Tribune Bay Park to Helliwell Park, which included around a thousand Garry oaks.

The 150 hectare (370 acre) property, locally called High Salal Ranch, was developed as strata title lots in 1979. There were many stages in this development, but the land included the largest stand of Garry oaks on the islands. Most of this forested area was to be held as common lands, while the rest was planned for private homes overlooking the bay.

At the east end near Helliwell Park are the "Thousand Oaks." According to *The Log*, a newsletter produced by the Friends of Ecological Reserves, this Garry oak stand was considered, "by far the largest contiguous stand of the Garry oak—Brome community located to date." It was also identified as the most northerly community, "in pristine condition, with no broom, [and] no damage to site," according to the British Columbia Conservation Data Centre (CDC). Of fewer than twenty Garry oak communities, "none approach the high quality, condition, size and ecological integrity of the site at High Salal Ranch," wrote the CDC's ecologist Carmen Cadrin.[7]

With rapid development undermining the integrity and beauty all along the coast of BC there was concern on all fronts. A *Vancouver Sun* reporter, Stephen Hume, wrote that the province was now facing "The Last Stand" of the Garry oaks, the rarest and oldest in the world.

Tony Law, a member of CHI's board, worked both as a director, and later as an island trustee to help save the oaks. Tony moved to Hornby Island in 1989 from Nova Scotia where he had a sheep farm and worked as an addiction counsellor. He had been involved in conservation since age fourteen when he volunteered at a local nature reserve in England. He served as an elected trustee for Hornby Island for twenty-two years.

Tony explained, "The covenants attached to the 1979 preliminary layout approval for the subdivision prohibited the removal of any vegetation or trees within a to be

Garry oaks and their associated meadow ecological community on Hornby Island, an ecosystem with over one hundred species at risk in BC.

designated oak grove area, stipulating that the layouts of lots at the east end of High Salal Ranch not conflict with the grove."[8] However the covenants, to be held by the two provincial ministries (Ministry of Environment and Ministry of Transportation), had yet to be registered when CHI first became involved.

Unfortunately, the initial development approval hadn't designated the oak grove area specifically. The covenants were not registered until 1996. The last stages of the proposed development included six homes that would be within half of the grove, with sea views in an "oak grove tree preservation area."[9] The Conservancy filed a lawsuit against the development for not following the initial plans. Unfortunately, they weren't successful.

Tony Law tried to get the Islands Trust Fund (now Conservancy) added to the covenant in 2006, to ensure the long-term protection of the oak grove and help manage the encroaching firs and grasses. "As it turned out," he explained, the Ministry of Transportation "required that the High Salal Strata Council approve the addition of the Islands Trust Fund to the covenant, and a couple of holdouts prevented the Strata Council's approval."[10] With the Province and occasionally regional districts having covenants on title to hundreds of properties, Tony felt that there was little likelihood that these covenants would be monitored, and thus respected over time. Tony's efforts to have the ITC registered on title as an additional covenant holder would have ensured that the restrictions were respected over time.

"In the end one acre building sites were created in the strata and most of the 370 acres remained intact, unfenced, and open for habitat and wildlife," former director Sheila McDonnell added. "There certainly was more opposition about the later lots that go right to the grove, which are quite intrusive in places. The strata has collaborated on some restoration practices since, such as removal of firs, etc., under a naturalists' guidance. The trail right-of-way stopped the houses from being built closer to the cliffs and impacting the visual elements of the cliffs from Tribune Bay to Helliwell. But the incursion of the last eight or so lots into the oak grove was wrong and did need to be fought. Even with some push back, many of the last eight houses are right in the oak grove, and these can't help but impact it."

Through this long struggle, the islanders managed to protect approximately half of the oak grove, along with creating a two metre registered trail right-of-way in front of the houses at the edge of the bluff. They set some cement blocks with low ropes along the right-of-way, but apparently, these have been challenged over the years by some of the strata's owners.

How difficult these two projects must have been for these stalwart directors. There were some positive outcomes, however. For example, they raised community awareness on the island and in the broader region, as people realized that these incredible places were not just up for sale, willy-nilly, with no thought for the wildlife, species, and ecosystems in which they were located. The tide was changing, and with CHI's persistence, large swaths of land were about to be protected.

Mount Geoffrey Escarpment Park

When Anna Zielinski and her husband Bob moved to Hornby in 1972, they learned from their neighbours Arthur Link and Jim Parsons, owners of the large property that lined the shore and went up the slopes of Mount Geoffrey, that they had purchased it to protect it. Both Arthur Link and Jim Parsons were professors of Chinese studies in California. Anna explained, "We also met a couple who owned the farm, located on both sides of the Ford Cove Hill. Bob and I had a dream to try and conserve the whole ridge from Shingle Spit to the top of Ford Cove Hill."

This group of neighbours drafted an agreement to establish a park that would include 69 hectares (170 acres) of the farm's uplands, the Link/Parsons land of 170 hectares (420 acres), and around 5 hectares (13 acres) of their own land, which would create a large contiguous area of protected land. "We developed this proposal and all the owners were in agreement, including the total price of $175,000. Unfortunately, this deal fell through as one of the partners backed out. That ended the first attempt at realizing this dream of protecting the whole area." Shortly after, the farm owners subdivided their uplands.

Anna Zielinski, Sheila McDonnell, and Tony Quin in 2022, directors of CHI who worked tirelessly to protect Mount Geoffrey Escarpment Park.

Anna and her husband then reached out further. "Early on we met two fellows who were well placed in two government ministries. We went to talk to them about our dream and the possibilities of making it into a park. They felt very confident they could raise money through provincial and federal parks' ministries, and were very keen to help us."

Anna then joined the board of Conservancy Hornby Island and they made a second attempt to protect the lands. Hoping to determine a price, they tried to contact Link and Parsons, and their son Vance, whom they had now added to the title as a co-owner. Unfortunately, the owners weren't accessible then, which ended the second attempt.

In 1996 CHI tried again to acquire the property. Tony Law was now an elected trustee. He told me, "Vance Link, with whom I had kept in touch, came to my door one day saying he was ready to explore the property being acquired and protected for conservation."

Anna, as a director of CHI, pursued the Pacific Marine Heritage Legacy Fund (PMHLF). This federal/provincial conservation fund for the south coast region was highly sought after. Having contacted staff within the provincial government, Anna learned that they were well aware of the Link/Parsons property and were giving it priority. With the help of both Tony Law, then an island trustee, and Tony Quin, the president of CHI, they put in an application for funding. "This gave us the impetus and confidence to go ahead," Anna explained. CHI started raising awareness, pledges, and funds.

Well into CHI's fundraising campaign, Anna learned that the Province's $30 million, which was to be added to the $30 million in federal funds for the PMHL program, were not yet in place. "The effort made by the island made it clear that we were all in support of this purchase, as we had raised pledges and money. But we had to return all those donations. It was a lot of work and a shock."

With no funds to support this third attempt, the owners listed the property for $3.9 million. There were several reactions. One islander expressed his opinion. "Well you know what I'd do if I had that land. I'd put a runway on the top bench and develop homes facing west and people could fly in."

Anna took me to meet Tony Quin, the CHI past president who worked closely with her to acquire the Link/Parsons land. I recalled his crinkly smile and laughter from years ago when we met through my work with the Land Trust Alliance of BC. Though his memory was thin, his humbleness and fortitude made me glad I had taken the time to meet with him. As he was losing his memories and some of his physical stamina, I felt a renewed impetus to record the stories and history of these founders of local island land trusts and commemorate these local champions who have conserved so much on the islands.

Several years after their third try, CHI got the news that the PMHL fund was now in place. Full of hope and confidence, CHI began their fourth and final campaign to raise local funds to contribute to the now available PMHL funds. The directors and members of CHI set up booths at the farmer's market, selling sheepskins, roses, and quilts, gathered a variety of auction and raffle items, and took pledges and donations to raise the funds to conserve the Link/Parsons land.

Tony Quin, then president of the board of CHI, took the lead when they were working to acquire the property. With his partner, Carol Martin, he owned a rose nursery. He also worked as a regional planner. With these connections, he had many contacts with both wealthy people and government officials. These are very useful traits to have for a successful acquisition campaign.

Tony Law, in his role as the Hornby Island trustee, also worked hard to protect the land. He told me,

> On a cold, wet, windy, and cloudy day I met the potential partners—BC Parks, TLC, the Comox Valley Regional District, CHI, and the Islands Trust Fund (now Conservancy). The visitors got off the ferry shaking—not the best day to see the land. Fortunately, some years previously, I had walked the property with Bill Turner of TLC, and he raved about it. He went on to take a key role in working with Vance, so that he was able to take advantage of the federal government's Ecological Gifts Program in making a partial land donation. TLC also donated funds for an ecological inventory and appraisal of the proposed park, which were needed to move ahead.

With strong community support, CHI and the Hornby Island community raised $300,000 toward the acquisition. In 2004, after four attempts, they finally created the Mount Geoffrey Escarpment Park. Thanks to Conservancy Hornby Island's impetus and their dedicated fundraising and relationships with other partners, the stunning 170 hectares (420 acres) that occupy a major part of the southwestern coast of Hornby Island are now protected forever. With the adjoining Mount Geoffrey

Regional Nature Park and the connected Crown lands, this is now an extensive network of protected areas over all of Mount Geoffrey, with trails that weave through the area, some for bikes, some for walkers, and others for horseback riders.

Mount Geoffrey from the ferry between Denman and Hornby islands.

Jan Bevan, another director of the Conservancy at the time, was elated about the acquisition. "When I come home on the ferry in winter to Hornby, the whole side of the island is dark. I heave a big sigh of relief—we saved it!" After Jan and I looked through the files for the Mount Geoffrey project, she told me, "I have hope for the future because we did succeed, with so many tries and so many setbacks." She exclaimed, "Persistence was key!" In 1993, Jan replaced her partner, Robear LeBaron, as director on the CHI board when he was serving time for protesting at Clayoquot Sound—another Conservancy member related to the protests at Clayoquot!

Several years earlier, in 1989, the Comox Valley Regional District obtained a license of occupation over the adjacent 336 hectares (830 acres), establishing the Mount Geoffrey Regional Nature Park. It includes a mature Douglas-fir forest, coastal bluffs, and several small seasonal wetlands and creeks. In 1992 the Province agreed to transfer it under the Free Crown Land Grant program. By 2004 the land was finally transferred as a regional park.

The CVRD also obtained a permit to build and maintain the trails in the adjacent Crown lands. Their management plan states, "An extensive 22 km trail network stretches through Mount Geoffrey Nature Park. Add to that the Crown land and Escarpment Provincial Park trail networks and you have 50 km of trails. Mount Geoffrey Regional Nature Park, the Escarpment Park and adjacent Crown lands, together cover approximately 36 percent of Hornby Island."[11]

The two and half kilometre stretch of trail along the waterfront at the base of Mount Geoffrey is one of my most treasured walks along the shoreline of the Salish Sea. While moored at Ford Cove in my sailboat years ago, I often walked along the lower trail even before it was protected, heading for a shower and to do laundry at Shingle Spit. Soothed and inspired by the curving trunks of arbutus, large Douglas-fir, towering bluffs above, and occasional glimpses of mink and otter seen along the shore, I feel so grateful to the people of Hornby Island who cared so deeply and worked so hard to conserve this large extensive area for all people, for all time.

Conservation Covenants on Hornby island

Tom Knott, who initiated the local Conservancy, explained how he came to have a conservation covenant on his own land. He told me that he felt pressured by a neighbour who asked if he could cut some of the Garry oaks higher up on his land. "With many of the lots near me heavily logged, I've found myself the legal custodian of the last privately owned natural space near the end of the ridge—a forest corridor important to animals and plants." He added, "If I didn't protect it now, there could potentially be no refuge for these species after I'm gone."[12] In 2012, Tom registered a Natural Area Property Tax Exemption Program (NAPTEP) covenant on his 5.6 hectare (14 acre) property on Hornby Island through the Islands Trust Conservancy (ITC).[13]

> The Islands Trust's Natural Area Protection Tax Exemption Program (NAPTEP)[14] was created under the *Islands Trust Act* in 2002. The program applies to all the islands within the Islands Trust Area. The conservation covenant must be held by Islands Trust Conservancy (another conservancy can act as co-holder), and the covenant area must be at least 5 acres to apply. Generally, the covenant allows for a 65 percent annual reduction in property taxes on the covenanted area.

Another landowner in Tom's neighbourhood put a covenant on her 6.12 hectare (15.1 acre) property. The covenant restricts what they and future landowners can do on specific areas of the property, ideally protecting the ecosystems on the land forever. Tom exclaimed, "I'm very pleased with the way this is working out. I do have a slight exemption to the no-use clause because I can cut wood for firewood, under rules established by a forester."

The local Conservancy is registered on title as a second covenant holder on these two covenants. A covenant monitor comes every year to walk around and make sure the landholder has respected the covenant's restrictions, and other than natural progressions, the land is still being protected. Anna, who joined me during my interview with Tom, said, "It's very reassuring that the covenant is there, and watched carefully."

She also told me about the property next to these two where the owners had planned a covenant, but the realtor at the time suggested it would depreciate the land's value. There have been many studies undertaken to review this opinion.[15] For the neighbouring properties, multiple studies reveal that protected green space increases the value of surrounding properties.[16] The *Assessment Act* prevents BC Assessment from considering any additional impact to the assessed value of a property with a NAPTEP covenant. This is an unusual situation, as the assessed value remains the same, yet there is a 65 percent annual tax exemption applied to the assessed value of the covenanted area.

However, with the increased values of land today, and especially on larger properties, a conservation covenant that is not under the NAPTEP program may in fact impact the market value of the land, depending on the restrictions. Kate Emmings, the current manager of the Islands Trust Conservancy, explained that "over the last five years we've had covenants that have ranged in value from $315,000 to $1,265,000 (sizes of 4 hectares to 45 hectares with the size not always correlating to the high value.) In these cases, there is a federal program, the Ecological Gifts Program, which can eliminate the taxes generated from such a deemed disposition." Donating a conservation covenant to a land trust is a powerful way of protecting specific

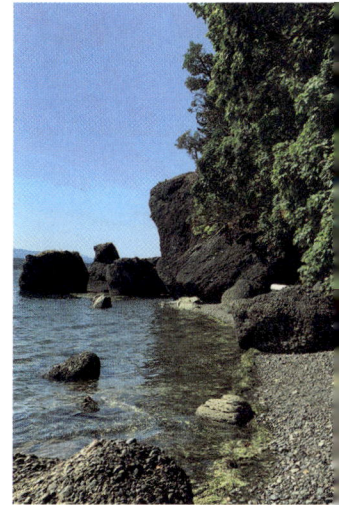

Sandstone and conglomerate rocks line the shoreline in Lambert Channel between Ford Cove and Shingle Beach.

areas on a property. However, it is essential that landholders seek professional tax advice to understand the programs a covenant could be registered under and its tax consequences.

Thanks to these dedicated local people, working with land trusts and conservancies, and regional and provincial parks staff, almost 36 percent of Hornby is now in park status.

Parks and Protected Lands on Hornby Island

Mount Geoffrey Regional Park: 336 ha	Mount Geoffrey Escarpment Park: 187 ha
Mount Geoffrey Crown Land: 400 ha Helliwell Provincial Park: 69 ha	Tribune Bay Provincial Park: 72 ha
Community Parks: 7 ha	Conservation covenants: 4 ha

Hornby Island: 2,996 ha	Total protected: 1,075 ha	36 percent protected

(23 percent protected if Mount Geoffrey Crown land is not included)

Current CHI Initiatives, Including Marine Protection

After all the successful conservation of terrestrial land on Hornby Island, a transition to the protection of the surrounding marine areas was a natural evolution. I met Grant Scott and Cath Gray from CHI during my 2021 trip. I walked up from where I was anchored at Tribune Bay to meet them at the local market. Grant Scott, CHI's president at that time, has a varied background in forestry, reforestation projects and conservation, land use planning, and treaty negotiations with First Nations. He was inspired to join Tony Quin and his wife Carol in saving what became the Mount Geoffrey Escarpment Park. This led him to join the Conservancy as a member, and later he became the president.

Cath Gray, who was the executive director at the time I met her, arrived on Hornby in 1988 with her partner, Mike. She was a web director for several magazines such as *Canadian Living* and *Canadian Gardening*. For many years she travelled to Toronto monthly. With her background, she knew how to get the word out, pull all the pieces together, and help move the organization forward in new directions.

As Grant explained, "We had big herring runs then that people saw directly. It's the last run on the coast. There used to be five major areas, but overfishing, mainly, then climate change has had an impact, and now this is the last one. It was so hugely dramatic every year in March for people here. So we decided to focus on the marine side of things." The herring fill the seas around the island with a luscious chalky blue milt full of sperm, which attracts the females to lay their eggs on the beaches, eelgrass, kelp, and rocks.

Cath's partner Mike Berman was on the CHI board, and had a legal background. Between the three of them they dreamed up a Marine Conservation Initiative. They created the *Hornby Island Marine Conservation Atlas*, using resources from local and marine knowledge holders. They hired a cartographer to assist with making maps. They held public gatherings to share the basic maps and the stories they told. Grant said, "We were surprised at how interested people on Hornby and elsewhere were in the herring run that happens every March, turning the ocean glacier-white."

CHI developed a strategy to change the laws and the politics around the herring fishery. Acquiring data from the Province and First Nations, they advanced a deep understanding about the herring, both the year round and migratory schools, their life cycles, and the spring fishery—which is all about getting the roe (eggs). Unbelievably only 10 percent is used for human consumption, with the other 90 percent ground up for fish farm food, livestock and pet food, and fertilizer.

Thanks to archaeological evidence and local knowledge, we now know herring was once the primary source of food from the Salish Sea. Archaeology can really help build a baseline, along with a historical record of species. Dr. Ian McKechnie from the University of Victoria, a specialist in zooarchaeology (the archaeology of animal bones) and historical ecology, found that herring was once the backbone of the coast's abundant economy—for both humans and as the main sustenance for a network of species.

Herring fishing during the opening in Lambert Channel between Hornby and Denman islands with sea lions and humans both vying for the catch. SIMON AUGER

> Recent research by McKechnie and colleagues showed that in archaeological sites from Washington State to SE Alaska, herring has been hyperabundant for millennia. In archaeological sites in the Salish Sea, herring bones can represent 80–100 percent of the fish bones present in middens. Yet overharvesting of herring began over 100 years ago on the BC coast, reaching its peak in the mid-20th century. Management of herring fisheries on the south coast takes place in the context of a species that was depleted in numbers largely before data began to be systematically collected.[17]

CHI is working hard to advocate for change, asking other local conservancies and scientists to support their call for a review of current priorities and policies and a Marine Conservation Plan for the waters surrounding Hornby Island.

As part of their campaign, they invited experts from the larger Salish Sea region to a special event, called HerringFest. Cath explained their approach. "We see it as a celebration of the wonder of it—not government is bad. We went through a phase of focusing on shutting the herring fishery down. Now we want to work with First Nations and recover it—make it positive rather than scream, 'shut her down, shut her down!' You get one shot with the media and that's it. We call it a Herring Recovery Plan. Gord Johns, our MP and Fin Donnelly, a former MP, have been promoting it in Ottawa."

The atlas and HerringFest have drawn huge attention to herring as a focal species. Grant described it as akin to the Spirit Bear in the Great Bear Rainforest. Drawing on Grant's experience with First Nations in the '90s, CHI started working with the W̱SÁNEĆ Nation, who haven't had a herring run in decades. Some Indigenous Knowledge Keepers joined in on some of the educational sessions of what is now the annual HerringFest. They have added an art show, with live poetry, songs, and guided boat tours to take people out to be among the herring and their predators. "Adding the close-up, in-person and the visual elements," Cath explained, "creates a great educational event and fundraiser."

In 2019 Bob Turner, a videographer and board member of the Bowen Island Conservancy, made a remarkable video of the herring spawn off Hornby Island.[18] It highlights the amazing number of different species that gather for this once a year event, which feeds almost everything from tiny shore crabs to eagles and sea lions.

Thousands of marine birds gather for the event. "Aggregations of 30,000–60,000 waterbirds occur each year during herring spawn and over 100,000 were observed in March 2019."[19] Some notable bird species include the western grebe and harlequin duck, both whose numbers have declined significantly in the past decade. The area is designated as the K'omoks IBA (Important Bird Area), which includes the former Comox Valley IBA, Baynes Sound, and Lambert Channel IBA areas.

Personally, I'm really worried about today's absence of the herring runs around the Salish Sea. I first moved to Lasqueti Island from Salt Spring Island in 2009 and saw my first herring spawn in 2012. I photographed herring galore on the beach near my home in Boat Cove. Since then, I've not seen any here. Over in French Creek, on Vancouver Island, where I catch the ferry to Lasqueti, the beaches those first years were covered with herring eggs over a foot thick. I watched locals come with wheelbarrows and bags to get them for their gardens. Lasqueti's resident archaeologist Dana Lepofsky told me that in 2016 the herring in French Creek drew "thousands of sea birds (Franklin's gulls [mostly], glaucous-winged gulls, dunlins, and western sandpipers) munching on herring eggs washed up on the beach. This is four weeks after the initial herring spawn—showing us again just how important herring are to our marine ecosystems."[20]

Cormorants are one of many seabirds that depend on the herring for their survival in spring. SIMON AGER

In spring of 2023 I saw no sign of the eggs on the beaches at French Creek. Similarly, the turquoise waters that reveal a herring spawn around Hornby Island were much smaller than in prior years. As noted in the Mayne and Saturna island chapters, protecting the ocean and its marine life is significantly more challenging than protecting terrestrial areas, with their land titles available to acquire in our current system of private property.

CHI has identified three designated Marine Conservation Areas around Hornby. "The purpose of the Conservation Areas are to make people aware of the high marine values both below and above the surface of the ocean, and to enforce regulations to preserve the marine ecosystems."[21] One of these is the vast area of Helliwell Park, now 2,872 hectares (7,097 acres), which runs all the way from Flora Islet on the southeast side of the island around to Maude Reef in Lambert Channel.

BC Parks notes that this area, which includes all of the southern waters of the island from low water mark out to 80 metres, is managed as a Marine Protected Area with commercial fishery closures of anchovy, surf perch, pile perch, sea cucumber, octopus, scallop, squid, red urchin, Pacific oyster, and green urchin. They also state that local divers have implemented a voluntary closure on all marine life. However, there is still an allowed fishery of transitory species such as salmon (when permitted) but not territorial species on the bottom such as rockfish. There is a Rockfish Conservation Area between Maude Reef and Savoie Rocks inside the Lambert Channel on the west side of Hornby Island. All Rockfish Conservation Areas are closed to recreational fishing including halibut and salmon.[22] However, commercial fisheries of some species are still allowed. Anna, whose son is a diver, reported that "unfortunately there is no one patrolling this marine component and the rockfish population is declining rapidly." CHI, like other conservancies including Galiano, are actively working to educate local fisherfolk about the dwindling fish by disseminating educational posters at the marina and at other related locations.

Hornby has two salmon bearing streams, including Beulah Creek which leads to Little Tribune Bay. In 2019, they supported a project constructing a series of rock riffles, spawning platforms, and pools, and added large woody debris to allow the small coho fry, three-spined stickleback, and cutthroat trout to have better access to areas, adapt to seasonal high-water flows, and contain more water during the summer. The local Hornby Island Community School and other supporters planted native seedlings along the restored creek.

Beyond marine protection, the Hornby Island Conservancy has another major initiative. Their Trees 4 Tomorrow project is a tree planting and educational initiative across the Salish Sea region—to help fight the effects of climate change. Choosing sub-species that they hope will be better adapted to the changing climate, they acquired and then planted trees on Hornby, Galiano, Denman, Gabriola, and in the Comox Valley. In 2022 they planted Garry oaks, in partnership with the Garry Oak Meadow Preservation Society, a species that can for now withstand the droughts we are experiencing. They also held their first ForestFest in October 2022, and are planning them annually in future.

Conservancy Hornby Island has a strong vision for the future: a Herring Recovery Program put in place; increased orcas and salmon; collaboration with First Nations; and planting thousands of trees—with a focus on climate change. Along with forage fish surveys, bat surveys, videos, and a strong social media presence, this Conservancy has helped acquire and protect land for the future and instilled in their community an awareness of the fragile and unique place that they are so lucky to live in.

CHAPTER NINE

DENMAN ISLAND
Conservation after Logging and Lawsuits

*"The spirit of resistance and refusal to accept the kind of exploitation that
was going on all around us contributed a lot to these little local actions."*
DES KENNEDY

MY ARRIVAL ON DENMAN ISLAND FELT A LITTLE LIKE CHEATING as I opted for
taking the ferry from Hornby Island instead of coming directly with my sailboat.
One thing Denman Island does not have is anchorages. I walked up past the string of
Hornby bound cars lined up the hill. I felt sorry for Denman islanders having to deal
with all these cars heading to Hornby on a daily basis. On this note, I was intrigued
by a recent newspaper story about seventy-five to one hundred protesters blocking a
contractor from clear-cutting one hundred trees in an area adjacent to the terminal
for a proposed expansion of the loading area. Here on Denman, islanders have been
successfully protesting the cutting of trees for decades.

John Millen, a long-time director of the Denman Conservancy Association (DCA)
greeted me in his electric car. As on the other islands, many of these conservationists
are among the first to embrace these new electric cars. Little did I realize then that
this bearded, soft spoken, neatly dressed gentleman had fought and won court battles,
and spent years negotiating with multiple parties over acquiring a single property—all
in the interest of conserving a bit of land for the public. Despite some local naysay-
ers, the Denman Conservancy Association along with their activist community are
pioneers in protecting land and fresh water on their island.

John drove me from the terminal to a 1910 heritage school building—the office
and meeting space for the DCA. There I met with three other founders of the Denman
Conservancy, each as formidable as John. This large open school room was stacked
with books they had collected to raise funds for their land trust. I was pleased to see
that the full collection of seven Denman maps created for the *Atlas of the Islands in the
Salish Sea* in 2000 were hanging on the walls. Over the course of the morning, this
foursome regaled me with stories of their local and powerful Conservancy.

Des Kennedy, a well-known award-wining author of numerous books explained,
"Many of us were involved in the Strathcona Park blockades in 1989. Denman provided half the arrestees. I was also in the Clayoquot blockades, which had the largest
number of protesters at the time. That spirit of resistance and refusal to accept the
kind of exploitation that was going on all around us contributed a lot to these little
local actions as well." Des's book, *The Garden Club's Kumquot Campaign*, is a hilarious
and brilliant account of our culture's relationship to the natural world in a semi-
fictional novel about the protests.

John interjected, "I think Clayoquot caught a lot of attention, but on Denman there was a strong environmental ethic prior to that. Weldwood started logging the Komas Bluffs and was stopped by Denman islanders in 1984. People on the island were concerned about forest practices as early as that."

Anne de Cosson, another founding director, explained that the Clayoquot arrests were formative. Her husband was arrested in Clayoquot too. Like many of those who went on to found land trusts on Galiano and Salt Spring, these actions on public lands outside their island moved them to found their own local conservancies, where they had the power to make change.

Anne, an art historian, moved to Denman in 1979, where she became an avid gardener, planting apple trees, and then helping start the island's Organic Producers' Association.

A neighbouring property, called Lindsay Dickson, drew her in. It was one of the oldest farms on the island with large old growth trees and an intact forest. "I was just interested in the beauty of the property next door. It was just talk at first. A few people said, 'let's try to buy it, and sell off a portion, as a way of purchasing the land.' That was how I came to the Conservancy. Coming here, being near the beach, with the amazing property next door, it expanded my thinking about the possibilities. It also raised a fear that it could be sold and all chopped up. I remember a neighbour and trustee telling me, 'trying to purchase it won't work. It's too not Denman Island.' So protecting some land somehow all started to become very important and more real."

Des added, "Here in the '70s, it was like paradise. A relatively undeveloped population on an island, 30 percent owned by Weldwood in tree farm, but they couldn't get their logs off. The ferry wouldn't work, and they had no water access. Things took a radical turn in the '80s. The ferry got bigger, and they went and did stupid logging on the Komas Bluffs. The one that shouldn't have been logged most was done first. All that land we used to gather mushrooms in, and hike and bike through, was not our land. Then we discovered all that land was subdividable too!"

Mounting pressure on the island and a population boom through the '80s and '90s was the turning point. Prior to the Denman Conservancy's formation, the Ratepayers Association handled public issues, such as negotiating the setback of 50 acres of the Beaver Pond, a wetland area that was set aside through lobbying the government. The Ratepayers also started up a Forestry Committee. However, their lobbying for policy changes turned out to be fruitless. As on Salt Spring and Galiano islands, the regional government with their mandate to "Preserve and Protect," had no say over how forest lands were being logged. Nor did the Ratepayers have the ability to protect the land, not having charitable status or the mechanism to acquire property.

Anne drew from another formative experience. "I got more aware of the land around me, having also travelled in India. I had seen that every inch of India seemed to be used and overused. I came back and realized what an amazing thing we have on Vancouver Island as a whole, and Denman Island especially—with pockets of old growth forests. I feared that we were all going to start polluting and changing the land. There were very good farmers who were taking care of their land, in an old-style, small scale. We have more arable land and more water than most of the other Gulf Islands. So it's a special island."

Past and current DCA directors that I interviewed on a warm summer day in 2021. From left: Des Kennedy, Jenny Balke, John Millen, and Anne de Cosson.

There was one more catalyst to the founding of the Denman Conservancy Association. In the late '80s, the Province published a "Crown Lands Opportunity Study," which included options for selling these lands to the highest bidder. At that time, 2–3 percent of Denman was in parkland, and 5 percent was in Crown land. As Des explained, "the Ratepayers battled against the alienation of those lands, but there was an overall sense that if we don't get more land in conservation on this island, we are really, really in trouble."

In response to the threat that Denman's Crown lands would be sold, Des and another stalwart director Patti Willis produced their own report on the island's Crown lands. "This woke islanders up to how little land there really was in conservation," Des added. When the government's report stated that the highest and best use was housing on the island, the Forest Committee pointed out that most of it was water. Ken Millard from Galiano helped them initially address some of these myths, including that the Weldwood lands were open for public access.

With tensions mounting, Des decided to take action. "My partner Sandy and I ended up having a little project to purchase additional acreage around Pickles Road pond. At the time, it was just individuals in the community doing it, but the real impetus for starting the Conservancy were Anne and Susan-Marie Yoshihara, who went to a conference in Richmond and learned about US land trusts. We said, let's try to do that then."

Many people were at that conference, stimulating the formation of many land trusts in BC. Ron Pither, with his West Coast Islands Conservancy, was at the Richmond conference too. The Denman group invited him over to the island to help them set up their land trust. Bill Turner of TLC The Land Conservancy of BC told them they could do anything they wanted. Both Bill and Ron were founding directors of the Land Trust Alliance of BC. Anne added, "Galiano was ahead of us. They were our mentors, but it wasn't common, and we were doing it!"

The Formation of the DCA and Protection of the Inner Island Nature Reserve

The Denman Conservancy Association (DCA) was formed as a society in 1989–90 with a mandate to acquire land. The focus in the beginning was both the large Lindsay Dickson property on the island and what they called the Pickles Road project. The Pickles Marsh area was identified by islanders starting in 1977 and through the early 1980s as an area needing conservation. This 9.4 hectare (23.2 acre) property is located in central Denman Island south of Chickadee Lake. It is made up of two pieces of land, connecting to a long, narrow wetland property held by BC Parks.

Shortly after their founding, in 1991 the fledgling Conservancy raised the needed funds and acquired part of the Pickles Marsh, which became known as the Inner Island Nature Reserve. This was the first property protected by the DCA, and they donated it to the Islands Trust Fund (Conservancy). The Nature Reserve became the first of the Island Trust Conservancy's now over thirty-four Nature Reserves on the islands. The DCA and the Nature Conservancy of Canada, the national land trust active on some of the other islands, registered a conservation covenant over the Inner Island Nature Reserve land.

Jenny Balke, the fourth founding director I met that day, is a veterinarian and biologist. She, along with others of the DCA, created the first management plan for the property, and then revised it in 2020. These management plans generally include the history of the place and how it came to be protected. They also include descriptions of ecological attributes, the cultural context, connectivity to other areas, and the management issues that need to be considered.

The Inner Island Nature Reserve includes part of Pickles Marsh, as well as three connected creeks. The Islands Trust Conservancy described the context that makes the nature reserve an outstanding candidate for protection: "Located within 640 hectares (1580 acres) of protected forest land, the Reserve is a critical link connecting large areas of forest, wetland habitat, and the drainage system of a broad freshwater catchment area."[1]

Jenny was initially drawn to the island because of its vibrant community.

The Inner Island Nature Reserve on Denman Island, DCA's first conservation campaign, transferred to the Islands Trust Conservancy as their first nature reserve. JOHN MILLEN

There were these incredible powerful people, like Anne leading the whole organic thing. There are the people in the Conservancy, the hermitage, and then there's Des, a very dynamic leader, a great speaker, and Susan-Marie, an incredible researcher. There were other people, such as Jim Bolen, who started Greenpeace. In a meeting with Dave Fraser, Jim Bolen stood and said, "I'm here to speak for the seals." I thought I'd died and gone to heaven. I had this incredible feeling that Denman's people were really different. I remember the forestry committee folks had a battle going, whether you could save the land by managing it, or if you had to own it. Do you try and control people or do you control the land? I wasn't sure what camp I sat in, but I wanted to do the education part.

Protecting the Commercial Forest Lands

In 1995, Weldwood, owner of 30 percent of Denman Island, created a stir when it suddenly announced that it had sold all its coastal properties. This included its Denman acreages, ~1,538 hectares (3,800 acres), which were sold to Hancock Timber Resource Group, a subsidiary of the Boston based John Hancock insurance giant. The Ratepayers executive and the Denman Forestry Initiative met with the Hancock Group three times in hopes of buying the land for a community forest. However, Hancock announced that clear cutting and thinning would commence in November 1995.[2] Hancock's representatives met with some of the DCA directors and with some of the people from the Pacific Marine Heritage Legacy (PMHL) fund, who persuaded Hancock that the two areas, the Railway Grade Marsh and Komas Bluffs, had significant environmental values. But the PMHL fund was focused on the south islands at the time, so DCA continued discussions about registering conservation covenants on these areas. But then "in 1997 Hancock abruptly sold its holdings to Northland Development who in turn sold them to Mike Jenks (4064 Investments Ltd)," Des said. "Included in these land sale agreements was the requirement to register covenants on both the marsh and the bluffs."

Both the Islands Trust and the DCA initiated legal battles to protect the forests and trees on these private lands. The Islands Trust was denied the ability to enforce their development permit areas, which would require some level of sustainable forestry. Yet, the little local Denman Conservancy successfully sued and settled out of court against Jenks and 4064 for cutting in the areas that were within the proposed covenant area, established in the sale agreement.

The whole community wanted control of the logging that was going on. Louise Bell, a former Denman Island trustee, was writing a book about the issues but unfortunately died before completing it. In summary, the Local Trust committee (Trustees from Denman Island) went to court to uphold five bylaws they had enacted to restrict logging, without a development permit, on private lands. In 2000 and again in 2001 the Supreme Court of BC denied their case. "The British Columbia Court of Appeal held that the local government on Denman Island (the Denman Island Local Trust Committee) did not have the statutory authority to regulate the cutting or removal of trees on private lands on Denman Island."[3]

The Islands Trust's mandate to preserve and protect the islands was thus decapitated by the Province's unwillingness to give authority to the rural, regional government to regulate tree cutting on private lands. Many hearty souls have attempted to change or appeal this lack of control of massive deforestation on the islands, so far without success.[4] This very issue has surfaced again recently in an overall review and revision of the Islands Trust's Policy Statements. On these small local islands, there are still people who are so fearful of government "overreach," including a few local representatives elected by islanders, that objections continue to this day against regulating any kind of oversight over logging on the islands. On the other hand, there remains considerable animosity over why the Islands Trust has been given a mandate to preserve and protect the islands, without the legal authority to do so. This untenable reality is yet another reason for the conservation of land by land trusts. Their ability to register a voluntary conservation covenant on the land that runs with the title into the future, or to buy or acquire it outright through sale or donation, is a saving grace for the islands!

Des remarked that this was a lesson learned. "We won some and lost some. The Provincial government is not interested in having curtailment on how logging happens in this province. The one we didn't win was the ability of the Islands Trust to have significant input into logging on private land. The Trust spent so much money fighting for that. But the sad truth is any municipality has more control over tree cutting than the Islands Trust."

However, some success was achieved by the local Conservancy with the notation for registering a conservation covenant on the sale agreement that Jenks signed. "In July of 2000 Jenks began logging in the Railway Grade Marsh proposed covenant area. In response to the ensuing uproar, Hancock and Comox Timber Ltd. concluded an assignment of rights to DCA, allowing DCA to sue and settle out of court, claiming damages for intrusion into the Railway Marsh system." Des explained, "This assignment of rights carried forward and was negotiated with one of Jenks's 4064 partners, and eventually led to DCA acquiring what is now known as the Settlement Lands."

Denman Island Provincial Parks

Due to the sale from Hancock to Northland and then to 4064 Investments Ltd. in the late 1990s, Jenks and 4064 now owned 30 percent of the land on Denman. John described the deal that eventually became the Denman Provincial Park in the north and central area of the island. "Jenks's lands were almost all zoned for forestry, one house per 160 acres. The developer to whom Jenks sold wanted to do more development than what would have been permitted. With significant help from interested Denman islanders, the developer made a deal with the Province to create the Denman Island Provincial Park by trading some of their land for density. The Province put all these blocks they had as Crown land into the park, especially the wetland (Pickles Marsh adjacent to Inner Island Nature Reserve), so by 2010 they had created this large 561 hectare (1,386 acre) Provincial Park."

Another provincial park, on the north side of the island, is Fillongley Provincial Park. Previously it was privately owned by George Beadnell, who settled here from England at the turn of century. He donated the 26 hectare (66.7 acre) property to the Province in 1953 on the condition that he be allowed to live there until he died and that they name the park Fillongley. His request for a life estate was honoured, and he was buried on the property in 1958. Little George Creek is a salmon spawning stream that runs through the park. The park includes Beadnell's imported deciduous trees and native wildflowers in an area once the site of a bowling green.

Settlement Lands and Covenants on Railway Grade Marsh and Komas Bluffs

It took six long years and a series of tedious legal negotiations to remedy the rampant cutting of trees in the Railway Grade Marsh area, originally identified for covenants when they were owned by Hancock.[5]

The Marsh area and the Komas Bluffs were both ecologically sensitive areas that Hancock had originally agreed to protect.

Denman Conservancy Association v. 4064 Investments Ltd.: A Summary of the Case History

Denman Conservancy Association (DCA) sued 4064 Investments Ltd. for breach of a land purchase contract. DCA asserted that 4064 had been obliged by the contract to place covenants on two areas and, having not done so, proceeded to aggressively log one of those areas. After six years the parties settled this case on November 6, 2006. As a result, DCA holds conservation covenants on two large, ecologically valuable areas on Denman Island and has title to an additional 156 acres of land. The Settlement Land includes a significant wetland and is an important link in a network of already preserved lands and adjacent Crown lands. The constant support of the Environmental Dispute Resolution Fund (EDRF) since August 2000 has been a major factor in sustaining DCA's volunteers through their years of struggle with the case.[6]

The ~63 hectares (156 acres) of the Settlement Lands are surrounded by the Denman Island Provincial Park. The Inner Island Nature Reserve is situated within the bottom southern area of the park. Even though the Settlement Lands had been logged, this connectivity between different conservation areas is an important way to provide protected corridors for wildlife, forests, and streams. This mix of Inner Island Nature Reserve, DCA's Settlement Lands, and the Denman Island Provincial Park have undergone extensive restoration work over the years.

Railway Grade Marsh is an ecologically sensitive area that DCA went to court to protect. JOHN MILLEN

Jenny explained that because the Province obtained title that included the Railway Grade Marsh, the covenanted area is now in the park. It is unusual to have a conservation covenant on a provincial park, because the Province usually refuses any fettering of their lands—another reason that many donors choose to give their lands to a land trust/conservancy.

She also explained that the Komas Bluffs is in the process of being divided into 4 hectare (10 acre) parcels. The bluff stretches for three kilometres on the eastern edge of the island, facing the Salish Sea. With desirable locations like this, I can see why they fought so hard to defend the conservation covenants. Jenny told me that it's a lot of work to monitor covenants on ten parcels instead of one. She put a positive spin on that though, by saying, "It's good for education, because you get to bug them about the continuing need for stewardship."

"A number of us from the Conservancy went with Jenks and walked the Bluffs," Des said. "Jenks asked if the Conservancy would endorse an application to put fifty lots along the bluffs in exchange for a large inland acreage (before he'd logged it.) I said, it's our policy not to lobby or get involved in development procedures. But when I look at the devastation he wrought, I think maybe we should have said yes. And there may be a lot more trees standing, but there is that feeling of trade-offs." This question of negotiating with developers through supporting trade-offs is a common discussion within land trusts.

The Pentlatch, Qualicum, K'omoks, and Sliammon people had temporary or permanent summer camps on Denman Island for activities such as hunting deer, fishing for salmon and herring, and harvesting clams, oysters, and herring roe. Interestingly, one of the largest and most complex pre-colonial fish traps was unearthed by an earthquake in 1946 at neighbouring Union Bay on Vancouver Island.[7] Tragically, the Pentlatch people were one of many First Nations that were devastated by both the 1780s smallpox epidemic and then a second wave of smallpox in the 1860s that killed between 50 to 90 percent of the population. Today, Taystay'ich is one of the Indigenous names for what is now called Denman Island.

Lindsay Dickson Nature Reserve

European settlers arrived on Denman and the surrounding Comox Valley in the 1860s. In 1878 John Graham took up land on what became the Lindsay Dickson property.[8] The Grahams were from New Brunswick and made their living by a combination of logging and farming. The property was hand logged in the early 1900s. The family also created a small orchard and ran a small dairy. Most of their land was left untouched.

Many islanders described the property, with its very large trees and forest, as having a quality of permanence to it. It had been in the hands of the Dickson family for over one hundred years. Dr. Lindsay Dickson and his wife visited the island while on a trip from England, and he took a fancy to the place. He built a new house and lived here in retirement for a number of years before turning the farm over to his son Gerald and returning to England. Later Gerald, his wife Laura, and their youngest son Clive returned and farmed in a small way. Clive continued to live in the old home that was built around 1920.[9]

Anne de Cosson and many other Denman islanders wanted to protect some of the Lindsay Dickson lands since before the founding of the Conservancy. The concept of establishing a nature reserve at this site was originally proposed to the owners in the late 1980s by the Residents and Ratepayers Association of Denman Island. Protecting the Lindsay Dickson forest was one of the initial goals of the Denman Conservancy Association after its formation in 1990–91.

Des described the onerous negotiations that led to the Lindsay Dickson Nature Reserve in 2001.

> Little did the original board members know that the conservation of the Lindsay Dickson property would take ten years of dedicated and often frustrating work. In 1993 the new owner expressed a tentative willingness to sell or trade the land. Scientists, journalists, funding agencies, park representatives, government representatives, and many other interested parties were shown parts of the forest and all expressed support. The project became an exercise in patience and perseverance as the owner and the government negotiated endlessly over the value of the property and lands for trade. Islanders raised over two hundred thousand dollars. The Denman Conservancy, supported by the island as a whole, acted as a go-between, mediator, and cheerleader.

The ten-year-long negotiations included successful discussions with six different environment ministers for its protection. These negotiations with government agencies took place amidst talk of land trades, changing owners, and clearing of some large trees. Eventually ~4 hectares (10 acres) were subdivided off including the family residence with its waterfront. There were also a significant number of prime Douglas-fir trees which were selectively logged from the western half of the property before the purchase.

John reflected, "It is not all we had wished for but it is a fine conservation legacy for the Island and the Province." This early conservation success was initiated by the DCA, yet John said, "In the end the Province completed the negotiations, days before the NDP government lost the election, transferring the title to the Islands Trust Conservancy (Fund)." The Lindsay Dickson Nature Reserve is now a 52 hectare (134 acre) property with a conservation covenant held by DCA. Further, the Conservancy undertook an extensive management plan, and to this day, manage the reserve for the Islands Trust Conservancy.

One noteworthy aspect of these negotiations involved the lands that were in the Agricultural Land Reserve (ALR). All lands in the ALR where land trusts and landowners agree to register a conservation covenant must be approved by the Agricultural Commission before it can be registered on title. When the Agricultural Land Commission staff came to assess the lands, they were impressed by the age of the trees—some were over one hundred years old. Consequently, DCA ended up with an unrestricted covenant on the part of the property on which these large trees grew.

Winter Wren Wood—The Small Yet Crucial Success

In 2000, in the midst of negotiating with 4064 Investments, a small 2.4 hectare property at the edge of Chickadee Lake came up for sale. During our tour, John took me to see Winter Wren Wood, which leads to the west side of Chickadee Lake. The site straddles a public road and provides traditional access to the lake. Though it was mid-summer, the coolness and quiet of the area made me feel sheltered as we walked down the trail crossing the marshy site where people can launch rowboats and canoes.

The tenacious directors were hesitant to raise funds to purchase this property for $85,000, in the midst of other negotiations. Yet, its public community benefit brought considerable support and attention.

This is the first property that DCA chose to own outright, in contrast to the Lindsay Dickson and Inner Island Reserves. The DCA holds the title, while the Islands Trust Conservancy holds the conservation covenant. According to John, there were some early lessons associated with its purchase. At times people have been found camping out in the area, so they found a local warden who keeps an eye on things. John told me it gets lots of use from students and other islanders, and with its riparian ecology, it supports scientific research and public workshops. Situated adjacent to the Denman Island Provincial Park, it is an important ecological link between two sections of the park to Chickadee Lake.

Morrison Marsh Nature Reserve

During colonial settlement, farmers often drained marshes and swamps to create fields for agriculture or pasture. Many of the areas in the south end of Denman are very wet, and the Morrison Marsh property, immediately adjacent to Boyle Point Park, shows signs of this type of activity.[10] The property was logged by Weldwood in 1979 and replanted. In 1985, Ducks Unlimited Canada, with provincial parks staff and shoreline residents, installed a variable crest weir and outlet to control water levels in the marsh.[11] However, a beaver dam has maintained higher water levels ever since.

DCA identified the marsh and its surrounding forest as an area needing protection in their 1999 Island Legacy Project. In 2000, the property was purchased from 4064 Investments by a private owner with the intention of placing two conservation covenants over the property, one for conservation and the other to allow for residential use. The DCA obtained a grant to help with the cost of preparing the conservation covenants, baseline studies, mapping, and surveys. However, with the use of the Section 99 subdivision process only available at the time through the Islands Trust Fund

The Winter Wren Wood—a small yet crucial success.

(Conservancy), the owner gifted the larger section of the property to the ITC. DCA holds a conservation covenant on the nature reserve land and, since March 2008, they have been managers of the reserve.

The Morrison Marsh Nature Reserve is 51.73 hectares (127.77 acres) and provides a network of low impact trails leading to the adjoining Boyle Point Park. As a large key wetland, it is home to a number of endangered and threatened species. The DCA has been working to put a culvert under the road at the end of Morrison Marsh because the downstream wetland has been drying up since its remaining headwaters and Graham Lake are used for domestic water supply. This would help the painted turtles, and other amphibians who have been seen attempting to cross the road to get to the other side.

Central Park

Denman Island is approximately the same size as Manhattan Island, New York. New York City has a Central Park of 340 hectares (840 acres). The directors of the Denman Conservancy wanted to connect everything up, from the vicinity of the Old School to Chickadee Lake to create something of a similar size. That would be five quarter sections all in conservation or park status, ~800 acres. The section that DCA acquired from Jenks and his 4064 Investments was at the south end of the new Denman Island Provincial Park, directly in the centre of the island. It had just been logged, though it was reported by these land trust directors that it wasn't exactly clear-cut. John said, "If they couldn't make a buck off a tree, they left it." This is an example of conserving lands for local community needs, rather than based on typical larger conservation priorities, often prioritized by national or provincial agencies. One of the Conservancy's directors decided to buy it, so it could be acquired expeditiously. John told me, "She raised the bulk of the money and we paid her back. So we fundraised enough to repay her, which took about three years."

John took me through Denman's Central Park, where I noticed some trees growing back, good trails, and wetlands. Because it was late August, the ponds were looking dry—right down to the bottom. John explained that Denman Island has all these streaky wetlands throughout. The old logging roads have been turned into trails. John explained that along the property's Beaufort View path, one can see all of Denman Island and, on the western horizon, the Beaufort Range.

Louise Bell, a long-time Islands Trustee, approached the DCA directors with a request to create a green cemetery site at Central Park. Green burial grounds have been gaining popularity. "One of things we said when we started campaigning to purchase Central Park was that this was one possible use for it," John said. One hectare from Central Park was donated by DCA to the Denman Island Memorial Society in 2010 for a natural burial cemetery. "The idea overall is as the cemetery fills up, it is allowed to return to a forest. The layout of the burial area is supposed to last one hundred years, which is about right the way its filling up. There is a covenant on it which ensures that the land can only be used as a natural burial cemetery, and it describes protection measures such as only allowing native plants and requiring the retention of some old growth stumps. The idea is

These sentinels mark the entrance to the Green Cemetery lands within Central Park.

to be able get a much more rapid colonization of the area (where the stumps are) because they will lead to more regeneration."

As part of John's tour of the island's protected sites, we walked through this area. I was captivated by the three large wooden statues at the entrance, looking to me like angels or guardians. The low-impact effect of no headstones, large stumps, and the curving memorial structure with mounted plaques in the central area, made it feel like a sacred memorial ground. I looked at the first plaque in the second line, and saw the name of Louise Bell, who had recently died, responsible for the cemetery's creation.

In 2021, the Denman Conservancy finally met its goal to protect 800 acres (~324 hectares) of land.[12] It was a huge accomplishment, as Jenny explained. "What these incredibly dynamic people were willing to take on, especially with the Conservancy! So many people said, 'no you can't do that,' and everything they said—'can't do it, never been done before'—and now everything is done!"

The Valens' Brook Nature Reserve

Starting with Jenny Balke's vision of inspiring more landowners to protect areas along a stream, four generous landowners donated portions of their properties to the Islands Trust Conservancy.

These landowners used a simplified subdivision process to donate portions of their land along Valens' Brook, a precious salmon bearing stream with lush sword ferns which runs through mature forest into Baynes Sound. In 2012 and 2019, thanks to the generosity of Dr. Kal Holsti, Marilyn Wan, Luise Hermanutz, and David Innes, a corridor of protected areas now runs along Valens' Brook into Baynes Sound.

Pickles Waterfall Wetland/Raven Forest Lands

Shortly after my 2021 visit, the Denman Conservancy acquired Pickles Waterfall Wetland, another ~32 hectares (80 acres) of land for $1 million from Raven Forest Products Ltd. It was in important acquisition as this wetland provides habitat for at least five species at risk, plus cougars and other larger mammals which have been seen in the area. Des remarked, "Securing this conservation land rounds out a series of conservation campaigns and land acquisitions that spans the entire thirty-year life of Denman Conservancy Association. Contiguous conservation lands now extend from DCA's Central Park northward to Chickadee Lake and the main bulk of Denman Island Provincial Park."[13]

The Pickles Waterfall Wetland area was acquired with the assistance of the Government of Canada through the Natural Heritage Conservation Program, part of Canada's Nature Fund, and the Provincial Habitat Conservation Trust Foundation's Acquisition Grant, as well as DCA's Acquisition Fund, a grant from Islands Trust Conservancy's Opportunity Fund, in-kind support from Nature Conservancy of Canada, and funds generously provided by DCA members and supporters including Denman Island Chocolate and the Denman Climate Action Network.

Stewardship on Private Lands

The tenacity of the Denman Conservancy in protecting lands by acquiring them is matched by their ability to convince islanders to practice good stewardship on their own lands. John showed me a beautiful art piece near the community hall with its electric car charging station. The fern like sculpture includes over 150 names of people on the island who have taken the stewardship pledge. Jenny Balke is a passionate crusader who knows how to mobilize community awareness and education together with stewardship of the land. She told me how this successful project came about.

> Stewardship is very important—knowing how to live on the land and share the land with all the other species that have a right to be here, and need to be here. We did this big stewardship project for two years, modelled from the Cowichan Community Land Trust. We walked with landowners and talked about all the values on their land, and we held a number of workshops over two years. This covered over 1,158 acres! People wrote a volunteer stewardship pledge, making a map showing areas they were using and areas for conservation. This was right during the major logging. People were blocking roads, and we were running around—oh stewardship! Some people thought it was good to have something other than a battle going on.

The Stewardship Pledge program is the DCA's way of honouring landowners who care for native species by adapting their land use plans for the mutual benefit of all. The removal of the forests over the years on Denman Island resulted in the loss of myriads of forest dwelling species. Instead, dry shrubs, open spaces, and wet meadows resulted in the proliferation and immigration of sun lovers and open land species. With this change came the emergence of a once-thought extirpated butterfly in Canada called the Taylor's checkerspot (Cspot).[14] In 2005 biologists were surprised by the emergence of this typical Garry oak meadow species and with it even more rare meadow species—growing to eighteen meadow species at risk found on Denman Island. The Meadow Stewardship Program grew with the charismatic Cspot as their flagship species.

The Denman Conservancy Association— Leadership into the Future

All land trusts require financial and operational support to flourish. The DCA has come up with some very creative fundraising ideas. Their Home and Garden Tour has been an annual fundraiser that draws people both on island and from across the region. Initiated by Sandy and Des, it has become the sustaining fundraiser for the DCA. Des said that it has held on for years and made thousands of dollars. "You get 1,500-plus people coming through. We talk to a lot of people, and all the proceeds go to the island Conservancy. They get to see properties and homes that reflect a conservation ethic. We don't tend to feature the multi-million dollar houses that are popping up. We tend to feature the homes that grow out of the earth—my god here's a different way of living. We charge twenty dollars now for the weekend, and you can use your ticket at any time."

Jenny added that the Home and Garden Tour helps raise both money and awareness. Now they also have book sales at the Blackberry Fair each year which brings in

Creative Stewardship plaque sign outside the local community hall. It acknowledges the many landowners who have committed to stewardship actions on their own land.

Taylor's checkerspot butterflies were found on Denman island and were previously considered extirpated. Here it is on a Canada Endangered Species Stamp 2008.

a quarter of their annual income. In recent years, they are getting both financial and land bequests. "When I meet new people, they say, 'isn't it wonderful how all this land is here to wander on.' It's all of this work we've done. Give us money, help us."

Anne remarked that people who now come to Denman Island "very quickly become aware of the conservation ideals on the island. I think in general we've become known for our strength in conservation."

John agreed that they have been very successful in securing land for conservation on Denman. "The provincial park wasn't pushed by the Conservancy as much as the island in general, but it's been our success too!" As of September 2022, DCA has acquired five properties. Three more properties now owned by the Islands Trust Conservancy were initiated by DCA, with added conservation covenants held by the local conservancy. "And, we are still working to protect more of the Island by ownership and conservation covenants," John added.

This indomitable Conservancy, with the support of their island community, over the past thirty years has helped conserve nine properties. It also holds conservation covenants on four privately owned properties, plus five on the Provincial Park and Islands Trust properties, with another on three kilometres of the crest and face of the Komas Bluffs. This is a significant achievement, given the lawsuits and logging of lands that were to be covenanted. One of the things that this group of people stressed on that warm July day in 2021 when I met them was how much they appreciated, respected, and learned from each other—from how to speak in public meetings through to negotiating complex land deals, providing a natural burial site that links to restoration, and a successful stewardship program.

Yet, when I asked each one to comment on the future, they all expressed concern about the impacts on Denman's conservation lands from climate change and the need for affordable housing. The challenges are staggering. Yet, these strong and prescient people have led the way by resisting the destruction of nature, developing and using legal mechanisms to save land, and building a conservation ethic that increased the island's conserved lands from 5 to 25 percent during their watch.[15] With the protection and restoration of wetlands and forests, streams and habitats for endangered butterflies, painted turtles and humans, this to my mind, is a seminal basis of hope—connected conservation lands, there for the next generations to steward into the future.

Komas Bluffs, an ecologically sensitive site that was developed into ten parcels. DCA has covenants on three kilometres of the crest and face. JOHN MILLEN

CHAPTER TEN

QUADRA ISLAND
Saving the Heart of Quadra

*"The idea of a land trust went beyond just saving one piece of land;
it was a useful tool for Quadra Island to be more self-reliant."*
MICHAEL MASCALL

IN EARLY JULY 2022, I SET SAIL FOR COMOX. We were on our way to the Vancouver Island Music Festival. We were excited to be heading to this annual musical event which signals for me the beginning of summer every year. My friend Doane joined me on the first leg of this journey north to Quadra Island. After a night anchored in Hornby's Tribune Bay, we flew with full sails on a beam reach as a nice southeaster pushed us past Norris Rocks and Chrome Island. This turned out to be the best sail of the year, with *Tiddy Oggy* very tidily sailing at 7 knots, heeled over as we headed past Lambert Channel and over to Baynes Sound. Then as we entered the Sound, the wind died down in this narrow channel between Denman and Vancouver Island. We had to wait a while as the new cable ferry crossed over from Denman to Buckley Bay. The cable ferry is one of a kind on the coast, an experiment using a different propulsion system.

We spent the second night anchored at Henry Bay, at the top end of Denman Island. According to Rozen's *Halkomelum Place Names* thesis mentioned earlier, Henry Bay was called xwá7asxwem (place having harbour seals).[1] On shore, we were dismayed to see abandoned, ripped nets over many areas of the beach, left behind from commercial oyster growers. Denman islanders have been trying to bring this industrial waste to the attention of DFO for years. Imagine its impact on birds and other wildlife that forage on the beaches, not to mention people.

We walked over to the spit to view the open Strait—which looked so big and wide here reaching far across to Texada Island and the mainland. To the north was Sandy Island Marine Park, locally known as Tree Island. These name(s) are indicative of the extensive sandbars around the area and the gnarled trees open to the wind from the Strait. This park was established in 1966, formerly used by the Department of National Defense for military exercises. The large sandy shelf continues over to the head of Comox Harbour and then halfway out to Cape Lazo. This over one-hundred-year-old lighthouse on the shores of Vancouver Island helps mariners navigate safely through the sandbars and out to deeper waters.

After three days of camping and rabble rousing at the festival, while my boat sat captainless at the dock, I returned to stock up and head up to Quadra and Cortes. Heather was joining me again to travel north up the Salish Sea to meet the people who saved natural areas on their islands from logging and development.

We anchored off Denman Island's Henry Bay before heading to Quadra. This view is looking over to the mainland.

Quadra and Cortes are both within the Coastal Western Hemlock biogeoclimatic zone (not the Coastal Douglas-fir of the southern islands). Unlike the more populated islands in the south, these "Discovery" Islands are still being razed by commercial logging and industrial fish farms. Outside of the Islands Trust area (with its Islands Trust Conservancy), protecting the amazing diversity on these islands requires a bit more fortitude and creativity.

After stowing food and water below, checking the weather reports, I received the news that Heather was delayed. Instead of waiting for her, I decided to meet her on Quadra while there was a relatively calm forecast, with no place to tuck in should problems or high winds occur for a solo journey north to Quadra. It was hot and windless the whole way—a typical journey I've made over the years. Just me and *Tiddy Oggy* motored along at our usual slow pace: 4 knots an hour in a wide open sea in the summer's heat. I heard a swhoosh, and looked up from the cabin, where I'd gone to refill my water. There were three humpbacks—rising and falling in a crescendo of wave patterns. As much as I wanted them to come closer, they were focused on their own travels. Who was I to pull them in.

Humpbacks have made an amazing comeback in the Salish Sea since commercial whaling ended in 1967. The first humpback sighted since then was thirty years later—off Victoria in 1997. Since then, in 2022 the Canadian Pacific Humpback Collaboration reported 396 unique humpback whales travelling in the Salish Sea. DFO's monthly surveys reveal that humpbacks are in the region all year. That's an amazing recovery! Along with their increasing numbers in the Salish Sea, there are also a few vessel strikes, commonly occurring in November. I had a near collision myself a few years ago coming back from Hornby to Lasqueti when I saw a large wave right in front of my boat. I ran to the stern to cut my engine, and then turned to see a huge whale tail disappear behind my boat!

"Their presence is a reminder that we can rapidly change our values and actions to not only benefit species, but whole ecosystems," said Jackie Hildering, a representative of the Canadian Pacific Humpback Collaboration who echoed my own optimism on this clear summer day. "Humpback whales fertilize the ocean, leading to more food, more oxygen production, and more absorption of carbon dioxide."[2]

On the way up to Quadra Island is a small island of distinct interest—Mitlenatch Island. Now a BC Park, "Mitlenatch" is an Indigenous word with a number of meanings. In the Coast Salish language it means "calm waters all around." On a windless day like this, I could relate to its name. Mitlenatch receives less than 75 centimetres (30 inches) of rain each year.[3] This fragile, rocky island out in the middle of the Strait is often full of common glaucous-winged gulls and pelagic cormorants who nest here in spring. Scientists come here to study this unique island in the middle of the Strait as it attracts other unusual species of birds and native flowers. BC Parks acquired the island in 1959 from the Manson family of Cortes Island, who ran cattle and sheep on it from the 1890s. Here again, thanks to land conservation, was another protected oasis for the birds, and another chance for nature to restore itself!

I headed over to the east side of Quadra Island where I passed the bouldered shores of the southern panhandle, avoiding numerous buoys offshore that indicated some kind of marine farm. Six and a half hours after leaving Comox, I anchored at Drew Harbour, off Rebecca Spit for the night.

The We Wai Kai Nation (Cape Mudge Band) has a population of approximately 1,200 people with 40 percent living at the Cape Mudge Village at the south end of Quadra Island. Tsa-Kwa-Luten Lodge and the Nuyumbalees Cultural Centre are here, with ancient petroglyphs along the shores of this waterfront village. Three reserves are on Quadra, including one at Drew Harbour, where the We Wai Kai Nation operates the Rebecca Spit Campground. The other 60 percent of the Nation live in Campbell River.[4]

The next day I brought the boat over to Heriot Bay. I walked up the dock to meet Ken Roxburgh and Michael Mascall, two of the founders of the local Quadra Island Conservancy and Stewardship Society (QICSS). Ken rode up on his bike, got off, and removed his helmet. Another fit senior, Ken has a PhD in geophysics, and developed a software business in the era of early microcomputers. He did some logging on the West Coast, but when he moved to Quadra he turned his focus to conservation.

While waiting for Michael, we talked about the many boats anchored in the harbour. The two docks in the bay were full, including the government dock I was tied up at, three boats deep in some places. I felt that the island had a more rustic flavor than the Southern Gulf Islands.

As Michael pulled into the marina parking lot, I recalled his engaging manner. I already knew him from my years as the executive director of the Land Trust Alliance of BC as Michael was on the founding board. An active and engaging man, his background is in economics. He has been involved in cooperatives including serving on the board of Coastal Community Credit Union. If that's not enough, his volunteer work includes being chair of the board for the Sierra Club of BC, board treasurer for Habitat Acquisition Trust (HAT), and founding chair of the Quadra Island Foundation. Not to mention he helped GAIA Recycling get recycling off the ground on Quadra Island.

Michael barely sat down, as he began to explain how islanders felt at the time of their founding about a key property on the island that had come up for sale at Morte Lake. The community was concerned that the 23 hectare (57 acre) property on the lake might be sold to a buyer who would limit public access and possibly engage in commercial development. The rest of the lake was within a Tree Farm License (TFL) area: Fletcher Challenge, a lumber company, owned half the logging rights on Quadra Island. "There was a sense," explained Michael, "that we should do something about it. Let's put our money where our mouth is—sort of thing." He then went on to describe the establishment of QICSS.

Olivia Rousseau, our local doctor's wife, saw that this property was for sale by a family who owned April Point, a high end lodge. One of the family was Thor Peterson. She thought something could be arranged. They were asking $190 thousand. Linda and Dirk van der Minne were instrumental in the initial organizing. Dirk identified key elements on the property when he talked to Olivia. She was a vital person on the island in the '80s and '90s, publishing the monthly *Discovery Passage*, Quadra's only newsletter then. We recently had Guy Dauncey up, who talked about a couple of tools that might be useful for our island, and one was a land trust. I thought we

Approaching Mitlenatch Island, a BC Provincial Park that attracts glaucous-winged gulls and pelagic cormorants who nest here in spring.

QICSS past and present directors I met with. From left, Ken Roxburgh, Michael Mascall, and Janice McLean.

could do this, so Dirk and I took the lead. I talked to Ron Pither, and we evolved from there.

Not surprisingly, here was Ron Pither again, helping to start a land trust! He shared a copy of Galiano's bylaws as an example, and Michael saw that this was indeed a powerful tool for local people to protect land. "I wanted to help the community protect the environment from the industrial devastation of logging, which happens on half our island."

Michael explained that beyond acquiring the land, another impetus was knowing that Quadra islanders would get behind protecting nature through voluntary stewardship. Activities such as putting up nest boxes, becoming aware of ecosystems, and trying to keep these intact without harming the natural processes are all part of stewardship. Streamkeepers and other similar groups practice stewardship through their stream restoration and monitoring programs.

Quadra is a very large island, almost twice the size of its neighbour, Cortes Island. Both are plagued with areas still undergoing active logging. Yet there still are lakes, second growth forests, and incredible vistas looking over to Vancouver Island and the mainland—an insatiable draw for locals and tourists alike. Michael knew the local community would support goals of protecting land, adding trails, and increasing recreational use. Michael and Warren Peterson from April Point; Bill Pirie, who ran the local fish processing plant; and Dirk van der Minne all joined the founding board. Adding "Stewardship" to their name, the Quadra Island Conservancy and Stewardship Society was incorporated in 1990.

The group spent six weeks debating about whether to purchase the Morte Lake property or not. "We had a meeting at Quadra Elementary school, with all of us sitting in these small chairs." Michael said, "I had been on the island a couple of years at that point, and Olivia was my landlady. We had about forty people there. We raised $40,000 that night, showing considerable commitment. I invited the manager of the local Credit Union to help. She said, 'We'd be happy to lend money at 18 percent.' I said, 'Hmm maybe 14 percent would be good.' The going rate was 19.90 at the time. We negotiated an interest-free loan with Thor Peterson instead for one year."

The determined Conservancy raised another $50,000 in the first year. Ken added that a garden tour and series of guest speakers gave them a huge boost. David Suzuki had just moved to the island, so they invited him to speak at the first of what became an annual fundraising dinner. Michael described the first year's event. "The highlight was a banquet at April Point, with lots of wild salmon, roasted pig, and the guest speaker David Suzuki. We all got dressed up and paid our fifty dollars each to have dinner there. Suzuki came in jeans and a plaid shirt and felt underdressed on Quadra."

That was the first of three fundraisers. Each year thereafter, they organized one of these social events, each included well known speakers, such as Robert Bateman and Roy Henry Vickers. Another islander, Marjorie Rye, a keen gardener, suggested a garden tour as an annual fundraiser. As Michael explained:

We had seventy-five to a hundred people for dinner, raised money and offered things—books and art work for auction. At the end of the first year, we had to pay Thor Peterson out. So we asked the Credit Union if they would give us an interest free loan. They said, 'well no,' so we had to pay interest. At the end of the first year we went to them again, and they gave us the loan—interest free. They did this generously for two years, until we paid off the mortgage. In addition, George Murdoch, another founding director, organized a large art auction held at Tsa-Kwa-Luten, a lodge owned by the Cape Mudge Band. It was very successful in that it raised $18,000. So they were helpful and the whole thing went really well. We paid it off in three years. We raised the money for the interest for expenses: surveys and legal fees. In a gesture of good will, Fletcher Challenge gave us $10 thousand, but in the end we didn't need it. So we set up a GIS mapping project—pretty rudimentary as far as early GIS projects go. We used ArcView [software] to identify rivers and topography.

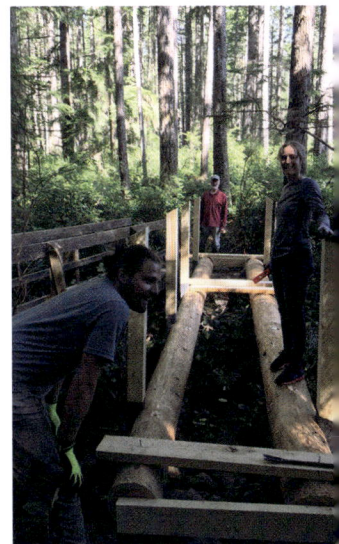

Bridge repair at Morte Lake with Gaspard Laniece, Ken Roxburgh, and Amy Vandal. KRIS WELLSTEIN

On purchasing the Morte Lake property, the QISCS contacted the Nature Conservancy of Canada (NCC), who agreed to register a conservation covenant on it. Because the covenant prohibits development, Ken said they had to get permission from NCC to rebuild the bridge on the property. He explained that the old bridge, originally built in 2004, was underbuilt and rotting.

Ken told me that the Trails Committee maintains trails and builds bridges on Quadra Island. Their standard for building bridges is based on forest service specifications, as some of the trails go through the TFL area around the lake. Ken explained further that the original trails were hard to walk on and almost impossible to ride. They received a grant from Tourism Vancouver Island for the local mountain biking group, which enabled the Trails committee to cover most of the costs. Ken noted, "Not only have they rebuilt the bridge, but they have also redesigned a major part of that trail in the last couple of years. The best part is that much of this work has been undertaken by young people, some of whom were mountain bikers."

The Trails Committee started with ten official legally gazetted trails that they maintain. Because they have been publicized in the official *BC Gazette*, the forest companies have to take them into account. One trail goes through the Conservancy's property. "It's the only trail we maintain that is on community (Conservancy owned) land. The other trails are on TFL land, and the committee has gone through the process of identifying them, so they show up on the TFL maps," Ken explained.

After QICSS acquired the property at Morte Lake, people started coming forward with ideas for conservation covenants. "One woman came forward and said she wanted to protect 10 acres on the point, at Shellalligan Pass." Michael explained that this area is south of Village Bay, on a northeast corner of the pass between Bretons Island and Quadra Island. "They talked to a lawyer in town, who didn't have a clue. It was the first one. It wasn't very solid and not very enforceable. But it was early days and innovation was starting with covenants. We thought sure, we'll hold the covenant." Michael added, "Maybe you want to take your boat through there."

Ken remarked, "the covenant said no old cars, and was pretty loosey-goosey." QICSS are the only covenant holders on title, of this their first covenant, but since then, they decided to strictly co-hold covenants with other organizations.

Michael, who just returned to the board of QICSS in 2022 explained their strategy. "We are a small local Conservancy with low resources, but we're willing to do the annual monitoring and be the local eye. It's a complimentary role so we can line up with a larger group. We decided as a Conservancy that we won't hold covenants without another major Conservancy behind us."

The local Conservancy now has two more covenants, both registered on properties a little north from Shellalligan Pass up Hoskyn Channel. The first is a 3.9 hectare (9.6 acre) covenant on a 160 hectare property on Bold Point that enabled the owners to cluster their homes and protect a wetland. The second is 22 hectares on Bold Island, which limits any subdivision.

Ken added that covenants are difficult to write. It takes a lot of thought to create something that fits with the landowner's desires, that works with both the ecosystems and the developed areas of the land, and is enforceable. A guide to covenant language is available for reference, written by Ann Hillyer, a lawyer with decades of experience helping land trusts design and write them.[5]

Despite the fact that conservation covenants are legal agreements registered on title, there are times when a landowner might want to do something outside the covenant's restrictions. The bridge at Morte Lake is a good case in point. If a landowner needs some exception to the covenant's requirements, they would need to contact the covenant holder(s) to discuss the project or activity and ensure that they are given a written letter of permission. If the landowner goes ahead without contacting the covenant holder, this could result in legal action. Conservation covenants are registered on title, so every realtor has a responsibility to ensure that the new owners are aware of any restrictions. There have been very few cases of covenant infractions in BC and across Canada.[6] Should the land or its features that are protected through the covenant be damaged, legal enforcement would likely require compensation, including restoration. In most cases, the landowner is able to work with the land trust to find a solution. Enforcement and its costs are one reason why small conservancies such as QICSS decide to co-hold a covenant.

The Conservancy then decided to expand their area of interest beyond Quadra to help people write and register covenants on neighbouring Read and Cortes islands. You'll read about Linnaea Farm's covenant and this historic farm and educational project in the Cortes Island chapter.

Breton Island on Quadra's east side has recently been protected by the Nature Trust of BC (NTBC). The owners donated it to the NTBC in 2021. MARKUS THOMPSON

The Nature Trust of BC— Conserving Land on Quadra

Breton Island on Quadra's east side has recently been protected by the Nature Trust of BC (NTBC). Jasper Lament, the CEO of NTBC, was eager to tell me about this recent acquisition.

A Vancouver native, Jasper brings a lifelong love of wildlife and three decades of biology, conservation, and non-profit experience to his role leading NTBC's successful conservation efforts. These provincial land trusts are a major boon in the world of conservation. They are there for people who prefer to work with larger organizations, with a long history and, often, connections to cross-border families. Local land trusts often make the initial contacts with landowners, being on the ground on the islands. At times, the local Conservancy works together with the province-wide larger land trust to raise funds for an acquisition.

Jasper described this 5 hectare island as a hotbed of bird diversity. "Northeast of Heriot Bay, the island conserves sensitive mature Douglas-fir communities and an herbaceous, rocky shoreline surrounding the shallow marine habitat." The area is known for its sea ducks, shorebirds, and at-risk species including the red-listed Brandt's cormorant and common murrelet, and the at-risk marbled murrelet, Cassin's auklet, great blue heron, horned grebe, and western grebe.[7] Jasper explained, "the island was owned by the Whitridge family for sixty years or more. This family from California had connections to the San Juan islands. Mr. Whitridge worked in BC as well and was an active supporter of land trusts in the western US. After his death, the family donated 100 percent of the value to NTBC. It is a wonderful gift from a conservation oriented family."

A National Park on the Island?

Michael relayed the following story about how Quadra was included in the Forest Resources Committee on Vancouver Island. He told me there were eight to nine different groups meeting together to find ways to limit the logging on Quadra. In addition to these groups, the committee included the woodlot owners and the local forest workers. The Commission on Resources and Environment (CORE) process was meeting on Vancouver Island. Michael explained that he was representing the conservation sector.

> I got Quadra Island included in that CORE process. I suggested we look at having a national park between Strathcona and Tweedsmuir Park from the north end of Quadra. It would go from Vancouver Island to Quadra Island. Parks Canada was very excited about this. At the time, 1993, Judy Lester, who was also involved in what we called the Save the Heart of Quadra Committee, and Ray Grigg, a writer about environmental issues, were trying to get Village Bay Lake made into a park. This was controversial as some people thought it was in their back yard. Because Parks Canada's interest was current, they flew over the area. Ray Griggs sent a letter to our MP, asking for support and two minutes later that letter, as indicated on the fax paper, went from the MP to Fletcher Challenge. Parks Canada got stopped in their tracks. Some of the land was in their timber lease area.

As Michael wrapped up his story, we were joined by Janice McLean, chair of the local Salmon Enhancement group on Quadra. Like a few of the many people I had interviewed, Janet was cynical about the state of the world. She did admit, however, that she was initially in favour of the concept of a national park on the island, but now she balked at the idea mainly because of the overloaded ferries dropping off too many tourists.

It's true that there are many recreational sites and provincial parks on Quadra Island. Rebecca Spit is one of the larger campgrounds on the island with 150 recreational vehicle and tenting sites. The small Rebecca Spit Marine Park adjoins the campground area. Its two kilometres of shoreline on both sides of the spit was purchased by the Province as early as 1959.

Rebecca Spit Park next to a large campground owned and managed by the We Wai Kai Nation.

While I was anchored off of the spit I noticed a couple of deer walking along the peninsula. It was late afternoon, and as they started to head back up the spit, I thought how in the heck are they going to get off the spit. Everybody's got a dog, off leash. Eventually I saw them turn around and go back. So I imagine they stayed until dark when campers and visitors had left. It was a visible reminder that unleashed dogs in parks are predators, in an area that is supposed to be conserved for wildlife. On an individual level, there's nothing wrong with dogs in parks, but on a cumulative level, the impacts are substantial. Because of this concern, the Bowen Island Nature Conservancy has decided to exclude dogs from their newly protected Wild Coast Refuge.

Provincial and Regional Parks on the Island

Main Lake, a large provincial park on Quadra Island, was established in 1997. According to BC Parks, it is the largest conserved freshwater waterway in the Gulf and Discovery Islands. It encompasses six lakes, connected by narrow, shallow marshes navigable by canoes and dinghies, with three of the six lakes requiring portage.

Further north up Quadra Island, along Surge Narrows is a provincial park, accessible by land through gravel logging roads. Across the channel, located just inland from Surge Narrows on Read Island, is the 1.86 hectare (4.6 acre) John Kim Nature Sanctuary, protected by the Strathcona Regional District, with a conservation covenant held by the Nature Trust of BC. Another 8.2 hectare (20 acre) property, just southeast of the Sanctuary, was acquired by the Nature Trust of BC and the Surge Narrows Community Association to conserve its mature forest, wetland, and stream ecosystems.

As a boater, I've been through Surge Narrows at slack tide—otherwise, it is a boiling cauldron of whirlpools cutting through this narrow slot. It leads to my all-time favourite anchorage at Octopus Islands Marine Park. Both places feel like a rare wilderness, still primarily intact with substantial forests along the shorelines and an astonishing diversity of marine life all along the islets and channels. If the waters are fairly calm, one can see exotic looking marine life in the shallow waters.

The Octopus Islands themselves are a series of small islands and islets (islands without trees). I always look forward to anchoring here, then paddling around entranced by the underwater marine life—giant sea stars, sea cucumbers, and nudibranchs of all shapes and sizes. You would be lucky to see the giant Pacific octopus if it doesn't practice its escape artistry. It is the largest and longest-lived octopus in the world, known to be quite brilliant (in looks and intelligence).

The original Octopus Islands Marine Park was established in 1974. It is 862 hectares (~2,130 acres) in size (404 hectares of upland and 458 hectares of foreshore) at the junction of Quadra, Sonora, and Maurelle islands. The Octopus Islands are off of Waiatt Bay, a large bay popular among boaters. It is surrounded by Quadra's forests on both sides. At the head of the bay, after a brief portage or hike, a surprise awaits, as one looks out on the Johnstone Strait side of the island from Small Inlet Marine Park. Between the two bays is a trail that leads up to Newton Lake, a popular swimming hole.

This site has been a popular area for over four millenia! Archaeologists have confirmed that clam gardens in Kanish and Waiatt Bay date use by Indigenous people in the area for over 4,000 years.[8]

Shoreline at Octopus Island Marine Park.

The far, outer end on the north side of Waiatt Bay has been logged, but further into the bay lies a new conservation site that has expanded this marine park by 400 hectares. The Quadra Island Conservancy and Stewardship Society helped raise funds for the extension of the park up the northwestern side of Waiatt Bay in 2014. Ken explained that it is a wonderful success because they joined with another island group, Save the Heart of Quadra Parks. Together they raised $200,000 toward its purchase which connected these two provincial marine parks (Octopus and Small Inlet).

Ken said, "Groups on the island, including the Sierra Club, were after the provincial government to make it part of the park. Eventually in 2012 the government came through and said we'll work on it. We need you to raise some money locally. The two groups raised $200,000 as a contribution to the $6 million purchase. Spearheaded by Judy and Susan Lester, they had the usual fundraising events, including auctions. The most successful was a thousand dollar club. We thought that rich people would contribute more, but that wasn't the case."

The BC Marine Parks Forever Society contributed an additional $433,000. The Vancity Foundation and Vancity Credit Union provided a $186,940 contribution as a carbon offset. The Province contributed the rest of the $5.85 million purchase price.[9]

Ian Atherton, the negotiator for BC Parks at the time, explained to me during our interview that the owners, Merrill and Ring Forestry from Washington State, were the oldest forest company operating in BC. They had ten family members within the company. Ian detailed how they convinced the family members to donate some of the cost. "We had a tax accountant who was familiar with conservation lands. She did some research and came back and said the tax benefit to an American donor involving Canadian land was 10 percent more advantageous than a Canadian donating the same land. We went back to the owners and told them that, so they donated. The Province issued ten receipts to each of the owners, rather than through the corporation."

The Quadra Island Stewardship and Conservation Society Today

Ken described the various ways that the local Quadra community has supported the QICSS in various forms. "The community got together and formed this Conservancy. They got together to raise money for the park. The same thing is true for this bridge. The whole community is involved. The Trails community is paying for the bridge. The tennis group is paying for a pond liner, and it just goes on and on. We're just a vehicle."

It's very fulfilling to see a community support conservation. However, Ken echoed comments I'd heard on other islands. "Some of these hardworking founders and directors simply burn out! You get excited about a project. But how do you keep people engaged? That's where a paid person to keep it going is important. Then the directors won't burn out. They can then have a life, other than just volunteering. I think that's something we've learned."

This evolution from a volunteer only land trust to one with paid staff is a natural development, especially when an organization has annual responsibilities such as monitoring covenants and managing other lands. Depending on the financial support the organization can draw from the community—through donations and through grants, they can hire locals, or seek experienced people who may end up moving to the island. This keeps these small local land trusts vibrant with professional biologists and administrative staff who take the load off the volunteer directors. Staff can often organize local events and keep a website up and active. The additional load of organizing meetings with landowners to discuss conservation options, registering and monitoring covenants, and drawing in potential donors can then by handled by experienced directors. Imagine doing all of this work with only volunteers!

Succession is another issue Ken promptly added. "One of the roles of a leader is to find someone to replace themselves. These initial groups get together, they have energy and they do so much, but then we all get old and move on, and the next group is different." Like many of the other islands, the QICSS is not the only organization on the island needing board members and volunteers. Hiring young people can help free up the volunteer directors. This is one way to involve the next generations, for small projects or as part or full-time staff. All of this needs funding and support.

The Quadra Island Conservancy and Stewardship Society is helping to conserve lands on Quadra Island thanks to people who, like Michael and Ken, are on the front lines—voluntarily offering their professional services. Thankfully, they are joined by other organizations, larger provincial land trusts like the Nature Trust of BC, and BC Parks. BC has more biodiversity than anywhere else in Canada, yet more than half of the province's assessed species have low or dwindling populations. Our downward spiral can only be reversed if we conserve and steward more land!

While pondering these thoughts, a light wind beckoned me back to my boat. After repairing a few rips in the jib, Heather and I prepared to head over to Cortes Island.

Sunset from Rebecca Spit, the night before heading to Cortes Island.

CHAPTER ELEVEN

CORTES ISLAND
Individual Islanders Count

*"To counteract the feeling of environmental despair, registering
a covenant on our land was something we could do."*
GEORGE WEST

BUOYED BY A LIGHT BREEZE ON THE MORNING of our departure from Quadra Island, Heather and I put up the sails and headed toward our next destination—Cortes Island. After a bit of flogging, (the sails, not Heather), we sadly started up the engine and motored the 9.5 nautical miles toward Gorge Harbour on Cortes Island. We wove through Uganda Passage on one of the lowest tides of the year. Neighbouring Marina Island's Shark Spit lifted its sandy shores and reached out toward Cortes, leaving only the smallest passage for vigilant boaters to cross, observing all the green and red markers that are the foundation of marine navigation.

I learned the next day that wolves swim across Uganda Passage during these low tides. They then travel down to the bottom of Marina Island to feed. Many locals have reported sightings of these wild wolves as they cross the swift current pass.

After entering Gorge Harbour, we squeezed into a small cove and anchored on the east side among large floating marine farms. Next to us was a colourful wooden sailboat built by a man I had met and talked with years ago. I remembered clearly his smiling face as we chatted about boats and where Heather and I might access the shoreline. That turned into a fruitless task, so we moved over to the public wharf for the next night. We saw thirty of the ubiquitous Canada geese, including one albino and another with an orange beak. We also spotted ten oystercatchers, a kingfisher, and over a dozen of the barn and violet-green swallows.

I spent some of the next day with Sabina Leader Mense, a warrior-like woman who is in it for the long haul—working to protect networks and corridors of land on Cortes Island. She explained, "Marina Island is an important source of seasonal food resources for Cortes's wild wolves—extensive clam beds at Shark Spit and harbour seal pupping grounds on Marina Reef, where the wolves feed on placenta and weak pups. An important wildlife travel corridor across neighbouring Cortes lands connects the wolves to the shore of Uganda Passage where they swim across to Marina Island at slack water. Cougar also use this corridor."

Cougars, wolves? Had I finally found the wilderness I was seeking? Cortes Island, like Quadra, has a north end, primarily designated Crown land (traditionally viewed by the Province as available for commercial logging), and a south end, where the people live. The forests on Cortes were logged in the 1920s and then again in the

Tom Trebett welcomes us to Gorge Harbour. Seen here in his dory, *Soaring Gull*, with his ketch, *Good Tidings*, behind. The hull was built on Galiano by the Fosters and Tom completed this colourful sailboat himself.

1950s. Much of Cortes Island's northern regions are Crown lands under negotiations between the Province and the Klahoose First Nation, for future management. Other lands already designated as "private lands", included ~890.31 hectares (2,200 acres) of prime bottom land, that were bought up by MacMillan Bloedel in the late 1950s and designated as private managed forest lands. A subsequent cascade of corporate ownership presently has these lands owned by Island Timberlands and managed by Mosaic Forest Management.

I learned that a community forest group was started thirty years ago in order to promote more ethical logging practices. In 1996 the Cortes Island Forest Committee retained Herb Hammond to create an ecosystem based conservation plan, to learn what was what, ecologically. Herb is a master at helping locals understand and map different habitats and ecosystem-defined areas, similar to what he did on Galiano Island. The group, now renamed the Cortes Island Ecoforestry Society revised the ecosystem-based maps.[1] These maps were used as a basis for creating an ecosystem based Forest Management Plan. Eventually in 2012 the newly designated Cortes Forestry General Partnership, a fifty-fifty partnership between Klahoose First Nation and Cortes Community Forest Cooperative, was given tenure to most of the Crown land to operate as a Community Forest.

Cortes Island is within the traditional territories of the Klahoose First Nation, Tla'amin Nation, and Xwémalhkwu (Homalco) Nation. The Klahoose First Nation's traditional territories span from Cortes Island to Toba Inlet. Most of the community lives in Squirrel Cove. In addition to partnering with the Community Forest group, the Klahoose own and run a Wilderness Resort, Klahoose Coastal Adventures, and the Gorge Harbour Marina Resort. The Klahoose First Nation are both in Stage 4, an agreement in principle, of their respective treaty agreement with the governments of British Columbia and Canada.[2]

The area we moored inside Gorge Harbour is known as Sa'y'ilh, meaning "two waters in one" because the salt water mixes here with fresh water from the numerous streams and springs. There were two Klahoose village sites inside the harbour, abandoned when the Klahoose people were ushered onto reserves before 1900.[3]

Sabina Leader Mense moved to Cortes in 1990 with her husband. An ecologist by training, she initially found the concept of land ownership at odds with her own ecological values. Like Misty MacDuffee on Pender Island and Briony Penn on Salt

Spring, she embodies a passion and enthusiasm that is hard to keep up with! She showed me maps of the island, indicating places that connect, and a vision to protect a network of areas at a landscape level so that the cougars, wolves, bears, deer, and other wildlife could cross over these lands and access habitat they need to survive. I had only a brief time with her as she was preparing for a major sailing trip to the central coast.

In her first years on Cortes, Sabina was fortunate to meet an influential woman, Gilean Douglas, a poet and author. Gilean had bought ~157 hectares (140 acres) in 1949 on Uganda Passage, that she called Channel Rock. Over the next two decades, she wrote a descriptive, lyrical book, called *The Protected Place*, about her experiences living on the waterfront at the pass there. Sabina explained how this early pioneer of conservation on Cortes protected her own place in 1993.

> Gilean covenanted her private land holdings: 40 acres as a wildlife refuge to protect the important wildlife travel corridor (connection to Uganda Passage) and the remaining 100 acres to allow for a conservation minded residential component. This was prior to 1994 when conservation covenants became a tool that registered non-profit organizations could use in BC. So she was ahead of her time. In her early nineties, Gilean made a concerted effort to locate a future conservation owner of Channel Rock. Before Gilean died, she sold to Gifford Pinchot, from a family of noteworthy conservationists in the US. Gilean's legacy of conserved lands at Channel Rock continues to be an inspiration for many Cortes private landholders.

In the early '90s, a group of people arrived on Cortes with plans to develop an ecoforestry and sustainable agriculture program and protect some of the 127 hectares (314 acres) of the land they had acquired. The property had been pre-empted in about 1887 by the Manson Family. Then it transferred to a colonial family, the Hansons (who sold Mitlenatch Island to BC Parks). Robert and Penny Cabot were familiar with land trusts in the US and secured some funding through the Trust for Public Lands to acquire the lands on Cortes. Several others joined this group of hardy individuals, and together they began building cabins and setting up what many called a hippie commune. This group soon morphed into a non-profit organization, Turtle Island Earth Stewards (TIES). Their vision included designating some areas suitable for ecoforestry and agriculture with other areas set aside for natural succession. Over time, the group divided, with some members of the group moving elsewhere, leaving the farm to those who continued to actively farm the land. Eventually the remaining group created an alternative school, which was well attended by those on the property and beyond to the wider island.

The remaining group formed the Linnaea Farm Society. However, they had no legal tenure on the land. An agreement was reached with TIES to transfer the lands, subject to having a registered conservation covenant on the title. As TIES was equivocating, a group of Linnaea farm people went up to the TIES AGM in mass, hoping to get enough votes to approve the transfer to the Linnaea Farm Society. After an anonymous donor gave $10,000 to TIES, they finally reached an agreement.

Sabina explained how she met Shawn Black who was living on Cortes at the time through their shared love of the land. Shawn was working for the Klahoose First Nation, assisting with treaty negotiations as their researcher and treaty coordinator.

Previously Shawn had worked as a treaty researcher with the Gitxsan Hereditary Chiefs in Northwestern BC near Hazelton. He got to know some of the people who lived on Linnaea Farm. They asked him to join the Linnaea Farm Society board and help them write a conservation covenant. Their vision was to protect some of the lands on the farm and allow for other uses including residential, agricultural, and forestry. In my conversations with Shawn I asked if he had a template which they used for the covenant, being early days since Section 219 of the BC *Land Title Act* had changed to allow conservation organizations to hold conservation covenants. Shawn told me he did not have a template. Because a section of the land was in the Agricultural Land Reserve, they had to get permission from the Agricultural Land Commission to register the covenant on the title. The conservation covenant contained provisions that restricted farming to organic farming methods only and protected the agricultural land on the property from other land uses. The Linnaea Farm Society was able to get the Agricultural Land Commission (ALC) to agree to the covenant, including the organic farming only clause. Shawn remarked that the ALC was clear in their decision that they did not want this to become a precedent.

Having the ALC agree to a covenant on Agricultural Reserve Lands is a difficult task, given that the ALC feels responsible for ensuring that agriculture can continue in perpetuity on agricultural reserve lands. However, over the years a few land trusts have succeeded in convincing the ALC to accept a covenant, even in a few cases that included forests, for example, surrounding agricultural fields which are essential for water retention and to sustain the insects needed for fertilization and growth.

In 1999 Linnaea Farm Society registered a conservation covenant on the full 127 hectares (314 acres) of the farm. The Quadra Island Conservancy and Stewardship Society and TLC The Land Conservancy of BC agreed to co-hold the covenant. The property has four zones: agricultural, forestry, residential, and protected, each with different allowable uses. Michael Mascall from QICSS recently monitored the covenant. His report documents their educational centre, which houses a wildlife centre and a museum of natural history with around one hundred taxidermied birds and animals. In 2021 when I was there the centre had a display about the wild wolves, bear, and cougars on the island. Tamara McPhail, the farm's current executive director, told me they recently restored an area of the farm, creating a wetland.

Back in 1999, Sabina and Shawn had considered starting a land trust for Cortes Island to hold covenants like Linnaea's on the island, and to help raise funds to conserve other areas. They reached out to several individuals in the community, and with positive encouragement, in 2000 they registered the Cortes Land Conservancy Society. However, after five years they found it difficult to find and keep people willing to sit on the board. Sabina told me, "The vision was so big and during those years everybody was fighting fires—building a community health clinic, establishing food security, protecting Crown forestlands, etc. We made a decision to let the Society status go and continue as a working group."

Shawn Black eventually moved to the interior and went to work for TLC The Land Conservancy of BC. Sabina continues to run the Cortes Land Conservancy Working Group, working with an extended community that includes TLC, regional land trusts, surveyors, realtors, GIS analysts, foresters, First Nations, and the local community—all championing land conservation on Cortes Island.

Sabina was inspired by the maps Herb Hammond produced in his ecosystem based conservation plan for Cortes Island's Crown lands. The *Protected Landscape Network* map identified critical "cross-island linkages"—harbinger to today's science of connectivity conservation. Creating ecological corridors for cougars, bear, and other species is a key priority in curbing the loss of biodiversity and helping species adapt to climate change. Linking protected and conserved areas, we can help species move, interact, and find habitat and food on the land and sea across the islands. With less than 4 percent of wild mammals still in existence, linking corridors is essential for their survival.[4]

Protecting one of Cortes Island's most important wildlife travel corridors has been one of Sabina's long-term conservation goals. Gilean Douglas's Channel Rock covenant and the Cortes community purchase of the Whaletown Commons park, protect much of this corridor, but the critical linkage between these two protected areas remains unprotected. That single private landholding is the focus of Cortes Island's next conservation covenant.

"I just finished a baseline on this 25 acre landholding," Sabina explained. This is not only a major wildlife travel corridor, it is also a riparian corridor with a stunning forested swamp. There are twelve ecological communities at risk on it, in addition to beautiful bluffs, and veteran trees. The landholder plans to covenant it." Sabina added, "I'm just trying to help people out. I've got a quote for the survey. I do flat rates for my baseline work. I charge for three days, but I can spend up to three weeks."

Sabina's approach is to talk to all interested people, walk the land with them, and discuss ways to protect the land, while they still live on it and use it. As she explained it, "What I'm working on now is focusing on the connectivity of protected lands across the landscape. This is one of the most exciting projects underway, especially to see how many people it's attracting." She feels that there is huge potential for land conservation on Cortes.

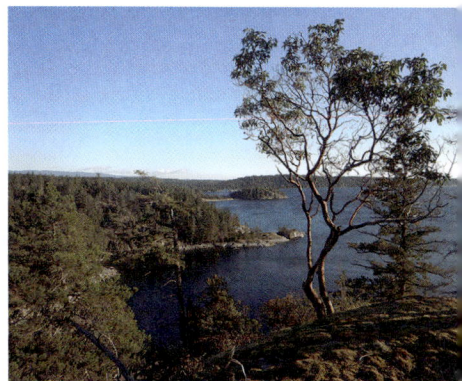

An area of protected places along Cortes Island's coastal bluffs, creating a natural legacy for the future. SABINA LEADER MENSE

Conservation Covenants—A Powerful Tool

In our current system of land tenure one can hold title to the land, but it is only temporary, as it will eventually transfer to others. However, the land itself is under the stewardship of that landholder, whose actions can have long ranging impacts on the future condition of the land. You can't do much about logging on tree farms or a TFL license on Crown lands, but you can covenant the land you own or hold, and that takes precedence over zoning and future subdivision. You can protect its ecological forests and marshes by working with a conservation organization.

Mary Gordon and George West are a couple who protected their forested land on Cortes through an innovative conservation covenant. Purchasing the land in 1981, they moved to the Island to live full-time three years later and set out to build a home base from which they could both live and work. Over the next forty years, they developed an awareness of how ecologically rich and complex the land was on which they lived. This diversity included not just the iconic large animals like wolves and cougars but, equally important to the ecosystem, the small forest floor dwelling reptiles and amphibians, the latter of which were particularly sensitive to disturbance by humans.

The wetland at this covenanted property has attracted a rare newt. GEORGE WEST

Down the road from their property is Hank's Beach, with its forests previously clear-cut by industrial logging companies. The couple really noticed the difference between the two areas. Their land had never been clear-cut, so it had a diversity of types and ages of trees, together with a rich understory of salal, huckleberries, oceanspray, and a diversity of mosses. In industrial forests, natural regeneration is replaced by a plantation of even-aged trees of the same species, and chemical sprays are used to keep "competing" vegetation at bay. The forest floor of such areas supports little biological richness.

I found Mary and George inspiring with their strong environmental ethic, professional backgrounds, and amazing creativity, which was evident in their unique home design. George, a lawyer, has served on various boards including the Silva Forest Foundation and, for a while, TLC The Land Conservancy of BC. Mary, a geographer, was a faculty member of North Island College for twenty years, which included running a community learning centre in Mansons Landing and establishing and running a similar centre with the Klahoose Nation. The couple own a 6.7 hectare (16.5 acre) property with ten acre zoning. They fear that in the future that zoning might change, allowing for three five acre lots. With development on the rise, they worry about the trend for people to build additional housing without subdividing. Their goal is to protect the ecosystems on their land, while still allowing for the buildings and life on the land.

George explained, "We realized that the ongoing changes on a small scale, even on Cortes Island, are substantial. If we look at the all parcels around us, and the changes over the recent years, they've gone generally from seasonal use to full-time use. They've gone from individual owners, to multiple individuals owning one parcel." This couple's goal is to protect in perpetuity the small yet valuable ecosystems within which they live. With this in view, they contacted TLC to see if they would hold the covenant.

Mary explained some of the things they considered once they decided to register a conservation covenant on the property. "Part of the covenant process for us was to choose if we wanted to separate out the residential area, and have that legally surveyed and not form part of the covenant area, or to have the covenant protect the entire property and recognize a residential polygon that is defined at the outset and will not get bigger." Their property includes their beautiful hand built log home, with two additional out buildings. "You can have some disturbance of the buildings, but the footprint of the building can't get larger, and you can't increase the number of buildings. So that's our vision with the fundamental principles of being able to live in the natural environment in a pretty non-obtrusive way."

George described their work to register a conservation covenant over the land. They saw the community expanding rapidly, clearing more and more areas of forest and disturbing other natural areas. He said it countered the feeling of environmental despair, because it was something they could do that would have long-term benefits. "We are not trying to create a park. We are trying to create a model, an example, to live on the land sustainably, maintaining a healthy, fully functioning ecosystem, as an aspect of a larger ecosystem."

George shocked me with figures about how much humans have been squeezing out the wild over the relatively short time of human existence. "Of all the mammalian biomass on the planet, 36 percent is human, 60 percent are farm and domestic animals, and 4 percent is wild. So we've gone from 100 percent of the mammals on the planet being wild down to 4 percent, with an implicit acceptance of their ongoing eradication."

George added that they do heat with firewood and the covenant allows them to take up to four cords a year. The covenant requires a letter of approval to negotiate this, and once they sell, the subsequent owners would have to renegotiate with TLC the amount of firewood allowed per year.

When TLC agreed to hold the covenant, Mary and George hired Laurel Brewster to work with them to write it to suit the land holders, the lands and the buildings, and still have it cover the whole property. In 2000 Laurel began to study conservation covenants, while completing her master's thesis under Simon Fraser's Faculty of Resource and Environmental Management. While working on her master's degree, she helped Joel Solomon, who lived on Cortes, design covenants for a conservation development he was working on through his organization, Renewal Land Company.

Through his company, Joel purchased several hundred acres of land that Weyerhaeuser was selling. Over a period of five years, Laurel worked for Renewal Land Company to help create a conservation focused subdivision (Siskin Lane) that resulted in twenty-five residential lots, a large conservation area, a public park (Cemetery Road Park), and a network of public trails (managed through a statutory right-of-way that was donated to the Strathcona Regional District as part of the subdivision).

Another residential development with conservation covenants was arranged on a property held by Treedom Ventures. Carrie Saxifrage, one of the residents, explained, "The covenant is on the entire ~33 hectares (82 acre) property. There are three areas, each with different restrictions. The restrictions on the Delicate Bluff Area, half of Treedom's waterfront, allow public trails to the beach known as Brigitte's Beach. All other use of the two acres of ecologically delicate bluffs is prohibited. The restrictions on the protected forest area allows forestry activities that enhance the old growth characteristics of ~16.2 hectare (40 acres) of second growth, mostly Douglas-fir forest. The restrictions on the remaining half of the property allow management primarily for residential use while maintaining ecological integrity as a secondary goal. The covenant is held by TLC, and there are currently six co-owners with two acre house sites."

Laurel has continued to work on drafting covenants including one she designed for Hollyhock, a well-known retreat centre on the island. She also worked with George West and Joel Solomon to create one for Hank's Beach, which was acquired as a public park through a large philanthropic donation. This property was previously owned by Weyerhaeuser. During our conversation she explained that the management plan, which she helped write with Sabina and Briony Penn, is where public use issues are addressed, such as trails, maintenance, washroom facilities, etc. Laurel continues to work on covenants on other islands in the region.

For Mary and George, the costs of the covenant became the impetus to find a solution for what is typically one of the most expensive aspects of the process—the need for a legal survey to define the covenant area in terms precise enough to satisfy the legal requirements of the Land Titles Office. They strongly feel that if conservation covenants are to become a more mainstream tool for land conservation, then the process must be one which people can afford.

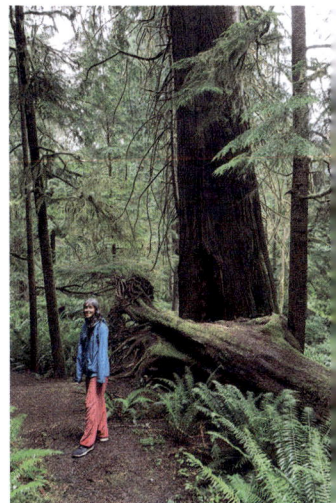

We hiked into the Whaletown Commons land that islanders spent twenty years trying to protect. It was eventually acquired by the Strathcona Regional District's Park Acquisition Fund in 2014.

Together with Laurel and the staff of TLC, they developed a process that used the existing drilled deep well, adjacent to the house, as the centre point of a 60 metre radius that circumscribes an area that becomes the residential polygon of the covenant, subject to fewer restrictions than the remainder of the parcel. All land outside the residential radius is fully protected and will be allowed to mature by natural succession to become a mixed-age, old growth forest.

Identifying the residential area by this method meant that a legal survey to define the different areas within the covenant was no longer necessary. Perhaps best of all, the process of using boundaries defined by GPS rather than legal survey pins was accepted by TLC's lawyers and by the Land Titles Office.

By avoiding the expense of a formal legal survey, the cost of developing and registering the covenant was cut approximately in half compared to what it would otherwise have been. The remaining costs of hiring professional help to develop the Baseline Inventory and to develop the actual covenant, together with a $15,000 endowment to TLC to cover monitoring costs into the future, means the process is still seen by many to be an expensive one. But as Mary and George point out, the cost of the covenant process is not particularly expensive compared to other costs incurred in home ownership.

A conservation covenant protects much of Mary and George's ecologically rich land.

He said, "A few years back we replaced all the decks around our house, and it cost $15–$20,000 dollars, similar to what the covenant cost us. But in fifteen years, the decks will need to be replaced again, but the covenant is there protecting this parcel of land ostensibly forever. We are happy with that."

When Mary and George gave me a tour of their land, I was surprised by how much diversity there was, with its varying ecosystems including a bluff, forest, and wetlands. Mary said, "What I really love about our place is it's not like a plantation. We have incredible understory—oceanspray, salal, huckleberries, ferns, mosses, and other native plants. Here's one of the original old growth stumps—the size of them is huge. There's other trees, and an incredible stand of second growth now. This is one of the remaining remnant old growth trees. It used to be taller, parts of it are coming down. We have such a lack of knowledge of ecology in our society. Some people have come through and said, why don't you clean this up? Generally people don't understand what is a healthy, diverse understory."

I could really relate to Mary and George's vision, dedication, and understanding of the innate connections between the overstory, the trees, and the understory that contains so much diversity. There are plants, mushrooms, flowers, moss, fungi, and underground mycelium, not to mention all of the insects, amphibians, birds, mammals and more—all interconnected species in a small area that creates an incredible web of life. In the wetland I saw tree frogs peeking up and a small snake disappear into the sedge. The "plant blindness" that is so pervasive today could be replaced with a renewed awareness. We simply need to get out of our heads and look around!

RECENTLY A FLEDGING Community Foundation was created on the island, with a mandate to secure land for social and conservation purposes. Sabina went to them to introduce the work of the Cortes Land Conservancy Working Group. She encouraged the new Foundation to think about supporting private landholder's conservation goals (which ultimately effect conservation of the greater Cortes landscape) through an endowment fund, rather than simply purchasing a single property for conservation. Sabina told me, "It took off like wildfire with the Foundation. They had no idea how much influence their money could have in supporting the conservation of extensive local lands. I showed them the geographic positioning of lands where I have contacted landholders. This simple idea has surprised them and is growing into the most exciting thing."

An endowment is primarily allocated to support the land trust with the legally required annual monitoring of the covenant (monitoring covenants has costs—travel to and time on the property, producing photographs, maps, and reports, etc.) She gave the example of TLC, who ask for an endowment of $10 thousand or $20 thousand for a new covenant. They place that money into the Victoria or Vancouver Foundation, and the annual interest pays for the monitoring costs—in perpetuity. If the Foundation were to put up $250,000 to support endowments, the interest could cover the monitoring costs for several different landholder covenants on the island and surveys (if needed) or appraisals.

Sabina assured me that there are multiple landholders willing to register a conservation covenant. She feels that many landholders with large ecologically rich acreages on Cortes have an Aldo Leopold land ethic. (Leopold is regarded as the father of wildlife ecology and the wilderness system in the US.) "Lands here are of provincial and regional significance. I focus on this when talking with people, in terms of what we have within the larger context." For this very busy and active woman, her most important role is being on the land and helping find legal advisors and other land trusts for residents to work with. "Our most important role is to create the relationships with the landholders."

This Mothertree is on a private property in an area that Sabina Leader Mense hopes to protect with a conservation covenant. SABINA LEADER MENSE

Regional and Provincial Parks on the Island

In addition to the private landholders who have protected land through covenants, the Strathcona Regional District has created several larger parks on the island in addition to the typical beach access areas they have acquired.

The earliest is a large 250 hectare (618 acre) Kw'as Park along the shores of Hague and Gunflint Lakes that they acquired in the late 1990s. Small patches of old growth and veteran trees remain in the park along with sensitive bluff ecosystems.

In 2005, the regional district obtained a License of Occupation over the Crown land that makes up the large Carrington Bay Park. It includes a tidal lagoon with shoreline, riparian areas and streams, along with a second growth forest and sensitive bluff ecosystems.

Hank's Beach Forest Conservation Park was acquired by the Strathcona Regional District in 2011. The Park's conservation covenant is held by TLC and protects the natural features of the park in perpetuity. "The park is ecologically significant in that its inland and coastal bluffs form important habitat and a wildlife corridor for many species including black-tailed deer, grey wolf and cougar. The property contains an active great blue heron rookery and several sensitive ecosystems where rare species and plant communities are also represented."[5]

Above Whaletown Road is the Whaletown Commons, a Regional District park that islanders spent twenty years trying to extract from Island Timberlands. It was eventually acquired by the Strathcona Regional District's Park Acquisition Fund in 2014. I walked along this 28.3 hectare (70 acre) riparian area noting its salmon bearing stream, second growth forest, veteran trees, and wildlife corridor. It is an oasis of nature among growing developments in the area.

Many regional governments have been setting up Park Acquisition and Conservation Funds all across BC. This is a separate fund usually created by a regional district with a small portion of its annual property taxes. It is a great way to raise funds to help conserve natural areas, and in some cases like in the Capital Regional District as mentioned in the Salt Spring Island chapter, in collaboration with local land trusts.

There are a few provincial parks on the island as well. Mansons Landing Park, established in 1974, abuts Mansons Landing and Hague Lake. I found the sandy shore off the Landing a welcome anchorage in fair winds, with the large lagoon inland and long peninsula offering a fascinating opportunity for exploration.

Smelt Bay Park is along the waterfront on the southern peninsula of the island and provides twenty-two camping sites. A long, narrow sheltered inlet at the north end of Cortes is popular with boaters and avid hikers. Háthayim Marine Park is an undeveloped marine wilderness park that includes lakes, estuaries, a saltwater lagoon, and an old growth forest. Boaters must be prepared for reversing tidal rapids, steep sided fjords, and tidal flats.

Parks are great for recreational and educational purposes. BC Parks, with their various classes (A, B, C), focus on protection of ecosystems and habitats, while others are focused on public recreational values, including camping. Regional parks have public access in mind when they acquire land, and other public amenities as well, including groundwater and riparian protection. The Island Trust's Nature Reserves are protected for their habitat values, national parks habitat and public recreational values. There are also educational reasons for conserving land, such as this far-sighted vision for the Children's Forest on Cortes Island.

The children of Cortes are lucky to have leaders within the Forest Trust for the Children of Cortes Island Society (FTCCIS). CHRISTINE ROBINSON

Forest Trust for the Children of Cortes Island Society

Briony Penn gave a talk on Cortes in 2009 to support and inspire Cortes islanders to defend their forest lands against Island Timberlands imminent logging plans. That sparked the creation of the Forest Trust for the Children of Cortes Island Society (FTCCIS), founded with the mandate to purchase, protect, and provide education and research. With acquisition their key goal, the FTCCIS has targeted the site of their youth programming for over ten years. Their goal is to protect approximately ~243 hectares (600 acres) within the James Creek watershed, immediately adjacent to Carrington Bay Park. Conservation covenants will be placed on the lands upon purchase.

Recent negotiations with Mosaic Forest Management (new managers of Island Timberlands and TimberWest forest holdings) to purchase five parcels of contiguous forestland have reached a key milestone, with successful negotiations for the two parcels immediately adjacent to Carrington Bay. Mosaic has placed the remaining three

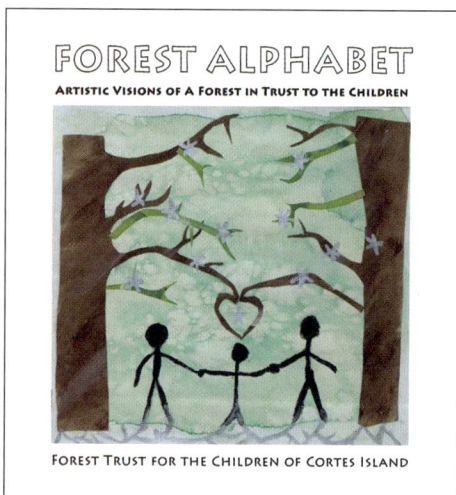

FOREST ALPHABET
ARTISTIC VISIONS OF A FOREST IN TRUST TO THE CHILDREN

FOREST TRUST FOR THE CHILDREN OF CORTES ISLAND

properties into a carbon offset, Big Coast Carbon Initiative that will provide protection for the next twenty-five years, allowing the Forest Trust Society to continue to raise funds to purchase these parcels for the children.[6]

The FTCCIS hosts monthly family forest walks, workshops in natural history, streamkeeper stewardship activities, and community bioblitzes with renowned flora and fauna experts such as Andy MacKinnon (forest ecologist), Paul Stamets (mycologist), and Suzanne Simard (forest ecologist). Mentorship, leadership, and empowerment are the focus of the Society's work with youth; the *Forest Alphabet: Artistic Visions of a Forest in Trust to the Children* was written by youth to bring attention to protection of the "Children's Forest" in perpetuity.

CONSERVATION COVENANTS have proven to be a very powerful tool to protect natural areas for private landholders on Cortes as elsewhere. Even though the total amount of protected land may not be large, they are still an incredibly useful tool for connecting landscapes and protecting ecologically important areas.

Given the dire state of the planet today, every bit of nature conserved counts! Cortes has attracted incredibly creative people who have incorporated land trust methods and legal tools. Thanks to the dedication of a few stalwart individuals like Sabina, Shawn, and Laurel, creative landholders like Mary and George, Joel, the Linnaea Farm Society, and Hollyhock and organizations, including TLC The Land Conservancy of BC, the Strathcona Regional District and the Forest Trust for the Children of Cortes, there are now many protected areas on the island. They have created small parks and trails, conserved ecologically sensitive areas, and worked with the larger conservancies to ensure that Cortes Island's trajectory is distinct from destructive logging practices. Most importantly, they have given it a vision that includes wildlife.

We headed into Gorge Harbour on another calm summer day. The harbour is known as Sa'y'ilh, meaning "two waters in one" because the salt water mixes here with fresh water from the numerous streams and springs.

CHAPTER TWELVE

SAVARY ISLAND

Saving the Big Wild Heart and Lots More

*"I ended with a quote from Joni Mitchell's famous song about paradise lost.
There was silence in the crowd. That was the moment SILT was born."*

LIZ WEBSTER

WE LEFT THE SMALL SANDY ANCHORAGE off of Mansons Landing on Cortes Island early. We had a long way to go ahead. The inner lagoon's entrancing tidal entrance receded just as we were heading out. It was a silvery blue flat calm day, so it looked like we were in for an all-day motoring journey. Travelling well outside the rocky shoreline along the southwest coast of the island, we set our sights on Savary Island.

Savary is a thin sliver of an island, a unique and ancient sand dune rising up as an island surrounded by underwater rocks—not the best anchorage for any vessel except a small fast speed boat with no keel. With calm waters forecast for the next few days, we neared Savary Island's south shoreline. Heather and I looked for a large fir that Liz Webster, co-founder of the Savary Island Land Trust, told me marked the front of her small cabin where she suggested we moor. With a ~7.5 metre (20–30 feet) deep sandy bottom and local moorings all around, we dropped the anchor, hoping we and the boat would be safe to spend the night there. With no shelter from the open sea, the close-knit and lightweight moorings could spell disaster as the winds and tides change things around.

Once I'd anchored, and then tied a stern line to an available mooring, we rowed to shore to meet Liz Webster, a dogged advocate for conservation on Savary Island. Normally accessible by small boat or water taxi from neighbouring Lund on the mainland, there is no BC Hydro to offer easy electricity. So, once I found our host, our first conversations revolved around solar panels and heat pumps to reduce firewood use, similar to many conversations on Lasqueti Island.

Savary lies within the traditional territory of the Tla'amin, Klahoose, and Homalco First Nations. There are two Indigenous names associated with the island. One is qɛyɛ qʷən, meaning fresh water spring.[1] According to Erik Blaney, a Tla'amin Nation's executive council member, ʔayhos (Savary Island—pronounced: ay-hos) was where "our ancestors not only placed our loved ones to rest on the island, but families were also raised here, wars fought, resources utilized and managed." The island is shaped like a serpent, with its crescent shaped form barely rising above the ocean's surface. Drew Blaney, Tla'amin Nation's culture and heritage manager, expanded on this origin story: "this serpent was taking too much from the neighbouring Mitlenatch Island, and so the transformer transformed ʔayhos into an island, which is a constant reminder for our people to not take too much."[2]

A rare sand dune system makes Savary Island ecologically unique among the islands of the Salish Sea. DEAN V'ANT SCHIP

Ecologically, Savary Island is unique among all the islands in the Salish Sea because of its rare dune ecosystem, towering cliffs, and large old growth cedars. North Thormanby Island, a much smaller island southeast of Lasqueti, has huge sweeping sandy cliffs and sandy beaches with numerous small lots as well. In contrast, though, Savary has a very unusual orientation in the Georgia Strait. Its longest shorelines face south and north, leaving it wide open to erosion from the prevailing winds in both summer and winter.

In the rare coastal Douglas-fir ecosystem, its red cedars, arbutus, and a number of western yew trees help stabilize its sandy soils. R. S. Sherman, an early local surveyor and naturalist, documented the island's ecology in his book *The Ecology of Savary Island*, from his visits to Savary starting as early as 1892. He described the island's high sand cliffs and stabilized gentle slopes of meadows as headed by an unusual shore pine and salal forest. With sandy beaches and close proximity to the mainland, boosters saw a chance to make their fortune.

The Union Steamship Company brought visitors to the Sunshine Coast and Savary from 1889 to 1959. Advertising their excursions to Savary as equivalent to a South Sea Paradise, the *Capilano* made stops there for twenty-five years, until it was wrecked near Savary Island in 1915. A second *Capilano* operated for another twenty years. It was promoted as a recreational paradise and tourist destination for more than half a century.

Unfortunately, Savary was subdivided in 1910 into 1,700 small 15.24 metre (50 foot) city-sized lots. A group of real estate developers, called the Savary Island Park Association, bought and then sold some of the lots. They built the Savary Inn and attempted to provide a communal water supply, planning to sell many more.[3]

Liz described the trajectory of its development. "Very few of the lots were developed and Savary was a pretty sleepy place for nearly a century. I came in 1994 and at that time only 450 lots were developed. Today there are 1,000 developments on an unregulated and unserviced migrating sandbar." Planning is under the authority of qathet (formerly Powell River) Regional District. According to Liz, the Islands Trust rejected Savary in the 1970s because of the number of small lots and the associated planning challenges. The island continues to be a recreational paradise for people

SILT Conservation lands

1. Indian Point Deer Sanctuary
2. Rowan Forest
3. Sunset Trail Forest
4. Rodgers Rd Wetland
5. Old Growth Forest
6. Gouin Family Forest
7. Savary Island Road Forest
8. Tennyson
9. Hodgins Forest
10. MacDougall Forest
11. Macdonald/Hannay Nature Reserve
12. Daryl Duke Memorial Forest

Savary Conservation Lands

Savary Island Land Trust
Province of BC
Nature Trust of BC
Crown land perimeter

Savary Island / Ayhos (Double Headed Sea Serpent)

from all over the world. In the early years small cottages, tents, and cabins were the norm. Today many larger developments are being built. The lack of planning, zoning, or even building codes in such an intensely subdivided environment has made Savary vulnerable.

Savary was formed from glacial sediments, layered over a bed of clay. A granite outcrop at Mace Point, known locally as the "anchor of the island," helps to stabilize and block the sand and gravelly clay from blowing back into the sea. The south shore is lined with eroding tall sand cliffs, the subject of many paintings. According to Jim Spilsbury (a legendary writer on the BC coast), he and other local children were employed to plant broom to stabilize the lower slopes![4] That broom is now rampant on the island, competing for soil with the native vegetation.

In the middle of the island, is a large 137 hectare (350 acre) unsubdivided District Lot 1375—the only intact district lot left on Savary. The island was divided into tiny lots on both east and west sides of District Lot 1375. Today, the area is called the Heart of Savary Island. It is a mecca of incredibly rare dune ecosystems, intact archaeological sites, and endangered species. The main road bisects this large section, with an old growth cedar forest and old growth Douglas-fir trees, including a very large gnarled one locals call the Spirit Tree. Islanders had used the trails running through this central area so long that they considered it theirs. That was all about to change!

In 1995 a ninety parcel, gated community was proposed by Roger Sahlin's RRR Construction and David Syre's Trillium Corporation. These Washington State developers each owned 50 percent undivided interest in the land and planned an airport and private airplane hangars, so that distant landowners could fly into their imagined development.

Along with another 3,000 odd people that travel here each year, Liz Webster came from nearby Powell River for the summer. "My first summer was a total dream, because I wasn't working. I fell in love with the island. I just got on my bike and explored the whole island. I had bought my cabin, and it was very Zen. It was beautiful. Time was so sacred. It became my sanctuary. The next year was when a bylaw proposed by the local government, put forward by two developers, was going to turn the heart of the island into this gated community, with ninety parcels covering rare and sensitive ecosystems."

At the time, Liz was an instructor at Malaspina College. In her second summer, she got a job driving a taxi on the island. Her cab quickly turned into an information highway. She said people would get in her truck and when they reached the centre of the island would gasp and ask, "What is happening with this land?" Being a newcomer she knew little about the land and with all the questions she got from long-time property owners every day she became curious and eventually got on the phone to the Regional District to find out. Pretty soon she was carrying copies of the proposed bylaw for the development around in the taxi and asking people what they thought about it. That same year Liz met Sherwood Inglis, who had spent his summers on Savary as a child and then bought his cabin in the 1960s, the oldest one on the island. Liz told me, "Sherwood was an island heritage buff and interested in protecting the great treasure that Savary was." Together they began hatching a plan to create Savary Island Land Trust (SILT) and try to save the Heart of Savary.

> People kept saying somebody has to do something about it! So I encouraged everyone to go to the public hearing, which was August 1995, at Duck Bay under the fir trees. We didn't have any community hall on the island, so that was where meetings happened. So the hearing happened and the directors from the regional district came over to listen. Lots of people spoke from the over two hundred people at the meeting. I didn't speak at the beginning, because I first wanted to hear what people were saying, but I had prepared my own reasons why this was a bad idea. The Regional District planner had said that the bylaw would help to protect the island's sensitive ecology. I asked how more roads, more development, and houses on top of sensitive ecosystems would help protect the island's sensitive ecology. I ended with a quote from Joni Mitchell's famous song about paradise lost. There was silence in the crowd. For me, that was the moment when SILT was born.

Liz explained that the next day Hartland MacDougall, a Savary islander and the first chair of Heritage Canada called her. He told her that he agreed with her sentiment and asked how he and his family could help. He became a founding director of SILT, and many years later donated a ~1 hectare (2.5 acre) forest to SILT under the Ecological Gifts program.

By this time, Liz had started a business called Savary Cycle and Recycle with customers from all over the island. Every time she visited a customer, the topic of saving the Heart of Savary came up. People felt so strongly about protecting this land it inspired Liz to dedicate her time and energy to save the island from the proposed ninety parcel subdivision.

A year after the meeting, Sherwood and Liz rode their bikes all over Savary seeking out potential board members for SILT. The land trust took another year to officially register, but by 1996 they had a full board of high powered directors.[5] These included Wynn Woodward, sister to Kip Woodward, the chair of the Nature Trust of BC at the time, whose family had been property owners on Savary for four generations. Daryl Duke, founder of TV station CKVU and director of the *Thornbirds*, *I Heard the Owl Call My Name*, and *Tai-Pan*, joined the board. Daryl had been coming to Savary since he was a child. His great uncle was R. S. Sherman, author of "The Ecology of Savary Island."

Forested sand dunes, salal, and Douglas-fir trees in "sacred valley." LIZ WEBSTER

Supported by this highly talented board, Sherwood, Liz, and later Paula Butler led the fight to acquire the Heart of Savary. Initially a founding board member, Liz and the rest of the board worked tirelessly to save the property from the proposed desecration.[6]

In 1999, in the beginning of their efforts to protect the property, the islands in the Salish Sea Community Mapping Project invited Savary to join the other islands in this millennial project. Sponsored by the Land Trust Alliance of BC (LTABC), it provided a small honorarium for both the coordinator and the artists. The stunning dark blue *Savary Island Map*, created by graphic artists Kathy Kebale and Tony Wypkema has formed one of the key pieces of education and fundraising ever since. This initial map shows the many species found on the island along its outer edges, with insets picturing the sandy geology and rare plants on Savary. The island is portrayed as covered in forest, but overleaf, it reveals the cadastral cutting up of the island into its eastern and western blocks of tiny lots, with the large District Lot 1375 in the middle.

Since then, they have used the map to create placemats, featuring varying themes, starting with information about the campaign to protect the Heart of Savary. They later developed other educational placemats featuring varying themes and to show different elements of the island including a wild flower map, the rare sand ecosystems, and the location of the bigger trees, each with an update about the campaign to protect the Wild Heart of Savary on the back. Like many other islanders involved in that millennial mapping project, Liz views the mapping project as central to all of their work.

The "Spirit Tree" on Savary Island. DENNIS INNGERSOL

When the Sahlin/Syre development proposal came forward, there had been no scientific inventory done on the island. "We knew intuitively that these were very special places that needed protection." Fortuitously, Liz met Kathy Dunster, a plant ecologist and dune specialist at an LTABC conference in Nanaimo. She invited her to visit Savary in March 2000. Kathy wrote the first analysis of the large, undeveloped property in the centre of the island, a report that highlights the island's rare dune ecosystems and the excellent aquifer in the centre of the island. The forest was identified as having old growth, more than 250 years old, and a mature second growth forest more than 80 years old, and a rare plant community that had never been named before. The area was also identified as having the largest groundwater recharge zone on Savary. With only three shallow perched aquifers and four springs, accessing fresh water can be a challenge.

According to Kathy's report, "the property provides one of the best examples of the geography of coastal dune ecosystems in Canada. Along with the dunes is a unique, complete, and therefore very rare, plant successional sequence: beach, beach strand, foredune, dune meadow, young dune forest and older forest."[7] The only other dune ecosystems of this nature are found in a few hectares of Point Pelee National Park in Ontario and another in the Sand Lake dune system near Cape Lookout on the Oregon coast.

Inspired by the report, several provincial and federal scientists from BC's Conservation Data Centre, Environment Canada, and BC Parks made a field trip to the island accompanied by the report's author, Kathy Dunster. "At one point, we had ten scientists here at once," Liz exclaimed. "We went through the whole island in two days; lastly we visited DL 1375." For several years afterwards university, government, and independent researchers visited the island and wrote scientific reports about the forest, its rare dunes, plants, and geology. The BC Conservation Data Centre encouraged the Province to include Savary in the Sensitive Ecosystem Inventory.

"We wrote a letter to the Nature Trust of BC asking them to join us in the campaign and included all these scientific reports." Liz added, "We also contacted the Nature Conservancy of Canada and hosted an NCC potential benefactor on Savary."

Like many of the other islanders detailed earlier in this history of conservation in the Salish Sea, Liz became aware of the Pacific Marine Heritage Legacy (PMHL) fund. She told me that at that time, the boundary was south of Texada Island, so Savary wouldn't be able to apply. SILT began lobbying the government and some key people who had places on the island. Working at Malaspina College, she heard about a BC public caucus meeting to be held in Powell River. She got herself on the roster. She made her presentation, and at the lunch after, David Anderson, the current BC minister of environment, announced that the PMHL boundary had been moved further north to include Savary Island.

Liz told another colourful story about a taxi ride she gave to Gordon Wilson, their MLA at the time.

> One day the taxi went down to the wharf, and Gordon Wilson, our MLA, was at the end of the dock with his groceries and no ride. I drove him down to where he was staying, near where you are anchored today. It was the slowest ride, because I had a lot to say. I had a good long talk there, filled him in on what was going on, as he was in power at the time. Later on he ended up being quite helpful, directing some provincial funds from the Georgia Basin Ecosystem Initiative to the cause. I don't know if I would have gotten involved in starting SILT and saving the Heart of Savary, if I hadn't got the job driving land taxi on Savary that summer. Because it was really all the voices of Savary islanders who told me "something has to happen here" and it was really the love of Savary and a lot of perseverance that drove the campaign. I was not looking for a project when I moved to Savary. I was going to teach in the winter, and spend my summers off relaxing and rejuvenating on Savary. I've been working on Savary Island conservation ever since!

The SILT board did everything they could think of to protect the area. One board member contacted the owner/developers directly and asked if they could buy it. When a negative answer came back, they went and spoke with the (then) Powell River Regional District to request a development permit be put on the property, so if they did go ahead, they would have to meet all the requirements of the development permit.

As the community became more aware of the developers' threats to the island, many began expressing their opposition to them, especially at public meetings. The developers submitted a second subdivision application, this one for thirty-six ten acre lots. Since at the time Savary had no planning and not even an OCP, the subdivision application was subject to the approval of the Ministry of Transportation. SILT submitted all of the scientific papers about DL 1375 to the numerous referral agents for the second subdivision application and met with the Ministry of Transportation approving officer. Eventually, the application was approved with twenty stringent conditions attached.

Liz expanded on that. "There was a lot of conditions because at the same time, the land was established as a Heritage Conservation Area. It had the most significant archeological and ecological features on the island. We started raising money. We had live art auctions at the Woodwards."

By now, both federal and provincial agencies recognized the importance of protecting the area. In a newsletter to islanders, SILT published the news that the Nature Trust of BC (NTBC), the oldest land trust in BC with links to these agencies, was on board. The executive director of the Nature Trust, Tom Lester, told SILT that "the Nature Trust endorses the conservation of the critical forested dune complex on Savary and will provide whatever assistance it can to promote its conservation."[8]

In the meantime, SILT had acquired six of the smaller lots on the island, dedicating them as nature reserves. Then in 2001, a generous donor gave SILT a beautiful ~4 hectare (10 acre) piece of forested land on the west side of the island. With SILT's outreach and fundraising building a strong reputation, these primarily donated lots became the centre of the land trust's successful work.

A year later, in 2002, SILT announced the good news. Quoted in the *Powell River Peak*, Tom Lester said, "On the strength of a magnificent donation of an eco-gifted property from two individuals who wish to remain anonymous, we were able to structure a deal that saw the Crown contributing $2 million from the Pacific Marine Heritage Legacy initiative, along with $100,000 from the Georgia Basin Ecosystem initiative through Environment Canada. That, combined with some money from the Nature Trust, was used to acquire the undivided 50 percent interest and the full interest of the second partner's property."

When the 50 percent interest was protected in 2002, Sherwood, Paula, and Liz, exhausted, resigned from the board. After a six month break, the board then hired Liz as the executive director, one day a month, to run SILT. She explained some of the creative and very successful ways they raised funds.

> We had been educating people, getting them to buy art. So we came up with Savary Stock to provide the operating funds we needed to keep the doors open and provide paid support. This big event, Savary Stock, is a huge auction with a barbecue and beer gardens at one of our board member's places. The biggest event drew eight hundred people. Because we wanted to bring in more and younger people in the community, we started a music festival, every other year. When we started out the entrance fee was five dollars. In the last year we had so many people, we took the tickets online and boosted the price to twenty-five because we wanted to have less people. It was just too overwhelming. We had over six hundred, which was manageable.

University of Victoria professor, Dr. Thea Cacchioni, who became the chair of SILT for five years, spearheaded the development of Savary Stock. During my visit to the island, Thea told me, "There were so many people on Savary who loved the island and cared about nature, who were not participating." She explained, "We tried to think about a fun, family centred event that could help raise funds and bring a fun spirit. With Bronwyn Schoner, the niece of Ed Henderson from the band Chilliwack, we worked to organize an all-day music festival and art auction. Savary Stock raised thirty-five thousand to fifty thousand dollars in one day! There were kids events and all age events. So that was a big success, and my contribution. I had a daughter to look after, so I left just when the Save the Wild Heart campaign picked up."

Liz explained that in 2010 the remaining developer, Roger Sahlin, took the NTBC to court asking the court to divide the land so that each party would have their own interest. The court ruling divided the land into a four strips of land with the Nature Trust and the developer getting alternate pieces. The SILT board was shocked and horrified by the court decision which did not take into account any of the ecological significance of the land. A meeting was held with the SILT and NTBC executives. SILT asked the NTBC to appeal the court decision and offered the assistance of SILT trustee and litigator, Christopher Harvey. The NTBC agreed with the condition that SILT raise the $50,000 needed for the appeal. Liz had just returned from a Land Trust Alliance of BC workshop on fundraising at the Naramata Centre and got busy. In one week, Liz told me, they raised the money and the NTBC agreed to appeal the decision. Sadly the appeal was not successful.

However, Liz told me about, "a new trustee on the Nature Trust of BC board and subsequent chair was another Savary islander, Doug Christopher. Doug's father Gordon was instrumental in the acquisition of the first 50 percent interest of DL 1375 for the Nature Trust of BC. Doug worked tirelessly and with the patience of a saint over the sixteen years towards the really challenging goal to acquire the remaining 50 percent interest in the land for conservation."

Some years later, in 2015, the remaining developer of District Lot 1375 went into bankruptcy. According to Liz, this led to the formation of a subgroup, the Friends of Savary. Most were members of SILT who were skilled business people with experience in acquisitions. In December 2017 the Friends of Savary DL 1375, comprised of Savary islanders Peter Armstrong, John O'Neill, Doug Christopher, Dan McIntyre, and Kip Woodward, successfully negotiated an agreement to purchase the remaining land in DL 1375 from the Sahlin family.

"Ultimately they struck a deal to buy the land for 3.5 million dollars," Liz said. "The Friends of Savary and SILT kicked off the fundraising by collectively contributing $1.8 million. We had to raise the remaining 1.7 million plus another half million extra for an endowment. We raised the bulk of that in six weeks—every penny from Savary. Together, we raised four million in six weeks—in 2018! But in reality, it took twenty-one years to finish this project. It's a good thing I didn't know that when I first started."

In 2018 the Nature Trust of BC announced its acquisition of the last 50 percent interest in the property. It was the longest acquisition the Nature Trust had ever undertaken. Two additional Savary Island donors added another twelve ~0.4 hectare (1 acre) waterfront parcels to the mix, so the entire ~142 hectare (350 acre) area was protected. It took over two decades of incredible effort and generous donations from this island community with the strong support of the Nature Trust of BC, who now hold the title. The Nature Trust of BC honored Friends of Savary leader John O'Neil and Liz Webster with the Conservation Champion Award of the Year for 2018 at their Gala Dinner in Vancouver. In 2023 the chair of the Nature Trust of BC is another Savary islander, Peter Armstrong, who was one of the Friends of Savary and a dedicated supporter of SILT.

Danielle Dalzell, a SILT board member, described their final success: "After 21 years of work on the part of the Savary Island Land Trust, with the tenacity and generosity of the Friends of Savary, as a community we came together to save the heart of Savary Island. It is a remarkable legacy to leave for future generations, and a story we should all be proud to be a part of."[9]

After completing the acquisition, they had another big party with five hundred guests and music by the Adam Woodall Band and special guest Colin James. Colin was happy to perform, having run on that land for exercise when he was on his own property on the island.

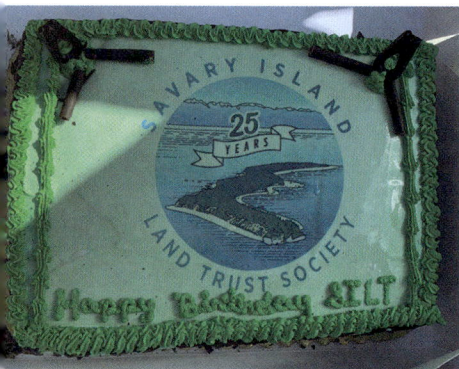

SILT was celebrating its twenty-fifth anniversary at the beach when I visited.

After years working to protect the Heart of Savary, SILT took on a new focus to acquire more conservation lands in all parts of the island. Recognizing a need to redirect and re-energize SILT the existing members approached some of the original board members to rejoin them. At the top of their list were former chair Sherwood Inglis, as well as land donor and litigator Christopher Harvey. They developed a new strategic plan which focused on a land acquisition framework, and educational initiatives. A gift from the Armstrong Family Foundation established a Savary Island Nature Legacy Fund and began to raise funds to help in further land acquisitions.

The day I went to Savary, a stunning coincidence came to light. It was SILT's twenty-fifth anniversary! Liz took me to the beach in front of five properties that had been donated to SILT over the years. They were having a party with a birthday cake, kid's games, and educational presentations. For their anniversary, they made T-shirts and created an auction with twenty-five pieces—one for each year. Their auctions have been a foundational support for keeping a part-time administrator moving the ball forward. Liz told me they ordinarily have sixty to one hundred works donated by the artists. Last year's auction raised $26,000. Dianne Cacchioni, a photo based artist who works on handmade paper and other media, stressed how wonderful it has been to contribute many pieces to Savary Stock over the years.[10]

By the time I visited in 2022, SILT had already acquired twenty-two properties. With another lot every 22 metres, Liz explained that some donors buy their neighbouring lot, to give them some privacy. SILT has also encouraged property owners to amalgamate their lots and reduce density. I walked the beach here on the north side, facing Lund, with the Rowans, a couple of early donors who had donated one of the first properties.

This enthusiastic couple told me, "Because we thought Savary was destined for disaster with 1,700 plus lots, we realized one way around that is to buy adjacent properties and amalgamate. There's also selfish reasons—we don't want another big house next to us. We bought the lot on the other side, and re-jigged it and gave the remainder to SILT. Everybody is so happy. We've been members a long time. Just think what the Heart of Savary would have been without SILT."

As I walked the beach with Liz, I asked her if she has hope for the future. She stressed the same thing I've heard from so many others I'd met. She hopes the younger generation will carry on the torch. Not surprisingly, this stalwart leader has been getting more young people involved in the organization. Their current chair is a young woman biologist named Maddie Beange. Her grandfather was one of the donors of twelve waterfront parcels that were added to the NTBC acquisition.

When SILT began, there was no protected land on unique Savary Island. Today more than 43 percent of the island is protected. I talked with several SILT supporters who came that day to enjoy the beach and join in the celebration. Walter Riemann, the current treasurer, explained that being on the board is a creative outlet for him. His goal is to keep the organization supporting Liz so she can continue to do the "incredible work" she has done over the years. He told me that he is looking at the future and how they can bring in the next generation.

I was caught up in this land trust's excitement as they explored the beach's creatures, celebrated their incredible success over twenty-five years. Danica, who runs the nature-based education programs, was leading a game the children play, called "I notice, I wonder, it reminds me of." With displays and games and a warm summer breeze, the beach was full of people.

Thea, the current chair, said something to me earlier in the day that stuck as we travelled back to Liz's place for dinner. She suggested that land trusts have a unique role to play in working with First Nations to acquire land for conservation. As I considered my return to Lasqueti Island, where an incredible archaeology project has enveloped the island in the past two years, I wondered what other roles land trusts might play in reconciling First Nations' traditional land stewardship.

ʔayhos Savary Island was quite heavily populated by the Tla'amin people until the mid-nineteenth century. Archaeologists confirm that the island was one of many preferred mortuary landscapes of the Tla'amin Nation.[11] In 2022 when a building site was being excavated, an ancestral burial and related archaeological artifacts were unearthed. In a media release about the project, the Tla'amin Nation asked that owners who are building conduct a Traditional Use Survey (TUS) before digging to ensure development is conducted in a respectful manner. Identifying archaeological sites is still a voluntary act in BC, even though doing so doesn't threaten the current owner's title.

As I headed back to the boat that night, the weather changed. Heather and I experienced a very windy night in a rolling open anchorage, reminding me how tentative our lives are. With each year, these incredible leaders in the conservation movement on the islands are passing on. I was delighted to be able to record the successes of this amazing Savary Island Land Trust, with its formidable executive director and strong team of voluntary directors and very supportive members and donors.

The next morning, everything had changed, yet again. It was a glorious morning, flat calm, as we set out for our home on Lasqueti Island. It was the end of another year of cavorting around the islands, meeting other founders of land trusts and learning about their successful conservation of land and hope for protection of the marine life in the Salish Sea. Several attempts to create national Marine Conservation Areas (MCAs) around the Salish Sea have unfortunately floundered. Over the past two years, I witnessed and avoided anchored tankers, and increases in tanker traffic from virtually no tankers twelve years ago. What a change! Proposals for new container ports and the dreaded Trans Mountain Pipeline (TMX) are moving ahead with their associated increase in ships and oil tankers that will be travelling in the

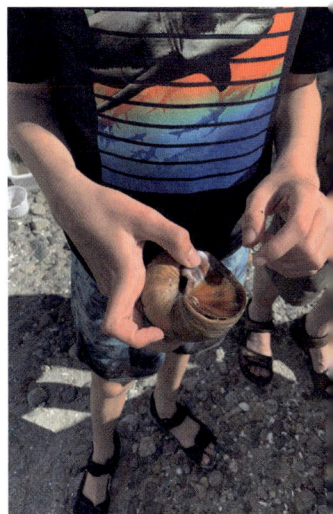

Kids were exploring the shoreline's fascinating creatures, such as this moon snail.

Salish Sea. Clearseas Centre for Responsible Marine Shipping provides these projections. "In an average year, 32 Aframax or Panamax oil tankers visit Vancouver, which is slightly more than one every two weeks. Once TMX comes on stream that number will rise to an estimated 380 Panamax and Aframax tankers or just over one per day."[12] Thousands of people have protested, written letters, and tried to stop these potential disastrous threats to the health and ecological integrity of the Salish Sea. Howard Macdonald Stewart of Denman Island writes in his seminal book, *Views of the Salish Sea*, "even an imperfect integrated coastal zone management (ICZM) process would be a marked improvement over the current free-for-all in which local interests are consistently steamrollered by powerful forces with deep pockets and governments they influence."[13]

As I headed for home, I looked around. With humpbacks now plying these waters, delighting almost everyone from all walks of life with their exuberance and return to the Salish Sea, I wondered, how can we turn this ship around? I was looking forward to heading to the new Átl'katsem/Howe Sound Biosphere Reserve and the final islands in my conservation journey—Bowen, Gambier, and the newest island conservancy on Keats Island.

Arbutus at Sunset Trail near Thah teq (Indian Point), on Savary Island. KATE HENDERSON

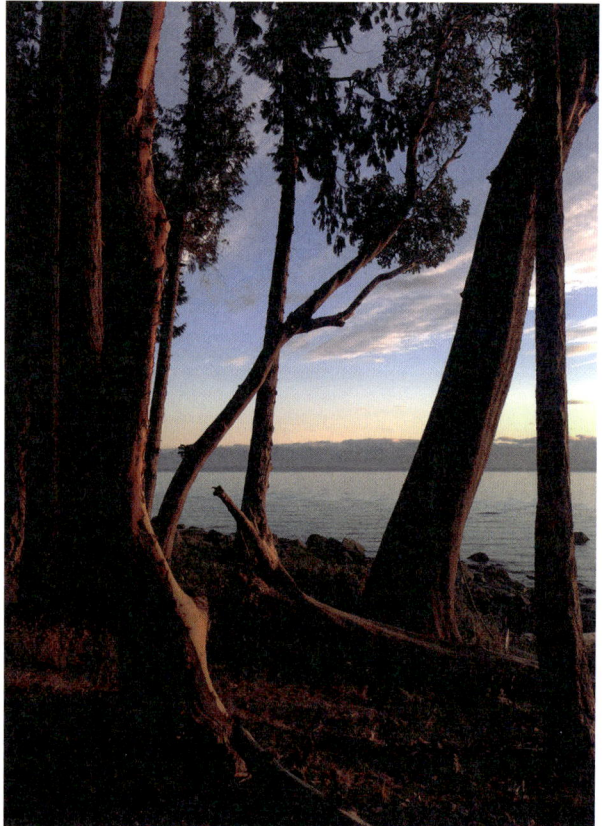

CHAPTER THIRTEEN

BOWEN ISLAND
Big Trees and Big Parks

*"Community is the way forward—connecting people
to their home place, so they know it better, and through
that knowledge comes care and stewardship."*
BOB TURNER

I COMPLETED THE LAST LEG of my conservation sailing journey in July 2023. Sailing downwind through a lumpy northwester, it took six long hours to reach my destination—Bowen Island on the outer reaches of Howe Sound. Squamish Nation Elders unveiled a new sign at Snug Cove welcoming visitors to Nex̲wlélex̲wem, Bowen Island, in 2021. It was a fitting gesture given that the island is an integral part of Squamish territory. Another Sk̲wx̲wú7mesh sníchim (Squamish language) name for Bowen I'd heard is Xwlíl'xhym, meaning "fast drumming ground" referring to the sound of running deer.[1] Sk̲wx̲wú7mesh (the Squamish People) hunted deer, collected clams, caught salmon and herring, and gathered many native plants on the island. Today, there are still numerous deer, travelling between some of the residential zones, through neighbouring protected places to the extensive Crown lands on the island.

Surprisingly, Bowen Island, in the Coastal Western Hemlock zone, has a higher level of mature and older forest than the islands in the Coastal Douglas-fir zone.[2] Given its proximity to Vancouver's three million people, one would think the island would be more suburban. The saving grace is the Crown lands, found on three high peaks—Mount Gardner and Mount Collins—plus the large 395 hectare ecological reserve on Apodaca Peak in the southeast side. The latter rises next to the small marine access at Apodaca Provincial Park. These Crown lands comprise 40 percent of the island's land base.[3] Due to these high mountain peaks and the logging which happened earlier than on the more remote Gulf Islands, 58 percent of the forests are between 80 and 250 years of age.[4] I nestled in the shade of these forests on my hot summer visit, and stood in awe at the base of one of the biggest trees I'd found on the islands. Unlike the drier Coastal Douglas-fir, Bowen and Gambier have far more rain than the islands they face across the Salish Sea.

When I arrived at Snug Cove and its neighbouring Kwilákm (Deep/Mannion Bay), I was struck by the extent of development, with numerous close-knit houses and many private docks. At Snug Cove, hourly ferries arrive full of day trippers, residents, summer residents, and contractors. Just up from the terminal is a hub of commercial stores and restaurants that I hadn't seen on any other island beyond Salt Spring Island. A bald eagle called my attention to the forested south shore of Snug Cove. Low flying herons and seals draped on the rising rocks of Kwilákm's southwest shore revealed a

Standing in front of a huge Douglas-fir on Bowen Island in the Coastal Western Hemlock zone, one of the wettest zones in Canada. SUE ELLEN FAST

continuous rock embankment that leads to a public causeway installed a century ago, behind which is a lagoon and the island's Terminal Creek.

On leaving this busy core, I could see some of the rural character that two women from one of the early settler families had been working to protect since early in the last century.[5] Marion Moore and Jean Jamieson, two of five sisters born on Bowen Island, grew up on the Collins farm near Snug Cove, carrying bottles of milk down to the old general store. The Collins sisters and others formed the Bowen Island Heritage Preservation Association (now Bowen Heritage) in 1989 to stop the Metro Vancouver Parks from destroying the historic Davies Orchard cottages in Crippen Regional Park. Like many land trusts in the US and in Canada, some of the early conservationists on Bowen Island started out focusing on preserving heritage conservation. This heritage generally focuses on settler history, and often leads to protecting some of the surrounding natural areas. Today, we are starting to recognize and include Indigenous cultural history as well as settler history.

As grown women, Marion and Jean wanted to ensure that Bowen Island retained its character, distinct from the suburban and urban neighbouring communities, and not become a bedroom of Vancouver. Not surprisingly, these two women joined the Cape Roger Curtis Trust Society, becoming two of its first donors in the long-time campaign to preserve the large ~243 hectare (600 acre) section of lands at the southern edge of the island, facing the open Salish Sea.

There is a substantial midden that runs across the front of what is known today as the Festival Field in Snug Cove. Farther up the shoreline are the old steamship playgrounds—where people would come from the city and compete in three-legged races and hold company picnics. An array of boats and water taxis provided access to Bowen Island then. The island has been a recreational destination for Vancouverites throughout the twentieth century. Initially the Terminal Steamship Company provided access, followed by the Union Steamship Company who promoted Bowen as a recreational destination. The Union Steamship Company built some 180 cottages, along with picnic grounds and a Dance Pavilion to bring people to the island for picnics, camping holidays, and moonlight cruises. After the Second World War the economy began to change, especially after ferries started bringing folks to the island in cars. By the 1950s the resort era ended. There are a few heritage buildings and some of the original fruit trees from 1887 still standing. Today, the new Union Steamship Company Marina welcomes visiting travelers and boaters to the historic lawns and docks, located on a dredged and filled tidal flat. Unlike some of the other Gulf Islands across the Strait, Bowen Island has limited agriculture. Hence it thrives mainly on bringing people from the mainland to drive, hike, or bike up the mountains and along the island's now protected parks. In the 2021 census, Bowen had 4,256 full-time residents.

After the Second World War and the arrival of the Blackball Ferries, later acquired by BC Ferries, the Union Steamship Company started to sell some of their cottages, including one along the waterfront—sold to the grandparents of a pioneer conservationist, John Rich.[6] For more than fifty years John Rich's family has lived in the same house near Snug Cove. He's seen a lot of change. Early in our conversations he remarked, "if it wasn't for the threats to the natural environment and enjoyment of it as a natural place, I'd probably be a retired carpenter." Instead, John lived a far from quiet life, as he went on to be the chair of the Islands Trust for six years. After that he became a lawyer and worked with several First Nations on litigation of historical claims and aboriginal rights. Today, John is on the board of the Bowen Island Conservancy.

Crippen Park—Bowen's First Park Land

John moved with his wife to live full-time on Bowen in 1973. "Kim and I were just putting roots under us," he explained, "when we found that a developer wanted to put thousands of houses on the neighbouring property and urbanize the place." Stan James, a developer with a deplorable track record, purchased 607 hectares (1,500 acres) of the former Steamship lands—stretching from north of the largest lake on the island, Killarney Lake, down to the former resort lands near Snug Cove.

James bought the land by securing private mortgages at 25 percent interest rates, counting on a quick sale of some 3,000 housing units, golf courses, etc. that would generate the funds for payments along with a very substantial profit. A pro-development director of the Greater Vancouver Regional District (GVRD) implemented a zoning bylaw that would allow 10,000 quarter acre lots and a lodge on Bowen Island. Shortly after, in 1969 the provincial government's 10 acre freeze on the islands resulted in the GVRD and the Province putting a hold on the bylaw. John had much to say about the antics that the developer, Stan James, used as the people holding the mortgages started to get concerned.

> James owned the community's water system as well, as part of what he purchased, and he was threatening to cut off the water. He also threatened to cut off access to his property, which had been used for recreation forever by Bowen residents. The first thing he did actively was close a causeway that goes between the lagoon and Deep Bay. In order to get from Deep Bay to Snug Cove you have to walk on the causeway. Lots of people lived on the other side, and the community had been using it for over fifty to sixty years. So he built a chain-link fence. People hauled it down. That's when I became active in 1975 in Bowen affairs. We were particularly affected by the causeway closure, and I had a problem with his attitude and proposal. We formed a committee for causeway access—to fight back. This got me more involved in the local political scene. Then I got involved in the local Advisory Planning Committee. Using that springboard and level of interest I ran in 1976 for the newly minted Islands Trust, with another new trustee supportive of putting an official community plan in place which would include recreational and conservation values.

With the developer under duress from the mortgage holders and the new official community plan that called for rural rather than urban development, James decided to start logging, from Snug Cove over to Killarney Lake, the largest lake on Bowen. The community had always seen this area as environmentally and recreationally significant. With virtually no control over actions on private land, John convinced the three general trustees, appointed by the Province, to request a stop work order to stop the logging under the *BC Environment and Land Use Act*. The *Act* was a lucky route for Bowen, as John said it was only used three times across the province, then rescinded.

John described the intense days during the community's protest against James. "In the winter of 1977, James was trying to get a logging operation in. He got a cat too large to go on the ferry, so it was delivered to Sandy Beach/Deep Bay. A smaller logging show came on the ferry with a skidder and small cat with about four guys. They went to a place where the contractor had things stored. Everyone knew logging was imminent—the beginning of the next week, so we had three to four days. Along with others in the community, we decided to have a demonstration and try to interfere with the logging and hope the Province would agree with our resolution for the stop work order."

Stanley Burke, a member of a Vancouver family who, with a couple of other families, owned a ~243 hectare (600 acre) piece of land on the southwest corner, was sympathetic to the struggle. He owned various small newspapers and had worked for the CBC. He asked John what they planned to do. "'Show up and stand in front of the bulldozers,' we said." John described the resulting dramatic event.

Burke said, "make it presentable for TV. Use fire extinguishers and stop the engine. He sent us a bunch of fire extinguishers. He sent us a bunch of media too, and at 7:00 AM fifty people were standing out where the logging was going to start. Up the street came *The Sun, The Province,* three TV and one radio station. They were pissed off to come for householders and hippies—but we were delighted. The loggers showed up and a bulldozer driver. And we stood in the way of things. This small outfit started their machines and drove forward, but the driver told his guys to stand down and get out of the way, but the bulldozer driver was storming. Stan James's manager showed up, who was a great big guy, and very hostile. He showed up, drunk, and with coffee and something you could smell in it. We tried to make a deal with him—to stop until we meet to negotiate plans for the land. He agreed to that, and we wrote it out and both signed. We were pretty naive. Then he realized what he had done, and he tried to snatch it back—the TV gets the action. The agreement was to stand down, but the bulldozer driver doesn't agree. He doesn't have the keys though, as someone has taken them. Assuming things had settled, someone throws the keys back to him, because of the agreement. But he starts his bulldozer and drives into the crowd with people on his blade—a potter, and a thirteen-year-old gal. He drives trying to shake them off. The whole crowd is running along beside. TV cameras are getting it. He stops at the precipice. The potter's wife climbed over the track and grabbed the driver, who punched her, following which the potter climbed over the machine from the blade and slugged the driver. This is all on national television news that night. Just as this was happening, a radio operator came in and said, "the stop work order just came in."

Beaver Wetland on Killarney Creek, Crippen Regional Park. WILL HUSBY

John explained how the land eventually became a Regional Park. A group of islanders created a society, the Park and Store Use Society, with its goal to establish a park and save a heritage building, which is now the library. John felt "this was a long shot because the Province wasn't making parks in those days, and the GVRD had just adopted a park plan with no more room in it. But that didn't discourage people on the island, and we lobbied and negotiated to do whatever we could. Eventually we managed to work with the GVRD to make a deal with the Province to purchase ~283 hectares (700 acres) out of James' holdings. At that point his mortgages were held by Crippen Engineering—who got burned badly. They had a stop work order and an angry community. The GVRD chairman, Jim Tonn, sealed the deal with Crippen when he suggested, 'how about two million and we'll call it Crippen Park?'"

Today, Crippen Regional Park is 240 hectares including Killarney Lake, all along Terminal Creek leading down to the lagoon behind Kwilákm (Deep/Mannion Bay). The park also includes extensive trails leading from north of the lake down to the lagoon to the older causeway. It contains the Terminal Creek Hatchery, fish ladder, and Bridal Veil Falls—out to Snug Cove and beyond to its end at Dorman Point. The acquisition of Crippen Park is a perfect example of how local people, with patience and persistence, can conserve land in their own communities.

Bowen Island Conservancy—Working in a Municipal Setting

The 1969, 10 acre freeze on land development for the islands was followed by a freeze on Crown land development on Bowen, initiated by the Bowen Island Improvement Association (BIIA). In 1971 the Province transferred land use planning to regional districts. On Bowen, the Greater Vancouver Regional District (today Metro Vancouver Regional District) would now have planning authority. Regional districts were to develop official community plans (OCP) that established zoning, which would then lift the 10 acre freeze. The BIIA worked with the Advisory Planning Commission to create a draft OCP that "recommended a slow growth policy to ensure that the island remained a 'restful refuge' for residents as well as tourists."[7] With developers planning extensive subdivisions on Pender, Mudge, and Bowen, the New Democratic Party (NDP) government of the day established the Nunweiler Commission, with a mandate to gather evidence and make recommendations for protection of the Gulf Islands. In 1974, the newly elected NDP government maintained Nunweiler's recommendations, and the Islands Trust was enacted with planning authority now transferred to this regional body.

The GVRD no longer had planning authority, so some islanders felt that its services to Bowen were limited. In 1999, with political alliances changing like the tides, after several referendums, 70 percent of the less than 4,000 residents on Bowen at the time voted to bring in the only municipal government on the islands within the Trust Area.[8] The political shenanigans from the pro-development side backing or standing as elected councillors with the proponents of conservation and careful development at the other end of the spectrum provides an ever-changing political vision on the island. The Islands Trust, the Bowen Island Municipality, and Metro Vancouver Regional District (formerly GVRD), in addition to the province and the federal government, all have differing powers and authority on the island.

Around this time the Bowen Island Improvement Association inadvertently lost their society status by not filing their annual report on time. Quick to take advantage of this oversight, the pro-development side filed papers for their group in the name of the Bowen Island Improvement Association. Thus, a very different political group acquired the name. In response, the old group adopted the new name of the Bowen Island Alliance. About ten years later they changed it to the Bowen Island Eco-Alliance to reflect their goal of protecting the island's ecological environment.[9] In 1996, the Bowen Island Eco-Alliance invited Des Kennedy, a Denman Island author, to come to Bowen to talk about his consuming interest in gardening and to introduce his latest book. Some Bowen islanders were aware that he was a director of the Denman Conservancy as well, so they asked him to stay and talk with another twenty-two or so Bowen islanders. They listened intently as he explained how conservancies can give power to locals to protect land, outlining some of their goals, successes, and programs.

The attentive group formed a steering committee, contacted other Gulf Island conservancies, including the newly formed Gambier Island Conservancy, and the current manager of the Islands Trust Fund (Conservancy), Lisa Dunn, to explore options and review constitutions. Considering the existing organizations on the island—the Forest and Water Management Society, the Bowen Island Eco-Alliance, and the Bowen Nature Club—they realized that a conservancy had its own unique role to play including "the ability to work formally with the provincial and federal Conservancy bodies, to educate Bowen Islanders about the advantages of protection, and to prioritize areas for protection on the Island. Of particular note was the existing public (Crown) land on Bowen and the Island wide opinion that some of that land might be better protected. In addition, people felt that a Bowen Island Conservancy could play a role in supporting research into conservation activities on the Island, and allow interested individuals to tap into the continuing flow of ecological and forestry research grants."[10]

Dave Witty led the official community plan development on Bowen. With considerable experience, he was active nationally in land use planning, including being the chief planner for Parks Canada for a while. He was at the Des Kennedy talk and joined the founding board.[11] During a phone interview with Dave, he described their impetus.

The thing that brought it together was Anne Ironside. She was a driving force in everything she touched in life. She and her husband had Ashoka House, a retreat centre where people came and reflected. She was quite a progressive thinker, and I ended up meeting her through UBC—we touched base and hit it off. I knew lots of people then. I chaired the Crown lands group, knew Sue Ellen Fast and her husband Will Husby. I can still see myself sitting on the floor, in a deep circle and we talked—and that was her approach. Through that, we developed a collaborative and integrated approach—ensuring that Bowen was developed in the right way, sitting beside the Vancouver monster. I knew about land trusts from my land use background, so it wasn't a new idea. It was the right idea at the right time—like-minded people sharing interests.

By the summer of 1997 the Bowen Island Conservancy (BIC) officially registered as a society. They added the goal of direct land acquisition along with the ability to use other legal tools and to act as a charitable land trust.

Like many other conservancies, the BIC had its first "office" at the home of the new directors, Julian and Kathy Dunster. Julian is a registered consulting arborist, professional forester, and professional planner. Kathy is a plant ecologist and a director of the Land Trust Alliance of BC for many years. The new Bowen Island Conservancy's (BIC) work overlapped with the Forest and Water Management Society (FWMS) who was doing the field work, data gathering, and mapping for a Crown lands inventory. Julian was locating and mapping the creeks, streams, and wetlands on the Crown lands, with the assistance of two of Vicky Troop's (a professor at Capilano College's environmental planning program) students. After receiving funds from ESRI, an international geographic information system software company, they put it all into digital GIS format. A data sharing agreement was signed between BIC and the Province to ensure that the more accurate ground-truthed GIS data was used to update government maps.

All this volunteer work culminated in *The Crown Lands of Bowen Island* report published in 2000, which then instigated the protection of the Mount Gardner watersheds. It was also used to stop the reopening of mining claims on Mount Gardner.[12] The new Conservancy was then armed with the science to take up the case for conservation of the Crown lands. The change of governance from a Local Trust Area to an island municipality in 1999 helped put weight behind the argument to protect Crown lands for their ecosystem services and public benefits.

The FWMS continued to do the background science and data collection to help inform the work of the Conservancy. The early 2000s focus on fresh water and watershed protection led to a team of islanders, including several working for the Geological Survey of Canada, engaging the community in learning how precious water is on Bowen. The result was the publication in 2005 of an illustrated poster packed with information useful to readers of any age or background. Knowing where the waterbodies and wetlands were, some previously unmapped or features found to be in the wrong location on government maps, helped in the creation of the *Bowen Island Map* for the Islands in the Salish Sea mapping project. This led to more ecological inventory work as background for protection of the Crown lands and private lands under threat of speculative land development.

After *The Crown Lands of Bowen Island* report was complete, one of BIC's early projects was creating a wetlands inventory. Funded by the Islands Trust Conservancy

Sue Ellen Fast with her map of Bowen's protected areas, heading to the Fairy Fen Nature Reserve.

in 1999, it resulted in the publication of the *Bowen Island Wetland Inventory*, completed by Karen Golinski with field assistance by Kathy and her daughter, Flora Dunster. This work helped the Conservancy identify specific areas, such as the future Fairy Fen Nature Reserve, that needed protection and informed their future Greenways Plan.

The day I met Sue Ellen Fast, she came bouncing down the public dock to meet me, her rolled up map of Bowen Island in hand, ready to show me what was what. She has been walking through the alleyways of various societies and levels of government on Bowen Island since the early '90s. She is also one of the most positive people I interviewed. She spent much of her adult life working in wildlife habitat education. She first came to Bowen Island through educational work she was doing with the Greater Vancouver Regional District Parks (GVRD). She told me, "in 1989 I first came to Crippen Park wearing a Park uniform, and I was stopped on the road. It was a very stormy time." Sue Ellen told me she later moved to Bowen because of the fabulous people she met on the island while working on joint events.

Now a permanent resident of the island, Sue Ellen joined the local Parks & Recreation Commission because of its new parks mandate. One of her major goals was to help acquire parks and establish public accesses to beaches. Because of Sue Ellen's work with the local Commission, Anne Ironside asked her to replace her as chair of the new BIC. She held this position for the next nine years.

Sue Ellen described how their Greenways Plan spanned Bowen Island, from one side to another, and envisioned protecting natural areas at all elevations. She drew a picture of the watersheds of Bowen Island with her hands, describing three upside down tea cups—the mountains—slowly draining their water into the two lush valleys on the island in the dry season. Sue Ellen explained how things developed.

This Cape to Cape Greenways Plan links up small parks, riparian areas, with bigger parks, like Crippen and the Crown lands. We are lucky to have these undeveloped lands, all the way down to the water's edge, so wildlife could come from the land to the sea, to keep the connections of wild natural areas and wildlife corridors open. It was a concept helpful in a surprising way. When we shared this on a map/diagram with my husband Will, he created the plan as a map on the computer. I discovered after the fact, Mayor Bob Turner had taken that map to UBCM and presented it at meetings. This concept map found its way into Metro Vancouver Regional District's (MVRD) Regional Growth Strategy, in a different format, but with the conceptual linked natural spaces. That was helpful because it set the stage for Bowen in MVRD's Regional Growth Strategy. It helped make Bowen part of a Conservation and Recreation Area for the larger region, outside the urban containment area—where people could get away, and nature was protected. Conservation was a theme, and it helped shape the way Metro Vancouver Regional District has envisioned and now helps to create parks and protected areas on Bowen Island.

For many years the Bowen Island Conservancy worked on watershed education, heron protection, vegetation restoration in the local parks, and developing the wetlands inventory. Like other islands, they also led public walks, submitted articles to the local paper, and invited key speakers to their AGMs. Sue Ellen said, "The BIC became quite involved in advancing the Parks Plan, which we would present to council about the benefits of rezoning of parks, beach access, etc. Because the municipality at that point only had a very small staff, we had a hand in many parks, trails, and greenways."

While Sue Ellen traipsed me around to all their protected sites, Crown lands, and parks, I learned that there are several heron nesting colonies on Bowen Island. I'd seen several herons flying low over Kwilákm while I was moored there, and learned that nearby and busy Snug Cove was one of the nesting sites. She also told me an interesting tidbit that made my earlier sightings of so many herons on the other islands' bays make sense! I had previously learned that herons need over 2,000 calories of food a day to raise two to three chicks (about what an adult human needs), and that they usually nest near healthy eelgrass beds.[13] Sue Ellen added to that by stipulating that herons are much more accepting of humans in their neighbourhoods than eagles are. With these kinds of survival needs for just one species, the Bowen Island Municipality has taken one step further by recently approving a Conservation Development Strategy that recommends nature needs half. This 50 percent nature protection goal has been taken on by other municipalities, including the Regional District of Nanaimo.

Adult great blue heron on nest in arbutus tree. TRUDY CHATWIN

Among the many places that Sue Ellen took me to was one of BIC's early restoration projects at the municipality's Quarry Park. On both Bowen and neighbouring Gambier Island, a few nature reserves and parks were created through subdivisions. Sue Ellen told me that John Reid is an unusual developer on Bowen because he understands natural processes and often provides 50 percent dedicated parkland with his developments. So much so, that in the municipality's early days, an owner of a large property hired John to help him develop a plan to restore the destroyed wetland and fish bearing creek that he had used as a quarry for a source of soft aggregate materials. A three-way agreement was made between John Reid and the Province and the Bowen Island Conservancy to revegetate the area and make Quarry Park function as wildlife habitat and as a park with trails. Several developed ponds needed to be opened and bridges installed to allow for the slow dissemination of water through creek channels. Eroding slopes that sent down torrents of rain needed to be stabilized and planted with seeds, wetland plants, and native shrubs. With the help of numerous volunteers, the BIC spent four hundred hours installing plastic mesh, planting and protecting tree seedlings, and adding other green biomass to hold down the gently sloped hills. The park is now a living expression of collaboration and successful restoration, which surely would have pleased Anne Ironside. As we walked along this restored area, I was impressed with the resulting wetland, bridges, trails, and forested areas. Next to the adjoining Crown land, and the future ITC Fairy Fen Nature Reserve and then to the Cape Roger Curtis lands, Quarry Park became the gateway to the Greenway.

Bowen Island's Crown lands are still in the Province's annual allowable cut—the amount of timber that is permitted to be cut annually from a particular area. A few years ago BC Timber Sales (who allocate logging rights on Crown lands) were thwarted by the Islands Trust and the Municipality of Bowen Island, the Squamish

First Nation, in addition to the local community who "offered to have a demonstration going to the meeting site." The Province is required to consult with the Squamish First Nation and have visual quality objectives in place if it is to consider a license to cut, so it cancelled the proposed lease. Even with the biodiversity crisis and carbon that trees sequester, the Province continues to lease Crown lands for logging, as we have seen on Quadra and Cortes islands. With logging on Bowen put on the back burner for now, development continues to be the largest threat to the conservation of natural areas on the island.

Another outstanding conservationist on Bowen Island is Bob Turner. With a background in geology, Bob is currently on the Bowen Island Conservancy's board. Bob is also an incredible videographer. His conversational, narrative, video explorations of nature around Bowen of the herring runs near Hornby, and now his focus in the larger Salish Sea region, brings intriguing close-up shots of underwater creatures and of nature in the Salish Sea into people's homes.[14]

A National Park on Bowen Island?

In 2008, when Bob was the mayor of the Bowen Island Municipality, the municipal council invited Parks Canada to come to Bowen to consider creating a national park on the island. Bob told me the process of determining if the community was open to a national park brought surprising results.

> That Parks Canada was considering a national park on Bowen Island set in some people's minds, certainly mine, that maybe there was a higher purpose to the Howe Sound region than just being the recreational backyard to Vancouver. The National Park initiative set in motion a very big process on Bowen. A year and a half of community consultation and investigation inspired a lot of people to realize the value that Bowen Island could be as a protected area. Parks Canada brought a conservation culture that people on the island hadn't experienced before.
>
> Parks Canada's National Park initiative, even though it failed in the end, inspired a larger view of conservation possibilities throughout the larger Howe Sound region. Bowen Island Council took the National Park question to a referendum and the community narrowly (54/46 percent) voted against it, so Parks Canada discontinued their initiative. Many people opposed the park idea because they feared that Ottawa bureaucrats would have control over large parts of the island, and island life would change dramatically. But among many, there was a sense that a National Park is a new powerful approach to caring for the land. I think the National Park initiative was one of the events in the Howe Sound region that set the stage for the success of the biosphere initiative. People paid attention. It inspired a lot of people, including myself.

Outreach—Educational Tools to Inspire Stewardship

During my interview with Bob, he explained that a mountaineer named John Clarke taught him about communicating with the public. Back in the late '90s John was a well-known mountaineer and, as Bob said, a "remarkable guy, having summited more peaks in the Coast Range than any other climber." He had an accident with another well-known conservationist, Randy Stoltman. Randy had written a book, the *Hiking*

Guide to the Big Trees of Southwestern British Columbia, highlighting their locations and importance. He proposed a conservation area in the Squamish River watershed. Sadly, Randy was killed by an avalanche while out with John on mountaineering trip. The tragedy led John to turn his attention to conservation education. As Bob explained:

> He gave a lot of talks to school groups. He had a giant collection of photographs from the Coast Range, and from ancient forests. He had a wicked sense of humour— he'd show a picture of an old growth forest, and say," well that's what happens when you don't cut your lawn for 1,000 years." He had memorable lines, such as "there are valleys in Southwest BC where the grizzlies don't know that Columbus has arrived." Everyone who listened to John got drawn into the conservation movement in some way. He worked with the Squamish Nation and artists from the Roundhouse Community Centre in Vancouver to run the Witness Program. For ten years in the 1990s the Witness Program would take a convoy of cars from downtown Vancouver up the Squamish River on summer weekends. They'd take people, many who had never been camping before, to big sandbars in the rive. Everybody set up their tents, and Squamish Nation members would host a welcome circle. Over the course of the weekend, they would run hikes in the ancient forests, along the river, or workshops such as drum making or storytelling. The whole purpose was to introduce people to this wild landscape, and to walk them into an ancient forest and a clear-cut area, to experience the difference. John didn't sermonize, he helped people experience things and then let them come to their own conclusions.

American dipper at Terminal Creek Lagoon. WILL HUSHBY

This story underscores the engaging and humorous style that infuses Bob Turner's videos and photography. Bob told me that working with John Clarke and the Squamish First Nation gave him a new awareness and commitment to "home place." "I had never encountered a people who, as they say, have been here since time immemorial. Squamish members would say to me, 'you white guys can come and make a mess of this place and then move on. But this is our home, we can't move on.' I was profoundly moved by that commitment to place. And John led me to that sentiment too. It's been something I've committed to ever since."

Bob worked on the team to gain designation for Átl'ka7tsem/Howe Sound as a United Nations Educational, Scientific and Cultural Organization (UNESCO) biosphere reserve for five years and remains an honorary director on the board of the newly minted Átl'ka7tsem/Howe Sound Biosphere Reserve.

Inspired by the Hornby Island Marine Atlas, several BIC directors developed a Bowen Island marine atlas in 2019. Len Gilday, Will Husby, Susan Munro, and Bob Turner initiated this marvelous atlas, *Exploring Bowen's Marine World*.[15] The result of tremendous effort by many Bowen islanders, the marine atlas is intended to foster public awareness of and engagement in local marine conservation issues. The atlas depicts some Squamish Nation's use and place names on Bowen Island, coves and bays where winter sea ducks congregate, streams, eelgrass, and salmon spawning beds, and the threats and best practices needed to protect the marine and connected terrestrial world around Bowen Island.

A related web-based exploration of Bowen's largest estuary and bay describes its history and place name: "For thousands of years, the Squamish People harvested shellfish in the estuary where Terminal Creek, Nex̱wlélex̱wem/Bowen Island's largest stream, drains into the sea. They called this place Kwilákm: Clam Bay."[16]

This innovative map and media site features award winning photography by Will Husby matched by a video with snorkel donned Bob Turner traveling from the freshwater of Terminal Creek, downstream to the brackish waters of the lagoon, and into the sheltered saltwater of Kwilákm. Within the hub of Bowen Island's human centre at Snug Cove and Kwilákm, the creatures and habitats featured in both Bob's video and Will's photography are a testament to nature's resilience and diversity even in the midst of a human centre.

Another important organization within the Salish Sea community is the Marine Life Sanctuaries Society (MLSS). This group has been advocating for greater protection of coastal marine ecosystems for decades, initiated by Thetis Island's Andy Lamb and Bernard Hanby. Over the course of thousands of dives, Lamb and Hanby determined that rockfish have been declining significantly over the last twenty-five years. As a result, the MLSS proposes many more marine protected areas, especially no-take sanctuaries.[17] No-take zones are marine protected areas that do not allow any fishing, mining, drilling, or other extractive activities. The society reports that the Rockfish Conservation Areas designated by DFO in 2002 over the entire coast of BC have, unfortunately, seen slow success due to non-compliance and general lack of awareness.

Glen Dennison, a citizen scientist and diver, found twelve glass sponge reefs in Howe Sound. Further dives revealed that rockfish prefer sponge reefs for foraging and nursery habitats. There is a glass sponge reef off Bowen's Dorman Point, a sponge aggregation off September Morn Beach and another off Gambier's Halkett Point. Elements of protection of these sponge reefs have followed, with a few federally protected sanctuaries now in place. These sanctuaries prohibit crab traps, downriggers, and any heavy things that will break the sponges. Sue Ellen remarked that along with this federally protected marine sanctuary in place, people on the island have seen whales in the are, giving her hope that things can turn around.

MLSS has secured funding from DFO, the Howe Sound Biosphere Region Initiative Society, and BC Parks to greatly expand their citizen science scuba monitoring of rockfish and lingcod, including at the shallower glass sponge reefs.

Cape Roger Curtis

At the south edge of Bowen Island lies Cape Roger Curtis, considered the jewel of Bowen Island. Once a single property, its 255 hectares (631 acres) include open forests of arbutus, the rare and unique seaside juniper, and coastal bluff ecosystems, fringed by riparian areas, with mussel and eelgrass beds offshore. The Bowen Island OCP set goals for the protection of sensitive upland areas including the shoreline, foreshore, and offshore areas. The Cape was specifically designated important for its recreational and environmental values. The area requires a development permit to protect the public interest. Its extensive trail system of old logging skid roads turned to forest trails were commonly used by Bowen islanders for decades to access the Cape.

The Bowen Island Conservancy has worked to protect the Cape since its formation in 1997. In 2002 they created a separate organization, the Cape Roger Curtis Trust Society (CRCTS), with two hundred members dedicated to protecting the Cape's unique ecosystems and environmentally sensitive areas. The society was devoted to a

Diane Reid over Dorman bioherm, off Bowen Island—one of twelve glass sponge reefs located by 2022 in Howe Sound. ADAM TAYLOR

broad community-based goal to include recreation and public access through a series of trails, illustrated in the Cove to Cape Greenways concept sketch. The initial goal was to purchase the lands for conservation, but in 2004 before sufficient funds could be raised, the land was sold to a professional development consortium, the Cape Roger Curtis Joint Venture.

The company's plan at the time included rezoning that would allow for greater densities than the original 58 lots—up to 480 units, a village with an 80 room inn and restaurant, and 464.5 square metres (5,000 square feet) of commercial area with a school, playgrounds, community centre, and amphitheater. This created an increasingly acrimonious debate within the Bowen community. CRCTS noted on their website that "events were turning confrontational (locked gates erected to keep out local hikers, the brazen cutting of a gruesome 'driveway' off of Whitesails, etc.). The CRCTS proposed alternative solutions in the form of their Wild Coast Two plan."

Eventually the company withdrew their rezoning plans five years later and applied for the final subdivision of fifty-nine lots. The development was approved providing that a 30 metre "do not disturb" protective covenant be registered along the shoreline and that they create three public access points at road ends linked to a public trail.[18] After some of the lots were sold, the community and some of the municipal councillors continued their drive to protect the area, including resisting three very long docks that went against the official community plan.

The Wild Coast Nature Refuge at Cape Roger Curtis, the first nature reserve protected by the Bowen Island Conservancy. OWEN PLOWMAN

Wild Coast Nature Refuge— Acquiring a Small Jewel for Nature

In 2012, the Bowen Island Conservancy recognized that they needed someone with an administrative background on the board. Peter Drake, the past president, asked Owen Plowman to join the board even though he was still working in Vancouver full-time. When I spoke with Owen, he told me when he travels to Bowen he notices "the people who come here want to get away from the city. Yet when they move they think they're moving to a suburb, and ask questions like, 'where's the pool?' We have to educate people that it isn't a suburb. You can have all those things but your taxes will go up. If we keep knocking down trees and building structures the island will lose its character and charm—the whole reason for people coming here. Six years ago we did a survey, asking what it is people think is significant on the island. The overwhelming response was it feels like it has a quiet, natural beauty. We need to preserve that and keep the lens of conservation of the natural environment. I think that's the case on all the islands."

After twenty years of trying to protect Cape Roger Curtis, Owen found very generous donors who offered to help BIC acquire three of the lots. "The land was much loved by residents and used as a park. It was hard for people when it was taken over and divided up into chunks. But we got this donation and were able acquire 32 acres of it. That's an amazing feat for a volunteer organization and a great boon to the island. It can be enjoyed by visitors and residents, and it made a huge splash." Owen explained, "I did the negotiations back and forth with the development company. I was supported by a sub-committee and got legal advice. It was really a team effort."

The lots were on the market for six months before they made the offer. Director John Rich explained, "We made an offer to purchase four lots initially, and the owners said, 'we're not interested.' So we let the Bowen Island public know that these developers (who were not popular) were refusing to sell the land at market value. The goodwill of the populace is important to every developer, and that was our strategy. Indeed they reconsidered and said they would consider selling us three lots. So we re-jigged our offer—and made a deal to buy the three for a little over nine million."

For Owen Plowman, John Rich, and Bob Turner, acquiring the Refuge has been a major boon to the Conservancy's board. Now they have a deeper understanding of conservation issues and a commitment to land trust principles. Bob outlined many of the issues they have had to face, being owners of conservation lands.

> We have created a technical advisory group of biologists, reviewed the existing development, and converted it into a trail system. We hired ecologists to inventory the lands. We had to deal with the issue of whether or not to allow dogs. We did our research and looked at the impact of dogs on wildlife and decided, no, that didn't fit the mandate of a wildlife refuge. That was controversial internally, and we had to talk it through. It took some convincing and scientific research and review of papers, etc. We decided that our greatest contribution these lands could make to Bowen Island was as a wildlife refuge, and not just an additional park. We are inviting people and want them to come, stay on trails, and not bring their dogs or any other pets. We are intentional about protecting the coastal bluffs. There is a real blind spot in communities when it comes to dogs and wildlife. Particularly during the pandemic when more families have acquired dogs. They really have an incredible impact on wildlife, the scent they leave behind, basically a wolf, their smell is identical to that type of predator, and they impact nesting success for songbirds and impact the ground mammals and their use of wild spaces. It's a real consequence and they walk all over everything in a coastal bluff area—that can damage things so quickly.
>
> We are still babes in the woods, opening these lands to the public in May of 2022. We had no real knowledge of what's ahead of us in terms of getting tax exemption status, signage criteria, inventing our way into involving volunteers. Once you become a landowner, it's a watershed moment. Suddenly you look around and consider what else is possible as a land holder.

Will Husby is on the Technical Committee for the Bowen Island Conservancy's first nature reserve—the Wild Coast Nature Refuge. Calling himself a recovering entomologist, Will changed careers to become an environmental educator. Prior to moving to Bowen, he worked for Alberta Parks at a nature centre in Edmonton. Later moving to BC, Will found Bowen Island and married Sue Ellen Fast. Will is part of the Bowen Island Eco-Alliance which laid the footings for the Bowen Island Conservancy. With others on the team, he evaluates the properties that the Conservancy considers acquiring and is asked to determine the best steps forward in restoring some of the area. This includes addressing issues such as the existing roads and building sites, which were put in prior to it being acquired as a Nature Refuge.

Owen told me that the BIC just put a covenant on the Wild Coast Nature Refuge, with the Bowen Island municipality registered title. It prohibits any building, and the land may only be used for conservation purposes in perpetuity. Some of the lands within the Refuge that BIC acquired had already been identified by scientists as a biodiversity hot spot. One area of the Refuge is open to the public and another is off limits. When I went to the Wild Coast Nature Refuge, just opened in the spring of 2022, I was impressed with the work already done in carving out trails to protect the vulnerable plants and moss from trampling feet. I noted various techniques to protect the plants, such as doubled ropes and cement blocks, to laying out flat stepping stones.

When we toured the area, Sue Ellen commented on the recently renamed seaside juniper species, bending low over the ocean at the Refuge. Recent genetics research on the two species separated the coastal juniper from rocky mountain juniper. Seaside juniper (*Juniperus maritima*) is found close to saltwater near sea level and is endemic to the Salish Sea with its own unique adaptations to salt spray. It has different genetics as well.[19] Stands are found on Hornby Island, the Pasley Islets, and Cape Roger Curtis on Bowen, with the largest stand documented on Lasqueti Island.

The Wild coast Nature Reserve looking north. Trail markers help protect sensitive areas.

Bob Turner noted during our interview, "Now that we have land, we have alerted the community to the fact that we *can* hold land. We've already had other inquiries from individuals interested in donating some land. Secondly we are now looking at lands donated for conservation currently held by the Province. These are the Lieben lands on Bowen Island, a former artist's colony, and visited by a who's who of Canadian literature and art during the 1940s to 1960s. These lands were given to the Province as conservation lands, and the Conservancy hopes to acquire and manage them."

In the spring of 2023, the Greater Vancouver Regional District (now Metro Vancouver) purchased ~97 hectares (240 acres) of land at Cape Roger Curtis for $40 million, using a small portion of property taxes from a regional Park Acquisition Fund. With camping as part of their new park plan, there has been considerable concern from the local community and from the Conservancy, with its Nature Refuge next door.

Through 2022 to 2023, the Bowen community debated whether Metro Vancouver's proposal to develop Cape Roger Curtis was the right fit for the island. Among the issues debated were the higher risk of forest fires, shortage of potable water, overloaded ferries, and camp sites adjacent to a higher density neighbourhood. The influx of off-island visitors and impact on sensitive ecosystems, including the adjacent Wild Coast Nature Refuge and Fairy Fen Nature Reserve, was a concern of not only islanders, but also the Islands Trust. Opposition to the Metro Vancouver plan grew and on September 12, 2023, the Bowen Island Conservancy made an offer of up to $30 million to purchase the lands from Metro Vancouver. This potential transfer of ownership would definitely change the purposes of the park from the Regional District's recreational and camping objectives.

ITC Nature Reserves on Bowen Island

Sue Ellen Fast is currently an elected municipal councillor and Islands Trustee. In the recent past, she served on multiple committees including the board of the Islands Trust Conservancy. With the municipality having planning powers and the regional

Islands Trust providing services, Sue Ellen has been promoting the value and work of the Islands Trust for years. She gave me several examples of advocacy and partnership work the organization has done on behalf of Bowen Island. "At the request of municipal council, the Islands Trust helped stop BC Timber Sales logging, helped the municipality become eligible for some rural grant funding, and is assisting with efforts to prohibit motorized vehicles on Mount Gardner."

At the time the municipality was incorporated, the Cates Hill development was underway. There was a large public process, and eventually the developer set aside two triangular lots as protected areas. One went to the Islands Trust Conservancy and the other to the Bowen Island Municipality. As mentioned previously, research has shown increased market values in residential areas near parks. Hence there is an economic incentive for creating a protected area around a development as well.

The 9 hectare (22.2 acres) Singing Woods Nature Reserve, created in 1999 through this subdivision, borders on the Ecological Reserve and Crown land, creating a corridor near Snug Cove, Bowen's central village. The majority of the reserve is a steep north facing slope covered in a second growth forest of Douglas-fir, western hemlock, western red cedar, and bigleaf maple that had regrown after logging and/or wildfires approximately one hundred years ago. There are also older "veteran" trees scattered through the reserve that escaped early logging and fire. Along the base of the slope is a narrow bench dominated by a forested skunk cabbage swamp, including the headwaters for two fish bearing creeks, a small open marsh, and second growth forest on more level ground.

The David Otter Nature Reserve was donated in 2006 to the ITC as part of another rezoning and subdivision process. The 3 hectare (7.4 acre) property has a stand of 200-year-old trees, left from past logging. Two creeks link to the neighbouring Crippen Park. Through the federal Ecological Gift program, the owner received 100 percent exemption from a capital gains tax. The Bowen Island Municipality holds a covenant over the property. This small property is not accessible to the public.

Doug Hopwood, who was a contract monitor for the Islands Trust Conservancy for over twenty years, told me he enjoyed meeting some of the landowners and people who had donated properties on Bowen, particularly Isabel Otter who donated the property and lived next door. "They often walked the property with us. It was always nice to hear about how the property was doing and the changes."

Bowen has been one of the islands able to take advantage of the Province's Free Crown Land Grant Program, transferring a section of Crown land to the Islands Trust Conservancy for a Nature Reserve. Today, they are called sponsored Crown Grants and apply across the province.

When Sue Ellen took me through Quarry Park, and then through the Crown lands to the Fairy Fen Nature Reserve, she described it as, "looking down from the balcony—and down there is the eye of the bog—the dance floor" Because the BIC had done a wetland inventory, the specialist of that inventory described Fairy Fen as regionally significant. This identification of the unique and rare wetland species, which look like very small plants, added to the rationale for protecting that area. Sue Ellen added, "being above the Cape Roger Curtis development, it could have been at risk. We felt an urgency as a road or a dam could come in nearby. Part of the thinking

The Fairy Fen Nature Reserve, a bog ecological community with rare lavender tea plants.

was to protect the wetland, but also the area around it which could prevent logging and associated disturbances."

The creation of the Fairy Fen Nature Reserve became the pet project of a past president of the Conservancy, Peter Drake. Peter loved the area very much and worked with several partners on the project, including the eventual landowners, the Islands Trust Conservancy.

Alan Whitehead, another BIC board member, recommended in 2010 the boundaries of the Crown land parcel which became the Fairy Fen Nature Reserve. The 18 hectare (44 acre) property was acquired to protect this regionally significant wetland. It includes two wetlands, the headwaters of Huszar Creek, and its forest. Biologists describe Fairy Fen as being "one of the most undisturbed biologically diverse and ecologically rare fens in southern British Columbia. A fen is a wetland fed by ground or surface water and is neutral or alkaline in its chemistry. It supports a high diversity of plant and animal species" including Labrador tea, St. John's wort, bog cranberry, and even Western bluebirds.[20] Once the transfer was complete, Alan, who has an environmental consulting company, created a Management Plan for the Reserve. The Bowen Island Conservancy has been the manager of the Fairy Fen Nature Reserve ever since.

On our way out from the Fairy Fen Nature Reserve we crossed over the Crown lands before heading into Quarry Park. Along the way I watched a beautiful Douglas squirrel peak out from behind a large conifer directly at us. We don't have any squirrels on Lasqueti Island, so I was delighted with its proximity. Then a little further along we heard and then saw two young barred owls calling. I blessed them and made a silent wish that these Crown (public) lands will continue to stand for generations to come.

Bowen Island Conservancy Today

The current BIC president, Owen Plowman, suggested "there are covenants with the municipality all over the map. We don't have an easy way of knowing where they are. If you went to the municipal hall they wouldn't either. It could be along a riparian zone. The nature reserves are owned by ITC, but managed by us, because we're right here."

Unlike most municipalities and even the provincial government, a land trust takes the responsibility of annual monitoring of a covenanted property seriously. The Canadian Land Trust Standards and Practices have been set up to ensure that land trusts understand and follow the annual monitoring requirements that will uphold a conservation covenant. Annual reports, photos, and descriptions of any changes to the land ensure that a subsequent landholder cannot challenge the covenant. Having long-term protection at the heart of the conservation movement, registering a covenant on a protected property, or on another conservation organization's land, and ensuring that there is annual monitoring are other ways of building the public trust—their land trust will protect their land, or the parks and nature reserves, in perpetuity.

In 2023 the Bowen Island Conservancy published a map that details the island's protected places. Beyond managing the Wild Coast Nature Refuge, their newest project is developing a Biodiversity Strategy. On top of monitoring and managing the

ITC's Nature Reserves and their own, the Conservancy is at the threshold advocating for financial support to help their volunteer board secure paid help.

As I prepared to leave Bowen Island, I considered Bob Turner's perspective on the Salish Sea.[21]

> When I look at the future, I see how grim it is at a global scale. So I've done some pondering about how to take that on. I'm wonderfully inspired by the Ukrainian people today. I look at their willingness to fight for a better future against remarkable odds. I find inspiration in the idea that hope is not optimism but belief is worth working for. That's the kind of hope I really want to communicate in my own work, particularly to younger people who have a tough future ahead. My hope is that we can come together to build our community, and commit to this place—our land, ocean, and wild neighbours—and that is the way forward. For a long time, my community has been Howe Sound, and Bowen Island is part of Howe Sound. Recently I made a conscious decision that I want to expand my sense of home—the place I am willing to work on behalf of—to include all of the Salish Sea as well, and my movie making now reflects that larger sense of place. All of this intention has been inspired by Squamish Nation Elders who I've met, and their deep ties to the land. My wife and I know that Bowen Island is home. We're here. We're staying put. We've committed to this place.

As I relinquished the mooring at Kwilákm (Deep Bay/Mannion Bay) I felt a renewed commitment to focus on what I am for—rather than what I'm against. The passionate and steadfast people I met on Bowen Island helped renew my spirits, as I headed to an island I'd never visited before—deep in the Sound, which I thought at the time was the last island on my conservation journey—Gambier Island.

The Coastal Bluff Ecosystem at Cape Roger Curtis. A twenty-year struggle to protect some of the Cape finally resulted in success! WILL HUSBY

CHAPTER FOURTEEN

GAMBIER ISLAND AND THE ÁTL'KA7TSEM/HOWE SOUND BIOSPHERE RESERVE

Glass Reefs and Crown Lands

"You can only stop the logging if you make enough noise. My advice to anyone trying to protect trees from logging— get media involved quickly and as much as you can."
MARIA VAN DYK

ON ANOTHER HOT AND WINDLESS JULY DAY, I left Bowen and motored into the heart of Átl'katsem/Howe Sound toward Gambier Island. This was my first visit to this high mountainous island with its four peninsulas that nestle around deep southern bays. As I journeyed up the Sound, I was surrounded by jaw dropping, steep, rugged coastal mountains. After decades of extensive work, the entire Howe Sound is under new guardianship, being declared the Átl'katsem/Howe Sound UNESCO Biosphere Reserve in 2021. Átl'katsem (pronounced At-Kat-sum) is the Squamish word for paddling up the Sound, the southernmost fjord in BC. Gambier Island, like all of Howe Sound, is within the unceded traditional territory of the skwxwú7mesh (Squamish) Nation.

Gambier is the largest of the islands in Howe Sound. Among its key features are its three large mountains and ten watersheds. Unlike most islands, Gambier has some old growth forest. Of its 60 percent Crown land, 566 hectares are designated old growth management areas.[1] As of 2023, Gambier's extensive provincial marine park, regional district parks, and nature reserves protect 16 percent of the island, with an additional 10,828 hectares in protected marine areas, rockfish conservation areas, and glass sponge reef marine refuges.

Besides the coastal black-tailed deer, larger mammals live on or frequent the island, such as cougar, wolves, and the occasional black bear, along with the smaller squirrels and martens. In damp areas, one can find roughskin newts and Pacific tree frogs along with a very rare coastal tailed frog. One islander told me the wolves that had been on the island had disappeared after a couple of years. As noted in the Cortes chapter, only 4 percent of wild mammalian species are left on the planet. We are not the only lives that matter. Conservation of land and protection of the ocean is essential to protect the diversity of wildlife of this precious planet.

The Gambier Island population grew from only 60 residents in the '70s to 430 in 2021. Most of the island's residents live along or close to the waterfront at the south

end, with a few developments along the east coast. In addition to the residents, Gambier has four yacht club out-stations with docks and adjacent lands. Three sizeable outdoor youth camps have drawn participants from across the province for generations. Many Gambier islanders with recreational property have year-round homes on the mainland. Remarkable work by impassioned people has led to improvements in industrial practices affecting the larger Sound and significant protection on the island.

Elspeth Armstrong, one of the pioneering activists on the island, grew up visiting her grandparents on Gambier and traveling around the Howe Sound area. In 1968 she moved to the coast and bought a cabin in Gambier Harbour. "What's not to love about the area," she said to me. However, in her early years there was no fishing up at the north end of the Sound, due to mercury poisoning from the chemical plant, the Britannia copper mine, the log sort, the gravel pits, and the effluent from two mills, including the Port Mellon pulp mill. These industries blocked almost all life in the Squamish River estuary, and in the last century, the last herring was seen in Squamish in 1969.[2]

Determined to change things, she pursued several key legislative protections.

I was fortunate to know several scientists who were familiar with Howe Sound and its pollution problems. There was a pollution control board hearing, a public inquiry into the forest products industry. I believe the previous time they had done a review was twenty to thirty years before. Due to a mountain of information from several federal fisheries scientists, I made a submission to the formal hearing on pollution standards for pulp mills. My submission related to colour in the effluent that should be recognized and mills be ordered to rectify that situation. The whole idea was that these companies' effluents—both in air and water—should be considered a pollutant, and something should be done about it. I was the only woman, and it was good fun. They listened to me, as I had all the backing from the scientists that were working in the area, and they changed the regulations. We [scientists] were ecstatic that it became law/statute.

Elspeth became a Gambier Island Trustee just as the Islands Trust was formed. Working with an eight member committee, islanders drafted the first Gambier Island Community Plan, which later became the official community plan. It called for "a mixture of residential, nature preservation, farmland, private institutional, extractive industry, interior park, marine park, and forest areas."[3] The OCP included a call for a moratorium on Crown land timber licenses, further log booming and storage, and a limit on road construction. There are two large church camps on the island (Camp Artaban and Camp Fircom). A third, Camp Latona, was privately purchased recently, offering outdoor experiences for non-denominational youth. With these three large outdoor camps, recreation has been a key purpose for land protection on the island. The moratorium on logging is yet to happen, but a halt to mining came about through Elspeth Armstrong and her determined friends.

During her time as trustee, Elspeth gathered critical evidence about the industrial activities harming the larger Howe Sound area, especially industry's impacts on the estuary and its freshwater sources. In a brief she sent to Grace McCarthy, then provincial environment minister, she recommended that Howe Sound be designated a National Recreational Area. Elspeth outlined the many forces affecting the area, most notably its role as a recreation centre for all of the surrounding mainland region. She outlined the very sensitive nature of the Sound. "Enclosed bodies of water, such as bays, estuaries and fjords with their moderate water circulation, abundant plant and animal life are more susceptible to damage from water pollution than is the open ocean. Discharges of industrial waste into these semi-enclosed areas can seriously impair water quality which is essential for healthy marine life."[4] Under the Islands Trust banner, her brief compared it to an area in the southern part of New Zealand very similar to Howe Sound. They brought out legislation to protect that whole area, and she told McCarthy—this is what you could do for Howe Sound. With some of these industries still operating, and a potential for huge liquefied natural gas (LNG) tankers plying the waters from the top of the estuary, her words from this '70s appeal could still be applied today.

A few years later, she worked to stop the large open pit copper mine that was proposed on Gambier Island. With two other active women, one the current island trustee and the other a past trustee, she formed the Gambier Island Preservation Society. They brought in an astonishing membership of 2,000. She explained to me, by phone from Hornby Island where she now lives, that they hired a media company who took photographs of an open pit mine and made a twenty minute movie about how this could happen on Gambier. The film influenced people to fight back. John Rich, then chair of the Islands Trust, organized several jam-packed meetings at the Devonshire Hotel in Vancouver. Multiple presentations by the Gambier Island Preservation Society to surrounding municipalities, recreational, and environmental organizations resulted in municipal resolutions opposing the mine and petitions from some 6,300 people from across the Salish Sea.

The BC provincial cabinet also reviewed a recreational and visual analysis report that concluded that Gambier was "virtually devoid of roads and commercial development." The report's authors proposed a "wilderness type" of recreational experience on Gambier. The authors reported that only 18 percent of the Sound's shoreline was accessible for recreation. This could accommodate the 40,000 households in the lower mainland who owned a boat.[5] This recreational goal stood in sharp contrast to the mining company's plans to bring in 690 workers around the clock, eliminate Lost Lake and most of Gambier Creek, and a recreational reserve with shellfish and prawn beds. The goal was to build an open pit mine and tailings pond complete with constructed dams. This plan would consume 40 million litres of water a day and require a submarine pipeline from the nearby Sunshine Coast. Rather than outright turn down the mine, the Province waited for the exploration license to expire.

Jack Little, an emeritus professor from Simon Fraser University, chronicled the story of this battle in his recent book, *At the Wilderness Edge: The Rise of the Antidevelopment Movement on Canada's West Coast*. Throughout, he highlighted the indefatigable nature of Elspeth Armstrong. In the final hours, the Gambier Island Preservation Society, bringing in some property owners, the Catholic Charities Society of Vancouver, and the Camp Artaban Society, filed a lawsuit against the Islands Trust for failing to uphold the Gambier Island OCP. The judge dismissed the case, noting that remedies were not available to the Islands Trust even though "there is no doubt that if the project proceeds it will largely destroy the existing environment of Gambier Island as a recreational resource and with it many of the amenities now enjoyed by the residents and visitors to the island."[6]

As on Denman, the court again confirmed that the Islands Trust had no authority over Crown lands, logging and mining included, even though their mandate is to preserve and protect the islands. Thankfully, Elspeth and her colleagues eventually succeeded in their campaign to protect Crown lands on the island. The campaign's success was based on individuals working with their respective organizations, framing a consistent vision, gathering scientific evidence, and communicating and networking with their own and surrounding communities. These techniques worked to impact government bodies who have the authority to make change happen. Persistence was key!

Not surprisingly Elspeth Armstrong went on to join the founding board of the Gambier Island Conservancy.

Maria Van Dyk with the Brigade Bay Nature Reserve sign at Brigade Bay Marina. PETER SCHOLEFIELD

Early Years of Gambier Island Conservancy—Mapping and Inventory

In 1995 logging on a commercial woodlot was underway, development was also clipping along, and the Gambier Island Official Community Plan came up for revision. The time was ripe to form the Gambier Island Conservancy (GIC). Joining Elspeth were founding board members Maria Van Dyk, a computer specialist, and her husband Wolf Wiedemann, an accountant. They had recently built a house on Gambier, where they met Elspeth and another powerful woman living on the island, Lois Kennedy. With a PhD in science, specializing in embryology, Lois was an avid community activist. She roused the community to the task of protecting the communities natural amenities. With logging on Gambier a real threat, and a new OCP up for revision, the new Conservancy decided to identify and map areas to see what was there. They planned to advocate for the protection of identified sensitive areas.

The provincial government granted tenures for logging on the Crown lands on the island to smaller, local companies. The new Conservancy met with provincial forestry staff and studied the Forest Practices Code. I talked with Maria Van Dyk about these early years. "We started to understand all of this and stay on top and monitor the *Forest Practices Code*. They had to manage for visual values, and for other uses. With this understanding and knowing what tools were available, we hoped we could hold them to account and help us protect environmentally sensitive areas."

Lois Kennedy was a keen woman and did much of the stream mapping for Gambier. She used the Ministry of Environment's Streamkeeper's methodology, adding in fish habitat studies. As Maria described it, "because it's so rugged, only the lower reaches of the streams have fish habitat—up the mountains there are no fish, so lower fish areas are so valuable as a result. We identified them to their standards, and created maps useful for the future protection of important lands and habitats." Kennedy brought in university students to help. Over three years Vicky Troop, a professor at Capilano College's environmental planning program, had her students do major studies. The first year, they did an environmentally sensitive site study. The second year they undertook a wetland study, and the third year they reviewed forestry data and ground truthed some of the identified old growth areas.

The GIC raised many thousands of dollars to identify environmentally sensitive sites. Maria's specialty includes all aspects of computer science, including program design to management. She discovered that the Islands Trust knew little about the island at that time, so she set up a mapping GIS system for Gambier, using what was then considered the leading edge ESRI ArcView program.

With an opportunity to provide input to the OCP, these expert directors of the new Conservancy were off and running—gathering essential data, ground truthing, and putting their newly found coordinates on fish, streams, and old growth areas onto their maps—giving the land a voice. As Maria explained, "it was an opportune time to see if we could identify those things that were valuable, in order to protect them in the OCP. We hoped that the Islands Trust would incorporate our data in some way."

In her interview with me, Maria stressed how important it was to form partnerships and relationships with other entities like the Islands Trust and the regional district, especially on a small island like Gambier. After the Conservancy had completed its inventory and mapping work, it began sharing its data. Maria explained some of the challenges they then faced.

> I often found they reinvented the wheel. Often they may not remember that you had given them the data or could find it after. Unless you generate the data with their standards, how do you know that the data being given meets the standards identified—so I can understand from their point of view. However, I also felt disappointed, as often we were using a more updated system. You do the field work and research, document it and identify it, but you can't put in the legislation to protect it. Local government and the Islands Trust have that ability, so all you can do is give them the information and hope this will inform their program. I feel we did valuable work doing that. These are the tools you put together in the hopes of preserving land. You start somewhere.

Subsequently, the Islands Trust and its Conservancy arm completed numerous environmentally sensitive site studies for all of the islands. The earlier work of these pioneer mapping and GIS specialists provided the foundation for many Gambier Island maps.

During my interview with Peter Scholefield, the current president of the Conservancy, he explained that Lois Kennedy's environmental analysis and many of the subsequent maps were included in the Gambier Island OCP. "The maps we have from that are incredible—of the old growth forests, younger forests, environmentally sensitive areas and watersheds. It was a major feat."

Maria praised local Island Trustee Kim Benson who spearhead the Natural Area Protection Tax Exemption Program (NAPTEP) in 2002. "She was a very dedicated conservationist who worked many years to get the legislation in place, and she saw it through to the end." Thanks to Kim's perseverance, a landowner today can save 65 percent of their property taxes annually on the protected portion of their land every year, with a NAPTEP covenant on their title.

Maria also coordinated the millennial Gambier Island map included in the *Islands in the Salish Sea* artistic community mapping atlas. "There was lots of enthusiasm for the map. We printed it off and got different types made—lithographs and high-end Giclée prints. It was used as a fundraiser. Artist Gloria Masse asked that the Gambier map be owned by the community and hang at the community centre. Gloria, now approaching eighty, lives in Davis Bay and considers it one for her most valuable projects."

Sadly, some of the founders of the Gambier Island Conservancy have died, including Maria's husband Wolf and Lois Kennedy, who bequeathed $100 thousand to the Islands Trust Conservancy for future conservation on the island. In their footsteps, several other eminent people have taken up the hat Maria and Elspeth still doff from across the Salish Sea.

The Gambier Island Conservancy Today

Peter Scholefield is a retired meteorologist who joined the Conservancy in 2001. He worked for thirty years for the federal government, half time doing weather forecasting and the other half managing climate programs. In the last seven years of his career, Peter worked in Geneva, Switzerland, as head of the World Climate Data and Monitoring Program for the United Nation's World Meteorological Organization. Peter bought property on Gambier in 1996, near the Halkett Bay Marine Park and next to the United Church's Camp Fircom. Peter explained that Lois Kennedy invited him to come check on the tree restoration work that was being done along the creeks in the Brigade Bay subdivision when it was being developed. It was this type of conservation and restoration work that motivated him to become president in 2004.

In 2003 the GIC developed a brochure map showing all the interconnecting trails on Gambier, with a description of each. Maria and her husband Wolf produced the original trails map to help people find their way around the island. With no connecting roads, the trail map was essential to find locations and public access points. In 2019, the trail map was updated using a different base map and made available on the Conservancy's website.[8] In 2020, the Conservancy obtained funding from the Province to employ two island residents to GPS and improve the island trail network.

Gambier is within the Sunshine Coast Regional District (SCRD) which has two regional parks and several small community parks on the island. A network of trails passes through both Crown lands and private lands, granted through statutory rights-of-way. The regional district negotiated with landholders to register these statutory rights-of-way to be used for public access trails and public road easements. As on Bowen Island, negotiations with the Islands Trust and the SCRD for subdivision resulted in the creation of a number of parks and rights-of-way.

Nature Reserves on the Island

When I sailed into Brigade Bay, on the east side of Gambier, I met with Carol Petroski, who showed me two of the three Island Trust Conservancy's Nature Reserves. A part-time resident on Gambier and a member of GIC's board, Carol was a long-time employee with Mountain Equipment Company's (MEC) sustainability program. Having attended nearby Camp Artaban as a teenager, she now lives in the Brigade Bay subdivision development. Its approval resulted in the establishment of the two nature reserves.

Due to the high mountains on the island, most of the human developments are along the shoreline. In 2006, Coastland Wood Industries Ltd. and Mike Jenks received conditional approval to go ahead with a large sixty-eight lot waterfront subdivision along Brigade Bay on private land that had been previously logged. Carol explained that because logging had occurred along the creek beds, they were notified by the Province that this was illegal, so the developers had to mitigate their damages by replanting in the logged creek beds. The Brigade Bay Bluffs and Long Bay Wetland areas were donated to the Islands Trust Conservancy (formerly Trust Fund) as part of the Brigade Bay subdivision approval process. In January 2005, the ITC established the Brigade Bay Bluffs and Long Bay Wetland Nature Reserves. This is yet another island where Mike Jenks's logging and development plans resulted in protected areas and a community park, the Peter Shields Regional Park.

The ITC's management plan describes the Brigade Bay Bluffs Nature Reserve, 5.14 hectare (12.7 acre), as steep forest terrain, selectively harvested with some remaining larger veteran trees. The Long Bay Wetland Nature Reserve, 38 hectare (94 acre), is a much larger site. The wetland and tributaries are part of the headwaters of the Long Bay watershed and Long Bay Creek, a fish bearing stream. Prior to its creation, the developers used the north end of the Long Bay Wetland Nature Reserve as a quarry borrow pit for sand and gravel. With support from ITC, volunteers from the Gambier Island Conservancy have planted and caged native trees, or in some cases simply caged young naturally growing seedlings in both nature reserves, including in the quarry. The local Conservancy has been restoring these two nature reserves since it was appointed to be the manager of the nature reserves in 2009.

Doug Hopwood, a professional forester, along with his partner, Chris Ferris, had the contract for the annual monitoring of the nature reserves with the Islands Trust Conservancy for over twenty years. The varieties Doug recommended for planting were Douglas-fir, western red cedar, and Sitka spruce. On my visit to the nature reserves, I was impressed with the size of some of these planted trees—some up to 2.4 metres (8 feet) tall now. There is a lot of English Holly in the Long Bay Wetland Nature Reserve likely resulting from settler homesteads that had stood in the area from the 1920s to the 1980s.[7] Other native trees were growing tall there too, including large bigleaf maples, western hemlock, and red alders.[8]

Due to the previous logging, these two nature reserves required considerable restoration, such as "clearing of slash and channel blockages, de-compaction of

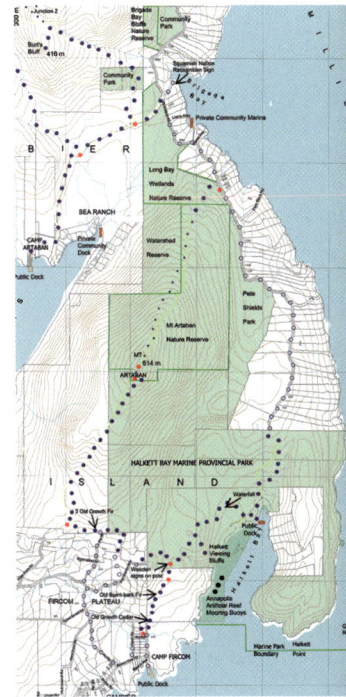

Gambier Island hiking trail.

The view east from the peak of Mount Artaban, an Islands Trust Conservancy's Nature Reserve, Gambier Island.
PETER SCHOLEFIELD

affected soils and re-vegetation of riparian areas." Habitat restoration is a field of its own today and organizations are trying different methods across different ecosystems. Even though some of the developer's planted trees in creek beds were not caged, some survived. The Conservancy's planted trees were caged to protect them from wildlife browsing.

After these two nature reserves were designated, Peter told me, "We in the Conservancy decided that we would work with ITC to establish another nature reserve that would connect all the land between the Long Bay Wetland Nature Reserve and Halkett Bay Marine Park. To get that land, we applied for the provincial Free Crown Land Grant program with help from ITC. To do so, we had to provide a legal survey of the land for the Province. In order for the Islands Trust Fund to establish and take ownership of a nature reserve, they required a management plan." With this in view, the Gambier Island Conservancy coordinated a fundraising campaign, raising close to $47 thousand, which exceeded the cost of the survey and management plan.

The resulting Mount Artaban Nature Reserve, at 107 hectares (264 acres), is the largest nature reserve on Gambier Island. It provides a natural contiguous corridor from the Halkett Bay Marine Park in the south to the Long Bay Wetland Nature Reserve to the north. The reserve itself had been logged in the lower elevation areas, with unlogged areas higher up. There are two ephemeral wetlands near the summit and two seasonal streams flow in the northern part of the reserve. It was transferred to the ITC as a Free Crown Land Grant in 2008 and is now fully protected from future logging or development.

When Carol took me on a tour of the nature reserves, she told me that between 2015 and 2021, the ITC helped support five volunteer restoration work parties to plant trees and remove invasive species on the two nature reserves, especially English holly which is prevalent in the Long Bay Wetland Nature Reserve.

The area is scattered with holly, thistle, and tansy ragwort. Carol explained that one worker was paid for three days in 2013 to remove some of the holly, which really made a difference. In addition to dedicated volunteers, with ITC's financial support, the local Conservancy hired two university students to spend one week in the summer of 2023 to eradicate some of the English holly. The Conservancy has been trying different methods to see which are the most effective. Some years they have pulled and stacked the branches, small trunks, and roots, and in 2022 they used a chipper. With many trees caged by the Conservancy, and years of eradicating invasive species, they are starting to see a healthy forest along the creeks and throughout these two nature reserves.

In 2013, the Gambier Island Conservancy and the Sunshine Coast Conservation Association were registered as joint holders of the conservation covenants on all three nature reserves. Similar to most of the agreements between the ITC and the islands, the local Conservancy and the Sunshine Coast Conservation Association monitor the nature reserves annually. In addition, the GIC and ITC have collaborated for many years on management projects for these reserves, including the removal of invasive species, planting and fencing trees, and assisting other contractors with additional work on site.

Skwxwú7mesh Úxwumixw (Squamish Nation) is active on Gambier Island, with cultural use lands identified on the northeast shore. The properties in the Brigade Bay subdivision have covenants that allow members of the Squamish Nation the right of passage related to use of lands or resources for traditional purposes.[9]

Successful Advocacy—Crown Land and Commercial Woodlot Logging

Gambier Island Conservancy's directors spent considerable time identifying and protecting Gambier Island's Crown lands, especially the Old Growth Management Areas (OGMA). In the early days, directors had many meetings with provincial forestry staff, reviewing aerial photos and then ground truthing their exact locations. However, Maria told me there was a change in the provincial government's ruling party, one which seemed less concerned with the protection of old growth. She explained, "It was very disappointing that after all the effort to work with the Ministry of Forests in the hopes of protecting Gambier's remaining old growth, provincial forestry staff moved most of Gambier's OGMAs to Anvil Island to meet their required protection targets, thus leaving Gambier's Crown land with fewer restrictions for harvesting. They also increased the maximum size of woodlots to expand the harvesting area. Removal of the OGMAs from Gambier Island and an increase in the maximum size of woodlots facilitated the planning of two large new woodlots with an expanded harvesting area."

In 2013, two decades later, the provincial government announced plans to log two new commercial woodlots, occupying about one third of the Crown land on the northeast section of the island. Peter Scholefield explained what happened next. "Their consultation with the community was inadequate, so many islanders were upset. When we got notification about this plan to log these two woodlots, we talked with the forestry people. They said, 'Sorry this has all been approved. It's in the system so there is not much you can do about it.' We didn't know what to do. Somebody suggested we go meet with Ric Careless, executive director at BC Spaces for Nature. So a couple of us went to Gibsons and met him. He said, 'Don't give up. You can do this. Start a campaign—get going!'" Peter described their concerted efforts:

> We embarked on campaign that took about one and a half years against the provincial government's plan. By 2014 they had already sent out notices and received applications from eight to ten companies to log. We held meetings, sent letters, developed brochures, videos, and posters. Bob Turner and his brother Tim Turner made a video walking through the areas to be logged. This took up a lot of our effort and time. As we got toward the end, we hired a lawyer, and drafted a letter to get an injunction to stop the logging. It cost $12,000 in legal fees. We had enough funds, but it drained our coffers to cover that. About a week before the case was to be heard by the Supreme Court of BC, we got a notice from the provincial government saying that they were going to postpone, leaving time for a public information meeting in faraway West Vancouver followed by another the next day in Horseshoe Bay. Over two hundred people went over to oppose the woodlots. Our legal counsel sent another letter and critically important, the Squamish and Tsleil-Waututh Nations sent letters to the provincial government as well, as they weren't consulted either. In the end we were successful. That land is still designated as woodlot, but there are no plans currently to log. We are thankful to Ric Careless for sending us off.

Facing extensive costs for legal action, and innumerable time spent on networking and meeting with others, it seems like a small victory, especially with no permanent protection in hand. With the Province now focusing on reconciliation with First Nations, Crown lands are no longer being transferred readily, along with the Free Crown Land Grant program many land trusts on the islands have used to help transfer lands into conservation status.

Early in 2021, a small group of Gambier Island youth, calling themselves the Gambier Guardians, alerted the community to plans to log a new cutblock containing old growth trees in the island's only operational woodlot, classified as W0039. This included some old growth forest and riparian areas in the headwaters of Whispering Creek. Bob Turner from Bowen made a video, *Why Log Whispering Creek? Cháʔelkwnech/Gambier Island, Atlʼkaʔtsem/Howe Sound*, to help stop the logging. The GIC launched a petition through Change.org, garnering close to 30,000 signatures. They also wrote letters to the Skwx̱wú7mesh Úxwumixw (Squamish Nation), Tsleil-Waututh Nation, the Ministry, and to woodlot owners themselves, asking them not to log in that area. The public response to GIC's petition, letter writing by many people in the region, the local woodlot owner's sensitivity, and meetings with the Squamish Nation and Province were all likely responsible for some good news. Peter reported, "In the summer of 2023, there has still been no logging in the headwaters of Whispering Creek."

Maria Van Dyk summed up her feelings about the many fights with the province over Crown land logging. "You can only stop the logging if you make enough noise. My advice to anyone trying to protect trees from forestry—get media involved quickly and as much as you can."

Bob Turner agreed. "In 2017, BC Timber Sales wanted to log provincial lands on Bowen Island. Both times big public protests compelled these plans to be withdrawn."

These campaigns show that with enough public attention and concerted action, locals and their supporters, working with partners and scientists, can slow down or even stop unsustainable activities such as clear-cut or old growth logging and mining that threatens the health of our communities.

In 2012, the GIC expanded its conservation mandate to the surrounding waters of Howe Sound, becoming a coalition partner with the Future of Howe Sound Society.

The Átlʼkatsem/Howe Sound UNESCO Biosphere Reserve

Ruth Simons, who is now the co-chair of the society that manages this UNESCO Biosphere Reserve, lives in Lions Bay and owns one of the properties at Brigade Bay on Gambier Island. Ruth credited Elspeth Armstrong and Bowen Island's Bob Turner as being key champions in initiating the recovery of the Sound. Restoration was a necessary element to receive the designation of the Átlʼkatsem/Howe Sound UNESCO Biosphere Reserve.

The Future of Howe Sound Society was initiated in 2012 by primarily a group of property owners on Gambier Island and around the larger Sound. Their goal was to raise awareness about the need to save Howe Sound from the many industrial projects threatening the recreational and ecological health of the area. There was another gravel mine planned across from Gambier near the estuary of McNab Creek. A year later, they convened a large rally, bringing in broad support across the mainland, from areas bordering the Sound and on the islands.

Whispering Creek where the very rare coastal tailed frog was found that has helped stop the logging of its habitat. MICHAEL STAMFORD

The local Conservancy participated as a partner in the Future of Howe Sound Society. Over 140 boats joined in the Save Our Sound Rally. The Burrard and Thunderbird Yacht Clubs, who have docks and a nearby camp near Ekins Point on the north end of Gambier Island, joined in along with the eight yacht clubs that have outstations in other areas of the Sound. It was a huge success!

Rather than reviewing ad hoc proposals such as the one for the gravel mine, two years later, in 2015, the Future of Howe Sound Society called for comprehensive planning for all of Howe Sound. Bob Turner explained some key steps and the people involved in the Biosphere Reserve's formation.

Ruth [Simons] took the idea of comprehensive planning and saw the biosphere idea as a way of creating a comprehensive vision for the Howe Sound Region. Ruth, Suzanne Senger with BC Spaces for Nature, Jan Hagedorn with the Gambier Island Local Trust Committee, and I headed to Tofino to visit the Clayoquot Sound Biosphere Reserve. We got inspired and went on and visited the Mount Arrowsmith Biosphere Reserve. We learned from them, gained some insights, and then really started to promote the idea with the Howe Sound community. Ruth, who led the charge and continues to lead the initiative, made presentations to the Howe Sound Community Forum (governments at all levels) and other organizations working in the area, and generally built an excitement around it.

Bob explained, "to get the designation, we had to complete this detailed nomination document requiring that we bring together a tremendous amount of information, as well as show that we were already operating like a biosphere community with a series of conservation initiatives showing the community is advancing on many fronts." Bob added that BC Spaces for Nature's Ric Careless had drafted a proposal for a Howe Sound wide conservation area that included a UNESCO biosphere reserve around 2010.

"Off we went, one by one to each of our local member municipalities, who voted to support the biosphere initiative in principle," Bob told me. "Then we approached the Squamish Nation, who were more reticent to commit until late in the game when they saw more of what a biosphere status would create." Today, the organization that leads and is responsible for managing the UNESCO Biosphere Reserve is called the Howe Sound Biosphere Region Initiative Society. The Society is co-chaired with a Squamish Nation elected council member.

In my phone interview with the Society's co-chair, Ruth Simons, I asked what restoration or conservation initiatives had happened since the days of industrial pollution and ecological damage. She told me, "After the pollution controls were put in place for the acid runoff from the old Britannia Mine, a significant restoration project began in the Squamish estuary, at the mouth of the Squamish River. The Squamish and Fraser Rivers are extremely important for the ecology of Howe Sound and the Salish Sea." She explained that the Squamish estuary itself had some of the log booming grounds removed and a gravel pit was removed. A piece of land that had been partially dug out in preparation for a coal port was filled in. Ruth added that the Squamish Nation has received significant funding to restore some areas, specifically removing barriers for fish all along the estuary. The Bowen Island Fish and Wildlife

Club have worked with their hatchery on restoring spawning channels on that island. With the *Riparian Areas Regulation* put in place, Ruth told me this has helped restore the health of the fresh water creeks.

Ruth told me the Átl'katsem/Howe Sound Biosphere Reserve will bring more capacity into the region, for volunteer groups and related organizations, and it has influence in terms of planning. A big part of the Biosphere's role, she added, is to educate people and protect biodiversity. Besides climate change and biodiversity loss, increasing human activities on the islands are some of the biggest threats to the entire Salish Sea region.

During our interview, I asked her to describe what she considers the key challenges. She replied, "As new generations of people come forward, how do we help them care, so these places are protected. Protection and conservation are also about what property owners need to do themselves. We need education and enforcement, because if we don't have that, it is human nature to push back. With fire and drought a serious issue, with larger homes instead of cabins and camps, there is more of an urban life-style here now. We need studies to show the impacts on the water tables from certain activities, and how trees and forest cover are important and can assist in protecting the natural value of the property."

When I asked Bob Turner how the Biosphere Reserve could help with conservation, he explained, "The great thing about biospheres is they don't create any new laws or regulations. They are aspirational. They don't take away any legal rights or jurisdictions. What they do is build a community sense of stewardship for the lands, built around principals of biodiversity protection and sustainable development and establish logistic support for those initiatives. The biosphere has created a real biodiversity focus, so conservation groups now have biodiversity objectives within a ten year plan as a vision—a guiding light. Most importantly, the Squamish Nation is a signatory to the Biosphere Region and the co-chair is an elected member of their Council and sits on the board as well."

Glen Dennison diving the Halkett Glass Sponge Reef. ADAM TAYLOR

Scientific Studies on Gambier of Significance in the Broader Region

In their work to protect the old growth and riparian areas along Whispering Creek, Mike Stamford, one of the GIC directors and a professional biologist, considered what possible species at risk could be in that particular area. Mike did an initial analysis in the creek, with funding from the University of Northern BC. Through his research he discovered an important and rare species at risk. The coastal tailed frog does not exist on either Vancouver Island or the Southern Gulf Islands.[10] This highlights the conservation significance of populations of coastal tailed frog on Gambier Island. Of significance is protection of its habitat, because this frog requires extensive old forest in riparian areas that sustain seasonally consistent cool and humid conditions for adult and sub-adult survival and dispersal. It also requires stable cool, clear stream habitats for reproductive success and tadpole rearing.[11]

Mike then took two university students under his wing to support their project to collect environmental DNA (eDNA) samples in all the major watersheds on Gambier.

Environmental DNA is DNA that is collected from samples such as soil, seawater, snow, or air, rather than from an individual organism. The Howe Sound Biosphere Region Initiative Society took the lead with the federal government's Priority Places Funding, along with funding from the Habitat Conservation Trust Foundation and the Islands Trust. The GIC participated in the project. During the summers of 2021 and 2022, they sampled of all seven major watersheds on Gambier Island. The ITC provided funding to pay for two Squamish Nation Archeological, Cultural, and Environmental (ACE) Monitors to join the students in the field to assist with collection of eDNA samples. As a result, the researchers found evidence of the coastal tailed frog and the Northern red-legged frog in at least five streams on the island.[12]

That's an exciting discovery, as protection of habitat for Species at Risk (SAR) is a federal requirement. These studies could now be added to the Province's records, which could help stop the proposed logging at Whispering Creek and in other areas in the region more permanently.

Amphibians are declining more rapidly than either birds or mammals, with an estimated 70 percent of amphibian species experiencing major population declines. Creeks and wetlands are key ecosystems, essential for any kind of biodiversity protection. Protection of wetland habitat is a priority, whether through private land stewardship, legislation to prohibit logging or development, or through acquisition of lands for long-term protection.

From 2018 to 2020, the GIC participated in the Salish Sea Nearshore Habitat Recovery Project. Under the leadership of the SeaChange Marine Conservation Society, eelgrass was planted in four bays. The Conservancy's president, Peter Scholefield, said, "It wasn't our project, but it was a pleasant surprise. We joined in and participated, as they consulted with us as to where they should go. Several of us got involved in the planting of the shoots of eelgrass and as a result, several areas were restored." As part of a large Salish Sea project, SeaChange Marine Conservation Society transplanted eelgrass shoots on several other islands, including Lasqueti and Bowen islands.

In 2022, Capilano University approached the Howe Sound coalition partners to initiate research with their students on some SAR analysis. With the Conservancy's guidance, forty students came to Gambier in the spring and set up eleven trail cameras and transects for study in the Long Bay Wetland Nature Reserve.

These associations with universities and other organizations offer golden opportunities for detailed survey work that can help provide the scientific backing to conserve natural areas. As on Galiano Island, where extensive program and graduate work is taking place, conservation groups and university or college students can benefit each other extensively by working together.

Collaborating with the Squamish and other First Nations offers some key insights. As Ruth suggested, "Today, we are really learning and appreciating more about how the Indigenous people live. In Howe Sound, the name Átl'katsem means paddling and canoeing to and from the islands. There are other names that the Squamish and other First Nations people use related to their land use. There are lots of areas with midden beaches and archaeology sites on them, showing how people had an abundance of food and how they used to cook. There is lots we can learn and share about how people lived off the land."

The islands and our larger world are so different today from when colonists first arrived 150 years ago. Development has transformed lands and habitats. To this day, industry is still destroying areas never sold or given away. With oral histories and growing archaeological evidence on Indigenous people's use of the area, it seems long past due to open our eyes and hearts to Indigenous people's perspectives and knowledge.

When Peter Scholefield, now just over eighty years old, took me for a hike into the Halkett Bay Marine Park, we walked down to see the Welcome Figure the Squamish Nation has put up at Camp Fircom. Facing the dock and beach near the camp, it reminded me of the Welcome Figures I'd seen at Burgoyne Bay, on Salt Spring Island, installed by the Cowichan Nation. These Welcome Figures and recognition signs are a growing physical reminder that Indigenous peoples have been living on these lands and waters for centuries.

Peter Scholefield by the Welcome Figure at Camp Fircom.

Peter led me further along one of Gambier's trails to measure some large trees. He would later upload the GPS locations, photos, and circumferences to iNaturalist, a digital application that identifies and records species. We made our way to a fork in the trail where signs indicated a trail to the peak of Mount Artaban that is within the Mount Artaban Nature Reserve, and to the right a second trail leads to the Marine Park dock and to a bluff in the provincial park that looks across Halkett Bay. We took that trail, and at the bluff's edge, we bathed in the beauty of the turquoise-coloured bay, with the protected and large Douglas-fir and western hemlock forests in the foreground and the impressive Coast Range mountains in the background. No wonder this area has been promoted as a recreational mecca for generations.

Having been so intimately involved with the Intergovernmental Panel on Climate Change (IPCC) in the last seven years, I was curious about Peter's thoughts on climate change. He told me that there are likely going to be changes to the jet stream, which creates the typical seasonal changes due to interactions between the cold arctic air with the warmer tropical air. This is sobering. He did offer some positive reflections. "What gives me hope is there is more recognition of the importance of preserving the environment in the broader public. Along with initiatives with the IPCC on climate change, people are more aware that continued growth and development is affecting the environment." Peter is a member of the Centre for the Advancement of the Steady State Economy, educating people about living within our current needs. "My personal hope is we'll gradually move in that direction, stabilizing populations, and the economy. Every politician talks about and promotes economic growth, but that invariably results in environmental degradation."

The Gambier Island Conservancy and its supporters and partners are doing incredible work on protecting Crown land, building inventories of species and ecosystems, and building bridges between other organizations and universities. The group is currently focused on maintaining their trail network, installing new signs thanks to grants from BC Parks and the Sunshine Coast Regional District, and promoting these trails among the wider public. Their hope is that when initiatives come up for logging or development, there is a contingency of people who are familiar with the island and its surrounding Howe Sound region that they will sympathize and object to unsustainable subdivisions and logging.

I was impressed with the depth of expertise, sheer number of supporters, breadth of participants, and incredible successes that this small island Conservancy and its wider community have achieved.

Marine Protection

Several important protected marine areas surround Gambier Island. On the day I arrived, I passed by the Halkett Bay Marine Park on the east coast of the island. Before the establishment of the park in 1988, Halkett Bay was a log booming ground. These booming grounds have been devastating to the marine life below. Linking the terrestrial area to its adjoining waters in a protected area is an essential conservation strategy. This large 448 hectare (1,107 acre) marine and terrestrial park includes shoreline camping areas, mooring buoys, and a dock. The dock was closed when I traveled through, due to sea lion damage. But the bay was full of boats and dinghies that could still access the shoreline. Peter Scholefield told me how the park began. The Ford family owned a large area of waterfront property along Halkett Bay. The family offered to contribute part of their property as park, keeping ~12 hectares (30 acres) for themselves. The Halkett Bay Marine Park is extensive. Peter's neighbour, Stewart Ford, the son of Denys and Marguerite Ford, told Peter that in about 1986 his father, mother, and aunt Joan Ford negotiated with the provincial government to sell at a below market price about 97.1 hectares (240 acres) of their waterfront property in Halkett Bay

California sea lions on community float in Halkett Bay. PETER SCHOLEFIELD

to the BC government on condition that the land be used to create a provincial park with a dock for public access. The rest of the park was established through a transfer of Crown lands.

An 136 hectare marine foreshore addition was added in 2016 to protect a rare glass sponge reef off the southeast shore of Halkett Point, located in only 30 metres of water. Glass sponge reefs are only found in fjords and on the continental shelf of the BC and Alaska coast. These ancient living structures had been recently found in Hecate Strait and Queen Charlotte Sound. Then in 1984 a local diver, Glen Dennison, discovered twelve new reefs within Howe Sound. According to the Marine Life Sanctuaries Society their locations "benefit from elevated bathymetry, whether as exposed glacial seafloor, pinnacles, seamounts or submarine ridges in areas of high silica concentrations and tidally-driven, near-bottom currents."[13] These cloud and fingered goblet sponges in Howe Sound build reefs by trapping sediments brought by currents into the sponge; then as they die their skeletal remains coalesce into a semisolid matrix. These reefs are important because they support large numbers of species, especially the rockfish that have been on an ever increasing decline in the Salish Sea.[14]

The Marine Life Sanctuaries Society (mentioned in the Bowen chapter) spearheaded the addition of this 136 hectare area off Halkett Bay. Because of the shallow depth of this sponge reef and sponge garden, it is one of only five diveable reef sites in the world! The society, originally formed in 1990, has a mission "to establish no-take marine sanctuaries that will protect all marine life in their natural environment, in perpetuity." Along with this significant goal, the society and particularly its current leader, Adam Taylor, host public workshops on the marine life of the area, host dives to the "city of glass," and work with other surrounding organizations, such as the Howe Sound Biosphere Region, Fisheries and Oceans Canada (DFO), the Underwater Council of BC, and Canadian Parks and Wilderness Society to secure Marine Protected Areas status and no-take zones along the coast. In 2022, two more areas around Gambier and several more in wider Howe Sound were designated Sponge Reef Refuges.[15] In addition to the Halkett Bay Marine Park, there are federal Rockfish Conservation Areas off the island's shores.

As I prepared to leave the island in my boat, I watched a cormorant and a couple of pigeon guillemots fishing, one with a small forage fish in its mouth. This was a great thing to see, and I wondered if the adjacent Halkett Bay Marine Park was helping other seabirds, fish, and numerous other creatures survive and thrive in the Howe Sound area. As I motored my boat away from this large primarily forested island, I marveled again at the turquoise blue colour of the ocean water derived from the rivers and glacial runoff in the summer from the Squamish River through its estuary into Howe Sound.

As I motored out into the sound, once again I marveled at the amazing tenacity of these mostly part-time residents on Gambier Island. They have fought fervently and voluntarily against industry and the Province to stop the impacts of logging, mining, and resource extraction at the expense of entire ecosystems, the wildlife, and people who depend on a healthy environment. As I know that there are plans for more industrial development at the headwaters of the Squamish River estuary, I prayed that more people would wake up to the tremendous impacts of LNG projects on the coast and across BC.

I crossed the Sound, avoiding the large BC Ferries plying their way across to Langdale, carrying thousands of passengers daily to the Sunshine Coast. I then headed into an anchorage at Plumper Cove Marine Park off Keats Island.

Keats Island Nature Conservancy Society

The Plumper Cove Marine Park was established in 1966. It includes both a wharf and mooring buoys, plus sixteen campsites. If you come by ferry from Langdale to Keats Island there is a two kilometre walk to these campsites. Little did I realize then, in summer, this is an intensely busy anchorage as the island is a mecca of recreational boaters and part time owners of cabins and larger homes. I spent the night listening to a cacophony of music, as neighbouring boaters enjoyed their weekend coming and going, with paddleboards revealing the new raised fin keeled hydrofoil that lifts the board right out of the water.

On returning home, I talked with Dan Rogers, a former Keats Island Trustee, who has had a property on the island for over twenty-five years. He explained that the island had an informal Conservancy group for a while, then in 2023 they formally registered the Keats Island Nature Conservancy Society. Dan told me that during the summer months the island can host upwards of 2,500 people with two large camps (Keats Camp and Barnabas) and all the recreational properties. This contrasts with only about forty-five full-time residents the remainder of the year.

In addition to the marine park, there are a couple of small Sunshine Coast Regional District parks on the island. In 2021 the Islands Trust Conservancy acquired the Sandy Beach Nature Reserve, 3.4 hectare (8.4 acre), through a subdivision and rezoning process. Keats Camp, a Baptist summer youth camp, operated by the Convention of Baptist Churches of British Columbia, was founded in 1926. Dan explained that the plan for over forty years had been to subdivide out the previously leased lots with many cabins. As part of a long process, the owners of the land were required to give a small piece for a community park, place a conservation covenant on the Salmon Rock area of the property, and transfer the larger Sandy Beach Nature Reserve to the Islands Trust Conservancy.

Located on the southwest shore of Keats Island (Lhek̲'tínes), the site includes 250 metres of beachfront, with suitable foreshore for surf smelt and Pacific sand lance spawning. The Sunshine Coast Conservation Association (scca) has a covenant on the property, co-held by the Land Conservancy of bc, and the Keats Island Conservation Society has agreed to work with the scca monitoring the site.

The new Keats Island Conservation Society's goals are to preserve and protect land and marine areas, educate people, restore land, and provide trail maintenance. As Dan Rogers explained, "As everywhere on the islands, waterfront owners naturally want to enjoy and recreate on the foreshore and on the waters in front of their land. In some cases this can lead to docks, seawalls, and other structures that affect the foreshore."

Seawalls particularly impact the shoreline, because they cause erosion, with the waves cutting away at the areas below. No matter what the regulations are, maintaining trees along the foreshore is important because they shade the shorelines where forage fish spawn. Trees, shrubs, and other woody debris help stop erosion caused by rising sea levels and the greater intensity wave action that climate change is bringing. In the absence of permits, only complaints can lead to enforcement regarding regulations. Dan added, "Most of the people are very respectful and appreciate nature's essential services."

With a couple of large, undeveloped tracts on the island, and growing awareness of the effects of climate change on these vulnerable islands, I wish this, the newest Conservancy on the islands in the Salish Sea, success in their mission.

With a calmer 10 to 15 knot southeast wind pushing me northward, I headed out the next day on my final leg, sailing on the Salish Sea, home to Lasqueti Island.

The Marine Life Sanctuaries Society spearheaded the addition of this 136 hectare area off Halkett Bay, which includes a No Fishing area to protect the rare Glass Sponge Reef.

CHAPTER FIFTEEN

LASQUETI AND SURROUNDING ISLANDS

An Island in the Middle of Everywhere

"There are so many generous people on the island who have chosen to gift their hard-earned money, time, or donated land to conserve these special places for the community and for wildlife."

GORDON SCOTT

OVER THREE YEARS, AT THE END of my journey to the islands, I returned to Lasqueti/Xwe'etay Island, my home in the middle of the Salish Sea. Lasqueti is cushioned between Texada to the northeast, and Vancouver Island to the southwest. In winter, the southeasterly winds howl unimpeded from as far south as Bellingham, creating rapid, high waves that challenge the most courageous of sailors. These extensive southeast winds have left shortened ancient trees at Squitty Bay on Lasqueti's southeast shores. In summer, northwesterly winds come from as far north as Read Island, at the top of Sutil Channel between Quadra and Cortes Islands. These northwest winds offer a breath of cool, fresh air in the hot summer months, over one of the hottest and driest islands in the Salish Sea.

I spent three summers sailing north, south, and—in the last year—east to meet the local people who had doggedly worked to protect places they held dear on their islands.

In 2021, I sailed from the south to Lasqueti, having rediscovered the beauty of the Southern Gulf Islands. The journey had been nostalgic in many ways—meeting old friends and reconnecting with the islands that I had often visited when I lived on Salt Spring. I was startled by the increasing development and industry around the calmer southern islands since I had been there twelve years ago. Yet, I was heartened by the many new parks and nature reserves determined people had worked so hard to protect.

On my return to Lasqueti from the northeast with my friend Heather the summer of 2022, we met a powerful southeasterly wind head on. As the seas picked up I steered my little craft into large three foot seas, finally ducking into the north end of Lasqueti's Spring Bay. Protected here from the tumultuous seas, I recalled the devoted independent people I had met in the northern islands. I looked west and thought of those on Hornby and Denman, our closest island neighbours, who fearlessly conserved valuable areas on their islands as early as 1990.

Then, in 2023 I sailed the final leg of my journey, riding the waves home from the southeast, after visiting Bowen, Gambier, and Keats islands in the newly designated

Átl'katsem/Howe Sound UNESCO Biosphere Reserve. Adjacent to the bustling metropolis of Vancouver, this teal coloured Sound holds its islands in its arms. I was enthralled by its astounding glass sponge reefs skirting its western hemlock forests. Gratefully, I sailed home to Lasqueti with a mild southeast wind blowing me back to Squitty Bay—the first place on Lasqueti Island acquired to create Squitty Bay Marine Park.

The Spanish explorers named this island in the middle of the Salish Sea Lasqueti Island in the eighteen century. Today it is also known by its Northern Coast Salish name Xwe'etay—meaning yew tree.[1]

Throughout the Northwest coast, yews were valued for their strong wood, used to make wedges. Among the Tla'amin people, "xweth" means wedge. Also referred to as ironwood, the wood was used for wedging planks off of living cedar trees. Luschiim (Arvid Charlie) from the Cowichan says that the wood was used to make clam digging sticks and bows, and the bark was used with its resin for medicines.[2] It is also known for providing the cancer fighting drug Tamoxifen, though today this is made primarily from a chemically synthesized taxol. Yews are usually found growing as individual trees, rather than in stands. The sinewy looking trunk of the reddish western yew tree leads up to an equally unusual cascading evergreen foliage that hangs like a chandelier.

ONE IS NEVER FAR from the sea on Lasqueti, surrounded by an archipelago of twenty smaller islands. Over the years, islanders have identified forage fish spawning habitat on several island beaches. These fish—sand lance and surf smelt—are a key food source for salmon. They also feed the sea ducks who dive down and pluck them up for dinner. Just today I saw three of the federally threatened marbled murrelets that need old growth, or at least large branches, for their nests. Lasqueti Island's forests are critical habitat for this rare seabird, which is declining in number due to logging of their nest trees.

The island's shorelines are laced with another unusual drought tolerant tree—the seaside juniper. Robert T. Adams, a professor and research scientist of evolutionary studies of speciation, has determined through recent breakthroughs in chemistry, mathematics, and DNA testing that seaside juniper (*juniperus maritime*) is endemic to the Salish Sea—in other words, it is only found in this region. Amazingly, the most extensive stand is on Lasqueti Island.[3]

Lasqueti/Xwe'etay has more intact contiguous forest, wetlands, and undeveloped shorelines than any of the other islands within the Coastal Douglas-fir zone. With the lowest level of human disturbance of all of the islands, it is ideal for conservation. Several large tracts of Crown land are scattered across the island, some of which the Province is now considering under varying forest tenures for reconciliation with First Nations.

Like all of the islands in the Salish Sea, Lasqueti is facing development pressures. Its permanent population in 2021 was 498, a 25 percent increase over the past five years. Because of the increasing number of part-time residents and summer visitors, the true population of the island varies considerably. According to the latest census, 40 percent of the island's dwellings are only seasonally occupied, with many more than the full-time residents spending time here for part of the year.

The Northern Coast Salish people's name for Lasqueti Island is Xwe'etay—meaning yew tree.

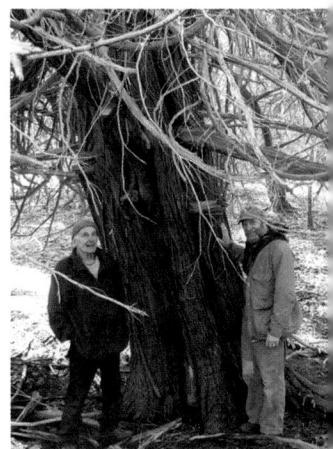

This large seaside juniper is flanked by Alfred Gaensbauer and Gordon Scott.

Squitty Bay Park

Squitty Bay Park was the first provincial park established on the island as early as 1988. The Nature Trust of BC negotiated a 5 hectare (12.35 acre) purchase of the peninsula that forms the outer eastern edge of the park from Dr. Peter Pearse. At the time, Pearse was a professor in UBC's resource economics department with extensive experience in the management of natural resources. One year after the initial purchase of the peninsula, Pearce sold the adjoining 7 hectare property to the Province. The Nature Trust of BC then leased its lands to BC Parks, thereby establishing the 12 hectare (30 acre) Squitty Bay Park.

Squitty Bay on the very south end of Lasqueti has been a popular community meeting place for generations.

Squitty Bay has been used for many years as an island gathering site for fishing, picnics, beach combing, weddings, and other celebrations. Many of its bays fill with logs swept from log booms in the southeast winds. The Lasqueti Island Nature Conservancy (LINC) holds its annual Squitty Bay Day here, celebrating the protection of the island's unique ecosystems. James Schwartz, one of LINC's directors, explains that "the funnelling effects of Juan de Fuca Strait, Puget Sound, and the Fraser Valley all play into the punishing gale force storms which blast the fir and juniper trees clinging to [Squitty Bay and] Young Point's rocky bluffs." Scattered among bonsaied trees are golden grasses and scant understory with fragile wildflowers among the rocks and cliffs. Browsed over a century by the island's feral sheep, wildflowers once filled the meadows, as described by Elda Mason in *Lasqueti Island: History and Memory*. The neighbouring Sangster Island and some of the Sabine Channel islands, free from most browsing sheep and deer, host an astonishing collection of wildflowers in the spring.

Conserving Jedediah Marine Park

After the establishment of Squitty Bay Park, islanders banded together to save a neighbouring island, Jedediah—the pearl in the necklace of the small islands and islets that surround Lasqueti.

There has always been a close bond between Lasqueti and Jedediah. In the early twentieth century, fisherman, loggers, and tug boat operators plied Bull, Sabine, and Malaspina Channels travelling through the surrounding waters to Lasqueti, Jedediah, and southern Texada Island travelling as far as Pender Harbour on the mainland. These pioneers lived by harvesting the abundance of nature around this once rich coast.

Harry John Foote, born in London in 1859, came to Jedediah to homestead at the turn of the twentieth century. With his wife Fanny, he built a large home, developed an orchard and gardens, and lived in Home Bay until they sold the island to Henry and Jenny Hughes. Many Lasquetians and neighbouring Bull islanders found their way to Jedediah over those early homesteading years as their families intermarried and shared tips, recipes, and techniques for living well off the land and waters.

Mary and Ed Mattice came to Jedediah Island, fell in love with it, and purchased it in 1949. Mary spent the first years moving back and forth between Jedediah and Seattle, where she owned a nursery. After several years of remote and occasional homesteading, she moved permanently to the island with her new husband, Al Palmer. The couple enjoyed several decades of life building their paradise home.

Together they restored the house and barns, maintained and expanded the large extensive gardens, planted fruit trees of numerous varieties, and kept one hundred sheep, chickens, ducks, goats, cattle, and their horse, Will. *Jedediah Days: One Woman's Island Paradise* chronicles Mary's compelling story of the years they spent there. Even though they spent considerable time gardening, canning, fishing, and harvesting, they maintained a vibrant social life, often visiting friends and neighbours in the surrounding area. The couple left the island in 1992. Over seventy years old, they continued to live on nearby Vancouver Island.

Determined to realize their quest to conserve the island's old growth trees, estuaries, meadows, and shorelines for future generations, they approached several federal and provincial agencies in hopes of turning it into a park. With the help of Bill Merilees, then with BC Parks, they negotiated an offer with the Nature Conservancy of Canada (NCC).[4] A few days before the agreement was set to expire, a representative from NCC contacted Chris Ferris, at that time the local Lasqueti Island Trustee, and told her they didn't have the money.[5]

Chris Ferris, Doug Hopwood, and several other earnest Lasqueti islanders formed the Friends of Jedediah.[6] Under its auspices, they mounted a fundraising campaign and lobbied for the island's protection. "One of my fondest memories is a benefit dinner on Lasqueti from the early days of the campaign." Doug recalled, "On a stormy night of wet blowing snow, the Teapot House was filled to capacity for a potluck banquet followed by an auction that raised over seven thousand dollars."[7]

Buoyed by their initial success, the Friends went on to apply for grants. They applied to MEC for $10,000. At that time MEC was giving grants to acquire lands so their members could have more protected places to explore. Doug exclaimed, "After a presentation to MEC's directors, a few weeks later, Sarah Golling, the chair of the MEC Board, called to say they were giving us $100,000!"

Along with the Friends of Jedediah, Doug and Chris continued to approach people for help. Over dinner with their local MLA, Leonard Krog, he promised to pitch it to his colleagues. At a book launch for Andy MacKinnon and Jim Pojar's *Plants of Coastal British Columbia, including Washington, Oregon and Alaska*, they met Jake Masselink, then the deputy minister of the environment. He advised them to go to the media and raise local funds to help the cause. Doug explained, "Chris and I had met Ian Gill at a forestry conference a few years earlier, and he brought a film crew to Jedediah and made a short feature that ran on CBC television. Articles in the *Vancouver Sun* and other papers soon followed. To our surprise, donations started coming in for amounts from ten to a few hundred dollars from as far away as Dallas or Dusseldorf, sent by people who wanted to be part of saving Jedediah Island."

Upon hearing about their campaign, Bruce Culver, brother of Dan Culver, who had recently died while climbing K2, contacted Mary and Al Palmer and explained that Dan had specified in his will that part of his estate be used to preserve a wilderness area on the BC coast. Dan had helped protect the Tatshenshini River, Khutzeymateen Valley, Clayoquot Sound, and Robson Bight. News of the Culver family's generous donation spurred on the campaign to acquire the island.

Doug described how interest spread. "There is a story about the day that Moe Sihota, BC's minister of environment at the time, met with the Palmers. While they

Home bay on Jedediah. The campaign to protect Jedediah was supported by people from Dallas to Dusseldorf, including especially the estate of Dan Culver, and BC Parks.

were talking, the phone rang. Mary listened for a minute, and then put her hand over the receiver. 'It's Bill Gates,' she said, 'offering $10 million. What should I tell him?'"

"'Tell him, no, thanks,' Sihota urged her. 'We'll come up with something.'"

In December 1994, the BC government announced the purchase of Jedediah Island for $4.2 million, a price well below market value. Funding came from: $1.1 million from Dan Culver's estate, $2.6 million the Province of BC, and from the Friends of Jedediah, the Marine Parks Forever Society, the Nature Trust of BC, MEC, Marine Trades Association, and Canada Trust.

Many Lasqueti islanders worked hard to protect this 243 hectare (600 acre) island, through letter writing, making personal contacts with media and government personnel, and through their own donations. The seed money from a roomful of Lasquetians grew into the $4.2 million purchase of Jedediah Island for a provincial park.

In my interview with Ian Atherton, the Province of BC's negotiator, he recalled the day he went to Jedediah to review the appraisal. He said, "I have a picture hanging somewhere of Will the horse looking over my shoulder as I reviewed the appraisal report." He laughed and promised to send me the photo. "I dealt with the family, and based on the significance of the property and of the discussions, it went well."

Ian Atherton reviewing the appraisal for Jedediah with the Palmer's horse Will overseeing. Where Ian gets his direction from—"the horse's mouth." DIANE MOEN

Doug completed the story. "The following year, the Friends of Jedediah were selected to receive the BC Minister's Environmental Award. Sheila Ray and I attended the ceremony at Government House on behalf of the group. But the honour of that award belongs to the whole Lasqueti community who came together with energy and imagination to keep beautiful Jedediah Island open to the public and preserved in its natural state."

In 2001, the Province dedicated the surrounding Crown islands and islets as the Sabine Channel Marine Park. This 95 hectare protected area encompasses a group of islands east of Lasqueti: Jervis, Bunny, and Jedediah, plus Fegan Islets and Finnerty Islands northwest of Lasqueti Island. Locals call them a String of Pearls, as they form a chain of more than thirty islands and rocky islets, with Jedediah Island being the largest.

Squitty Bay Park Extension and the Founding of the Lasqueti Island Nature Conservancy

Several of the founding directors of the Lasqueti Island Nature Conservancy (LINC) credit its beginning to both the protection of Jedediah Island Marine Park and the next conservation campaign on the island—an extension to Squitty Bay Marine Park.

Melinda Auerbach, a founding director, explained that as a child in Alberta she loved visiting relatives who had farms in small communities. She has always had a deep appreciation for nature and the countryside. She told me that later, while travelling in Europe, she noticed that there were areas that were developed and natural areas that were protected. She recognized that there have to be places where nature can't be encroached upon. Once she moved to Lasqueti, she set out to help do just that.

"I had been involved with two major acquisitions: first the 12 hectares (30 acres) of Squitty Bay Park, then Jedediah Island, without using an organization like a land trust." Melinda explained, "It seemed like there would be more legitimacy if right away you could spin into action as a land trust, as opposed to an ad hoc Friends of… acquisition of such and such a property. As soon as we started working on the property next door to Squitty Bay Park, we realized it was time to start our own Conservancy."

The desired parcel was next to the existing park, and at 39 hectare (95 acres), it was four times the size. It includes many hidden beaches and bays, a kilometre of coastline, and tree species that included large Douglas-fir, seaside juniper, large western red cedar, bigleaf maple, arbutus, and other species associated with the rare Coastal Douglas-fir zone. The absolutely stunning views look down Georgia Strait to Mount Baker and our sister islands in the San Juans.

Several of the Friends of Jedediah got together and registered the Lasqueti Island Nature Conservancy (LINC) in April 2007. Bonnie Olesko, another of the founders, told me that Dazy Drake had helped with acquiring the extension to the park. Dazy befriended the donor/landholders, Terry Tyler and Ingrid Iverson, and urged them to donate a portion of its value, offering the land at well below market price. This enabled the Province and the Lasqueti Island community to raise the funds to acquire it. Dazy was a very popular islander who helped start several organizations on the island, including the Nature Conservancy. She was renowned for her basket making and other natural fibre projects. Her legacy lives on, as another founding director of a conservancy who has since passed on.

Bonnie and her sister Darlene Olesko moved to the island in the early '70s from Portland, Oregon. In the mid-1990s Bonnie purchased a large farm at the south end. "I liked to run to that big field on the right heading down to Squitty Bay and do my stretches. It was important that we buy that property," she explained. "I had been with the Jedediah acquisition and realized it could happen. You can make change. And it wasn't a lot of money. It was incredibly inspiring."

Because it took a while for LINC to get charitable status, the society joined forces with several key partners. The Islands Trust Fund (now Conservancy) worked with Melinda and other LINC directors to organize fundraising and host events. Their goal was $250,000. The Province agreed to come in with the rest of the money along with other key funding partners.

Over 150 people contributed to the conservation of the extended park. The early directors of LINC and the ITC were busy, bringing in additional funding from TLC The Land Conservancy of BC, BC Marine Parks Forever Society, the Nature Trust of BC (who currently share ownership of the park with BC Parks), the Islands Trust, the Vancouver Foundation, the BC Trust for Public Land, the Powell River Regional District, and Tides Canada Foundation.[8] In a very short time, they raised $1,340,000 to acquire the property.

Just outside the western boundary of Squitty Bay Park the Xwe'etay/Lasqueti Archeology Project team found evidence of a small ancient Indigenous settlement dating to over 2,000 years ago. Dana Lepofsky explained, "Outside and inside the park boundaries are many Douglas-fir trees which have had slabs removed from their bark, possibly for their hot burning fuel. The trees have an impressive girth now, but they would have been much smaller in diameter when the slabs were removed—as evidenced by the fact that the 'natural' bark is splitting the slab scars as the tree increases in size."

I moved to Lasqueti from Salt Spring Island with my husband, Gordon Scott, in 2009. Having helped to acquire more than 10,000 acres of land with the Whatcom Land Trust in Washington State, Gordon is a seasoned conservationist. We met several years earlier at an Environmental History conference in Victoria where a couple of the "mapping queens" and I made a presentation on the islands in the Salish Sea Community Mapping project. Years later, we married and decided to move from Salt Spring to this more remote island to live off-grid, start a large garden, lessen our work load, and be closer to the nature we have spent most of our lives working to protect. Shortly after arriving, we joined the board of LINC, and we have been working with avid islanders to conserve its rare ecosystems ever since.

LINC was established as a society in 2007 and a charity in 2012. Provincially, we were registered to hold Section 219 Conservation covenants and a Section 218 Right of Way and then became an Ecological Gift Recipient. Within a few years, we started issuing quarterly newsletters and other educational materials about the natural features on Lasqueti and surrounding islands. LINC initiated what came to be a very popular annual Squitty Bay Day in the park in summer, to celebrate conservation and our community. Over the next few years, we drafted and registered three conservation covenants on the Islands Trust Conservancy's Nature Reserves with the Nanaimo and Area Land Trust.

Like other island conservancies, many volunteers from the community have been active removing invasive plants—spurge laurel—from a central area on the island. Like many other invasive species, this plant was introduced by early colonists and unfortunately, spread extensively. LINC has made significant progress, although eradication involves specific techniques. Simply cutting it, or trying to pull it out by the roots, only results in the growth of hardy new plants. With many deer and sheep browsing on the island, the ability for native plants to compete with these invasive species is practically impossible. Learning about successful techniques from the Invasive Plant Council of BC and other land trusts' experiences, LINC continues to manage invasive species, a significant threat to biodiversity in a changing environment.

Feral sheep on Lasqueti Island are a challenge for biodiversity as they eat understory plants and new seedling trees.

Islands Trust Conservancy's Nature Reserves on the Island

Doug Hopwood, who was integral to the protection of Jedediah and has been integral to many of the other Salish Sea islands' management and restoration plans, told me about his early days on Lasqueti. Doug grew up in Vancouver and moved to the island in the '80s. Once he arrived, he started running a portable sawmill. He told me, "Around that time there was quite a lot of interest in forestry because we had seen many 'log it and flog it' activities on Lasqueti. People were interested in finding out about alternatives."

Doug mentioned one islander who influenced him tremendously. "Amelia Humphries arranged for some forestry people from UBC to come talk to us, and that got me interested in forest ecology." Doug added, "that led to my interest in forest management and forest conservation, so after that I went to university."

Later, both Doug and his partner Chris Ferris became monitors for the Islands Trust Conservancy (ITC). For over twenty years, they visited the properties all around the islands and wrote up formal reports with photographs. The goal was to document the site's conditions and changes over time to provide evidence of a continual interest in the land. Today, the ITC employs two full-time people to monitor and manage the nature reserves and covenants.

Kwel Nature Reserve

Melinda Auerbach, one of the first Lasqueti Island Trustees and a founding director of LINC, was also inspired by Amelia Humphries. Melinda told me, "She was smart and a very charismatic woman from Texas. She had an ability to read material and present it in an easily understandable way, yet her passion came across, so you were inspired by what she had to say."

Amelia and Michael Humphries moved to Lasqueti in 1972 and soon became active on the island working an oyster farm lease in Tucker Bay.[9] With her husband, Michael from Ontario, she purchased the majority of a quarter section in Lasqueti's mid-island area, the island's centre for early homesteaders near Tucker Bay.

Because of its location in the middle of the island and its harbour, Tucker Bay has always been an important place. Doug recorded the context of the area in what was soon to be a new nature reserve's management plan. "Tucker Bay was the centre of activity in the early settlement history of Lasqueti Island. In 1913, the first public school on Lasqueti Island was built at the corner of Main Road and Tucker Bay Road, at the southeast corner of the property." A public dock was also built in 1913, becoming the main route on and off the island. The Union Steamships made a regular stop there until 1923. The school also served as a community meeting place, until the mid-1960s.

Concerned about the integrity of Lasqueti's forest, Amelia invited UBC professor Dr. Karel Klinka to speak to islanders about sustainable forest management.[10] Following this, she worked with a student of Dr. Klinka's, Donald McLennan, to create an ecologically-based management plan for her own quarter section.

Amelia's husband Michael became an Island Trustee, and later the chair of the Islands Trust. Tragically, Michael died in a plane crash years later. Amelia then subdivided their large parcel and generously donated 21.6 hectares (53 acres) on the corner of Tucker Bay Road and Main Road, the site of the former historic school, to the Islands Trust Conservancy. This became the Kwel Nature Reserve.

Because the property had been logged twice in the 1900s, the Kwel Nature Reserve is primarily mature, mixed second growth. Two hectares of old growth and several large, old Douglas-fir trees remain on higher areas of the property. These areas reveal exposed rocky bluffs with views out over the Sabine Channel and its many small islets, with Texada Island in the distance.

There is an interesting archeological feature on the site that has recently been identified by Dana and her team. "There are isolated patches of shell midden in the top of the reserve that are likely the result of several short term camps. Given the spectacular north looking views from this spot, these are likely 'look-out sites,' possibly associated with the small settlements along the coast below the reserve."

TLC The Land Conservancy of BC and the Nanaimo and Area Land Trust (NALT) registered a conservation covenant over the property in 2001.

In addition to Amelia's generous donation of the Kwel Nature Reserve, the island has two more very generous philanthropists.

A view of Mount Trematon from the John Osland Reserve. GORDON SCOTT

Mount Trematon Nature Reserve

Nancy and Alasdair Gordon spent much of the 1960s exploring the Gulf Islands by sail, anchoring often in Lasqueti's protected bays. In 1973, the couple, along with a group of friends, bought a piece of land and built a cabin on the island's southeast shore. The highest peak on Lasqueti—at 330 metres (1073 feet) in elevation—Mount Trematon was in clear sight. A lifelong mariner, Alasdair loved to climb the mountain where he observed the 360 degree view of the Salish Sea from the summit and watched the weather systems as they were moving through the Strait.

According to the couple's daughter, Jean, her father had a special interest in islands. "Alasdair grew up on the Isle of Skye, a child of Scottish naturalists and early conservationists. He was raised with a strong connection to the land and sea, and he spent his summers in a tent on the remote islands of the Outer Hebrides, assisting his parents in their field work."

The 58 hectare (143 acre) parcel on which Mount Trematon sits came up for sale in 2004. Alasdair saw the opportunity to secure and protect the land. In their lifetimes, he and his wife, Nancy—also a keen naturalist—had witnessed accelerating changes to the Gulf Islands, and they wanted to protect Mount Trematon from future development. The Gordon family bought the land in 2005.

The next year the Gordon family generously donated the entire property to the Islands Trust Conservancy to be protected. Jean explained, "My parents donated the land so that future generations could appreciate open access to its views, its ecology, and its remarkable landforms—from Trematon Creek with stickleback and otters, to the sunny meadow of Nootka rose, to the rocky outcrops with gumweed at the top."

The Mount Trematon Nature Reserve connects two large blocks of Crown land, including a large ecological reserve. Most of the property is forested, with approximately 15 hectares of original old growth forest, while the remaining sections have been selectively logged. There are two areas that were log landing sites, and an old homestead. The nature reserve includes Trematon Creek, which flows most of the year. Three spine sticklebacks have been found on occasion in the creek and in the adjoining Trematon Lake. The Conservation Data Centre has recorded a rare plant, hairy gumweed, located at the top.

Shortly after LINC gained charity status, it began to prepare a conservation covenant for the site, ensuring that the donor's statement of intent would be honoured. These conservation covenants are essential tools for protection, even in cases such as this, where one land trust is holding a covenant over another land trust's property. A conservation covenant can ensure that prohibited uses, such as cell towers, aren't located on the covenanted sites.

After many years, the Gordon family saw that new trees, some smaller trees, and the shrub layer was being severely impacted by browsing of the local deer and sheep. They encouraged LINC to work with the Islands Trust Conservancy to undertake a restoration project on Mount Trematon Nature Reserve. Jean and her sister Catriona Gordon drafted applications for funding to hire Dr. Cora Skaien, a forest and conservation specialist, to undertake a restoration project on the property.

The Mount Trematon Nature Reserve's Ecological Restoration and Plant Biodiversity Study began in 2021.[11] The Islands Trust Conservancy funded the construction of the large 1.2 hectare, 2 metre high fenced exclosure, with funding from the Habitat Conservation Trust Foundation (Conservation Economic Stimulus Initiative).[12] Many island volunteers planted two hundred native shrubs and some shore pine half outside and half inside the exclosure, thanks to additional funding from the Habitat Conservation Trust Foundation (Public Conservation Assistance Fund). After one year, the project team has observed dramatic increases in native species cover in both the dry forest and riparian forest habitat types. Surprisingly, we've noticed considerable natural regeneration of native seeded plants inside the fenced areas. Outside the exclosure there was less growth and reproduction success than inside the fenced area. The healthiest of the planted species surviving outside the fence are huckleberry and shore pine. Amazingly, Cora has recently reported that, "between 2022 and 2023, plants inside the exclosure grew on average 14 centimetres taller than those outside; plants outside decreased by 3 centimetres in the same period over the previous year."

LINC's current president, Gordon Scott, notes that there are things to learn from this project already. "What has become evident is natural regeneration has taken off in the exclosure. The transplanted shrubs are doing okay, but more importantly, the seed bank in the soil has come to life, allowing the ferns, alder, ocean spray, and flowering current to all just take off with the opportunity. By simply fencing, the result is tremendous. We're learning that perhaps it's not necessary to plant, to just put a fence up, and then see what comes back."

LINC's five year plan is to establish at least one shorter fenced plot within the Mount Trematon Nature Reserve that will be accessible to deer, but not the feral sheep. With herbivores a specific issue on Lasqueti, as on several other islands in the Salish Sea, this exclosure study is one of many that LINC and partners are considering for future restoration projects and the protection of biodiversity.

John Osland Nature Reserve

One of the most significant gifts of land on Lasqueti Island came from a local resident. Johnny Osland lived on Lasqueti for sixty-two years, until he was ninety-one. Johnny loved his land and lived a vibrant life, active in the community building boats and recording history. Inspired by the Gordon family's donation, and spurred on by Donald Gordon with whom he shared a great friendship, Johnny bequeathed his land in his will to the Islands Trust Conservancy in 2010.

The John Osland Nature Reserve is a spectacular area blanketed in a mature Douglas-fir forest that leads up to a summit with an expansive view of the Salish Sea over to Vancouver Island. A series of streams lead to a wetland-pond-lake complex nestled in the valley bottom. When Johnny cleared some of the lower wetland areas for agriculture, he dug a few canals to direct the water out to the natural stream that leads down to the nearest bay—Boat Cove. Just before the property was transferred

John Osland Nature Reserve before flooding. John Osland Nature Reserve is a large property donated through John Osland's will. GORDON SCOTT

to the ITC, a small dam was built, the drainage ditches were filled, and the field was flooded, creating a significant wetland and pond area. Birds and amphibians started recolonizing the area, and LINC, the ITC, and numerous volunteers installed nest boxes, built three fences along the riparian areas, and planted native shrubs to help restore the once agricultural fields.

In 2015, LINC and NALT wrote a conservation covenant to protect the unique wetland habitat on the property as well as the large stands of Douglas-fir, arbutus, shore pine, seaside juniper, and western red cedar. Naturalists discovered a rare plant, the giant chain fern on the site.

In the spring of 2022, beavers found the wetland. They increased the dam area, raising the water levels substantially to create what one would now describe as a lake. In the spring of 2023, islanders found thousands of Western toads along the water's edge, with many of the invasive bullfrogs nearby. Melissa Todd, a BC amphibian specialist, has reported, "to our knowledge, there are no reported occurrences of Western toads on any of the Gulf Islands except Lasqueti."[13]

The transformation of this land, from fields to wetlands and now to a substantial lake, is wondrous. Today one can visit the nature reserve and see hooded mergansers, buffleheads, Canada geese, mallards, swallows, eagles, and ravens flying above the forest and lake thanks to Johnny's generous spirit.

The old growth trees on Salish View Nature Reserve with Gordon Scott. LAURA MATHIAS

Salish View Nature Reserve

In 2017, LINC began work to acquire 11.6 hectares (28 acres) adjacent to Squitty Bay Park that leads up to a high ridge, now called Salish View. The property was owned by Wayne Bright, a former LINC director (and founder), who wanted to see more land protected for wildlife. The day that Gordon and I hiked up to the summit to look at the land, we saw a large falcon perched on the top of a Douglas-fir tree. Excited by this sighting, the 270 degree views of the Salish Sea, and the large old growth veteran firs on the property, we approached the LINC board about a potential acquisition.

Salish View's 11.6 hectares features towering cliffs that rise 160 metres above Lasqueti's rocky south coast to a prominent ridge. The property provides an extended conservation corridor from the seashore of Squitty Bay Park to the ridge top above it. Once acquired, LINC and its members would build a public walking trail to the summit. This was important as it would offer islanders the only public trail on the island. The property is home to many species at-risk including: five species of bats, but notably the yellow-listed brown myotis, plus northern red-legged frogs, common nighthawks, the olive-sided flycatcher, bat-wing vinyl, and leafless wintergreen.

In partnership with the Islands Trust Conservancy, LINC spent the next year and a half raising the funds to purchase the site. The campaign's fundraising events included three garden tours, coordinated by long-time islander and director, Wendy Schneible. An amazing gardener herself, she arranged the places where people wanted to see "what was growing behind closed gates." She acquired local beer and goodies and provided an opportunity for people to ask about the Salish View project. LINC directors took people on hikes so they could see the property we wanted them to help protect through their generous donations. A notable event was the Midsummer Night's Dream dinner, auction, and dance. With the theme of seeing an idyllic dream come true, it included a scrumptious dinner of local lamb and salmon, served by beautiful fairies to coincide with the theme. We danced to the Vancouver Island Gerry Barnum band and bid on auction items. LINC raised over $25,000 that night.

The ITC used a Section 99 subdivision to separate out the Salish View parcel from the landowner's larger property. The landowner offered a 20 percent donation off the appraised $300,000 value. Because the property would be registered under the federal Ecological Gift Program, the survey was paid for by Environment and Climate Change Canada. This program has been mentioned in previous chapters because it provides significant tax advantages. Capital gains taxes can be waived when an ecologically important piece of land is donated to a land trust or agency, a designated recipient of an Ecological Gift.

The Sitka and Clayden Family foundations provided additional financial support in addition to the 130 donors who supported the acquisition. The acquisition of Salish View Nature Reserve was celebrated by our community, LINC, and the ITC in August 2018 at Squitty Bay Day.

LINC arranged with the ITC to register a conservation covenant on the site in partnership with the Nanaimo and Area Land Trust (NALT) at the time the sale closed. This covenant prohibits towers or any other structures on the site.

Every conservation project has its own complications and challenges. Gordon mentioned several key features of the acquisition:

> A section 99 subdivision is a very helpful tool, as the landowner doesn't have to give up any road right-of-way. We didn't have to prove water or any of the other typical subdivision requirements. ITC was very helpful in navigating that, allowing us to focus on raising the money, making the case and talking to people. There was a bit of a struggle with the Agricultural Land Commissions' crude map that sliced off a small 10 foot section that should have been included.
>
> Now the property has the only official trail on Lasqueti, which goes from Main Road through Squitty Bay Park to the restoration site around the pond, where we've put a fence around it and planted many native riparian shrubs. Since then, we've seen some regeneration, which is good considering we've been in a drought for several years now. But we're keeping the sheep and deer out. We're seeing sword fern, Nootka rose, and oceanspray with thousands of sprouts shooting up next to the pond. It's an experiment, and we've learned a lot. The Islands Trust Conservancy have been a wonderful partner, helping with the legal costs, and funding the restoration and trail work. We also had great help with fencing from a Katimavik crew. We're grateful for everyone's help.

With Salish View acquired and protected in perpetuity as a nature reserve, with the added protection of a conservation covenant held by two land trusts, wildlife and people can traverse the over 100 contiguous acres around the south of Lasqueti Island, including both Salish View and Squitty Bay Park. Little did we know then, that the conservation area on the south end of the island was about to get much larger!

The BC Parks Foundation and Young Point

Yet even more conservation opportunities were to occur in the area as LINC started working with the newly founded BC Parks Foundation.

In 2012 a large meeting of people involved in environmental organizations, tourism, recreation, and First Nations took place. Ric Careless was at this significant meeting. During my phone interview with him, Ric told me, "We all agreed that we need to put together a unified effort to increase BC parkland. The provincial ministry responsible for parks have one fifth the funding compared to national parks. Really BC Park's funding hadn't grown since the '70s. In 2016 the group's campaign culminated with an announcement by then Premier Christy Clark about a future Parks Strategy. Funding would be added to BC Parks budget to increase infrastructure, including ten million that was designated for the startup of a new independent BC Parks Foundation."

Ric is one of the founders of the BC Sierra Club. In 1994 he was awarded the Order of British Columbia for his work on wilderness campaigns, contributing to the protection of the Pacific Rim National Park Reserve, Schoen Lake Park, Tatshenshini-Alsek Park, the Purcell Wilderness Conservancy Park, and Height of the Rockies Park helping to preserve nearly 5 million hectares of parkland in BC. He then went on to help found the BC Parks Foundation. Ric told me, "The BC Parks Foundation is an independent entity. It is a means to raise money from the public to enhance BC's parks system—not to supplant government's responsibility but to add to the offerings of the Parks capability. In 2017 we started up. I ended up recruiting a lot of the board, including Ross Beatty, the chair, and went on to draft the first strategic plan. The new BC Parks Foundation hired Andrew Day as their new CEO. Andy's background is in law and resource and environmental management. We picked up a couple key properties—Princess Louisa Inlet and Saturnina Island. A priority is the islands in the Salish Sea."

With the 10 million dollar start-up funds, the new BC Parks Foundation was able to jump into action.

Over the years, many people had talked with the owners of the large, undeveloped property that bordered Squitty Bay Park. I recall sitting in the owner's boat gazing up at a picture of their property—an aerial photo of over 101 hectares (250 acres) of contiguous forest. The Buttjes family inherited the property from their parents, Wilfred and Ria, who purchased the land in 1971, but divergent interests precipitated the decision to sell. They all agreed that ideally, it should become part of the adjacent Squitty Bay Park, in one form or another. LINC was delighted to find a province wide conservation organization that was willing to help.

Ric knew a member of the family and knew of the property. He connected them with Andy, and over the course of several years, they were able to negotiate an agreement. Andy connected with LINC, who also had the property on their radar. LINC helped engage the local community in support and fundraising. In a relatively short time, the BC Parks Foundation was able to successfully acquire the Young Point property.

The Young Point conservation area includes 5 kilometres of undeveloped waterfront, rocky shoreline bluffs, hidden pocket coves, many rare species, and some old growth trees. This extensive 103 hectare (256 acre) conservation area now links with

Young Point is one of the largest protected areas In the area 101 hectares (250 acres) acquired recently by BC Parks Foundation. GORDON SCOTT

Squitty Bay Park and the Salish View Nature Reserve to form a very large contiguous protected area on Lasqueti's southeast end.

Andy and the board of the new BC Parks Foundation are all movers and shakers across BC. In a little over three years, they have helped conserve twenty-five properties and raised over $100 million for conservation. Working with the foundation, LINC aims to have more land on Lasqueti and surrounding islands protected over the next few years.

Livingstone Forest Covenant

Because of their years of work in conservation, Doug Hopwood and Chris Ferris decided to protect the ecologically important areas within their ~15 hectare (38 acre) property on Lasqueti. They registered a NAPTEP covenant over two thirds of the forested and wetland portions of the property, leaving the home and arable land out of the covenant area. "We saw how a covenant can allow landowners to protect conservation values while retaining the use of the land," explained Chris Ferris. Even though a portion of the property was in the ALR, they were able to register the covenant. As Doug explained, "Because the ITC carried the burden of the process, they were able to get the permission of the Agricultural Land Commission, which took many years." Now they will be able to sell the land, knowing the natural values will be protected. It did carry a significant expense, Doug noted, with costs of $14,000 needed to survey the covenant area separately.

Previous owners of the property, Kate Livingstone and her family, had homesteaded a larger area around the property for sixty years. Kate Hackett, granddaughter of Kate Livingstone, shared in commemorating the family by installing a plaque on a rock on the property in August 2023. Doug explained that the Livingstone Covenant recognizes the family's long history in the area.

Protecting the forest and wetland has always been a priority for Doug and Chris. "We feel we achieved more durable conservation in the long run with the covenant," Doug explained. The carbon stored in the trees and in the wetland will be there for many years to come.

LINC—Looking Forward

With humans gobbling up so much of the planet's habitats, resulting in the extinction of species at an ever increasing rate, land conservation is becoming ever more important. Climate change poses a difficult challenge for conservation groups intent on long term management, such as: which plants or trees to use in restoration projects that will survive hotter temperatures and more droughts; which properties will be affected by rising oceans; which species will adapt and survive; and which will not, which wetlands will still exist decades into the future.

LINC has developed a strategic plan to guide the next five year's work to protect the island's ecosystems and habitats—while we have the opportunity. With many of Lasqueti's residents aging, it is inevitable that there will be changes in land ownership, which could result in more conservation. Capital gains taxes are a pivotal cost to landholders. As land changes hands, either through a sale or through a disposition to family members, a hefty tax is levied on the difference between its value upon initial purchase and its value when the title is transferred. Estate planning is needed to ensure that capital gains taxes don't force some heirs to sell inherited larger properties to a developer, if they wish to see some or all of it conserved for the future.

In 2023, about 12.5 percent of the Xwe'etay/Lasqueti and its surrounding areas are protected, much of that in the surrounding islands and islets. LINC's *2023–2026 Strategic Plan* sets a significant goal of protecting 20 percent of its land over the next five years and fully 50 percent in the next ten. That is close to the national 30 percent goal for the year 2030 set by the federal government.

Like many people I interviewed, LINC's president, Gordon Scott, has hope for the future. "The growing number of people who are aware of the importance of the environment and biodiversity gives me hope. I see the next generation coming on who have a great foundation of knowledge. They have big challenges, with some powerful players to struggle with, but they have initiative and enthusiasm. Here on Lasqueti, the next generation is tied to this place, which is a very valuable trait to have protecting land. They'll know it. I'm very encouraged by the young people coming on."

LINC, like other land trusts on the islands, has dedicated people on its board.[14] As with other local conservancies, attracting passionate and dedicated volunteer directors, especially young directors, is a challenge. Like many other land trusts, LINC has now hired a part-time administrative assistant to help with communications, donations, membership, and other administrative tasks.

Lasqueti is fortunate to have several residents who are retired university professors. Ken Lertzman, a resident on the south end, is well known to many in the forestry and conservation field because of his many years of research on forest ecology, policy, and management in coastal British Columbia. After thirty years, he is now professor emeritus of SFU's School of Resource and Environmental Management. Ken brings a wealth of knowledge to the LINC board, offering current research on topics of urgency for conservationists today, especially restoration and climate change.

I am seeing the impacts of climate change, especially on our dry island, with western red cedar, arbutus, and recently alders showing signs of stress. With Ken and Doug Hopwood's knowledge and assistance, I hope we can understand and then plan to adapt to these changes, for example by planting tree species that can withstand the droughts that we are now experiencing.

Xwe'etay/Lasqueti Archaeology Project

Lasqueti's deep history has come to life recently through a large archeological project run by Dana Lepofsky, a Simon Fraser University archaeologist, and her colleagues. This archaeological work is focused on finding and dating ancient clam gardens, fish traps, camps, settlement areas, and other isolated archaeological finds all around the island. The project includes members of the K'ómoks, Wei Wai Kum, Halalt, Tla'amin, and Qualicum First Nations. Working with First Nations, university students, and local islanders to identify archaeology sites, they have been reaching out to the wider community about their findings.[15]

I have attended some of the public gatherings with people from the island and the participating First Nations. Recently I witnessed a ritual cultural burning to honour the ancestors, hosted by Qualicum hereditary leaders Mark Recalma and Kim Recalma-Clutesi. Dana explained that "one of the primary goals is to "more fully honour, respect, and protect Indigenous heritage." As a result of the project, there has been a shift in people's thinking and an appreciation of the deep Indigenous history of the islands.

Passionate about her profession and people generally, Dana and her policy/planner research partner from SFU, Sean Markey, have discovered that there are archaeology sites on the surrounding islands anywhere people could have modified the landscape to make it liveable. She told me that Xwe'etay/Lasqueti was densely packed with people, especially around False Bay and China Cloud Bay. The oldest date of a site thus far is 6,000 years. She suspects the first settlements are considerably older than that. By 4,000 years ago, people seemed to have expanded to all the major, protected bays, and by 2,000 years, they were even living in areas that were more socially remote.

Dana expanded on what the team has uncovered. "We found an intertidal management feature on almost every beach we visited, especially on the northwest end of the island—where most of the ancient settlements are located. For instance, False Bay is lined with ancient settlements (visible today as shell platforms on which houses were built). Associated with these settlements, lining the foreshore, are rock features that are the remnants of the once carefully managed intertidal landscape."

There is an ecological concept known as "shifting baseline syndrome." This describes people's tendency to view what they see today as the norm, even if modern conditions are dramatically different than most of an ecosystem's history. This was first applied to thinking about how we perceive depleted fisheries.

Dana explained that this is similar to how we view Indigenous people's connections to the land, and results in a kind of cultural shifting baseline. "If we believe that the Salish Sea of the past was depleted as it is today, and specifically Lasqueti where we now have no herring, few salmon, no cultivated camas beds, and the like, then it is hard to imagine that Lasqueti—or anywhere in the world—could have sustained a large Indigenous population for generations. This kind of thinking results in erasing Indigenous history as well as ecological history."

To reset this kind of thinking, Dana and her extensive team—composed of local Lasquetians, First Nations's community members, and university researchers—are now documenting the island's ecocultural history through a sister project. Dana explained, "There is a layered history of settler history and ecocultural change which are linked. We want to help people understand that Indigenous history doesn't erase settler history and that they are layered and build on each other." By researching written and photographic archival documents, interviewing long time islanders, analyzing historic air photos, and modelling the location and size of past and current watersheds and wetlands, the group hopes to collate the "eco-cultural" landscape of the past and see how it has changed over time. Collectively, this information will help imagine other ways of living on the island—both in the past and how to be better stewards going forward.

As I journeyed to the islands in the Salish Sea, I came to see the fascinating differences among the islands. I also learned, as Mary Palmer highlighted in her book

Dana Lepofsky (left) invited people from the K'omoks, Wei Wai Kum, Halalt, Tla'amin, and Qualicum First Nations to join people living on Lasqueti Island to a community gathering at a very low tide to celebrate the large fish trap and clam gardens evident between Higgins and Wolf islands just off of False Bay, Lasqueti Island.

People at the top of Salish View during the conservation campaign. SHEILA RAY

Jedediah Days, that "Island people are fiercely independent, often stubborn, individualistic and opinionated beyond belief. But it's our way."[16]

There's some truth to that, especially on Lasqueti. Yet "our way" also includes very generous people who have donated land, volunteered their time, and donated their hard-earned money to conserve habitats for the future! The result is these magnificent lands on Xwe'etay/Lasqueti and its surrounding islands and islets including Jedediah, Trematon, Kwel, Osland, Salish View, Point Young, Squitty Bay, and more which are now firmly protected and treasured places for the community and its wildlife.

As I settle back into my home community on Xwe'etay/Lasqueti Island, in the middle of everywhere, reflecting on all the dedicated people I having visited, I feel so connected. We are harbingers in a world where everything is linked, and everything counts! We all share a love of the islands and the Salish Sea.

CHAPTER SIXTEEN

WAYPOINTS FOR THE FUTURE

"I learned that we have the power to organize, to create a land trust, to focus that awareness of the environment and do something to ensure that these places and values are around for our times and hopefully for the next generation."
CAROLYN CANFIELD

THE ISLANDERS WHO I INTERVIEWED over the last three years have shown enormous dedication, skill, and perseverance in the face of incredible challenges. This is the time to conserve precious habitats, wetlands, and forests. Looking at the maps at the beginning of this book, you can see how much has already been done, by people from all walks of life. I hope that their actions, stories, and voices will provide inspiration and hope that can bring us together over the next two decades, so we can realize the goals of conserving 30 to 50 percent of the land and waters that sustain us.

Public Involvement

The land trust movement has a long vision both culturally and ecologically that can help to address some of the harms we've created. It's not just about setting aside the ecological jewels, but also engaging people by connecting the community to nature—through hikes and workshops, through kids' educational programs, engaging newsletters, websites, auctions, garden and home tours, and through restoration projects. All people can support the protection of nature through their own actions, by volunteering or donating to conservation campaigns and providing general support.

Christine Torgrimson, formerly executive director with SSIC, stressed the importance of public access. "I think it's really really important for people to have access to natural places in a way that endears them to those places, so people remember that we are part of nature. What we do to nature, we do to ourselves. I think it's important to let people in, carefully of course, to cultivate that sense of love and desire to protect these places on the islands."

On the coast of BC, with its huge population growth and increases in land values, there are development pressures and recreational pressures on conservation lands. Carolyn Stewart, who now works for CRD Parks, reiterated that we need to educate people more about why we need to protect land. "Recreational use in park land is always the rub, because while we're trying desperately to protect the natural values, the area gets more people that recreate in it. We need to educate people about compatible recreation and how to protect parks so they are not loved to death. One of the challenges of protected areas in general is to get the word out about why they are protected, and how people can help to continue to protect them."

Resting Wood ducks at Killarney Creek, Bowen Island. WILL HUSBY

Eric Higgs sees restoration as another way to bring in the public. "The collective genius of the Galiano Conservancy is that it showed that restoration is a powerful part of the equation. They bought a completely (disturbed) and therefore cheap site and saw the long-term potential value of restoring it. Now they are converting agricultural land into the wetland and forest it once was. It involved hundreds of hours of volunteer labour, professional expertise, and it is leading the way. It took imagination and innovation."

Today, the Islands Trust Conservancy offers funds to local land trusts to undertake restoration projects on their nature reserves. They are providing service contracts (management agreements) to local land trusts to maintain these protected lands. This often attracts volunteers to the nature reserves. As Gordon Scott of the Lasqueti Island Nature Conservancy notes, "we are really grateful to the ITC as they work really responsibly and collaboratively. Without them things wouldn't be done nearly as well, because of a lack of funding."

Bill Turner, executive director of TLC The Land Conservancy of BC for its first twelve years, recalled that evidence of public support and financial contributions for acquisitions were important indicators for governments to support a project.

> Science is really important, but it's not what gets people really motivated. It's giving the land a voice—from their hearts. Public emotion usually is what makes it happen. Public dollars get great leverage because politicians pay so much more attention. I was meeting with the minister and we'd sit down and talk about the project. I'd say, this is what we need to do, because the public donated toward this project. You have to think about what Clayoquot did. It really was instrumental in helping with the Gowlland Tod acquisition because they needed a good news story. They did the Park Legacy in the Lower Mainland because they needed to do good things after being so beaten up over Clayoquot.

Collaboration

Today, conserving land requires collaboration with many partners. Initially, the landowner or landholder must be the first partner—open and willing to be good stewards and consider conservation options. With today's rising prices of land, we may need to bring in other potential partners, including Indigenous people, local and regional governments, provincial and federal parks, funding agencies, and other land trusts.

Carolyn Stewart, who was working for the Islands Trust Conservancy at the time of the Brooks Point acquisition on South Pender Island, recalled the multiple partners involved:

> The Alan Brooks family wanted to conserve the land as Alan was ill. He wanted to see it happen in his lifetime. They owned three properties. They made a gift of one using the federal Ecological Gifts program to reduce the family's taxes on the sale of the other properties. The partner groups raised the money for the second portion. These included NCC, ITC, TLC, HAT, PICA, and the Friends of Brooks Point. The second lot was given to another partner, the Capital Regional District, for a park. Then NCC and ITC drafted a conservation covenant over it. Several years later, another lot, one over, became available and the Friends of Brooks Point, PICA, the Victoria Habitat Acquisition Trust (HAT), and the CRD worked to raise the funds. Then the CRD bought the piece in the middle and now there is an extensive Regional Park at Brooks Point, made possible through the collaboration of many partners.

Jan Garnett, the BC regional vice president of the Nature Conservancy of Canada (NCC) from 1999 to 2010 agreed that it was important for local land trusts to reach out and search for partnerships. "Brooks Point was a good example. They established the scientific rarity of the site as well as the equally precious opportunity to conserve it."

During our interview, she commented on how NCC worked with the smaller conservancies. She explained that NCC was working during these years on the ecoregional assessments, showing connectivity in order to knit important ecosystems together into larger landscape projects. If projects on the islands were small they tended to refer them to the local land trusts."

Salt Spring Island's South & West Conservation partnership forged a different style of collaboration. It included the Province, CRD Regional Parks, and multiple island groups. Carolyn Stewart explained, "We got together every month or two to figure out how to promote conservation of the south and west parts of Salt Spring Island because it was so significant. We'd keep each other in the loop in terms of potential acquisitions that were going on—the Mill Farm Regional Park and Burgoyne Bay comes to mind." Scientific inventories of the area were created through the partnership. These were invaluable in terms of promoting the importance of protecting the area to larger funders and to the public who needed the rationale to donate their own funds to the project.

A recent example of a successful collaboration through partnerships between a local land trust and the province-wide Nature Trust of BC (NTBC) is the Cable Bay acquisition on Galiano Island. The Galiano Conservancy Association's incredible mid-island network of adjoining protected properties and their history of successful acquisition prompted the NTBC to partner with them on the acquisition. The 26.5 hectare (65 acre) Cable Bay property is adjacent to the Pebble Beach Nature Reserve. Zoned for a six lot subdivision, the landowner agreed to wait while the partners worked to raise the funds to acquire it. After several years, they succeeded, bringing in the lead donor, the Sitka Foundation, and then support from the Government of Canada through the Natural Heritage Conservation Program, several other foundations, and more than 150 additional donors. As Jasper Lament of NTBC said, "We were working with the community to protect a large chunk of waterfront property, building that connectivity, protecting high biodiversity in the coastal Douglas-fir zone, in an area of high threat surrounded by lots of private land. It's not common to have these opportunities to build connected conservation."

Increasing the public's awareness of the fragility, beauty, and need to protect nature is vital. Carolyn Stewart remarked that "another highlight while I was at the Islands Trust Fund (Conservancy) was the painting of the map and the other island maps for the *Atlas of the Islands in the Salish Sea*. That was a cool achievement done by many in collaboration. It was important to educate the public about what has been achieved."

Resident and transient orcas, a species at risk, visit the Salish Sea. MAUREEN WELTON

ANOTHER ESSENTIAL COMPONENT in conservation campaigns are the scientists and professionals. From biological and ecological assessments to mapping and report writing, hundreds of specialists have diligently donated their time, money, and professional expertise to the initial ground work. Kathy Dunster portrays the life of an individual scientist: "Identifying the often overlooked ecological values on a site that helped land trusts get a campaign going... Urgent late night phone calls. Field work in all weather and seasons... with almost impossible deadlines. And parachuting into different islands other than the one you live on because your outside opinion has validity there, where on island you were often ignored." These professionals deserve our thanks for providing the needed science to back up the often obvious opportunities to protect lands.

Cross-border conservation and collaboration is building momentum. The American Friends of Canadian Conservation (AFOCC) is leading the way. Estimates suggest that US citizens own close to 40 percent of the land on the islands. Prior to the establishment of AFOCC, US citizens would have to pay significant capital gains taxes upon donating their land.[1] Thankfully, several conservationists with roots in the US and Canada worked for years to set up this organization that now allows American citizens with land in Canada to receive the same types of tax benefits that Canadians donating land receive.

Bob Turner, of Bowen Island, mentioned that he has joined the Salish Sea Institute to widen his circle. He described some of the initiatives that he sees we could learn from in Canada.

If there was more opportunity for greater collaboration between land trusts across the border, I think that would be terrific. I'm paying more attention to restoration and rehabilitation work and really impressed that the State of Washington and the Environmental Protection Agency have set priorities for salmon restoration, and as a consequence major funding has gone into rehabilitating estuaries for salmon enhancement. Eelgrass beds are getting formal protection—all in the name of protecting endangered species or the name of salmon. The non-profit organizations right up to the state level, government agencies as well as the Tribes/Nations, are energetic in their environmental protections. I have a lot to learn from these American efforts. Canadians need to hear more about these partnerships. Canadians are attached to a wild west culture—resource extraction, economy—that's where the jobs are. South of the border, they have less wild spaces left, and less resources left to extract. That's why I'm joining with the Salish Sea Institute as they have things to teach us.

Jasper Lament of NTBC made a similar point. "I've learned from land trusts in the US. They are embedded in the communities they serve. Land trusts are a way of life there. That's not true as much in Canada, and we could learn from what they do there. It's remarkable how diverse their land trust movement is—regional, watershed, state, and national. We don't have that same depth and diversity in BC."

Financial Challenges and Opportunties

"The gap between demand and funds raised exists across charities of all sizes, but it is more significant for smaller charities."

CANADAHELPS GIVING REPORT, 2023

Kate Emmings, the current manager of the Islands Trust Conservancy, put the next stage's challenges this way. "As land trusts are starting to mature, taking on bigger responsibilities and complex ones, we need to embrace the challenges: funding crunches and expensive lands—looking at how to sustain what we do—talking about the next one hundred years, through having good practices in place, good strategies, and recognizing the role we play in terms of landscape conservation."

Individual philanthropy has played a significant role in land conservation. Many BC Parks on the islands, including Bellhouse Park on Galiano, Winter Cove on Saturna, Tribune Bay and Helliwell on Hornby, and Ruckle Park on Salt Spring Island, were gifts or partial gifts from individuals. On Lasqueti, two very generous landowners fully gifted their lands—one while living and another through their will. Other islands had similarly generous people who donated their lands, or part of its value for conservation.

Landowners with larger acreages, a bequest in a will, or a gift while living can result in an extraordinary legacy for the future. The challenge then is to manage these lands because they need to be protected from the growing spread of invasive species and the rising challenges of climate and ecosystem change.

Due to the rising price of land, covenants may be an even more effective way to conserve land. The costs of monitoring conservation covenants is ongoing. Laurel Brewster, who writes conservation covenants, commented on the landowner costs. "There are the landowners who struggle to come up with enough money for the covenant, including the survey, the baseline, and the endowment that some land trusts are now asking." But there are still a lot of people who care about the land. It's all relative, as George West mentioned in the Cortes chapter. We can come up with money for our own needs, such as new garages or decks with equivalent costs. To address these additional costs, Laurel recommends that philanthropists set up a large endowment—a pool for that region. Perhaps these types of endowments could work through the many community foundations around the province.

Acquisition, though increasingly expensive, is the most secure way to conserve land. Zoning does not protect land over the long term, because it can and does change. However, with rising land prices, the millions of dollars it takes today to acquire lands is an increasingly difficult challenge. Especially on the coast, the value of lands is increasing astronomically. Bill Henwood remarked that Parks Canada, back in 2003, would have liked to protect more, making the size of the Gulf Island National Park Reserve bigger. "We would have liked to add Samuel Island, the rest of Sidney Island, Moresby Island, but they are way out of reach now."

The general public, government agencies, and many foundations seem to be primarily focused on supporting humans first. Over the last thirty years, religious organizations have received 40 percent of Canada's charitable donations, with health and social services receiving 35 percent, and environmental organizations receiving 3 to 4 percent.[2] There needs to be a stronger understanding of the essential nature of the environment and the need to protect the natural ecosystems that are the foundations for all life. Even in local communities, people and municipalities are prone to giving far more public funds for sports arenas and food banks than conservation organizations.

Ian Atherton has been negotiating acquisitions for conservation for the bulk of his career. He explained that today there are several other "currencies" for acquisition. These include density transfer, where the density on one property is transferred to another. When a developer chooses to set aside areas for parks or nature reserves in order to receive approval for their development it is often referred to as mitigation. The Islands Trust Conservancy on both Bowen and Gambier islands have used this approach to create nature reserves.

A third currency is carbon credits. These are typically associated with forest lands. Ian has negotiated carbon credits for the acquisition of lands owned by Mosaic for the Children's Forest on Cortes Island. There are now blue/green carbon credits which apply to the marine areas, in addition to credits for protecting forested areas. At one point, there was a province-wide organization, Living Carbon. Its goal was to allow land trusts to combine properties so they could use carbon credits. Kathy Dunster and Dirk Brinkman were part of setting that up, along with Briony Penn, who today continue to work in this field.

According to my interviewees, BC is really lagging in terms of provincial funding for land trusts. Most of the directors with whom I spoke ardently said, "We need a fund for BC land trusts in terms of helping with acquisitions and capacity building. It's not just the money; it shows provincial government support. It has rarely shown support for land trusts." Surprisingly, our neighbours in Alberta are way ahead in terms of how much provincial funding is going to support the work of land trusts, which is true for other provinces as well. The BC Parks Foundation was set up in 2017 with a large endowment. With this core funding to back them, they have hired multiple staff and garnered additional financial support through private business connections, adding crowdfunding to fund specific acquisition campaigns. Thankfully, they have acquired extensive areas for future parks since their inception in 2017, in some cases working with local land trusts.

The recent announcement of $300 million for conservation financing from the Province will be a substantial jump-start for Indigenous-led conservation, including allocating funding for economic activities to replace existing Crown land tenures with First Nations for logging of old growth forests. The BC Parks Foundation will need to raise $150 million of this promised funding from the private sector. The foundation announced that "funds will be managed within the Foundation and overseen independently from government by a Strategic Oversight Committee made up of experts, half of whom will be First Nations." This funding prioritizes new Indigenous Protected and Conserved Areas (IPCAs). The foundation added that "Area-based conservation initiatives supported by the Fund will be led by or have the free, prior and informed consent of First Nations title and rights holders or delegated First Nation Organizations and provide opportunities to advance co-management of those conserved and protected areas."

Federally, the Government of Canada announced another 500 million in November of 2023.[3] This money is directed toward securement of 13,000 square kilometres of old-growth forest areas, and $104 million from the 2 Billion Trees program that will be specifically focused on the restoration of species-at-risk habitat, wildfire mitigation and recovery, and watershed health. This fund will hopefully move us toward achieving the national goal of 30 percent protection of land and water by 2030.

Federal acquisition funds in the last few years have been a real boon to the movement, especially through the National Heritage Conservation Program administered jointly by Wildlife Habitat Canada and the Alliance of Canadian Land Trusts.[4] Through an established agreement with Environment and Climate Change Canada, these organizations manage the Land Trusts Conservation Fund for habitat conservation and include land trusts' hard costs for acquisitions across Canada. As mentioned in previous chapters, often these federal funds require a non-federal match, such as regional or provincial government funds. Collaboration with larger conservation organizations may be a more complex but promising way to secure some of these larger funds.

However, raising money for acquisition and registering conservation covenants are not the only costs that a land trust must find. During our interview, Jan Garnett elaborated on the challenge.

> The role that land trusts play is critical to the planet. With accelerating climate change, their role is only going to become more critical. Collaboration rather than competition has to be way of the future, including collaborative fundraising. Locally driven projects that demonstrate community support have a better chance of success.

The Salish Sea conservancies are critical and do amazing work. What would make the biggest difference is some secure funding source. There are many legal risks running a conservancy, or any not-for-profit. Strong leadership is essential. Without sufficient funding, confidential records can be stored improperly, land management can be inadequate, time and money can be wasted in "putting out fires," and burnout becomes endemic. A greater focus on good governance is really important for land trusts—which is hard to do when they are struggling for money to just keep the work going. Provincial funding for the land trust movement would make a big difference, because land trusts are also enhancing and completing government parks' work in many ways but without some of the impediments of being in government. Core funding to support their work, and providing accountability for that funding, requires a staff person.

Female whimbrel, one of many migratory birds that breed on the Arctic tundra and winter on coastlines as far south as Tierra del Fuego. This female was seen resting and feeding on Pender Island's Brooks Point. MYLES CLARKE

Local land trusts face additional challenges. Many directors of the land trusts I spoke with mentioned that there is challenging competition with larger conservation organizations for existing grant programs. As Ann Eriksson of THINC put it, "there is a clear need for a sustainable funding model to assist smaller volunteer run conservation organizations. Many government programs, such as the federal Habitat Stewardship Program and the provincial Habitat Conservation Trust Foundation, have complex application processes which take a great deal of time to design and complete and are very competitive with larger conservation organizations." Funding for core staff would help these smaller organizations be more successful.

"Funding models are a barrier," added Rob Underhill of the Mayne Island Conservancy. "We are often focusing on the short term, and the reality is in the private landscape there is a high turnover of residents. Projects don't end. Education goes on, and restoration projects can be decades long. So this constant motivation to chase funding for short term projects, and not persist in maintenance of ones that require continued funding, means constantly jumping from one thing to another, rather than focusing on the important things that need to be done. Long term funding is needed."

Penny Barnes, the current executive director of the Salt Spring Island Conservancy, added a heartfelt motivational element.

Funding is a surprisingly difficult struggle. More governmental support is needed. This is not just for mental health—it's for ecosystem health and everything else. Government funding for these organizations is needed, not just to fund their projects, but to provide operational stability. If these land trusts, which are largely volunteer and community based, are providing something valuable to the community as a whole—then they do need to be supported to do that. Federal programs exist, but they are harder to access. Even with a great project, how do you fund it? Politically we're not as attractive as funding health care. We do seem to be at the bottom of the priority list.

The Galiano Conservancy has been able to secure operational funding by organizing annual member drives and events that engage the community and bring in needed funding for their staff. Denman Conservancy has developed their successful annual Garden Tour that brings in both financial support and public involvement. Along with basic annual support from their regional district, the Savary Island Land Trust has crafted fundraisers that bring in both members and funding for staff, but also for the many basic annual costs of keeping an organization afloat: financial reports and audits; offices and equipment; tools and materials; or legal reviews of covenants.

Nora Layard who worked with financial planners to develop what eventually became the *Green Legacies Guide* suggested, "we need intervention money—so loggers don't buy a property when it comes on the market. We need money to find a conservation buyer, or carve off a house site and protect the rest. We need innovative financing, another mechanism to buy the land, protect it, and re-sell with covenants on it—a Green Angels Chest." This type of financial support could attract philanthropists beyond the government support that is needed.

Kate Emmings, the current manager of the Islands Trust Conservancy, put it this way: "As land trusts are starting to mature, taking on bigger responsibilities and complex ones, we need to embrace the challenges: funding crunches and expensive lands—looking at how to sustain what we do—talking about the next hundred years, through having good practices in place, good strategies, and recognizing the role we play in terms of landscape conservation."

Reconciliation with Indigenous People and Land Trusts

An extensive two-year long archaeology project on Lasqueti Island has brought to light evidence that supports the oral history of thousands of years of Indigenous people's occupation. As a result, both our local and the wider community are now more aware of the long-term links to the islands with the Indigenous people who once thrived here. Dana Lepofsky explains the regional connections that have existed for thousands of years.

> Indigenous People living in the Salish Sea were connected through a common language, elaborate exchange systems, and marriage networks. People from eastern Vancouver Island, for instance, would regularly travel to the Fraser Canyon to harvest salmon in the territories of their Fraser River kin. Archaeologically we see these linkages in shared burial customs, region-wide artifact styles, and in traded items (e.g., camas from Vancouver Island found in an archaeological site in the Harrison watershed). In the past, there were a myriad of social connections that both maintained the Salish Sea as cohesive social-cultural region and linked the Salish Sea to other neighbouring cultural groups.[5]

Along with Pender, Mayne, Galiano, Salt Spring, and like many of the other islands, the Xwe'etay/Lasqueti Archaeology Project is bringing Indigenous partners to the islands to rediscover their roots here and to engage with islanders. In the marine world, these links are fascinating:

> There was a time—not that long ago on the scale of such things—when the marine intertidal zone flourished, supplying ongoing abundant and reliable foods for the many thousands of Indigenous peoples who lived along the north Pacific coast. In recent years, as we are all well aware, our intertidal ecosystems have experienced a decline in both species abundance and diversity. The decline has to do with a myriad

of factors including deposition of silts from upland clearing, dragging of logs through eelgrass beds, the introduction of invasive species (e.g., the Japanese oyster), and various kinds of foreshore development.

Another major factor contributing to shifts in intertidal abundance and diversity is the effects of removing the people who, for thousands of years, actively stewarded their lands and seas to ensure food harvests into the future. Oral traditions, memories, and the archaeological record demonstrate the extent to which Indigenous peoples in this region and, in fact, throughout the Pacific, have tended the intertidal landscape.

At the lowest levels of the intertidal zone are clam gardens (wúxwuthin in the Northern Coast Salish language). These are rock-faced terraces created by Indigenous People to expand and improve clam habitat at the zone where littleneck and butter clams thrive.[6] Our work on Quadra Island has shown that some of these gardens are at least 4,000 years old and that they provided a sustainable and abundant source of clams for generations. In fact, the team's experiments show that clam gardens have two to four times more clams than non-garden beaches and they increased clam productivity by 150–300 percent.[7]

A clam garden on Jedediah Island revealed at low tide.
DANA LEPOFSKY

I'd heard that Indigenous people had modified camas beds to increase productivity, but the idea that people could increase the number and quality of clams on the foreshore? These are astonishing findings that can have immense relevance in the world today as we find that food security is becoming more of an urgent need than ever before, and especially when we consider the vulnerable state of our ecosystems.

This archaeological evidence of the presence of Indigenous people on the islands is significant considering today's focus on reconciliation through conservation. TLC The Land Conservancy have acquired an island off of the Saanich Peninsula. TLC worked with the W̱SÁNEĆ Leadership Council on a landmark partnership agreement that transfers title of SISȻENEM (also known as Halibut Island), a ~4 hectare (9.67 acre) island off the east coast of Sidney Island, from TLC to the W̱SÁNEĆ Leadership Council as an act of reconciliation. Subsequently, the W̱SÁNEĆ Lands Trust Society (WLTS), now registered as a charitable society, has incorporated and recently received Ecological Gifts Recipient status. WLTS is the first Indigenous organization in Canada to receive land under this program. The W̱SÁNEĆ Leadership Council writes, "although the main goals are to help future generations of W̱SÁNEĆ access land for cultural purposes and to positively impact the environment through W̱SÁNEĆ stewardship, the WLTS will also seek land back for collaborative projects such as community housing and economic development initiatives."[8]

The land trust model is based on land title—a concept that has already caused alienation from territory. There are new relationships being forged between Parks Canada and the Indigenous Management board for the GINPR. BC Parks has recently chosen to remove the word "provincial" from many BC Parks. These new directions suggest some reconciliation will come through conservation. Some BC Parks are starting to be co-managed. All of us are living in a time of reconciliation. Engagement with First Nations is key and there are some great examples on the islands today.

Eric Higgs, who teaches restoration at the University of Victoria, explained how the Galiano Conservancy is currently partnering with Indigenous communities. "We have a restoration project called the forage forest, in partnership with the Penelakut First Nation. We are looking at traditional foods and medicines from the forest. We are building relationships on a level that people can accommodate. What's important; what can we do: for example, deer hunting where our Indigenous partners on the project can harvest, feed the people, and teach workshops. We are working to address an ecological challenge and a deep cultural one. The spirit of innovation is possible in ways government agencies can't take on."

During a workshop on collaboration with First Nations, Kate Emmings from the Islands Trust Conservancy described their efforts to acknowledge First Nations' rights to the use of the land in a traditional way with ITC's newer covenants. These new clauses may allow for harvesting of vegetation and animals, where there was traditional cultural access to that in the past. The ITC is also looking into including clauses that protect cultural sites of importance to First Nations, as those areas may have been damaged by building and human use. Another consideration is restoration activities where these important cultural sites are located. She mentioned that restoration might involve having an observer on site.

Announced in November 2023, the Stqeeye' Learning Society has bought a 4 hectare (10 acre) parcel of land of land on Salt Spring Island, where the Quw'utsun (Cowichan) village called Xwaaqw'um once stood. Their goals are to rebuild wetlands in the area of the former village, where logging and agriculture have damaged the landscape. Additionally, the plan is for the site to be a place for hunting and harvesting, practicing cultural rites, and land-based learning.[9]

These new relationships and collaborations with First Nations will bring both opportunity and challenges. During my interview with Briony Penn, she stressed that "BC has significant unresolved land issues. More collaboration with Indigenous groups and land trusts could be a model for trusts all over. A lot of nations develop alternative stewardship plans, such as creating carbon banks and a board that looks seven generations ahead. I think that's a great model, and will help us to get out of the boom and bust cycle. We need a change in governments and the *Indian Act* and the resource extraction mentality toward one based on looking forward seven generations."

Lessons Learned

I asked my interviewees what particular lessons they learned that might be useful going forward. The following poignant examples reveal that on the surface a mistake was made, causing stress, financial loss, and sometimes loss of public support. Yet on the other side of the coin, those mistakes moved the protection of land (conservation) ahead in monumental ways. To paraphrase the *I Ching*, challenges often turn into opportunities.

TLC The Land Conservancy had a period of financial turmoil. They had a $7 million debt when the courts came onto the scene. It took them three years to climb out of debt, after paying another $2.4 million to lawyers and the court appointed monitor.[10] With the shuffling of people and some loss of public confidence, the lessons learned became firmly established across the land trust field. Virtually all land trusts today have policies against going into debt, unless there are circumstances such as bridge funding (with accounts receivable or other monetary promises in hand). In addition, over the years, land trusts have developed a practice of raising 15 percent more than the cost of acquiring a property up front to help cover future costs, including long-term management.

In my interview with Bill Turner, formerly with TLC The Land Conservancy of BC, he described the level of risk that he was willing to take to acquire a property.

Briony Penn in Burgoyne Bay with Garry oaks all around. Briony rode topless in Vancouver to save this Garry Oak woodland on Salt Spring Island.

There is always the risk that you will not be successful in reaching a deal and that your investment in time and real costs will go nowhere. South Winchelsea [Island] is an example. I managed to raise $5,000 to pay for an appraisal and I donated the funds for the other costs. All of that would have been lost if we didn't get the deal. Then we had to raise the funds to buy the island. We took a mortgage on the island and then raised the funds over the next seven years. We raised part of the money before the closing, but I had negotiated a mortgage held by the owners over five years. We got great support from a wonderful couple from Vancouver and also from Robert and Birgit Bateman. It gave us a good start and several good connections. If we had not taken the risks, it never would have happened.

After the restructuring of TLC, they bounced back with a new executive director and policies aimed at protecting the long-term financial stability of the organization and the lands it conserves. Many attributed the mistake to taking out mortgages, resulting in continuing monthly payments with interest added. This is indeed a significant risk as it is very difficult to fundraise for a property that has in theory been acquired and protected. Briony Penn, who was not on the board of directors at the time, but did get involved in the restructuring, provides her insights:

The most successful thing TLC did—for better or worse—was pushing boundaries, looking at innovative ways to secure land (most of the time it worked). What people thought was wrong is incorrect. It really was too many staff and not enough members to support it. Bill's image of the National Trust was his base, but Britain has 52 million people and the National Trust has a membership of 2 million, whereas the population of all of BC was under 4 million at the time. We didn't have the membership base to support the overly ambitious goals he had. However, the great thing we achieved was the number of properties protected and at the time of the restructuring, we had 300 covenants and 52 properties. That didn't include those that were passed on, such as Burgoyne Bay, which Bill facilitated the acquisition of, which became a BC Park.

Jan Garnett described how NCC began to raise 15 percent more than the purchase price on acquiring a property. "We learned that land stewardship money had to be raised at the time that the project was being acquired, since afterwards it is very difficult to find. We gradually developed stewardship endowments for each region, with the hope that, one day, the interest on those investments would fully fund the 'forever costs' of owning lands in perpetuity. You can buy lands and waters, large or small, but unless you have the money to look after them, the ultimate success is limited. That was a huge lesson."

The Galiano Conservancy found it very difficult to pay off loans they acquired due to the need to find matching funds for a federal grant they received. Keith Erickson, the executive director at the time, found it very stressful and challenging for the organization. It was especially difficult for the directors who were responsible for the loan. However, in the end it had a positive outcome. "It forced our organization to become much more professional, more organized." Keith explained, "We brought in people outside the community and created relationships and expanded our partnerships." After five years of debt, they received an unexpected "bluebird" donation of a waterfront property. Through the sale of that property, they were able to pay off the debt and build an office.

Several others with the Galiano Conservancy raised another challenge, applicable for any charitable group, which is to rely too heavily on one champion. "Ken for a decade was talking about succession and how to move past him being primarily the key person on all levels, basically board chair and executive director, and it was always under-capacity. The only person motivated to do it was Ken, but he took it all on. Then he passed, and we had to adjust. We spent years bringing in policy and developing systems, revamping financial systems and contacts."

Chasing grants is an issue every organization faces. Because funding agencies and foundations require specific deliverables, and are focused on particular requirements and goals, the organization needs staff to run the projects, report, and then consider how to continue the work you actually need to do. Sometimes the grants can seem to lead the organization's work. A diversity of funding sources is key. That's a big challenge.

Tax Incentives

There are several programs that offer tax incentives that support the conservation of land that people can take advantage of, both for their own benefit and for their descendants. For large landowners, covenants are a great option to protect areas of the land and still be able to live there. The Islands Trust's unique Natural Area Property Tax Exemption Program (NAPTEP) offers substantial annual property tax relief while conserving land well beyond the time of the owner who sets up the NAPTEP covenant.

The federal Ecological Gifts Program offers another tremendous incentive for individuals who want to conserve some or all of their land. Although there are costs involved, the Program allows a landowner's descendants to keep some or all of their land, rather than be forced to sell it to pay the capital gains taxes that result from a disposition (change in title) of land. The Canadian government's Ecological Gifts program is an opportunity for people to receive tax relief for either gifting part of their land for conservation or to register a conservation covenant on all or part of it before they die.

These two programs have helped significantly to counter the rising costs of land and taxes and to benefit not only the landowner and their descendants but all of us through the legacy of conserved land.

Karen Hudson, the first executive director of SSIC, recalled an example on Salt Spring Island when the estate of a larger landholder was unable to protect the family lands. "Using the tools we have is important," she reiterated, "because in many areas, we're seeing a return to clear-cut logging. One example is an inheritance: the descendants weren't able to pay for the taxes on the property. One sibling couldn't buy out or pay the property taxes, so they sold it to someone who clear-cut the land. Despite the family wanting those areas to be protected, which was their intention, they weren't able to. Using these tools, we can help people feel they can do it—offering a motivation to do it, not just for a legacy, but because it will help their descendants as well.

Karen went on to mention how she learned about the various tools and techniques that helped her along in the early years from the LTABC's Seminar Series. Learning from others and reaching out for support and collaboration are essential.

Hope for the Future

Surprisingly, many of the islanders I interviewed were pessimistic about the future. Despite this they have carried on, 95 percent voluntarily, working to protect wildlife, ecosystems, and land for their communities for the future. In the early '90s there were a few parks, but today these precious islands now have 20 to 50 percent protected lands. I have renewed hope due to the inspiration and dedication of these founding directors and those who have followed their lead! It's thanks to these amazingly generous people that these islands have the conservation lands they do today.

We are at a crisis, an ecological crisis, and a social crisis. With an explosive population growth on the coast and the islands, and constant pressure for more housing, natural areas are at a high risk. Last year 100 thousand new people moved to BC—more in one year than the support of all land trusts put together.

Ric Careless, co-founder of the BC Parks Foundation, urges everyone to pick up the pace.

> Having been around for fifty years, the movement has to increase. We are facing risk to life as we know it; particularly human civilization hangs in the balance. How do we deal with climate change and biodiversity collapse? Canadians have generally felt there was no end to wilderness. Now we are under assault, so we must dramatically increase the pace. I'm really pleased that a businessman, Chip Wilson, gave $100 million to our organization. It allows us to operate on the scale needed—to up our game. In southwest BC and especially in the Salish Sea area, where development pressures are huge with the price of land skyrocketing, we need to move as fast as we can. We are lucky there was effort to preserve private land in BC, particularly in the '60s and '70s when we built the parks system. Without them, these natural areas wouldn't exist now. Instead they would be subdivisions, priced out of reach. So we need to move as fast as we can.

We are living in a transformative time. We are witness to and participants in this turning of the tide. The many people featured in this book plus the many more whose names and stories I have missed have spent years of their lives defending the forests and wildlife on these islands. Many of the people I interviewed responded to my question "What hope do you have for the future?" with an acknowledgement that their only hope is with the next generation—the youth. In the future, our children and grandchildren will carry on this torch we have lit—a torch of positive action. We hope that our actions to conserve land and protect the ecosystems that support life will have long-term value. The flora and fauna on these lands may change with the climate, but they will still be protected from logging, from development, from human actions that are all too often short-sighted. Having all these conservancies engaged and committed to protecting land is a positive force for the future.

We have all heard the warnings from scientists. They have been shouting out across the world since the mid-twentieth century. We all know that we must change our wasteful and consumptive habits. We can be creative in our actions, not being complicit to the ignorance and denial that are leading us to turn away from Mother Nature.

There is a mystery about life here on planet Earth. To paraphrase James Lovelock, the initiator of the Gaia principle, the best possible state for life to have happened by chance is as unlikely as emerging unscathed after driving blindfolded during rush-hour. It feels a bit like that's where we are headed these days—blindfolded by fear and cynicism. There is this complex interrelated mystery that sustains life, and we are part of it.

We will meet the challenges ahead by recognizing the deeper values that underlie our current problems, seeing the big picture, and choosing actions that sustain this living planet—Gaia. Close to home, there is an amazing diversity of life that surrounds us—the brown of a grasshopper turning into brilliant green as it jumps. The amazing world of amphibians, birds, insects. The whales, fish, and octopus and so much more are here to explore, understand, and protect. The stories in this book are waypoints for the future of conservation.

Welcome figures at Burgoyne Bay (Xwaaqw'um) once a Quw'utsun (Cowichan) village partially in the provincial park.

GLOSSARY

American Friends of Canadian Conservation US 501(c) 3 organization (a charity) offering US donors who support Canadian conservation the opportunity to make their gifts of land, or interests in land, cash and securities tax deductible. www .conservecanada.org.

Biogeoclimatic zones Biogeoclimatic Ecosystem Classification system initiated by V. J. Krajina and his students at the University of British Columbia that categorized fourteen different broad climatic ecosystems. They generally represent a geographic area with specific climax vegetation communities and soils. For a map and further info see https://cfcg.forestry.ubc.ca/resources/cataloguing-in-situ-genetic-resources/ about-bec-and-bgc-units/.

Conservation Covenant A written legal agreement between a property owner and a government body or one or more land trust organizations designated by the Surveyor General. The covenant sets out specific restrictions or requirements that the landowner will uphold to ensure conservation of all or parts of the land. It is registered on title under Section 219 of the *Land Title Act* and "runs with the land" in perpetuity along with a Section 218—a Statutory Right of Way (to enter the land and monitor the covenant).

Crown land grant transfer program Sponsored Crown grants transfer the ownership of identified parcels of Crown land from the BC government to municipalities and regional districts. The Islands Trust Conservancy was using this program until 2010, but has now discontinued its use as it is not in alignment with their current Reconciliation policy.

Density transfer "Two concurrent zoning amendments undertaken to increase development potential on one lot by removing or reducing the development potential on another lot. There is no net increase in density because the density that is transferred simply replaces that of the lot it is removed from." (Nanaimo Regional District)

Ecological Gifts Program Federal government income tax incentive program, giving the owners of land a 100 percent capital gains deduction for the donation of significant ecological land to a designated recipient (land trust or government agency) for perpetual protection. A "bargain sale" or "split receipt" is a partial donation of an interest in land—resulting in a significantly reduced price, usually with a minimum of 20 percent of its value. www.canada.ca/en/environment-climate-change/services/environmental-funding/ecological-gifts-program/overview.html.

Ecological Reserve Designated Crown land protecting rare and endangered plants and animals in their natural habitat.

Ground truthing Ground truthing methods involve visiting sites or sample sites for verification of aerial photos or other data.

Gulf Island National Park Reserve National park located in the Southern Gulf Islands. Created in 2003 and formally established in 2010, the park encompasses 36 kilometres of land and 26 kilometres of adjacent waters. https://parks.canada.ca/pn-np/bc/gulf.

Highest and best use The Appraisal Institute of Canada defines this as Definition. 2.8: "the reasonably probable and legal use of property, that is physically possible, appropriately supported, and financially feasible, and that results in the highest value." (Appraisal of Real Estate, Canadian Edition, 1992, p. 265.) This concept originated with early economists based on the idea of maximum productivity, i.e., maximum profitability. It can include timber values (rather than standing forest or trees) though more recently carbon values are also becoming a more accepted part of an appraisal.

Islands Trust Regional government for the 470 islands established by the Province in 1974. "The object [mandate] of the Trust is to preserve and protect the Trust Area and its unique amenities and environment for the benefit of the residents of the Trust Area and of British Columbia in cooperation with municipalities, regional districts, improvement districts, other persons and organizations and the government of British Columbia."

Islands Trust Conservancy A regional land trust, established as the Islands Trust Fund in 1990, today known as the Islands Trust Conservancy; works with landowners, local conservancies, environmental organizations, First Nations, municipalities, and other forms of government, charitable foundations, businesses, and private donors to protect land in perpetuity.

Land trust Also known as a Conservancy or conservation land trust; a charitable organization that may own land itself, or it may enter into a conservation covenant with a property owner to protect or restore natural or heritage features on the owner's land. Land trusts also engage in stewardship, restoration, and management of lands.

Life estate An interest in real property that a person is given for the duration of his or her life. This can include an interest in the use of a property, home, or cottage.

Natural Area Protection Tax Exemption Program (NAPTEP) An Islands Trust program, implemented by the Islands Trust Conservancy, that offers a financial incentive of an annual property tax exemption of 65 percent on the protected portion of your land. https://islandstrust.bc.ca/programs/natural-area-protection-tax-exemption-program/.

Official Community Plan Describes the long-term vision of communities, including a statement of objectives, and policies that guide planning and land use management as outlined in the Local Government Act section 875.

Pacific Marine Heritage Legacy Fund A fund established by the federal government ($6 million each year over five years) to assist with a federal/provincial program with the objective of creating an expanded and integrated network of coastal and marine protected areas along Canada's Pacific coast. It was to be matched by the Province of BC, but was primarily honoured through transfer of provincial parks and transfer of Crown lands to the Gulf Island National Park Reserve.

Profit à prendre Allows an agricultural or forest landowner to sell profit-making rights to a neighbouring landowner, in essence allowing an organization to hold the rights to farm, log, mine, etc. in the area over which the profit à prendre is registered.

Riparian Relating to areas surrounding or located on the bank of a natural watercourse, such as a river, creek, lake, or tidewater.

Sections and quarter Sections A section of land is a square mile in size, or 260 hectares (640 acres). A quarter section is 160 acres (65 hectares). That's the Land Survey system we inherited when the Royal Engineers marched across so-called unoccupied land to survey vastness into settler bites.

Strategic Lawsuits Against Public Participation (SLAPP) Strategic lawsuits against public participation, or strategic litigation against public participation, are intended to intimidate and silence usually non-profit organizations or individuals due to costly court costs.

Tree Farm License (TFL) A land tenure that assigns rights to harvest timber and manage and conserve forests, recreation, and cultural heritage resources on a specified area of land.

APPENDIX—ACRONYMS OF CONSERVATION ORGANIZATIONS

BIC—Bowen Island Conservancy

CHI—Conservancy Hornby Island

CLCWG—Cortes Land Conservancy Working Group

CRD—Capital Regional District

DCA—Denman Conservancy Association

FOBP—Friends of Brooks Point

FTCCIS—Forest Trust for the Children of Cortes Island Society

GALTT—Gabriola Lands and Trails Trust

GCA—Galiano Conservancy Association

GIC—Gambier Island Conservancy

GINPR—Gulf Island National Park Reserve

GLT—Gabriola Land Conservancy

HAT—Habitat Acquisition Trust

ITC—Islands Trust Conservancy

LINC—Lasqueti Island Nature Conservancy

MIC—Mayne Island Conservancy

NALT—Nanaimo and Area Land Trust

NCC—Nature Conservancy of Canada

NTBC—The Nature Trust of BC

PICA—Pender Island Conservation Association

QICSS—Quadra Island Conservancy and Stewardship Society

RCCF—Raincoast Conservation Foundation

SILT—Savary Island Land Trust

SSIC—Salt Spring Island Conservancy

SSIWPS—Salt Spring Island Water Preservation Society

THINC—Thetis Island Nature Conservancy

ACKNOWLEDGEMENTS

OVER THE COURSE OF THE THREE YEARS I was creating this book I met so many generous and dedicated conservationists—people who have devoted years, often decades, of their time and skills to the protection of the islands of the Salish Sea. On countless park benches and in hundreds of phone calls and email exchanges, these crusaders shared their heartfelt stories with me, and then entrusted me to weave them into a song of love that would carry the flora and fauna of their beloved islands into the future. It is hard to find the words to thank them all!

First and foremost is my dear husband, Gordon Scott. He helped me hold fast to my vision of collecting and sharing these voices, even when their magnitude and detail seemed overwhelming. Wendy Wickwire was a joy to work with, as she artfully edited my early drafts, making sure that the stories made sense, particularly to readers unfamiliar with the tools and practices of land trusts. I am grateful to Andrea Lister, an experienced editor, who guided me through the final drafts. Briony Penn and Kathy Dunster encouraged me to take on the project more than three years ago. I thank Kathy for her review of the manuscript and Briony for writing the book's foreword.

The following people deserve special thanks for their contributing voices and assistance:

On Gabriola: Rob Brockley, Kerry Marcus, John Peirce, Tom Cameron, Anne Landry, Norm Harburn, Dyan Dunsmuir-Farley. **On Thetis:** Ann Eriksson, Maureen Loiselle, and Laurel March. **On Salt Spring:** Maureen Milburn, Briony Penn, Fiona Flook, Bob Twaites, Bob Weeden, Peter Lamb, Jean Gelwicks, Christine Torgrimson, Karen Hudson, Nora Layard, Penny Barnes, Elizabeth White, Ashley Hilliard, Joan Makaroff, Kathryn Luttin, Debra Cobron. **On the Penders:** Jan Kirkby, Elizabeth Miles, Don Williams, Shelley Easthope, Lawrence Pitt, David Spalding, Paul Petrie, Graham Boffrey, Misty MacDuffee, Erin O'Brien, Doreen Ball, Angela Southward. **On Saturna:** Priscilla Ewbank, Susie Washington Smyth, Maureen Welton, Martin Wale, Richard Blagborne. **On Mayne:** Michael Dunn, Helen O'Brien, Rob Underhill. **On Galiano:** Loren Wilkinson, Gary Moore, Keith Erickson, Geoff Gaylor, Sheila Anderson, Chessy Miltner, Beth Thiessen, Risa Smith, Adam Huggins, Cedana Bourne, Judy Hayes, Bowie Keefer. **On Valdes:** Marja de Jong, Dan White. **On Hornby:** Cath Grey, Grant Scott, Anna Zielinski, Tom Knott, Tony Law, Tony Quin, Jan Bevan, Sheila McDonnell. **On Denman:** John Millen, Des Kennedy, Anne de Cosson, Jenny Balke. **On Quadra:** Ken Roxburgh, Michael Mascall, Janice McLean, Jasper Lament. **On Cortes:** Sabina Leader Mense, Mary Gordon, George West, Tamara McPhail, Shawn Black, Christine Robinson. **On Savary:** Liz Webster, Thea Cacchioni, the Rowans. **On Bowen:** Sue Ellen Fast, John Rich, Bob Turner, Kathy Dunster, Owen Plowman. **On Gambier:** Peter Scholefield, Elspeth Armstrong,

Ruth Simons, Maria Van Dyk, Carol Petroski, Mike Stamford. **On Keats**: Dan Rogers. **On Lasqueti**: Gordon Scott, Melinda Auerbach, Doug Hopwood, Ken Lertzman, Dana Lepofsky, Duane West.

I am indebted to Jasper Lament and Danielle Morrison of the Nature Trust of BC for developing the maps revealing the increase in protected lands on the islands from 2000 to 2021. I thank Jan Garnet, who was regional director with the Nature Conservancy of Canada in their early and expansive years in BC, for sharing her perspectives on the islands' conservation projects and NCC's involvement. Bill Turner deserves huge thanks. Through his founding years leading TLC The Land Conservancy of BC, he helped many local conservancies with their initial campaigns. I am grateful to many of the other stalwart board members of the Land Trust Alliance of BC (LTABC), as they offered support to land trusts across the province (in addition to their work with their own organizations) and to me in my role as founding executive director for thirteen years. I am particularly grateful to Ron Pither for bringing to my attention the outliers I could have missed in this history.

For their generosity with supplying wonderful photos, I thank Adam Taylor, Albert Normandin, Alex Harris, Dana Lepofsky, David Greer, David Spalding, Dean V'ant Schip, Debra Cobon, Dennis Inngersol, Diane Moen, Gary Geddes, Gary Moore, George West, Gordon Scott, Heather Crawford, Henny Schnare, Howard Fry, John Millen, Kate Henderson, Keith Erickson, Ken Lertzman, Kevin Oke, Kris Wellstein, Laura Mathias, Liz Webster, Marcie Welsh, Markus Thompson, Martin Wale, Maureen Welton, Myles Clarke, Owen Ploughman, Paul Petrie, Peter Scholefield, Rebecca Benjamin Carey, Ronaldo Norden, Sabina Leader Mense, Shari White, Sheila Ray, Simon Auger, Simon Henson, Sue Ellen Fast, Tamar Griggs, Trudy Chatwin, and Will Husby.

I am grateful to former employees with Parks Canada and BC Parks for their fascinating reflections: Bill Henwood, Kate Humble, Mel Turner, Wayne Bourque, and Ian Atherton. I thank Ric Careless, currently with the BC Parks Foundation, for his sage comments and decades of work protecting nature in BC. Rod Silver with the Habitat Conservation Trust Foundation was also a great support to land trusts over the years, and wholeheartedly encouraged me to write this book. Carolyn Stewart and Nuala Murphy and Kathryn Martell, from the Islands Trust Conservancy and CRD Parks staff, were also generous with their experienced contributions and review. And of course, everlasting tribute goes to those who initiated these organizations and conservation projects who have now passed on. Their voices and actions inspired future generations and have left a legacy for all time.

And last but not least, special thanks goes to my three crewmates during the journey—Heather Crawford, Doane Grinnell, and Jack Barrett—you offered support on the water that kept the whole project afloat!

ENDNOTES

Foreword

1 J. I. Little, "Like 'A Thousand Mosquito Bites': Forest Conservation as Social Movement on British Columbia's Salt Spring Island 1999-2001," *BC Studies* 213, Spring 2022, p. 87.

2 J.J. Merz, P. Barnard, W.E. Rees, et al., "World Scientists' Warning: The Behavioural Crisis Driving Ecological Overshoot," *Science Progress* 103, no. 3, doi:10.1177/00368504231201372.

Introduction

1 "This Mediterranean like bioregion is unique within Canada and home to the highest number of ecosystems and species at risk in the province, many of which are ranked as critically imperiled at a national and global scale. Approximately 9 percent of the CDF is currently protected, with 49 percent of the land base impacted by forestry, agriculture and urbanisation. Today less than 1 percent of the CDF remains intact as old growth forest, with forests over 100 years old covering only 4 percent of their former extent." (From CDFCP https://www.cdfcp.ca/)

2 Bert Webber coined the term, Salish Sea, in the 1970s, while working on oil-spill issues in the fragile inland sea from Campbell River, Vancouver Island, to Seattle, Washington. His intention to create awareness and a technological and scientific cross-border response to the single inland sea that is impacted by pollution and shares marine and terrestrial biodiversity was politically acknowledged in 2010, when the governments of Canada, British Columbia, and Washington all adopted the name. At a gathering of Coast Salish First Peoples in Victoria in 2010, the name was endorsed many years after a 1992 inter-nation declaration of our shared waters.

3 I use hectares with acres in brackets because lands in BC were surveyed using the imperial system and, until recently, most of the conservation groups I interviewed refer to land in acres.

Gabriola Island

1 Sam McKinnery, *Sailing with Vancouver: A Modern Sea Dog, Antique Charts and a Voyage Through Time* (TouchWood Editions, 2018), p. 41.

2 The Great Blue Herons I saw were coastal Great Blue Heron, *fannini* subspecies (*Ardea herodias fannini*) which is blue-listed in BC and is a Committee on the Status of Endangered Wildlife in Canada (COSEWIC) *Species at Risk Act* (SARA) species of Special Concern.

3 Dyan Dunsmoor-Farley, "Weldwood on Gabriola Island: Dancing with the Giant," PhD thesis, Athabasca University, 2013. Thesis on the impacts of globalization on the social fabric of resource dependent communities.

4 Dyan Dunsmoor-Farley, personal communication.

5 Dyan Dunsmoor-Farley, "Dancing with the Giant," master's thesis, p. 26. Auerbach recollects that while the purchase of the Weldwood lands was not subject to rezoning, the financing for the acquisition of the lands was subject to rezoning. "Kensington Capital, unable to put together a financing deal, sold off sufficient land (2000 acres) to a Gabriola logger, Mike Jenks, to allow them to complete the transaction with Weldwood. Clear-cutting the trees on the lands began immediately. The US investors retained the 800 acres for future development in accordance with applicable by-laws." (Melinda Auerbach, letter to Grignon, 2010). Ultimately Kensington sold its remaining 800 acres: a portion of the land was bought by the federal and provincial governments to be set aside for treaty negotiation, and another portion was purchased by developers.

6   Accessed from M. H. Turner, *Drumbeg Provincial Park and Gabriola Sands Provincial Park and Recreation Area, Master Plan*, August 1987; Lou Skinner, GaLTT, personal communication, September 28, 2023. "Both parks were previously privately owned rural properties. Gabriola Sands Park was established in 1960, following a donation by Mr. W. Coats and Mr. F. Ney on behalf of Gabriola Sands Resort Company. In 1972, the province established the foreshore of the two bays which border the park as a provincial recreation area. Additional Crown land was added to the park in 1983. Drumbeg Park was established in 1971, following the purchase of the property by the province. The park is named after the Scottish home of the former owner, Mr. Neil Stalker." (BC Parks.)

7   Madrone Environmental Services, *S'ul-hween X'pey (Elder Cedar) Nature Reserve Management Plan Gabriola Island* (Islands Trust Conservancy, 2021), p. 13–14.

8   Natural Areas Protection Tax Exemption Program (NAPTEP) is an Islands Trust Conservancy covenant program that gives owners a 65 percent tax break on their property if they covenant the majority of it. https://islandstrust.bc.ca › programs › natural-area-protection-tax-exemption-program.

9   "Skunk Cabbage," National Wildlife Federation, accessed February 3, 2023, https://www.nwf.org/Educational-Resources/Wildlife-Guide/Plants-and-Fungi/Skunk-Cabbage.

Thetis Island

1   Michael Rodway, R. W. Campbell, and M. J. F. Lemon, *Seabird Colonies of British Columbia, Part 4: Salish Sea*, *Wildlife Afield* 18, no. 1–2 (2023): p. 61.

2   David Lewis Rozen, "Place-Names of the Island Halkomelem Indian People," master's thesis (Department of Anthropology and Sociology, University of British Columbia, 1985), p. 93.

3   SeaChange Marine Conservation Society, https://seachangesociety.com/.

4   "The Coastal Douglas-fir covers a small area of British Columbia's south coast, including a band of lower elevation along southeastern Vancouver Island, the Gulf Islands, and a fringe of mainland along Georgia Strait. Victoria, Nanaimo, and Powell River are major urban centres in the area." The Ecology of the Coastal Douglas-fir, British Columbia, Ministry of Forests, 1995, https://www.for.gov.bc.ca/hfd/pubs/docs/bro/bro30.htm.

5   A video of the mooring system can be seen at SeaChange Marine Conservation Society. "Seafloor Friendly Mooring System," https://vimeo.com/395464992.

6   Joan Brown (Chief), Penelakut Tribe, letter dated July 8, 2021, https://pbs.twimg.com/media/E6Ly6BwxEAQsGeG.jpg; Angela Sterritt (@AngelaSterritt), "160 unmarked graves have been confirmed by Penelakut Tribe," Twitter, July 8, 2021, https://twitter.com/AngelaSterritt/status/1414763265989640194.

Salt Spring Island

1   The Crown Lands Use Coalition was an early group of individuals, organizations, and the Local Trust Committee with Linda Adams, CEO at the time, helping lead discussions regarding protecting these lands.

2   Maureen Milburn: "Gay's mother had recently passed away, and both she and her husband decided giving some of this inheritance to conserve this special place would have pleased her mother. The $50,000 extra was given by another local woman, Susan Bloom, who later gifted her estate for conservation to the Victoria Foundation."

3   Maureen Milburn: "Lloyd Rushton, CRD Chair at the time, and SSIC began a three-way dialogue with Pacific Marine Heritage legacy and the CRD. Through the leadership of Deitrich Luth we became part of the CRD Parks & Recreation and started the South and West Salt Spring Partnership Coalition."

4   Peter Lamb, *The Islands Trust Story: Celebrating 35 Years 1974–2009* (Salt Spring Island: Imagine That Graphic Design & Print Solutions, 2009), https://islandstrust.bc.ca/about-us/overview-of-islands-trust/.

5   Briony Penn, personal communication: "The South and West Salt Spring Partnership (SWSCP) met for three years up until the Prince's death in 1999. An account of this backstory is in the

2003 Burgoyne Bay Background Report for Burgoyne Bay Protected Area on SSI sent to BC Parks by Friends of Salt Spring Parks Society."

6   Mike Ho, "Chinese Dragons — Facts, Culture, Origins, and Art," China Highlights, updated December 14, 2021, https://www.chinahighlights.com/travelguide/article-chinese-dragons.htm.

7   Bill Webster, "Logging Sabotage May Spark Island War," *Driftwood*, August 1, 1990, A1; Susan Dicker Lundy, "$20,000 Reward Offered for Evidence," *Driftwood*, August 22, 1990, A1, A7.

8   Catherine McEwan and Chris Ling, "Community Action on Salt Spring," *Case Studies: Interactive Case Studies in Sustainable Community Development,* May 21, 2008, https://www.crcresearch.org/community-research-connections/crc-case-studies/community-action-salt-spring-island.

9   An account of this backstory is in the *2003 Burgoyne Bay Background Report* for Burgoyne Bay Protected Area sent to BC Parks by Friends of Salt Spring Parks Society.

10 J. I. Little, "Like 'A Thousand Mosquito Bites,'" p. 90.

11 Maureen Milburn: "The nude calendar was Ruth Tarasoff's idea as she had just been to Britain and there had been a calendar published there for an environmental cause. Ruth ran that campaign and Andrea collected the funds."

12 The Salt Spring Water Preservation Society contributed $100,000 and the Salt Spring Conservancy $34,000, leaving $303,500 for the water district ratepayers, representing a 9 percent increase in their annual rates. See Anastacia Wilde, "Rally Urges Watershed Protection," *Gulf Island Driftwood,* July 26, 2000.

13 Bob Twaites: "A pond and a creek in the watershed lands have been named after Tom Gossett and Mike Larmour as a testament to their years of hard work."

14 Catherine McEwan and Chris Ling, "Community Action on Salt Spring."

15 Conservation Covenants are different from common law restrictive covenants in that they are often held by one or more land trust organizations. (Whereas restrictive covenants are often registered between two landowners to protect something of joint interest, or to protect common land within a strata development.) A Conservation Covenant restricts uses, developments, or practices which would damage specific natural or cultural features on a single property. Compliance is monitored regularly by staff or by trained volunteers from the land trust that holds the covenant.

16 For more details and photos see https://saltspringConservancy.ca/protect/nature-reserves/mt-erskine/.

17 BC Systems and Ecosystems Explorer, https://www2.gov.bc.ca/gov/content/environment/plants-animals-ecosystems/conservation-data-centre/explore-cdc-data/species-and-ecosystems-explorer.

18 A profit à prendre allows an agricultural or forest landowner to sell profit-making rights to a neighbouring landowner. In essence this allowed the Conservancy to hold the rights to farm, log, mine, etc. that area, and take those rights away from the landowner. He could still walk there, but he couldn't dig or cut trees.

19 *The Heron* (Victoria: Islands Trust Conservancy, Spring 2023).

20 Recent grants from the Cerus Fund by the Foundation went to support the Islands Trust Conservancy's Opportunity Fund which was used for this recent acquisition. Many land trusts in the Salish Sea apply to the ITC's Opportunity Fund for things like appraisals or surveys to help landowners who wish to put a conservation covenant on their lands or make a partial donation of their land.

21 Canada's Ecological Gifts Program, https://www.canada.ca/en/environment-climate-change/services/environmental-funding/ecological-gifts-program/overview.html.

North and South Pender Islands

1   Georgia Basin Ecological Assessment and Restoration Society, https://georgiabasin.ca/puma.htm.

2   Georgia Basin Ecological Assessment and Restoration Society.

3   North American Breeding Bird Survey, Partners in Flight, https://www.pwrc.usgs.gov/bbs/about/.

4   Neil K. Dawe and Andrew C. Stewart, "The Canada Goose (*Branta canadensis*) on Vancouver Island, British Columbia," British Columbia Birds, *Journal of the British Columbia Field Ornithologists* 20 (2010), accessed November 29, 2023, https://bcbirds.bcfo.ca/volume-20-4/.

5   Canada Geese and Cackling Geese are migratory birds that are protected under Canadian law by the *Migratory Birds Convention Act*, 1994, which prohibits killing or capturing the birds or damaging, destroying, removing, or disturbing their nests, except as provided for under the Migratory Birds Regulations.

6   Peter Lamb, *The Islands Trust Story, Preserve and Protect*, Celebrating 35 Years, 2009, p. 3.

7   Lamb, *Islands Trust Story*.

8   "Conservancy Considered for Public Lands," *Island Tides,* February 1992, p. 1.

9   *Island Tides*, May 7, 1992.

10 Carrina Maslovat, *Medicine Beach (E,HO,) Management Plan Pender Island* (Victoria: Islands Trust Conservancy, 2018), p. 2.

11 Maslovat, *Medicine Beach (E,HO,) Management Plan*.

12 Written description of all three phases provided by Paul Petrie, August 1, 2021.

13 Tla'amin Elder Charlie Bob, June 16, 2013, quoted in The Lasqueti Island Nature Conservancy, *Newsletter*, Spring 2021, https://linc.lasqueti.ca/newsletters/.

Saturna Island and the Gulf Islands National Park Reserve

1   Saturna Island Marine Research and Education Society, https://simres.ca/.

2   Carly Chunick, Report on the Sencot'en Alliance's Participation in the Planning and Management of the Gulf Islands National Park Reserve, 2006, Environmental Law Clinic, University of Victoria, p. 20.

3   https://parks.canada.ca/pn-np/nt/thaidene-nene/info.

3   Chunick, Report on the Sencot'en Alliance's Participation, p. 42.

4   W̱SÁNEĆ Leadership Council, "From Fur to Forest," https://wsanec.com/avada_portfolio/fur-to-forest-2/.

5   W̱SÁNEĆ Leadership Council, "Removal of Invasive Deer a First Step toward Forest Restoration," https://wsanec.com/removal-of-invasive-deer-a-first-step-toward-forest-restoration/.

6   Parks Canada Restoration, "Sea Garden Restoration," https://parks.canada.ca/pn-np/bc/gulf/nature/restauration-restoration/jardins-de-la-mer-sea-gardens.

7   For more info on fish traps see "wuχoθɛn - Fish Traps," posted April 15, 2021, Tla'amin Nation, https://www.youtube.com/watch?v=Jww9zduMgb8; Andrea Bennett, "We Didn't Treat It as a Park. That Was Our Home," *The Tyee*, June 28, 2023, https://thetyee.ca/News/2023/06/28/Desolation-Sound-Not-A-Park-But-Home/.

8   Wildlife Habitat Canada, Land Trust Conservation Fund, https://whc.org/ltcf/.

9   Ken Lertzman, "Fact Sheet on Sheep," Lasqueti Island Nature Conservancy, 2022.

10 Sara J. Wilson and Richard J. Hebda, *Mitigating and Adapting to Climate Change through the Conservation of Nature, Land Trust Alliance of BC* (Victoria: LTA The Land Trust Alliance of British Columbia, 2008), p. 42.

11 Wilson and Hebda, *Mitigating and Adapting to Climate Change,* p. v.

12 Misty McDuffee, Raincoast Conservation Foundation, https://www.raincoast.org/2017/approval-of-trans-mountain-expansion-puts-fraser-river-salmon-and-salish-sea-estuaries-at-risk/.

13 Jason M. Colby, *Orca* (Oxford University Press, 2018).

14 Colby, *Orca*.

15 Saturna Island Marine Research and Education Society, https://simres.ca/.

16 "Commission of Inquiry into the Decline of the Sockeye Salmon in the Fraser River, Supplementary Argument," ISA Hearings Aquaculture Coalition, December 2011, p. 3.

17 Personal communication from interview. Susie expanded: "So they were created by an interim order under the Ministry of Transport, who nominally involved Parks Canada and DFO. Transport Canada is responsible for enforcement, which they do none, virtually. The other measures, no fishing is done by Fisheries and Oceans. The vessels slow down in the Port of Vancouver is done partly as a thought to protect the Southern Residents by Transport Canada, and its only part time,

and the Residents are here all year. It's voluntary, and some tankers slow down, but it should be mandatory, and it should be all year. They do it in Puget Sound, so they could do it here."

18   "Marine Protected Area (MPA) Networks: Guiding Principles," Fisheries and Oceans Canada, accessed November 3, 2023, https://www.dfo-mpo.gc.ca/oceans/networks-reseaux/principles-principes-eng.html.

19   BC Hydro News Release, December 20, 2004.

20   Point Whitehorn Marine Reserve, https://www.whatcomcounty.us/3681/Point-Whitehorn-Marine-Reserve.

21   Saturna Island Marine Research and Education Society, https://simres.ca/.

Mayne Island

1   Gulf Island Centre for Ecological Learning, https://www.gicel.ca/.

2   Tyee Bridge, *Heart of the Coast: Biodiversity and Resilience on the Pacific Edge* (Vancouver: Figure 1 Publishing, 2020). Excerpts can be found at https://www.nationalobserver.com/2020/10/27/features/kelp-sea-otters-urchins-starfish-ocean-forests.

3   "The Mayne Island Conservancy Celebrating 20 Years!," *Mayliner Magazine*, April 2023.

4   "The only persons or entities that may hold Section 219 Covenants are the Crown, a Crown corporation or agency, a municipality, a regional district, the South Coast British Columbia Transportation Authority (i.e., Translink), a local trust committee under the Islands Trust Act or any person designated by the minister. Private persons or entities may apply to the Surveyor General Division of the Land Title and Survey Authority for a ministerial order designating the person as being entitled to hold a Section 219 Covenant." Mccarthy Tetrault, November 2012, https://www.mccarthy.ca/en/insights/articles/covenants-respect-land-dont-be-so-negative.

5   A. M. Eger et al., "The Value of Ecosystem Services in Global Marine Kelp Forests," *Nature Communications* 14, no. 1, p. 1–13, https://doi.org/10.1038/s41467-023-37385-0; "Kelp forests are also estimated to sequester 4.91 megatons of carbon from the atmosphere/year highlighting their potential as blue carbon systems for climate change mitigation." Accessed through Nature Communications, April 2023, https://www.nature.com/articles/s41467-023-37385-0.

6   Nature Conservancy of Canada, https://www.natureConservancy.ca/en/where-we-work/british-columbia/featured-projects/salish-sea/edith-point-conservation-area.html.

7   Mayne Island has a history of agricultural use within the last century linked to the tragic story of the Japanese Canadians who were interned during the Second World War. In the 1920s over sixty first- and second-generation Japanese Canadians lived on Mayne. They were successful fishermen and farmers, and a thriving Japanese greenhouse tomato industry employed many islanders and kept a local school alive. The CPR steamship Princess Mary took away a third of Mayne Island's population in 1942. Although many Mayne islanders protested and tried to keep the greenhouses working, or hid their possessions in hopes of returning them to their owners, anti-Japanese settlement laws remained in place years after the war ended, and the Enemy Aliens Property Board ensured that Japanese lands and fishing boats were auctioned off cheap.

Galiano Island

1   Sum'nuw' (Montague Harbour) the encircling place, identified by name from Hul'qumi'num Treaty group maps, found in GCA's "One Island," Introduction, p. 8.

2   Test Excavation at Georgeson Bay, British Columbia, by James C. Haggarty and John H.W. Sendey. 1976. British Columbia Provincial Museum, No. 19 Occasional Papers Series. Quoted in The Bluffs 2018 Management Plan.

3   Roy L. Carlson, "Excavations at Helen Point on Mayne Island," *BC Studies* 6/7 (1970). Quoted from Bluffs Park Management Plan: 18, accessed May 23, https://galianoclub.org/club-programs/parks/bluffs-park/.

4   Rolf Mathewes et al., "Late Pleistocene Vegetation and Sedimentary Charcoal at Kilgii Gwaay Archaeological Site in Coastal British Columbia, Canada, with Possible Proxy Evidence for Human Presence by 13,000 cal BP," *Vegetation History and Archaeobotany* 29 (2020): 10.1007/s00334-019-00743-4.

5   Daryl Fedje et al., "Geo-Archaeology and Haíɫzaqv Oral History: Long-Term Human Investment and Resource Use at EkTb-9, Triquet Island, Núláwìtx̌ʷ Tribal Area, Central Coast, British Columbia, Canada," *Journal of Archeological Science* 49 (2023): 10.1016/j.jasrep.[2023].103884.

6   Galiano Club, "Bluffs Management Plan," 2020, p. 19, quoted from Hul'qumi'num Treaty Group, "Shxunutun's Tu Suleluxwtst: In the Footsteps of our Ancestors," 2005.

7   Galiano Club, "Bluffs Management Plan," p. 5.

8   Bluffs Deed of Trust 1988, accessed May 23, YEAR, https://galianoclub.org/club-programs/parks/bluffs-park/.

9   Personal communication with Ronaldo Norden, a resident on Galiano in the '70s.

10 Galiano Club, "Bluffs Management Plan," p. 18.

11 Gary Moore, "What Happened at Coon Bay, Roots and Branches of the Galiano Conservancy." quoted from the "In essence, our land was stolen from us. Though Hul'qumi'num people never surrendered or signed a treaty ceding away our land, several colonial actions dramatically altered access to our traditional lands and resources. First, access to our most valuable lands along the eastern coast of Vancouver Island and the Gulf Islands was limited when settlers pre-empted 59,000 hectares in the 1860s. More of our land was stolen in 1884 when the federal government handed over 268,000 hectares — 80 per cent of our territory — as payment for the building of the Esquimalt & Nanaimo (E&N) railroad on Vancouver Island." Accessed from the Hul'qumi'num Treaty Group, https://www.bctreaty.ca/hulquminum-treaty-group.

12 British Columbia Terms of Union, accessed May 23, 2023, https://opentextbc.ca/postconfederation/chapter/2-3-british-columbia-and-the-terms-of-union/.

13 Jesse Winter, "The Complicated History of Vancouver Island's Railway Corridor," *The Discourse*, October 2020, accessed May 23, 2023, https://thediscourse.ca/nanaimo/vancouver-island-rail-history-how-did-we-get-here.

14 Gary Moore, "Roots and Branches of the Galiano Conservancy Association," vol. 1, p. 2. For more details see https://watershedsentinel.ca/articles/vancouver-island-land-grab/.

15 Moore, "Roots & Branches."

16 Moore, "Roots & Branches," *Gulf Islands Driftwood*, May 18, 1972.

17 Ken Lertzman noted to me in 2023 that this term "mining" is still used: "Logging forest that is unlikely to grow back to its historical state (i.e., on very low productivity sites) or old growth that will never grow back to its late seral state is often referred to as mining (metaphorically anyway)."

18 Will Horter, Vancouver Island's Great E & N Railway Land Grab, *Watershed Sentinel*, December 2008.

19 Carolyn Canfield: "When Dunsmuir land was sold off—ancestors to MacMillan Bloedel—it was buying up smaller lumber companies. They were interested in saw timber and pulp. When the Managed Forest Act was adopted, the tax structure became important for the company. Managed Forest Land is taxed at an extremely low rate. Then when timber was harvested, they would have to pay a balloon tax for realizing the value. Crown land is leased, but the province wanted to provide an incentive for forest companies to continue to hold their lands, and not abandon it. 'We won't tax you until you turn a coin.' So when in the Land Use battle with MacBlo, we put it out to government that MacBlo was operating at taxpayers' expense holding it under Managed Forest land, and the public had invested in seeing that continue as Managed Forest land. CCA said we welcome you to continue to log. Let's figure out a way to do sustainable forestry. We won that battle, after the war was lost. The local timber manager did eventually agree to do selective logging—first time in the company's history. Jack flagged trees to come down, but within months, there were battles in Vancouver at MacBlo headquarters. No sustainable forestry—this was development lands—gaining residential development from the community who held the cards, because of the Islands Trust Act. No more discussion of sustainable forestry. It was ironic, people were getting arrested in Clayoquot. They were stereotyping. When newspapers wanted to write a story about David and Goliath situated on Galiano, they did not want to write that they were okay with sustainable logging. It didn't fit the cartoon. We were resentful that we couldn't communicate that to reporters. They wanted us to be tree-huggers."

20 Margaret Griffiths, "The Story of Galiano Island across Thirty Important Years," accessed May 23, 2023, http://galianostory.com/OVERVIEW.HTM.

21 Sheila Anderson: "The original Tree Farm Licence areas were removed from Managed Forest Classification—which meant they were held by the company for the purpose of doing forestry. Thus, they were eligible for subsidies to help for road building costs and taxed at MFL. In order to sell it, they had to remove it from that classification, as it doesn't transfer with sale. Then they marketed it."

22 https://galianoclub.org/club-programs/parks/mount-galiano/.

23 *British Columbia Park Act*, Chapter 309, 1979, I Interpretation, Appendix D.

24 MacMillan Bloedel Ltd. v. Galiano Island Trust Committee et al., (1995) 63 B.C.A.C. 81 (CA), paragraph 130, p. 41, accessed February 23, YEAR, https://ca.vlex.com/vid/macmillan-v-galiano-island-681204801.

25 Carolyn Canfield: "Our lawyer Greg McDade at Sierra Legal Defence said, 'You had every right to have a relationship with IT to influence the community," but we didn't. We had a near death experience through that lawsuit, as representatives on island were very vindictive. MB wanted to create a legal precedent that would apply in IT area and all Private Managed Forest land, most on VI, but some on the Sunshine Coast as well, from a real estate standpoint. GCA came out of big dream that we couldn't let go of community held land."

26 "Lands Owned by Galiano Conservancy Association," 2014, PDF supplied by Gary Moore.

27 Keith Erickson, "Protecting the Great Beaver Swamp," updated October 2014, https://galianoConservancy.ca/protecting-the-great-beaver-swamp/.

28 The Canadian Land Trust Alliance Standards and Practices, https://olta.ca/wp-content/uploads/202⅓s/cltsp_2019_en_final.pdf.

29 "Lands Owned by the Galiano Conservancy Association," 2014.

30 Ridington Jillian, ABC Bookworld, https://abcbookworld.com/writer/ridington-jillian/.

31 Rozen, "Place-Names of the Island Halkomelem Indian People," p. 72.

32 "Hwi'yu'nem ch – Welcome," Lyackson First Nation on Vancouver Island and Valdes Island, http://lyackson.bc.ca/.

33 Rozen, "Place-Names of the Island Halkomelem Indian People," p. 74.

34 Bill Merilees, *Newcastle Island: A Place of Discovery* (Heritage House, 1998), p. 33.

35 For more information on seabirds, check out M. S. Rodway, R.W. Campbell, and M. J. F. Lemon. *Seabird Colonies of British Columbia, Part 4: Salish Sea, Wildlife Afield* 18, no. 1–2, to be released in the Spring of 2024. The *Wildlife Afield* journal is published by the Biodiversity Centre for Wildlife Studies in Victoria, BC.

Hornby Island

1   "Hornby Island," *Marine Conservation Atlas*, 2nd edition, Conservancy Hornby Island, p. 3.

2   "Mt. Geoffrey Nature Park and Crown Land Trails Management Plan," Comox Valley Regional District, 2017, p. 6.

3   "Mt. Geoffrey Nature Park," p. 6.

4   "Mt. Geoffrey Nature Park," p. 7.

5   Founders of CHI: Bryan Beard, John Fletcher, Cathy Herbert, Richard Laskin, Sheila McDonnell, Betty Fairbank, Jan Gibson, Tom Knott, Dick Martin, and Elke Tietz.

6   From initial "Purposes of Conservancy Hornby Island."

7   Peter Grant, *The Log*, newsletter of Friends of Ecological Reserves, Spring 1993, p. 7.

8   Tony Law, internal memo to Conservancy Hornby Island, 200

9   Peter Grant, *The* Log, p. 7.

10 Tony Law, personal communications via email, July 2023.

11 "Mt. Geoffrey Nature Park," p. 1.

12 Quoted from *Islands Tides*, November 29, 2012.

13 Islands Trust, Natural Area Protection Exemption Program, https://islandstrust.bc.ca/programs/natural-area-protection-tax-exemption-program/.

14 "Property Assessments on Conservation Lands," Land Trust Alliance of BC, updated 2020.

15 Moura Quayle and Stan Hamilton, *Corridors of Green and Gold: Impact of Riparian Suburban Greenways in Property Values* (University of British Columbia, April 1999); Seung Kyum Kim

and Richard B. Peiser, "The Economic Effects of Green Spaces in Planned and Unplanned Communities," *Journal of Architectural and Planning Research* 35, no. 4 (Winter 2018), pp. 323–42.

16 https://info.bcassessment.ca/Services-products/property-classes-and-exemptions/conservation-covenants.

17 Ken Lertzman, "Shifting Baselines," Lasqueti Island Nature Conservancy, Fall 2020; Iain McKechnie et al., "Archaeological Data Provide Alternative Hypotheses on Pacific Herring (*Clupea pallasii*) Distribution, Abundance, and Variability," *PNAS* III (2014): E807–E816.

18 Bob Turner, *Herring Spawn! Serengeti of the Sea on Hornby Island*, https://youtu.be/v4dMyHzz_80.

19 Important Bird Area, https://www.ibacanada.com/site.jsp?siteID=BC272&lang=EN&siteID=BC272&lang=EN.

20 Visit www.pacificherring.org to learn from knowledge holders from Alaska to Washington about the cultural and ecological importance of this wee fish.

21 "Marine Conservation Areas on Hornby," https://www.Conservancyhornbyisland.org/marine-conservation-areas.

22 "Rockfish Conservation Areas," https://www.pac.dfo-mpo.gc.ca/fm-gp/maps-cartes/rca-acs/docs/protect-rockfish-protege-sebaste-eng.html.

Denman Island

1 Jenny Balke et al., "Inner Island Nature Reserve Management Plan," DCA and Islands Trust Conservancy, rev 2020, p. i.

2 John Millen, from the Denman Forestry Initiative Timeline.

3 The British Columbia Court of Appeal, Denman Island Local Trust Committee v. 4064 Investments Ltd., (2001) 161 B.C.A.C. 215 (CA), https://ca.vlex.com/vid/denman-island-local-trust-680983577.

4 Specifically Raincoast Conservation Foundation and more recently a group of land trusts working together to strengthen the Islands Trust Policy Review.

5 A detailed description of the case: https://www.denman-Conservancy.org/200%1/0½298/.

6 "Denman Conservancy Association V 4064 Investments Ltd.: A Case History," Denman Conservancy Association, last modified January 1, 2007, https://www.denman-conservancy.org/200%1/0½298/.

7 Terry Glavin, "Human Remains Found on Vancouver Island have Opened a Door into a Lost World," *McLeans Magazine*, November 26, 2020.

8 Winnifred A. Isbister, *My Ain Folk* (Denman Island: W.E. Bickle Ltd., 1976).

9 Isbister, *My Ain Folk*.

10 Meeri Durand and Ryan Durand, "Management Plan for Morrison Marsh Nature Reserve, 2007," Islands Trust Conservancy, 2007, p. 6.

11 Durand and Durand, "Management Plan for Morrison Marsh."

12 With the purchase of the 80 acres of Raven Land the Denman Conservancy finally met its goal to protect 800 acres of land. Please note this includes the Inner Island Nature Reserve (ITC) and 320 acres of Crown land that (in 2010) became part of the Denman Island Provincial Park. Even so, DCA owns more than half of the 800 acres. (John Millen)

13 https://www.denman-Conservancy.org/our-work/lands/pickles-waterfall-wetland-raven-forest-lands-conservation-area/.

14 Jenny Balke, *The Kingfisher*, Land Trust Alliance of BC, vol. 19, 2009, p. 16–17.

15 For a beautiful map of Denman's protected areas see https://denmanconservancy.org/.

Quadra island

1 Rozen, "Place-Names of the Island Halkomelum Indian People," p. 284.

2 Quoted from Adam Chan, "'A Second Chance': Record Number of Humpbacks Spotted in B.C.'s Salish Sea This Year," CTV News, December 2022.

3 Mitlenatch Island Stewardship Team, https://www.mitlenatch.ca/.

4   We Wai Kai Nation, https://wewaikai.com/about/.

5   Ann Hillyer and Judy Atkins (1st and 2nd eds.), Ben van Drimmelen (3rd ed.), *BC Conservation Covenant Handbook: A Guide to Best Practices for Conservation Covenants in BC*, revised 2023, West Coast Environmental Law Research Foundation and the Land Trust Alliance of BC, 2023.

6   In BC, few conservation covenant violations have gone to court. A sample are included in the above book, *A Guide to Best Practices*. A 1999 Land Trust Alliance (US) survey found that out of 7,400 conservation easements, 498 violations were reported, 383 of which were minor and got resolved without significant commitment of resources. One hundred and fifteen were major violations, but 94 were resolved without litigation and 21 cases resulted in lawsuits.

7   The Nature Trust of BC, "Breton Island," https://www.naturetrust.bc.ca/news/legacy-landscapes-breton-island.

8   For further info see Clam Garden Network, https://www.clamgarden.com/.

9   "This includes a bequest of $901,308 to BC Parks from John Locke Malkin estate, and $829,631 from the Pacific Marine Heritage Legacy trust." Quoted in the *Campbell River Mirror*, March 20, 2014.

Cortes Island

1   The Cortes Island Museum and Archives display, "Wayfinding", March 2023–December 2023. https://cortesmuseum.com/category/wayfinding/.

2   "hɛɬ toq tʊwa – I am from Squirrel Cove," Klahoose Wilderness Resort, accessed November 13, 2023, https://www.klahooseresort.com/about.

3   "There used to be a village site on the eastern side of the entrance to the harbour, and there was a second village site on the eastern side of the inner harbour which was abandoned before 1900." Dorothy Kennedy and Randy Bouchard, *Sliammon Life, Sliammon Lands* (Vancouver: Talonbooks, 1983).

4   "Prior to the dawn of agriculture eight to ten millennia ago, humans accounted for less than 1%, and wild mammals 99%, of mammalian biomass on Earth. Today, H. sapiens constitute 36%, and our domestic livestock another 60% of a much-expanded mammalian biomass, compared with only 4% for all wild species combined. McRae et al. estimate that the populations of non-human vertebrate species declined by 58% between 1970 and 2012 alone. Freshwater, marine, and terrestrial vertebrate populations declined by 81%, 36%, and 38%, respectively, and invertebrate populations fell by about 50%." Meghan K Seibert and William Rees, "Through the Eye of a Needle: An Eco-Heterodox Perspective on the Renewable Energy Transition," *Ecological Economics* 169 (March 2020).

5   Strathcona Regional District, https://srd.ca/services/parks-and-facilities/cortes-island-parks/.

6   Personal communications from Ian Atherton, appraiser, and Forest for the Children Christine Robinson.

Savary Island

1   "Photo History of Powell River," Traditional Place Names of the Tla'amin Nation Project, https://powellriver.ca/pages/photo-history-of-powell-river.

2   *Powell River Peak*, media release, November 14, 2022, https://www.prpeak.com/local-news/ancestral-remains-encountered-on-ihos-savary-island-6100844.

3   Michael Kluckner, https://www.michaelkluckner.com/bciw8savary.html.

4   Kluckner writes that Jim Spilsbury noted that children including himself were hired to plant broom.

5   SILT's founding members: Brendan Allen, Paula Butler, Daryl Duke, Norma Flawith, Sherwood Inglis, Anna Linsley, Hartland MacDougall, Rod Kirkham, Charles Pitts, Carol Wong, Liz Webster, and Wynn Woodward.

6   Well known Vancouver litigator Christopher Harvey joined the board in 1999 and gave SILT its first gifts of land: a waterfront property and an individual lot all at Thateq (Indian Point). Over the years Chris donated four more lots to SILT. Local naturalist and retired teacher Norma Flawith; college administrator Carol Wong; retired teacher Anna Linsley; Vancouver lawyer and son-in-law to Hart MacDougall, Rod Kirkham; economist Paula Butler; and writer and producer

Charles Pitts all joined the board united by the goal to save the heart of Savary. Some years later, long-time islander Paul Leighton, whose grandfather at one time owned the entire west end of the island, joined the SILT board as well.

7 Kathy Dunster, "Sand Dune Ecosystems on Savary Island, B.C. with particular reference to D.L. 1375," March 2000.

8 Savary Island Land Trust newsletter, 2001.

9 Danelle Dalzel, Savary Island Land Trust newsletter, 2018.

10 Some of the artists that supported SILT auctions for many years include Audrey Cappal Doray, Harry and Linda Stanbridge, Peter Wyse, and Anne-Marie Harvey.

11 Dalzel, Savary Island Land Trust newsletter, 2018.

12 https://clearseas.org/en/blog/how-the-tmx-pipeline-will-affect-marine-shipping-in-the-salish-sea/.

13 Howard MacDonald Stewart, *Views of the Salish Sea One Hundred and Fifty Years of Change around the Strait of Georgia*, (Madeira Park BC: Harbour Publishing, 2017,) p. 260.

Bowen Island

1 This place name is recorded from https://bowenislandmuseum.ca/first-nations-on-bowen/.

2 Islands Trust Conservancy, *Regional Conservation Plan*, 2018–2027, p. 59; Dunster & Associates Environmental Consultants Ltd., *The Crown Lands of Bowen Island: An Inventory and Assessment of Resources and Values*, November 2000, https://bowenislandConservancy.org/wp-content/uploads/2017%07/Crown-lands-report-Dunster-1.pdf.

3 Julian Dunster, "The Crown Lands of Bowen Island," November 2000.

4 Islands Trust Conservancy, *Regional Conservation Plan*, p. 58.

5 Verbal communication from Sue Ellen Fast, July 2023.

6 "By 1951, when ferry service to the Sunshine Coast had begun, Black Ball Ferries Ltd. (Canada) had four ships available to serve BC routes." https://www.sunshinecoastmuseum.ca/marine-transportation.html.

7 Jack Little, "Bowen Island's First Official Community Plan," *At the Wilderness Edge: The Rise of the Antidevelopment Movement on Canada's West Coast* (McGill-Queen's University Press, 2019), p. 81.

8 An extended version of this history is found in Irene Wanless, "Interview with Ross Carter," October 2006.

9 Irene Wanless for BI Archives "Ross Carter Final", a personal history .

10 Bowen Island Conservancy website: https://bowenislandConservancy.org/about-us/our-history/.

11 Founding Board Members: Anne Ironside, Julian Dunster, Jack Silberman, Dean Maidment, David Podmore, Sheilagh Sparks, Marja DeJong-Westman, Peter Busby, and Dave Witty.

12 Dunster & Associates, *The Crown Lands of Bowen Island*.

13 Connie Haist, "Great Blue Herons, Sentinels of Our Coast," Lasqueti Island Nature Conservancy Newtletter, vol. 14, Spring 2018, https://linc.lasqueti.ca/newsletters/.

14 Bob Turner, videos at YouTube @bobturner7642.

15 Bowen Island Marine Atlas, https://bowenislandConservancy.org/our-work/bowen-island-marine-atlas-project.

16 Bowen Island Conservancy, https://bowenislandconservancy.org/stories/discovering-kwila%cc%93km.

17 Sheila Byers, "The Marine Life Sanctuaries Society and Conservation of Howe Sound Rockfishes and Glass Sponge Reefs," *Discovery* 46, Nature Vancouver, 2018, p. 38.

18 Doug Hooper, Bowen Island Municipal Councilor, 2008–2011, letter to editor in Bowen's newsletter *Undercurrent*.

19 Stephen Partington, "Seaside Juniper – The Only Endemic Tree of the Georgia Basin," *Discovery* 46, Nature Vancouver, 2018, p. 48.

20 Islands Trust Fund press release, July 2010.

21 Bob Turner, "The Salish Sea – A Single Body of Life," https://youtu.be/PYlSyQoTIvo. "This is my second movie that explores the question of what makes the Salish Sea, our own back yard piece of the Pacific Ocean, so rich with marine life."

Gambier Island and the Átl'ka7tsem/ Howe Sound Biosphere Reserve

1 Islands Trust Conservancy, *Regional Conservation Plan*, p. 79.
2 Elspeth Armstrong, brief to provincial Environment Minister, 1974.
3 Quoted from J. I. Little, "Resisting the Gambier Island Copper Mine Proposal," *At the Wilderness Edge: The Rise of the Antidevelopment Movement on Canada's West Coast* (McGill-Queen's University Press, 2019), p. 117.
4 Little, "Resisting the Gambier Island Copper Mine Proposal."
5 Little, "Resisting the Gambier Island Copper Mine Proposal," p. 122. From Acres Consulting (a mining consultatnt) prefeasibility report.
6 Little, "Resisting the Gambier Island Copper Mine Proposal," p. 126.
7 Carrina Maslovat, R. P. Bio, and Laura Matthias, "Long Bay Wetland Nature Reserve Management Plan, Gambier Island, BC," Islands Trust Conservancy, 2019, p. 2.
8 Carrina Maslovat, R. P. Bio, and Laura Matthias, "Brigade Bay Bluffs Nature Reserve Management Plan, Gambier Island, BC," Islands Trust Conservancy, 2019, p. 13.
9 Cascade Environmental Resource Group Ltd., "Brigade Bay Bluffs Nature Reserve and Long Bay Wetland Nature Reserve Management Plan," 2005.
10 BC Ministry of Environment, "Management Plan for the Coastal Tailed Frog (*Ascaphus truei*) in Canada," Species at Risk Act Management Plan Series, Environment and Climate Change Canada, December 2015.
11 Sylvia Ascher, Samantha Wing, and Mike Stamford, Stamford Environmental, noted in "Gambier Island Coastal Tailed Frog Project: Field Sampling Summary and Preliminary Results, 2022."
12 S. N. Stuart et al, "Status and Trends of Amphibian Declines and Extinctions Worldwide," *Science*, 2004, https://doi.org/03061783.
13 Sheila Byers, "The Deep Sea Cities of Glass," *Discovery* 46, 2018, p. 30.
14 Sheila Byers, "The Marine Life Sanctuaries Society and Conservation of Howe Sound Rockfish and Glass Sponge Reefs," *Discovery* 46, 2018, pp. 38–39.
15 Keili Bartlett, "Five More Glass Sponge Reefs in Howe Sound," accessed August 2023, https://www.coastreporter.net/local-news/five-more-glass-sponge-reefs-in-howe-sound-protected-by-new-closures-4978227.

Lasqueti and Surrounding Islands

1 Lasqueti's Coast Salish name Xwe'etay is being accepted today: "Lasqueti's Coast Salish Name," Lasqueti Island, https://lasqueti.ca/archaeological-heritage/xweetay.
2 Luschim Arvid Charlie and Nancy J. Turner, *Luschim's Plants, Traditional Indigenous Foods, Materials and Medicines* (Harbour Publishing, 2021), pp. 68–70.
3 Stephen Partingon, "Seaside Juniper: The Only Endemic Tree of the Georgia Basin," *Discovery* 46, Nature Vancouver, 2018.
4 Mary Palmer, *Jedediah Days: One Woman's Island Paradise* (Madeira Park: Harbour Publishing, 1998), p. 220.
5 Doug Hopwood, "Protecting Jedediah Island – 25 years!," Lasqueti Island Nature Conservancy, vol. 21, Summer 2020, https://linc.lasqueti.ca/newsletters.
6 Doug Hopwood's recollection of some of the Friends of Jedediah: Sheila Ray, Sue Wheeler, Peter Johnston, Bruce Grant, Wendy Schneible, Ezra Auerbach, Melinda Auerbach, Dan Rubin, and Rosiland Hildred. But there were many more. Probably half the community contributed in one way or another.
7 From an article Doug wrote for the Lasqueti Island Nature Conservancy (LINC) on the celebration of Jedediah's twenty-fifth anniversary as a park, in which he reminisced about the acquisition.

8   The Squitty Bay extension Thank You poster lists the donors and funders of the Squitty Bay Extension.

9   Doug Hopwood, "Kwel Nature Reserve, Property Management Plan 2017," Islands Trust Conservancy, p. 8.

10 Hopwood, "Kwel Nature Reserve," p. 8.

11 Cora Skaien and R.P. Bio, "Mount Trematon Nature Reserve, Lasqueti Island: Ecological Restoration and Plant Biodiversity Study, Assessment of Different Recovery Strategies," September 2022.

12 The exclosure is intended to keep out mammalian herbivores, which is the centrepiece of an experiment in herbivory and plant recovery (Ken Lertzman).

13 Melissa Todd, reported in two issues of LINC's newsletter, vol. 18 and 26.

14 Current board: Gordon Scott, Wendy Schneible, Sheila Harrington, Ken Lertzman, James Schwartz, Duane West, Shirley Rogers, and Kaia Bryce. Founding board: Melinda Auerbach, Bonnie Olesko, Dazy Drake, and Wayne Bright.

15 https://www.lasquetiarc.ca/xwe-etay-project.

16 Palmer, *Jedediah Days*, p. 44.

Waypoints for the Future

1   The US Internal Revenue Service recognizes American Friends as a 501(c)(3) charity, so gifts of land, interests in land, or cash are tax-deductible against US income. American Friends of Canadian Conservation is a prescribed donee in Canada which means that gifts are essentially not subject to Canadian capital gains taxes. Visit the tax status page for more information about US and Canadian tax benefits.

2   David Lasby and Cathy Barr, "30 Years of Giving in Canada: The Giving Behaviour of Canadians: Who Gives, How, and Why?," Rideau Hall Foundation and Imagine Canada, 2018.

3   Government of Canada, press release accessed November 24, 2023, https://www.canada.ca/en/environment-climate-change/news/2023/11/government-of-canada-british-columbia-and-the-first-nations-leadership-council-sign-a-historic-tripartite-nature-conservation-framework-agreement.html.

4   National Heritage Conservation Program, accessed November 24 2023, https://whc.org/ltcf/.

5   Dana Lepofsky, "Lasqueti through Archaeology Eyes: The Island in the Middle of Everywhere," Xwe'etay/ Lasqueti Archeology Project, https://lasqueti.ca/archaeological-heritage.

6   Clam Garden Network, www.clamgarden.com.

7   Dana Lepofsky, personal communication.

8   WSÁNEĆ Lands Trust Society, accessed November 30, 2023, https://wsanec.com/w percentCC percentB1sanec-lands-trust/.

9   Kathryn Marlow, "Indigenous Non-Profit Buying Site of Former First Nation Village on Salt Spring Island," CBC News, accessed November 30, 2023, https://www.cbc.ca/news/canada/british-columbia/indigenous-stqeeye-xwaaqw-um-first-nation-village-1.7043800.

10 Andrew Duffy, "Abkhazi Gardens Zoning-Density Deal Could Send Cash to Land Conservancy Creditors," *Times Colonist*, March 8, 2022.

SELECTED BIBLIOGRAPHY

Bridge, Tyee. *Heart of the Coast: Biodiversity and Resilience on the Pacific Edge.* Vancouver: Figure 1 Publishing, 2020.

Charlie, Dr. Luschim Arvid and Nancy J. Turner. *Luschim's Plants: Traditional Indigenous Foods, Materials and Medicines.* Madeira Park: Harbour Publishing, 2021.

Harrington, Sheila and Judi Stevenson, *Islands in the Salish Sea, A Community Atlas.* Vancouver: Touchwood, 2006.

Hebda, Richard J and Sara Wilson. *Mitigating and Adapting to Climate Change through the Conservation of Nature.* Victoria: LTA The Land Trust Alliance of British Columbia, 2008.

Hillyer, Ann, Judy Atkins, (1st & 2nd eds.) Ben van Drimmelen, (3rd ed.). *BC Conservation Covenant Handbook, A Guide to Best Practices for Conservation Covenants in BC.* Vancouver: West Coast Environmental Law Research Foundation and the Land Trust Alliance of BC, 2023.

Kennedy, Dorothy and Randy Bouchard. *Sliammon Life, Sliammon Lands.* Talonbooks, Vancouver, 1983.

Layard, Nora and Murray Landa, et al. *Green Legacies, A Donors Guide for BC,* Victoria: Land Trust Alliance of BC and Give Green Canada, 2016.

Lamb, Andy and Bernard P. Hanby. *Marine Life of the Pacific Northwest: A Photographic Encyclopedia of Invertebrates, Seaweeds and Selected Fishes.* Madeira Park: Harbour Publishing, 2005.

Lamb, Peter. *The Islands Trust Story: Celebrating 35 Years 1974–2009.* Salt Spring Island: Imagine That Graphic Design & Print Solutions, 2009.

Little, J.I. *At the Wilderness Edge: The Rise of the Antidevelopment Movement on Canada's West Coast.* Montreal: McGill-Queen's University Press, 2019.

McKinnery, Sam. *Sailing with Vancouver: A Modern Sea Dog, Antique Charts and a Voyage Through Time.* Vancouver: TouchWood Editions, 2018.

Palmer Mary. *Jedediah Days, One Woman's Island Paradise.* Madeira Park: Harbour Publishing, 1998.

Pojar, Jim and Andy MacKinnon. *Plants of Coastal British Columbia, including Washington, Oregon and Alaska.* Tukwila, WA: Lonepine Publishing, Rev. 2022.

Rodway, Michael, R.W. Campbell, and M.J.F. Lemon. *Seabird Colonies of British Columbia, Part 4, Salish Sea.* Victoria: Wildlife Afield 18(1&2). 2024.

Rozen, David Lewis. "Place-names of the Island Halkomelem Indian People." Master's Thesis, Department of Anthropology and Sociology. Vancouver: University of British Columbia, 1985.

Stewart, Howard Macdonald. *Views of the Salish Sea: One Hundred and Fifty Years of Change around the Strait of Georgia.* Madeira Park: Harbour Publishing, 2017.

Websites of Note

American Friends of Canadian Conservation | http://www.conservecanada.org/

BC Species and Ecosystems Explorer | https://a100.gov.bc.ca/pub/eswp/

Canada Ecological Gifts Program | https://www.canada.ca/en/environment-climate-change/services/environmental-funding/ecological-gifts-program.html

Coastal Douglas-fir Conservation Partnership | https://www.cdfcp.ca

Important Bird Area | https://www.ibacanada.com

Islands Trust, Natural Area Protection Exemption Program | https://islandstrust.bc.ca/programs/natural-area-protection-tax-exemption-program/

Land Trust Alliance of British Columbia | https://ltabc.ca

The Canadian Land Trust Alliance Standards and Practices | https://olta.ca/wp-content/uploads/2021/05/cltsp_2019_en_final.pdf

Map Sources

Maps created by Danielle Morrison courtesy of The Nature Trust of BC

British Columbia NGO Conservation Areas Technical Working Group. 2023. BC NGO Conservation Areas Database – Fee Simple (secured as of December 31, 2022). Digital data files. Last updated Aug 9 2023.

Environment and Climate Change Canada. 2022. Canadian Protected and Conserved Areas Database. Accessed August 1, 2023 via https://www.canada.ca/en/environment-climate-change/services/national-wildlife-areas/ protected-conserved-areas-database.html

Government of British Columbia. 2023. ParcelMap BC Parcel Fabric. Accessed July 19, 2023, via https://catalogue.data.gov.bc.ca/dataset/parcelmap-bc-parcel-fabric

Islands Trust. 2023. Protected Areas. Accessed August 1, 2023 via https://islandstrust.bc.ca/mapping-resources/mapping/entire-region/

INDEX

ABOUT THE AUTHOR

SHEILA HARRINGTON is an author, sailor, and environmental advocate with a thirty-year career in the conservation field. She was the founding executive director of the Land Trust Alliance of BC (LTABC) from 1997–2011 and a director of the Lasqueti Island Nature Conservancy for over twelve years. She is co-author of the bestselling *Islands in the Salish Sea: A Community Atlas*, a finalist for two BC Book Awards and 3rd place winner of the BC Historical Federation prize. She edited and published *Positive Vibrations* magazine in the '90s and *Giving the Land a Voice, Mapping Our Home Places* and the BC *Kingfisher* magazine in the early 2000s. She currently lives off grid on Lasqueti Island.

GORDON SCOTT